Tatsuki Fujimoto

I love *The Menu*!

Tatsuki Fujimoto won Honorable Mention in the
November 2013 Shueisha Crown Newcomers' Awards for
his debut one-shot story "Love Is Blind." His first series,
Fire Punch, ran for eight volumes. *Chainsaw Man* began
serialization in 2018 in *Weekly Shonen Jump*.

15

SHONEN JUMP Edition

Story & Art **TATSUKI FUJIMOTO**

Translation/AMANDA HALEY
Touch-Up Art & Lettering/SABRINA HEEP
Design/JULIAN [JR] ROBINSON
Editor/ALEXIS KIRSCH

CHAINSAW MAN © 2018 by Tatsuki Fujimoto
All rights reserved.
First published in Japan in 2018 by SHUEISHA Inc., Tokyo.
English translation rights arranged by SHUEISHA Inc.

The stories, characters, and incidents mentioned in this publication are
entirely fictional.

Printed in the U.S.A.

Published by VIZ Media, LLC
P.O. Box 77010
San Francisco, CA 94107

10 9 8 7 6 5 4 3 2 1
First printing, May 2024

PARENTAL ADVISORY
CHAINSAW MAN is rated T+ for Older Teen
and is recommended for ages 16 and up.
This volume contains violence and gore.

CHAINSAWMAN

15

Hors D'oeuvre

Tatsuki Fujimoto

CHARACTERS

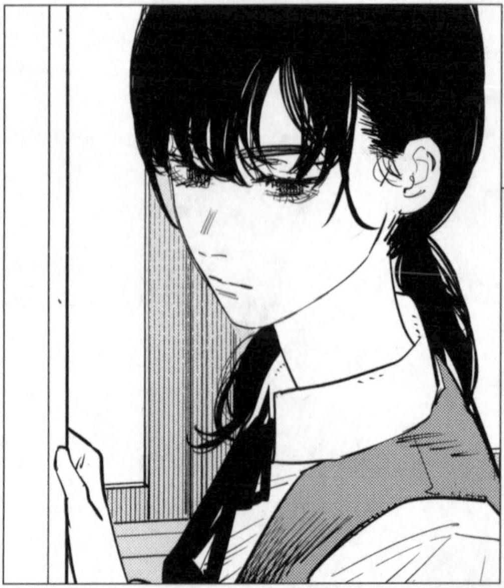

Asa Mitaka

A lonely, bullied young woman who doesn't fit in at school. She was killed by the Justice Devil, but came back to life when the War Devil, Yoru, took over her body. Asa hates devils—they killed her parents—and she's no fan of Chainsaw Man either. Her current battle? Handling Yoru!!

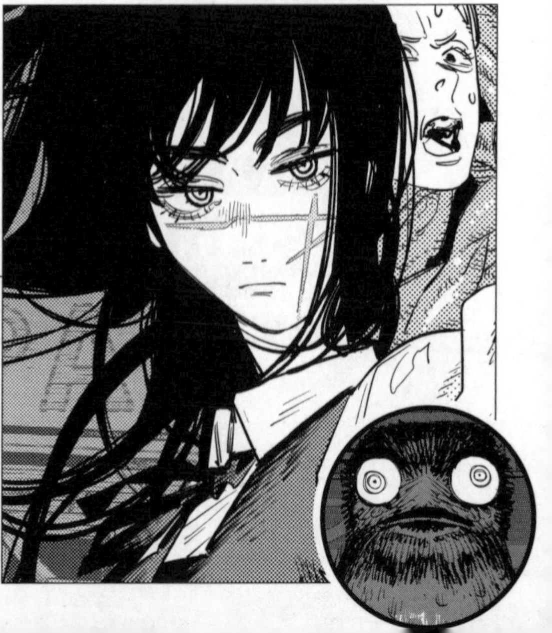

Yoru (War Devil)

This War Devil's true form is owllike, but she hopped into Asa's body and claimed half of the human's brain. See, she's on a mission to kill Chainsaw Man…but if she wants to track him down, she'll need help blending into human society. She has the power to transform things she kills into weapons.

Denji (Chainsaw Man)

Chainsaw Man! He carries the Chainsaw Devil in his heart (literally). High schooler by day, vigilante devil hunter by night. Kishibe from Public Safety entrusted him with the new Control Devil, Nayuta...

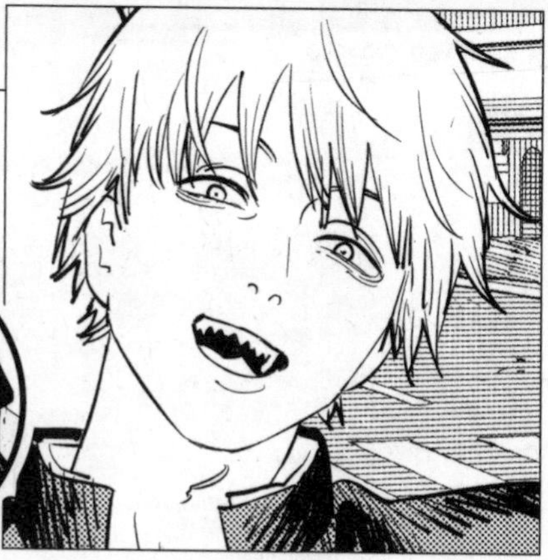

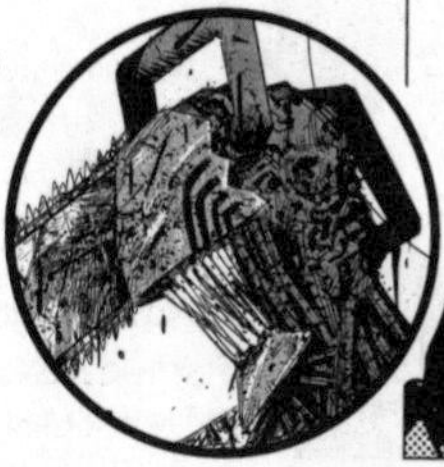

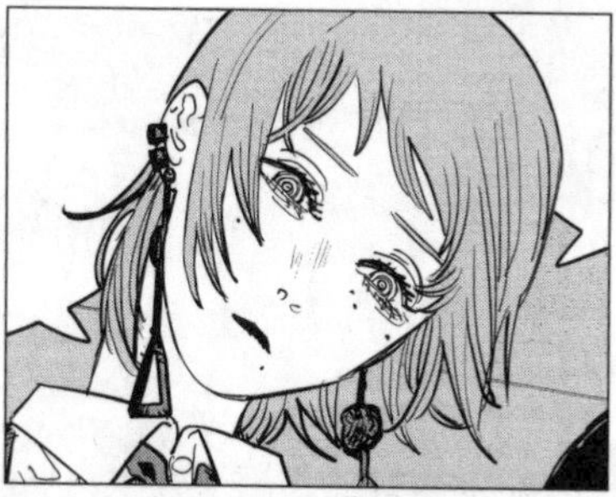

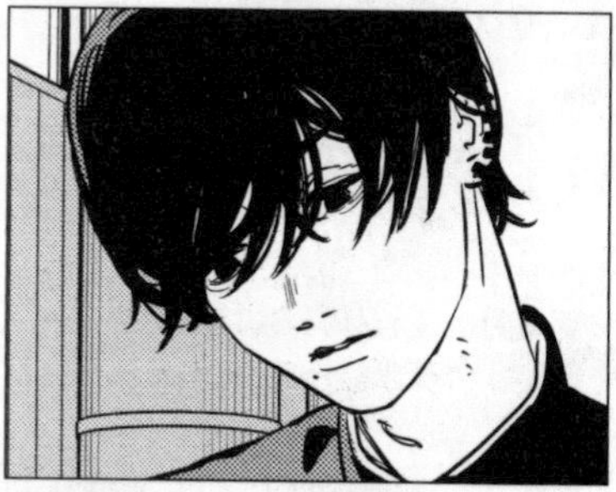

Fami (The Famine Devil)

A mysterious member of the devil hunter club at Asa's school. She's the sister of the War Devil.

Hirofumi Yoshida

A devil hunter who belongs to a particular organization. Wants to keep Denji's identity under wraps.

STORY

Asa Mitaka is a lonely young woman who doesn't fit in at school. Even the class president, the closest person she has to a friend, hates Asa so much that she makes a contract with the Justice Devil and murders her. But that's when the War Devil, Yoru, takes over Asa's body, giving her a second chance at life! Yoru's on a mission to find Chainsaw Man, and she claims she'll return Asa's body if they can kill him...

In order to turn Denji into a weapon, Asa asks him out on a date at the aquarium. However, due to the Eternity Devil sent by Fami, Asa, Denji, Yoshida, and others become trapped there. While things start looking grim, Asa is able to turn the situation around with some quick thinking. Afterward, Asa tries to become closer with Denji, but her failure at human interaction causes her to despair.

Meanwhile, Fami tells Yoshida of the terrible fate that is about to befall the world. And at the same time, a terrifying primal devil makes its appearance...

CONTENTS

Chapter 123: Hors D'oeuvre

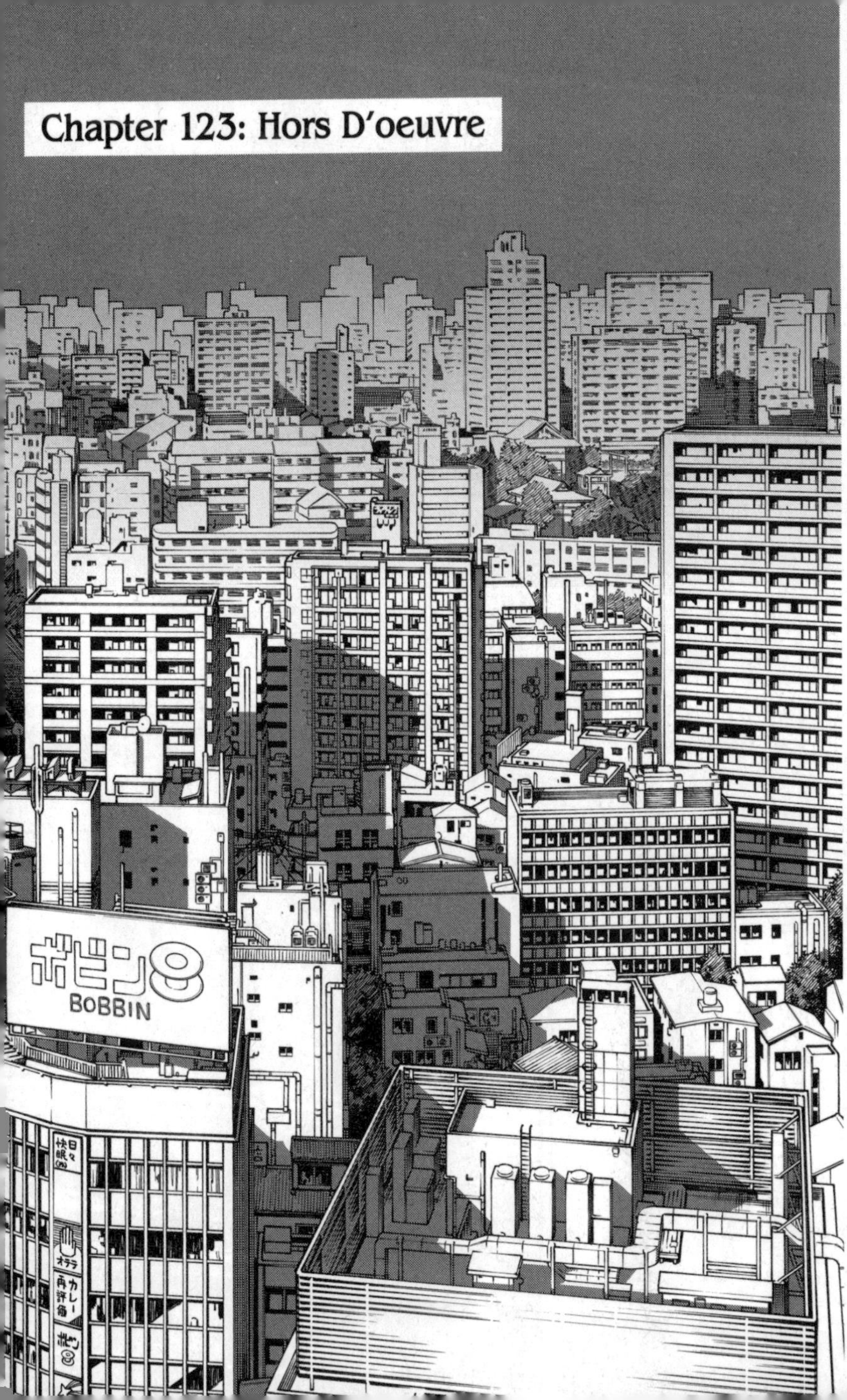
ボビン
BOBBIN

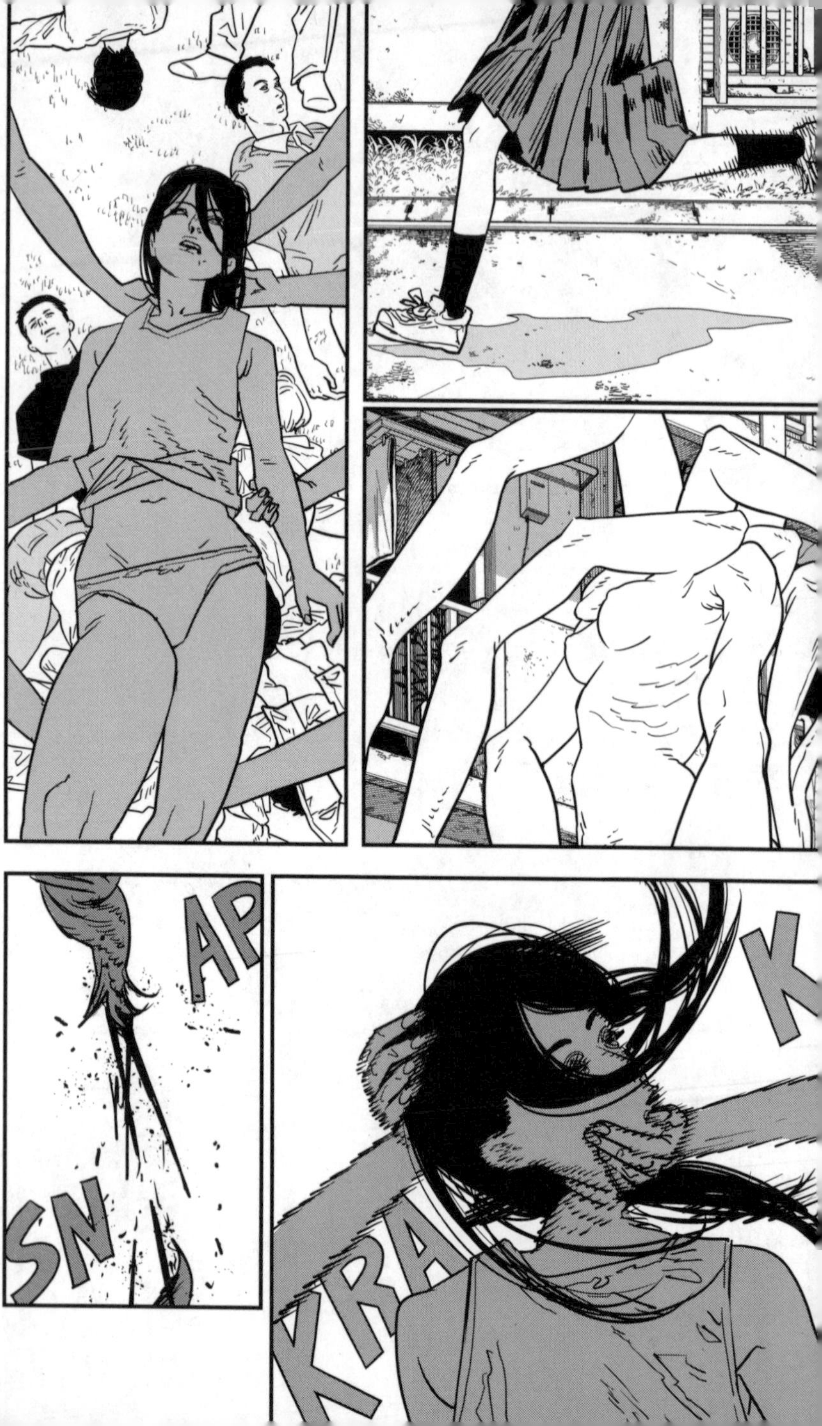
KRA
K
SN
AP

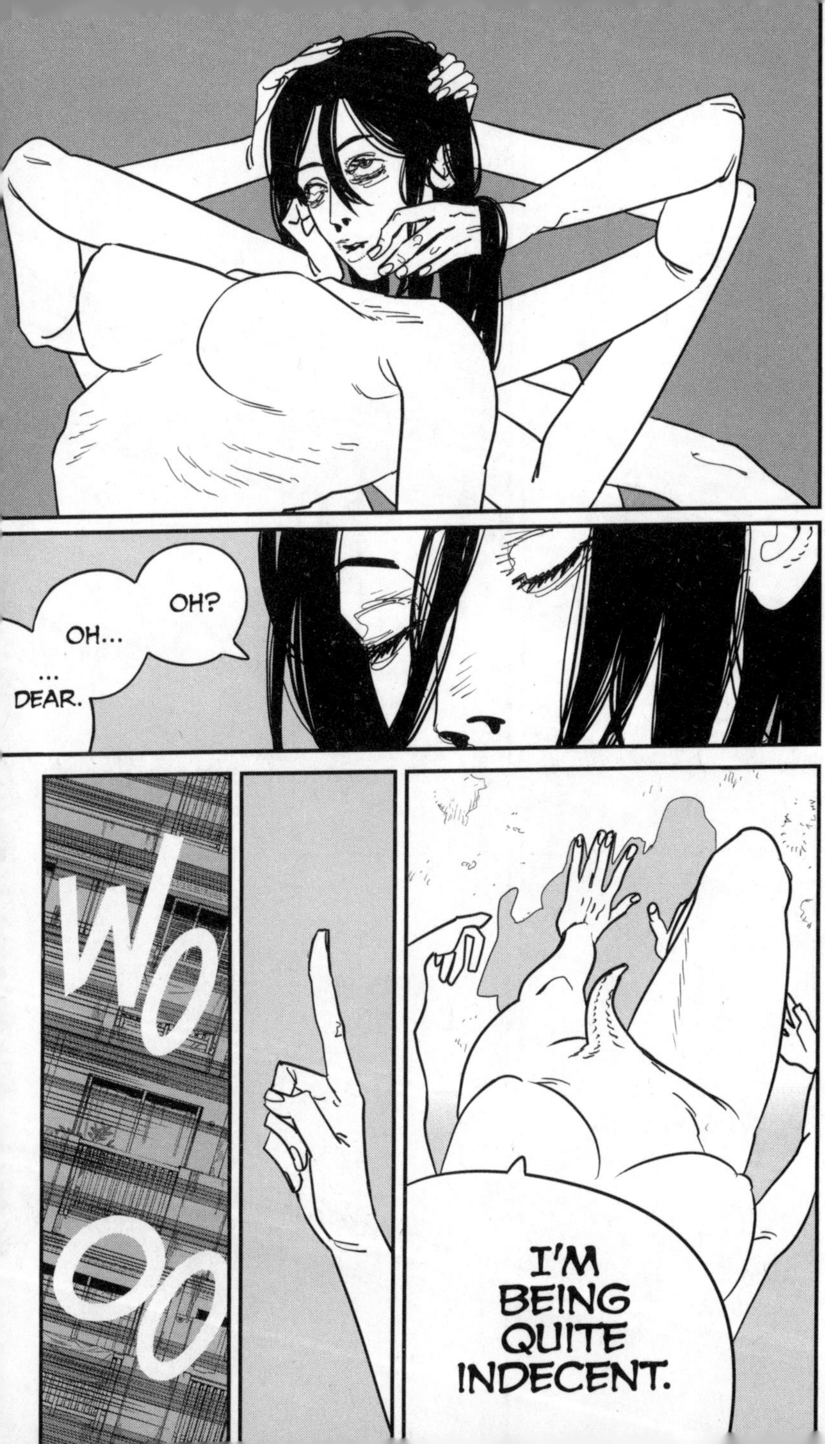
OH? OH... ...DEAR.
I'M BEING QUITE INDECENT.
WOOO

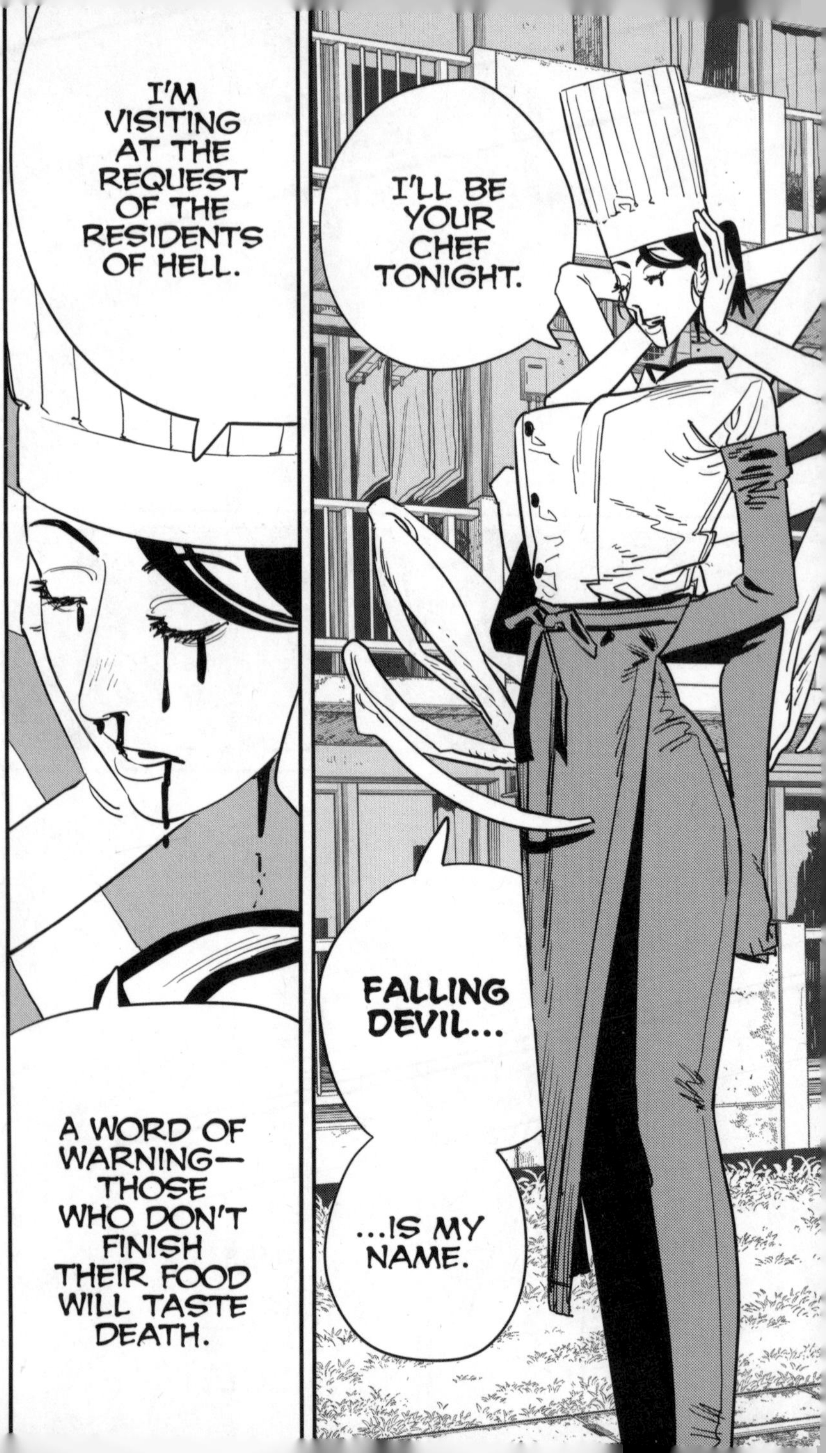
I'LL BE YOUR CHEF TONIGHT.
FALLING DEVIL...
...IS MY NAME.
I'M VISITING AT THE REQUEST OF THE RESIDENTS OF HELL.
A WORD OF WARNING— THOSE WHO DON'T FINISH THEIR FOOD WILL TASTE DEATH.

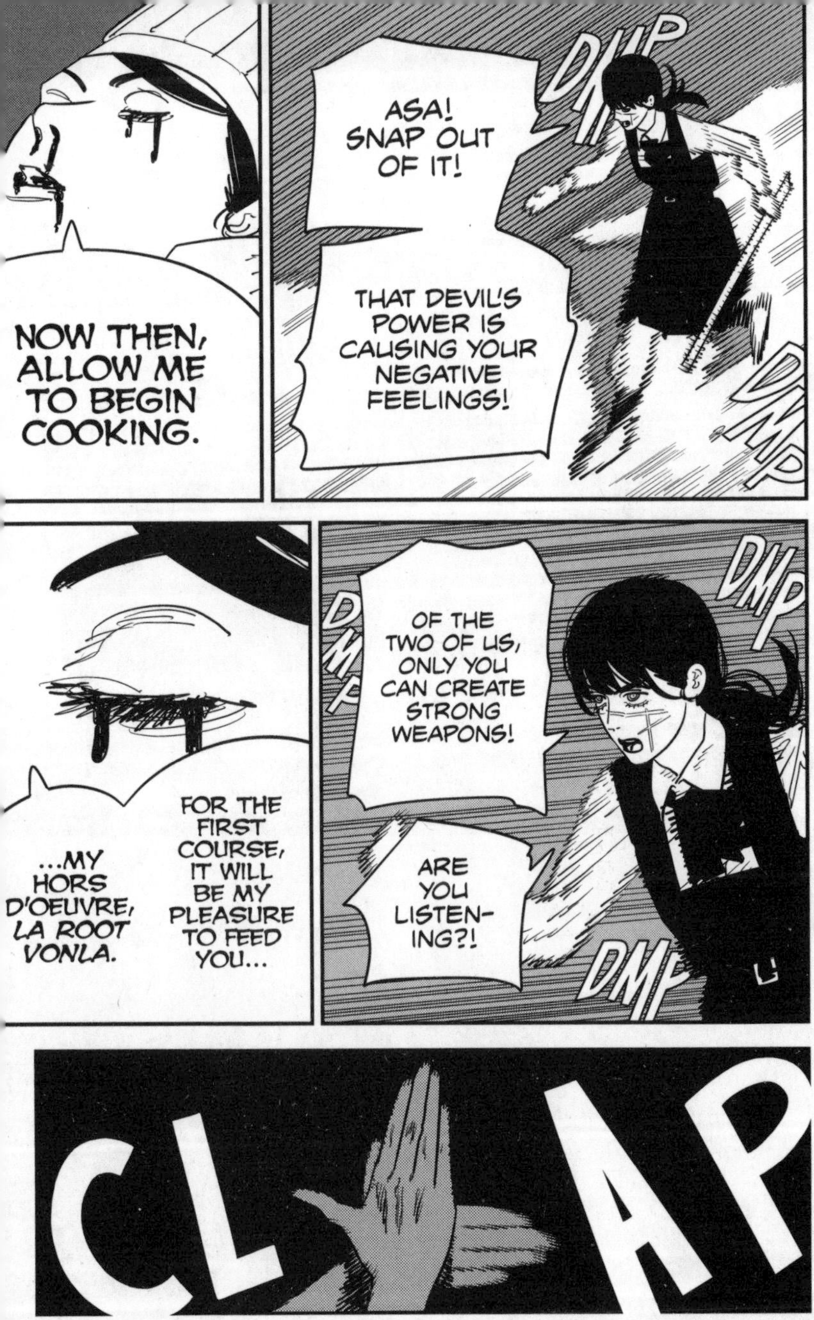
DMP
ASA! SNAP OUT OF IT!
THAT DEVIL'S POWER IS CAUSING YOUR NEGATIVE FEELINGS!
DMP
NOW THEN, ALLOW ME TO BEGIN COOKING.
DMP
OF THE TWO OF US, ONLY YOU CAN CREATE STRONG WEAPONS!
DMP
ARE YOU LISTEN-ING?!
DMP
FOR THE FIRST COURSE, IT WILL BE MY PLEASURE TO FEED YOU...
...MY HORS D'OEUVRE, LA ROOT VONLA.
CLAP

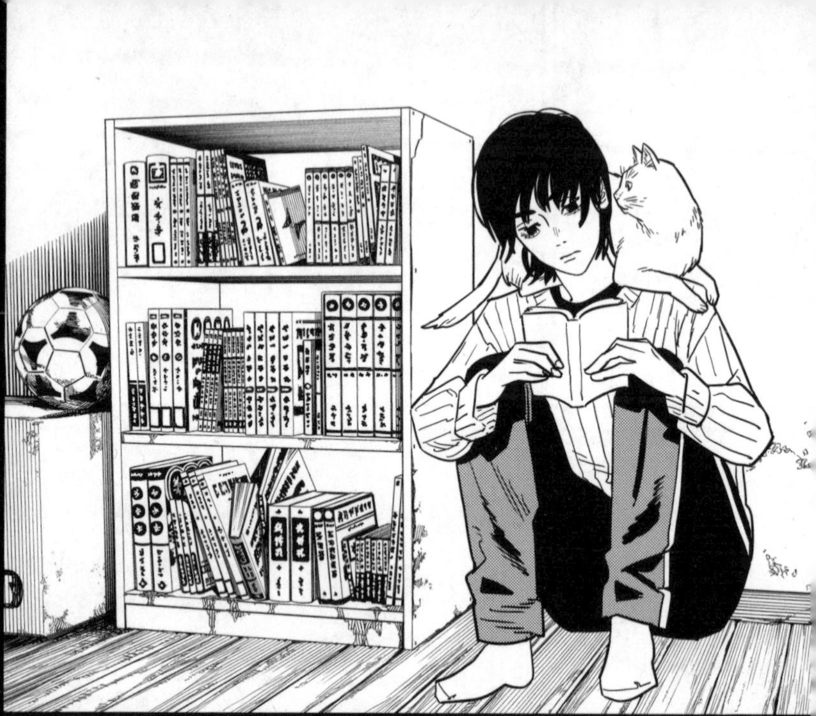
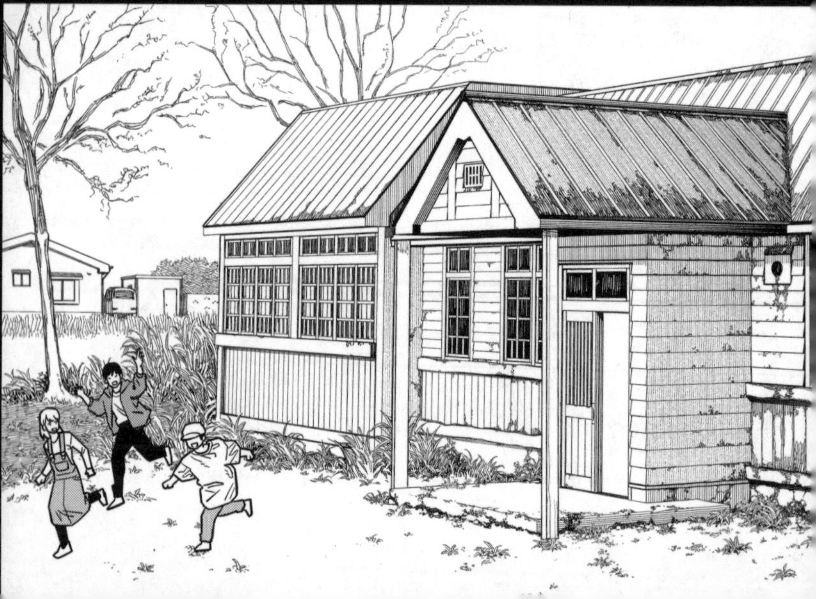

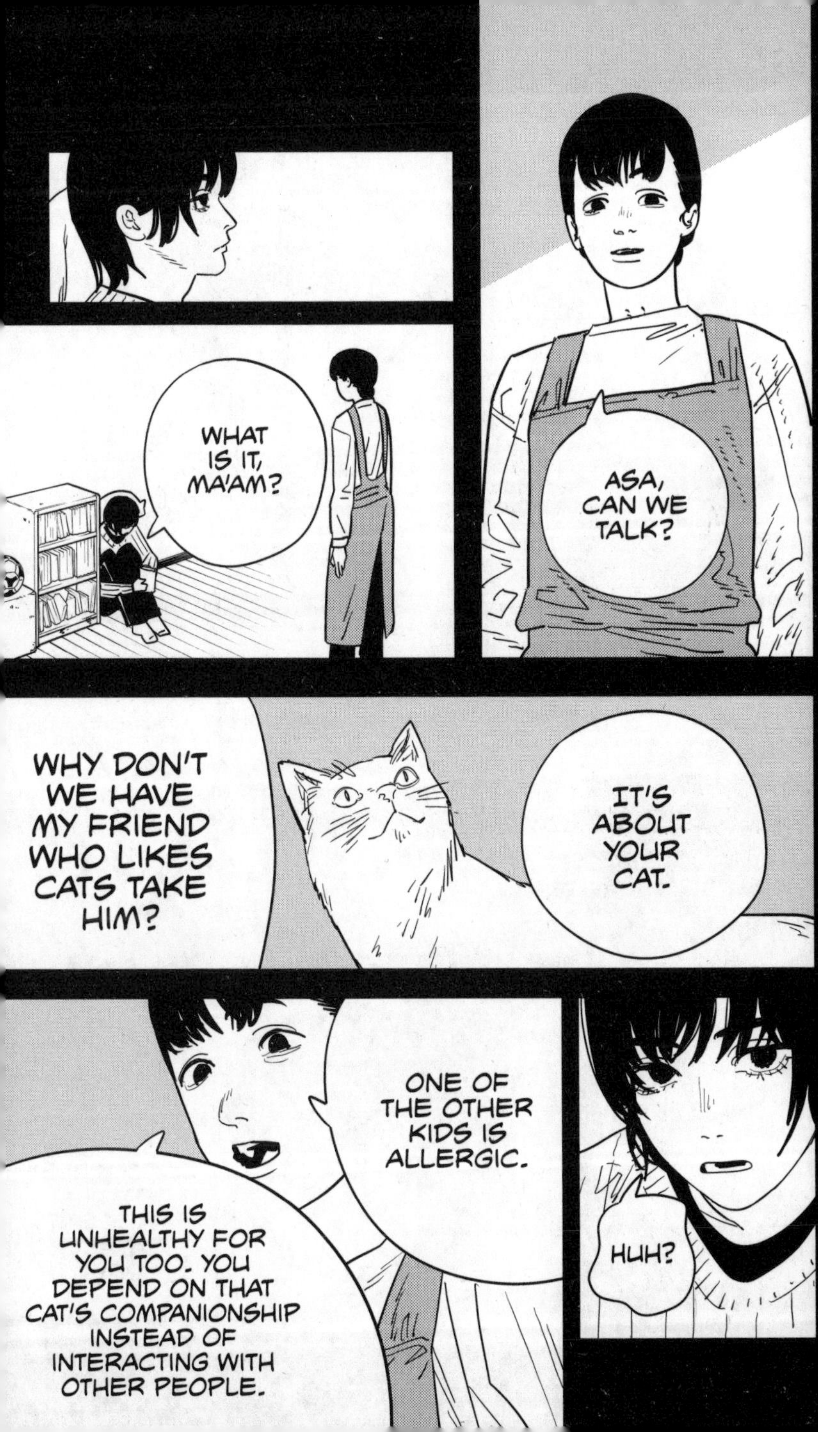
ASA, CAN WE TALK?
WHAT IS IT, MA'AM?
IT'S ABOUT YOUR CAT.
WHY DON'T WE HAVE MY FRIEND WHO LIKES CATS TAKE HIM?
HUH?
ONE OF THE OTHER KIDS IS ALLERGIC.
THIS IS UNHEALTHY FOR YOU TOO. YOU DEPEND ON THAT CAT'S COMPANIONSHIP INSTEAD OF INTERACTING WITH OTHER PEOPLE.

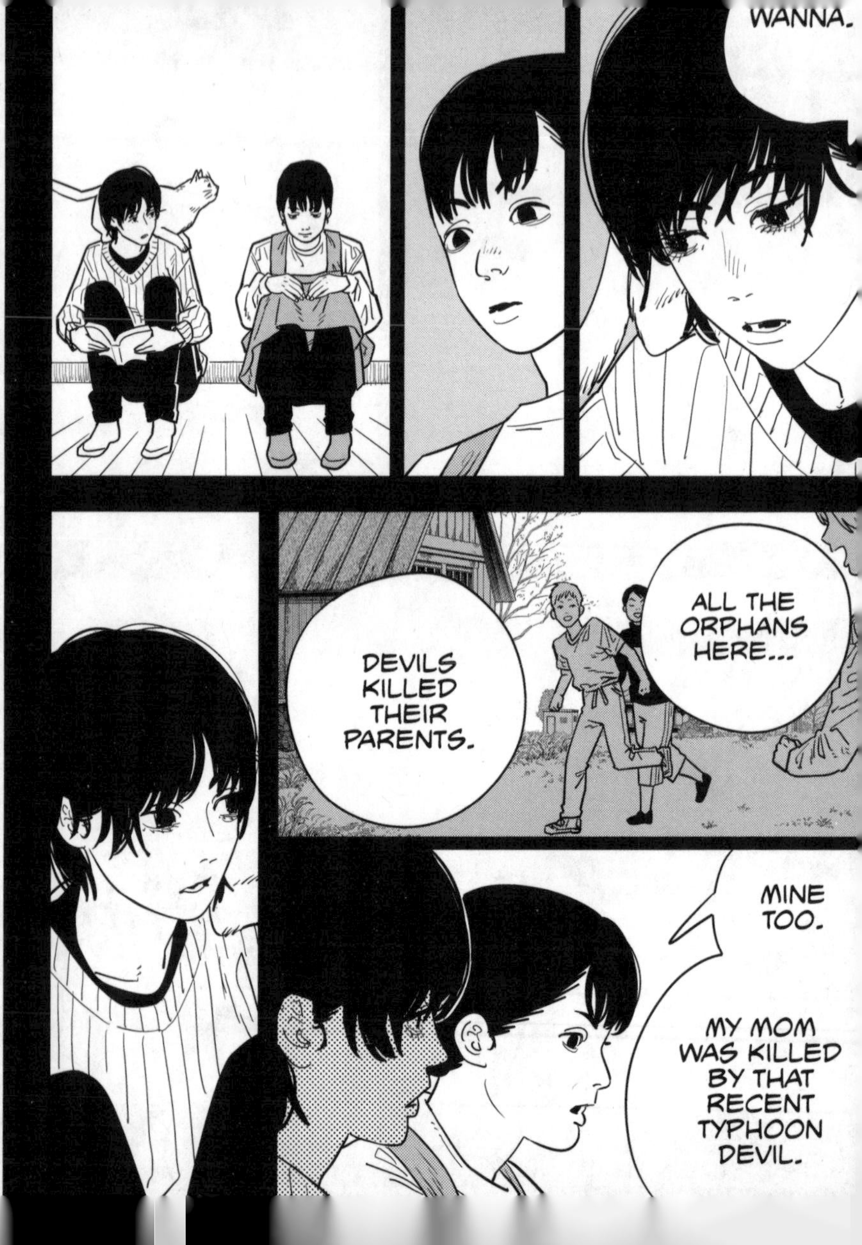
WANNA.
ALL THE ORPHANS HERE...
DEVILS KILLED THEIR PARENTS.
MINE TOO.
MY MOM WAS KILLED BY THAT RECENT TYPHOON DEVIL.

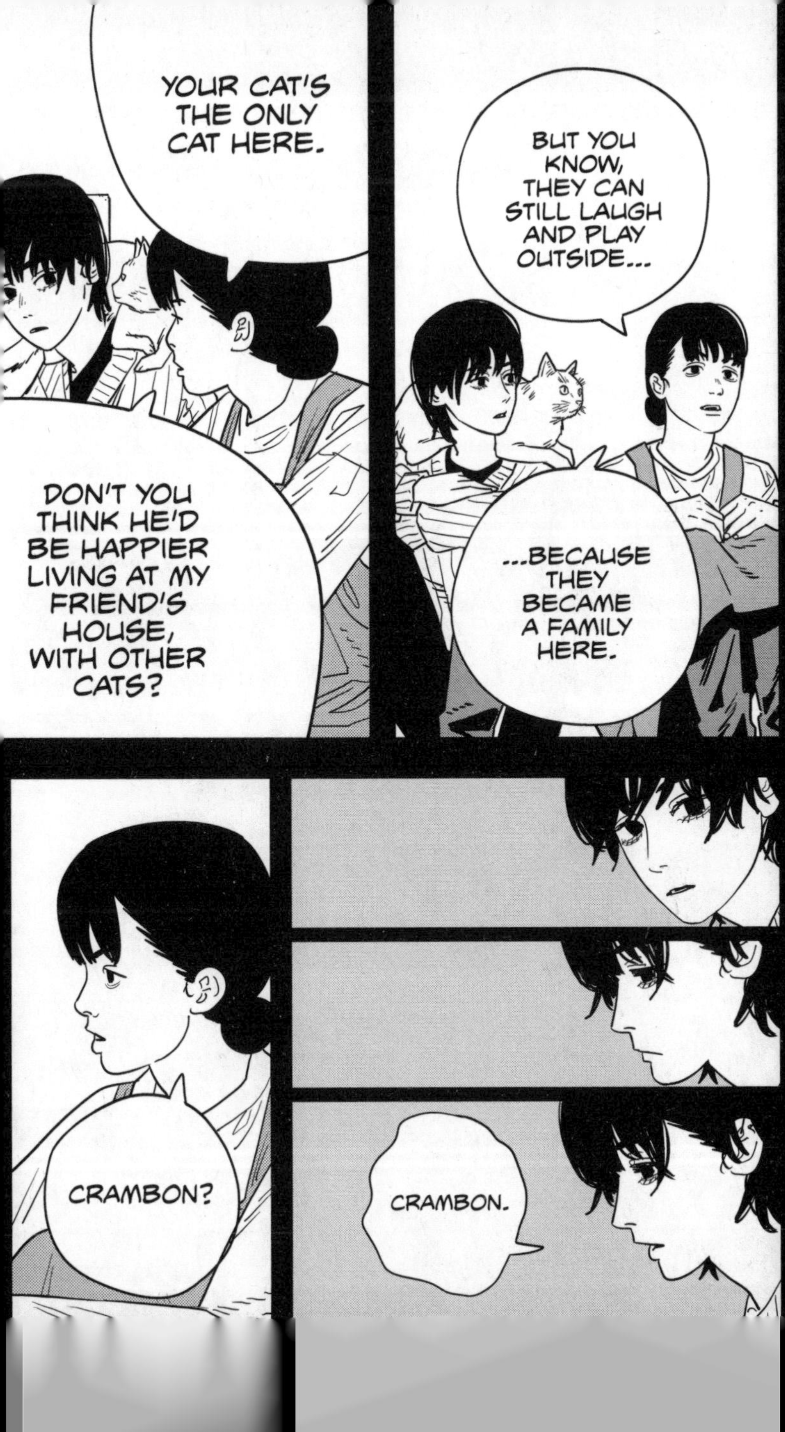
BUT YOU KNOW, THEY CAN STILL LAUGH AND PLAY OUTSIDE...
...BECAUSE THEY BECAME A FAMILY HERE.
YOUR CAT'S THE ONLY CAT HERE.
DON'T YOU THINK HE'D BE HAPPIER LIVING AT MY FRIEND'S HOUSE, WITH OTHER CATS?
CRAMBON.
CRAMBON?

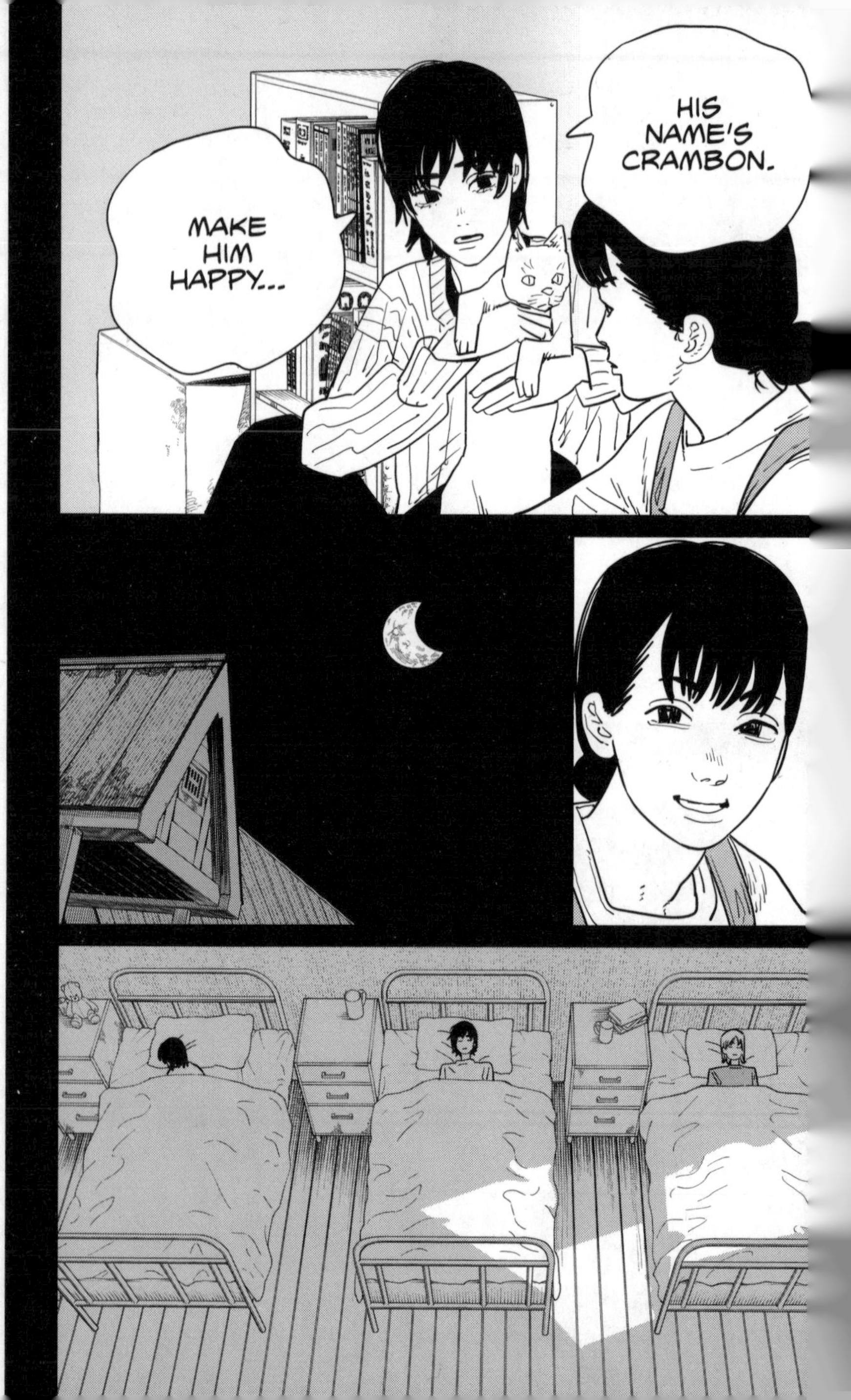
HIS NAME'S CRAMBON.
MAKE HIM HAPPY...

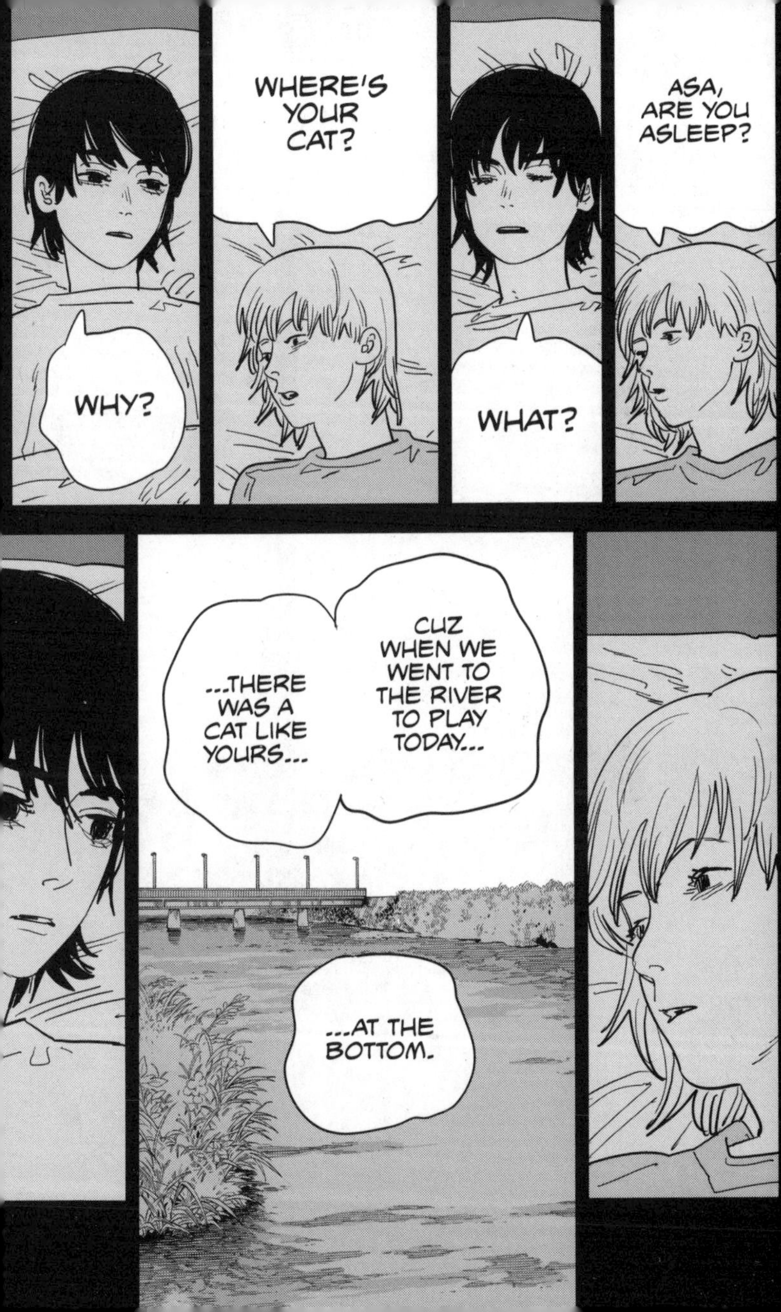
ASA, ARE YOU ASLEEP?
WHAT?
WHERE'S YOUR CAT?
WHY?
CUZ WHEN WE WENT TO THE RIVER TO PLAY TODAY...
...THERE WAS A CAT LIKE YOURS...
...AT THE BOTTOM.

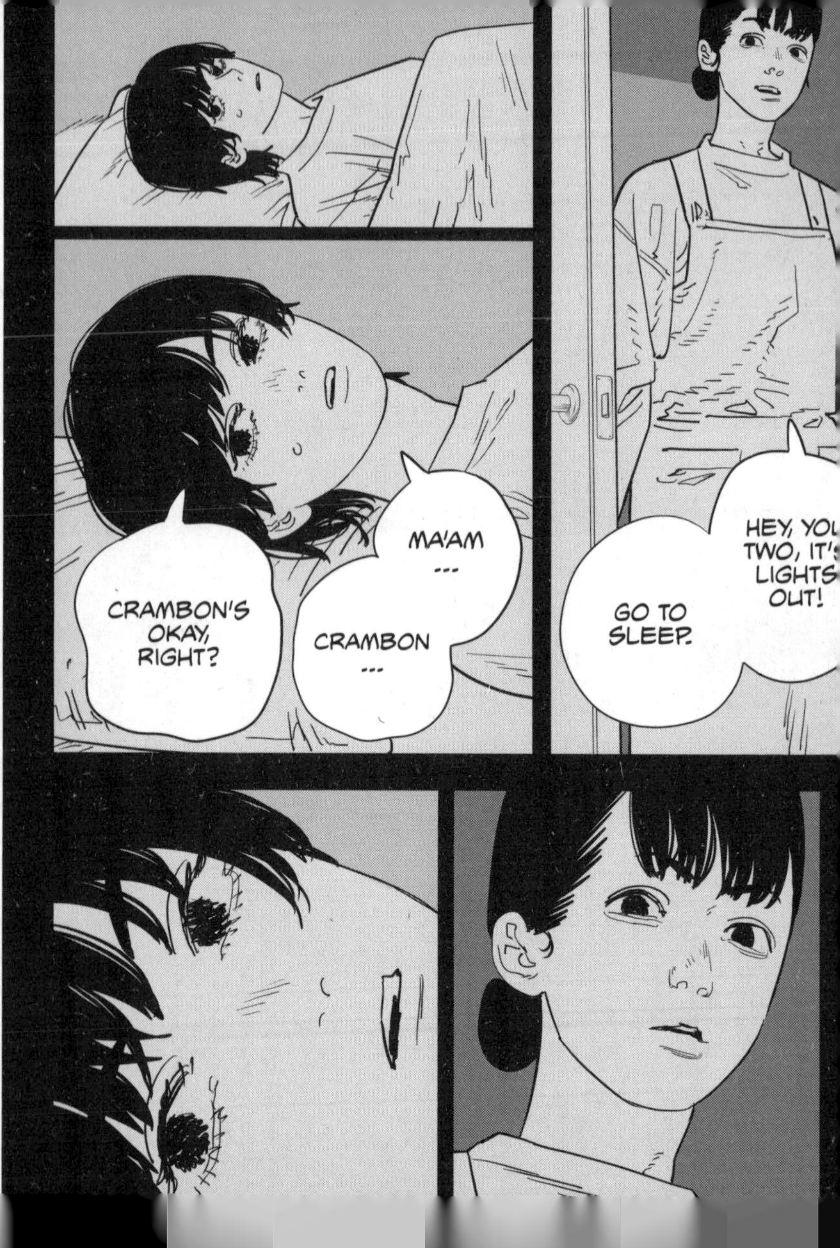

HEY, YOU TWO, IT'S LIGHTS OUT!
GO TO SLEEP.
MA'AM ...
CRAMBON ...
CRAMBON'S OKAY, RIGHT?

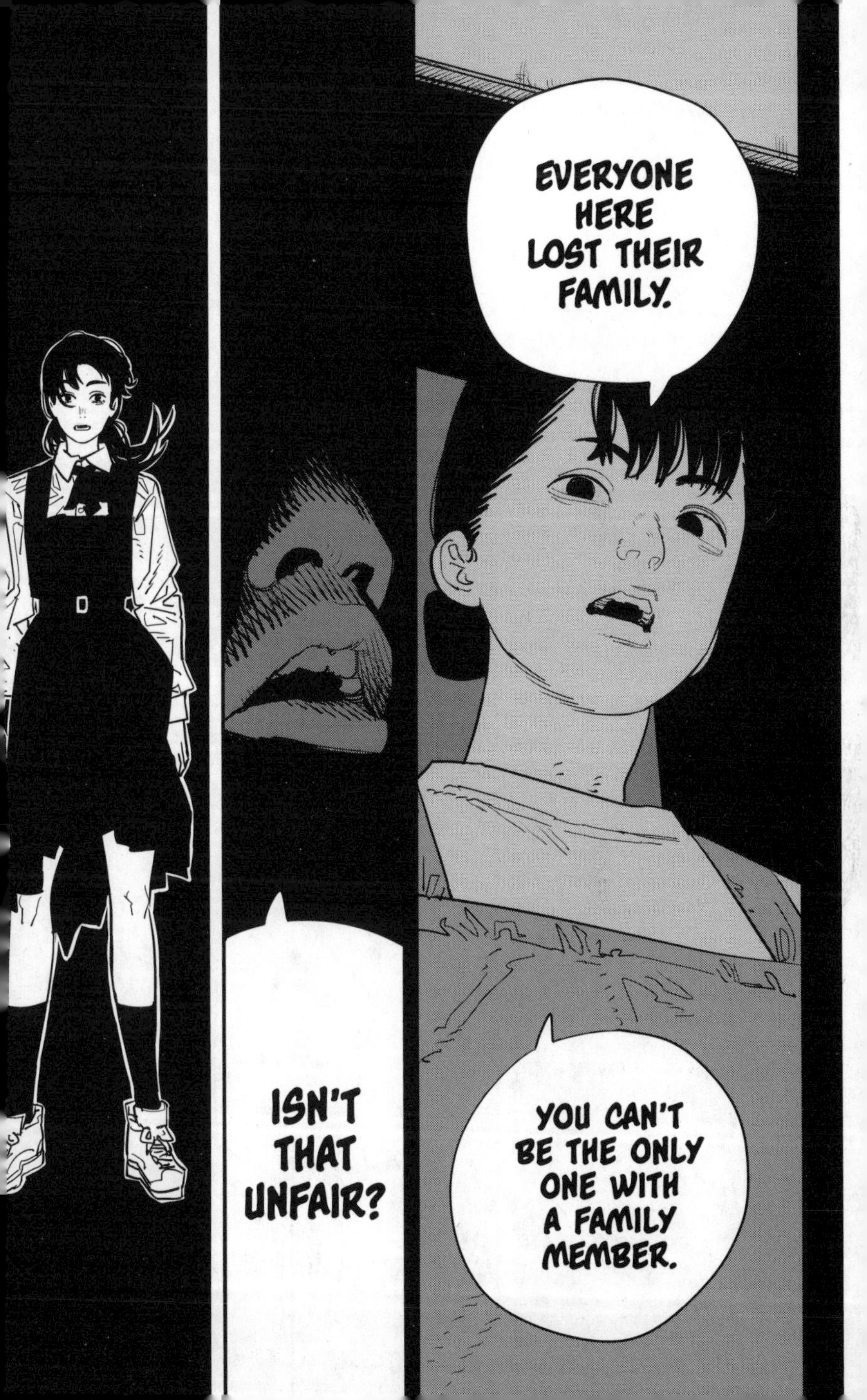
EVERYONE HERE LOST THEIR FAMILY.
YOU CAN'T BE THE ONLY ONE WITH A FAMILY MEMBER.
ISN'T THAT UNFAIR?

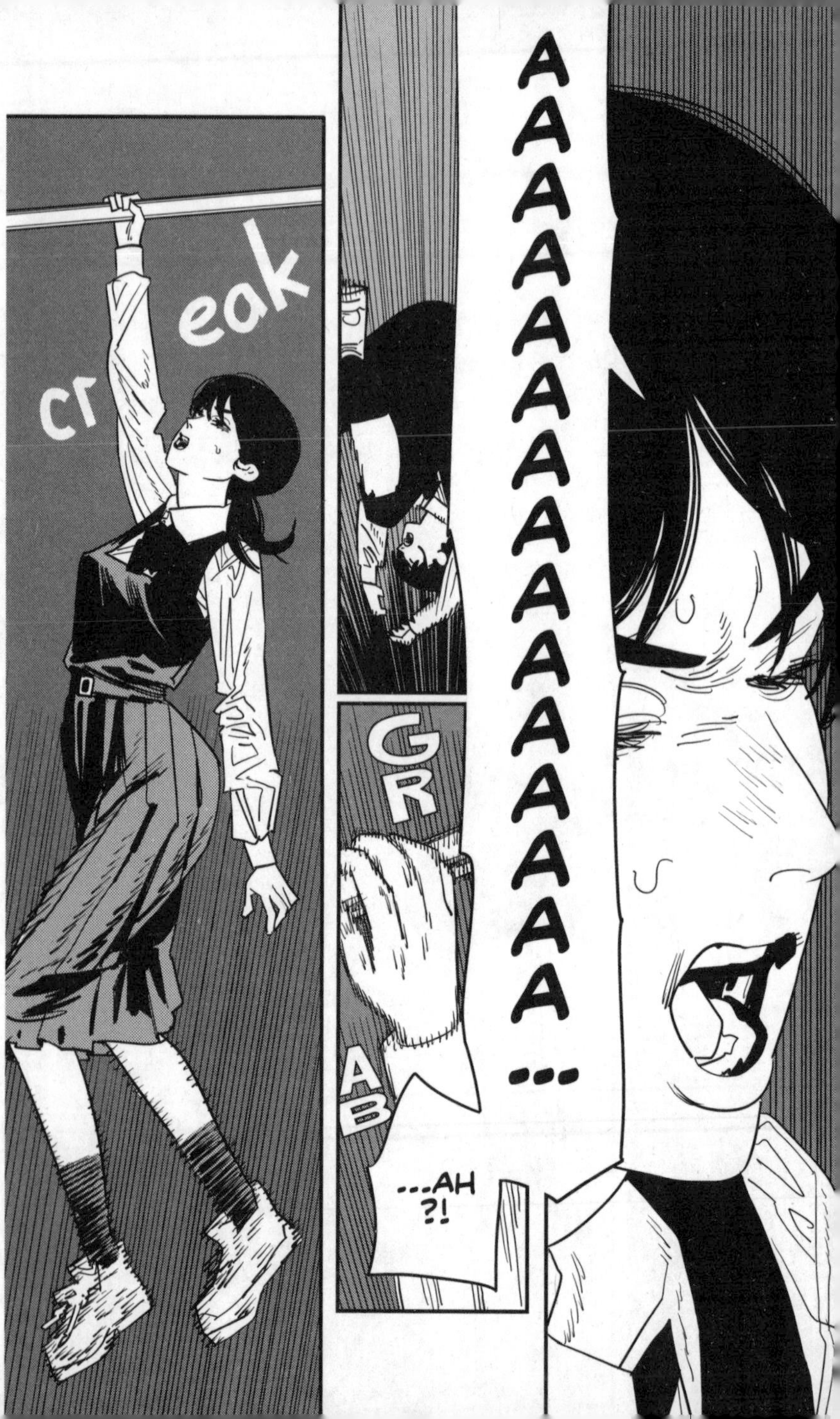
AAAAAAAAAAAAAAAA...
GRAB
...AH ?!
creak

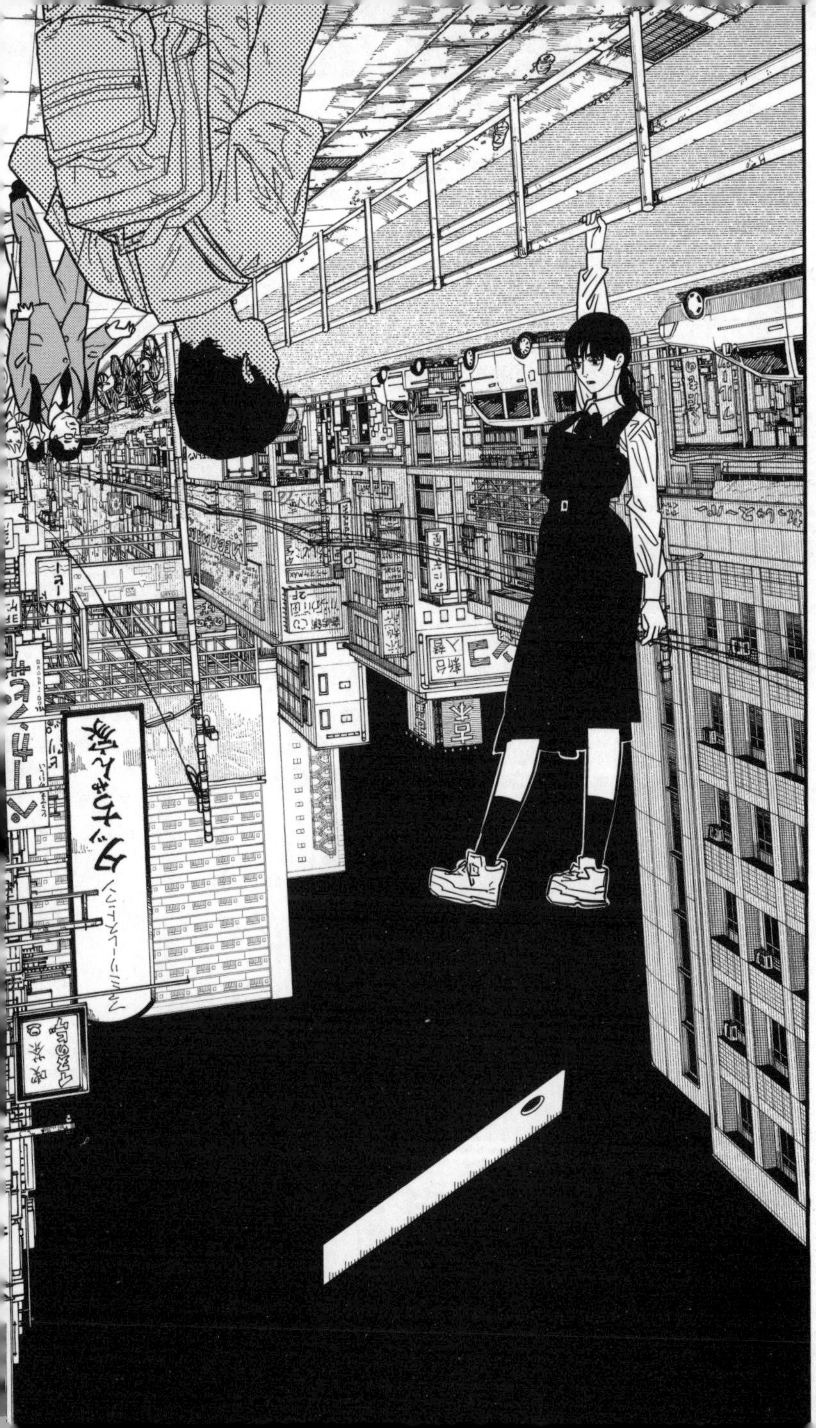

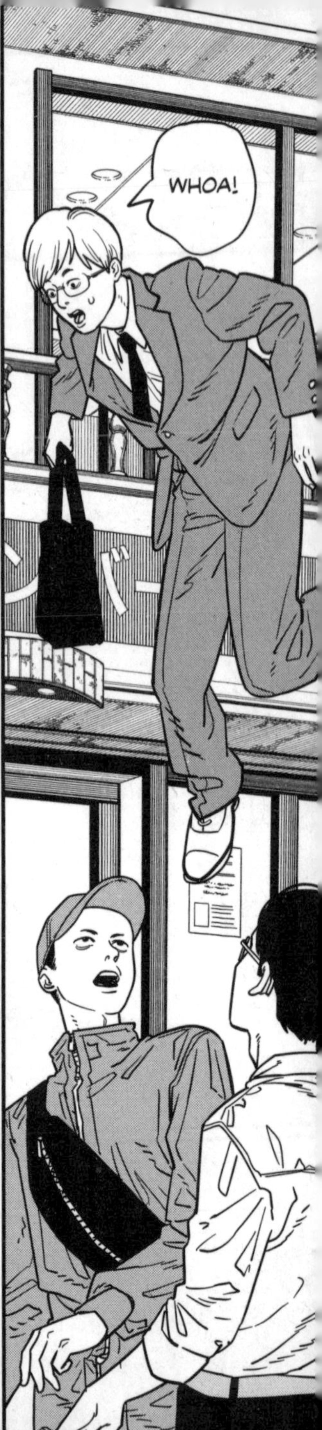
WHOA!
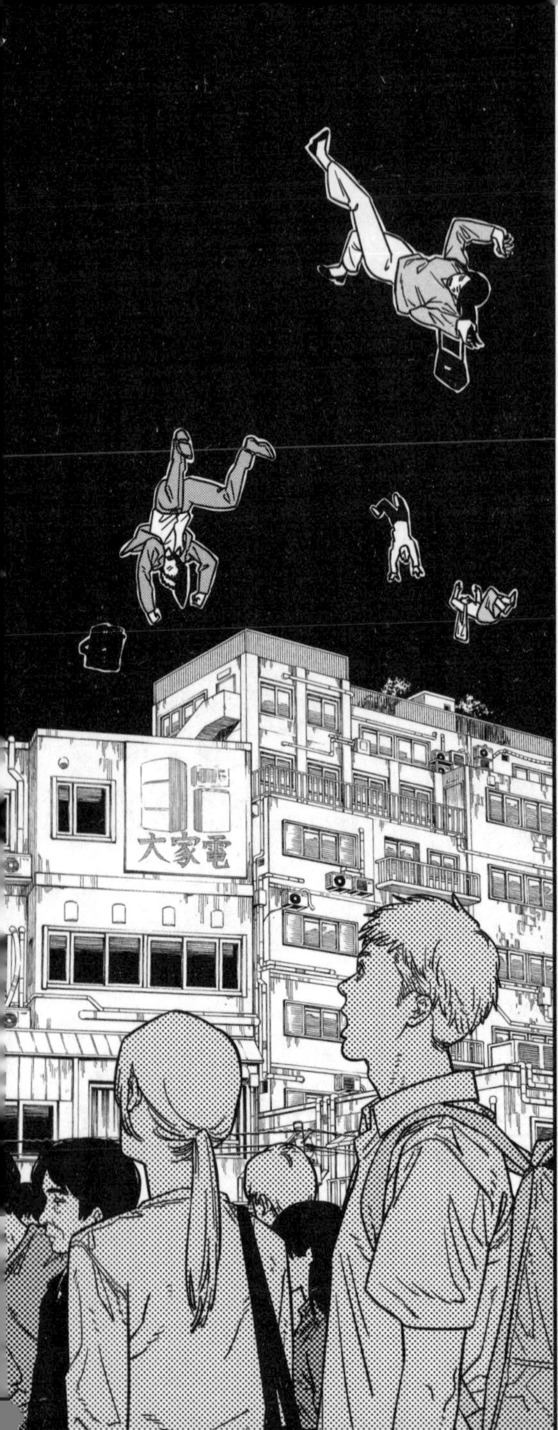
大家電

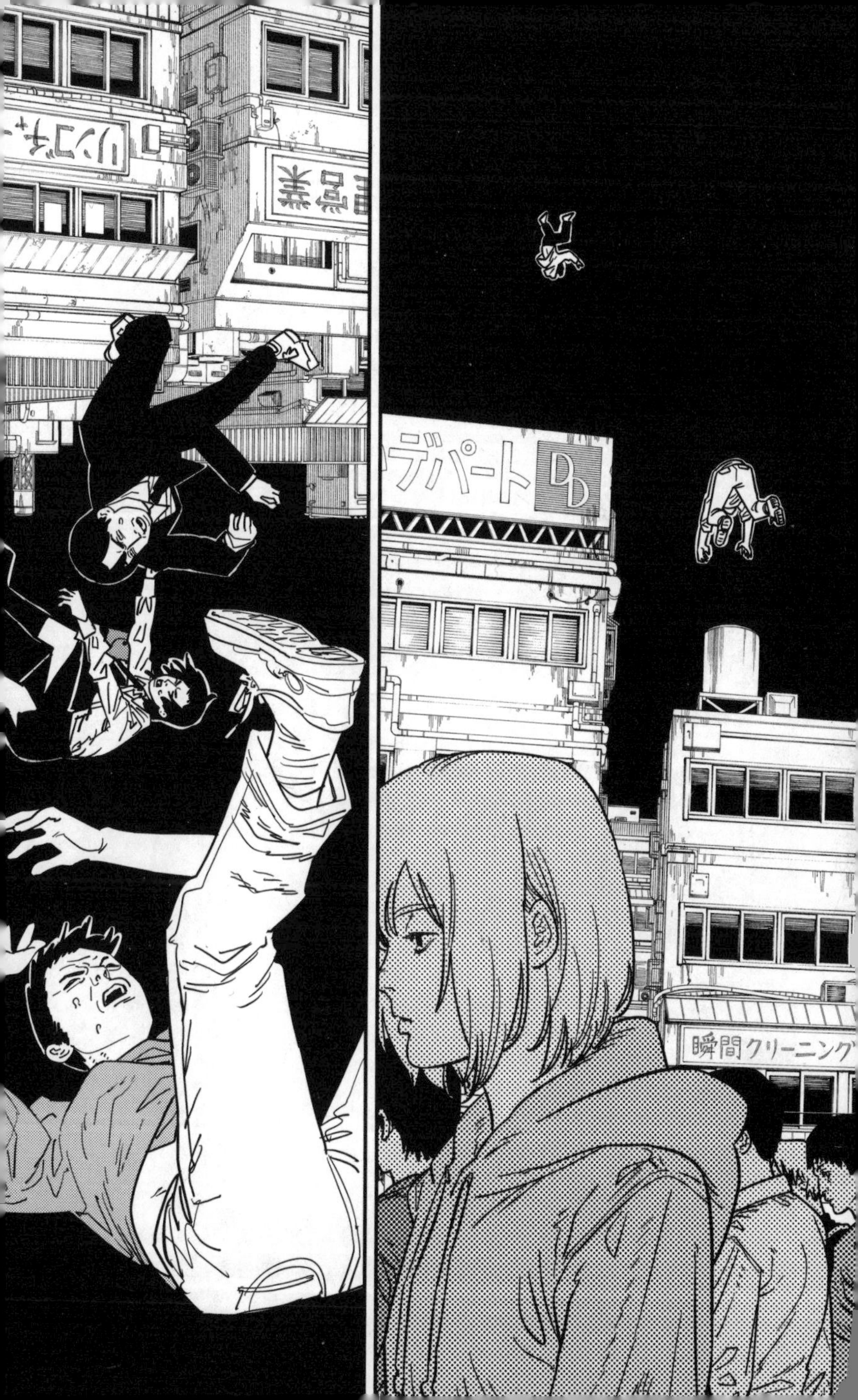
デパート
DD
瞬間クリーニング

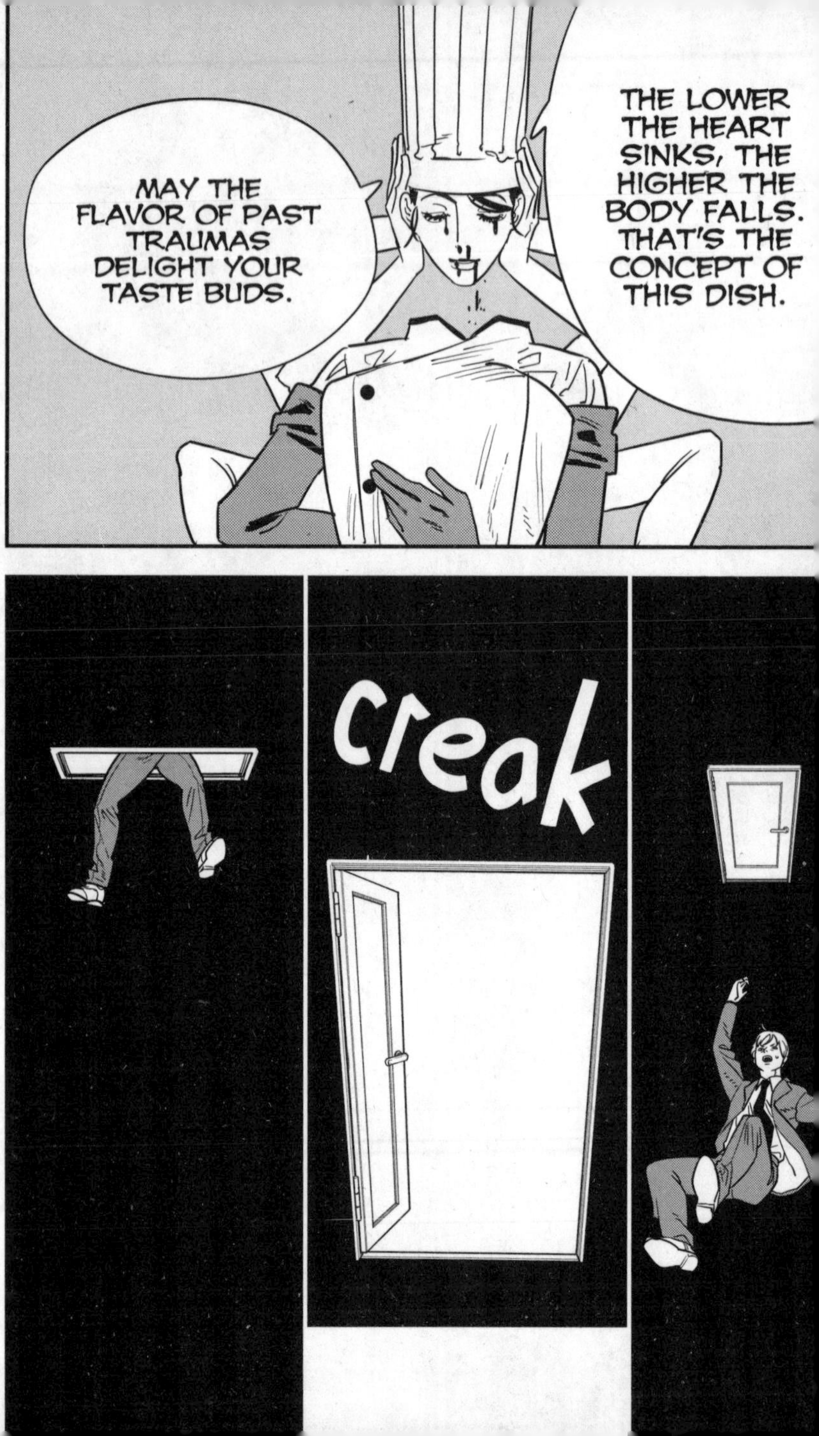
THE LOWER THE HEART SINKS, THE HIGHER THE BODY FALLS. THAT'S THE CONCEPT OF THIS DISH.
MAY THE FLAVOR OF PAST TRAUMAS DELIGHT YOUR TASTE BUDS.
creak

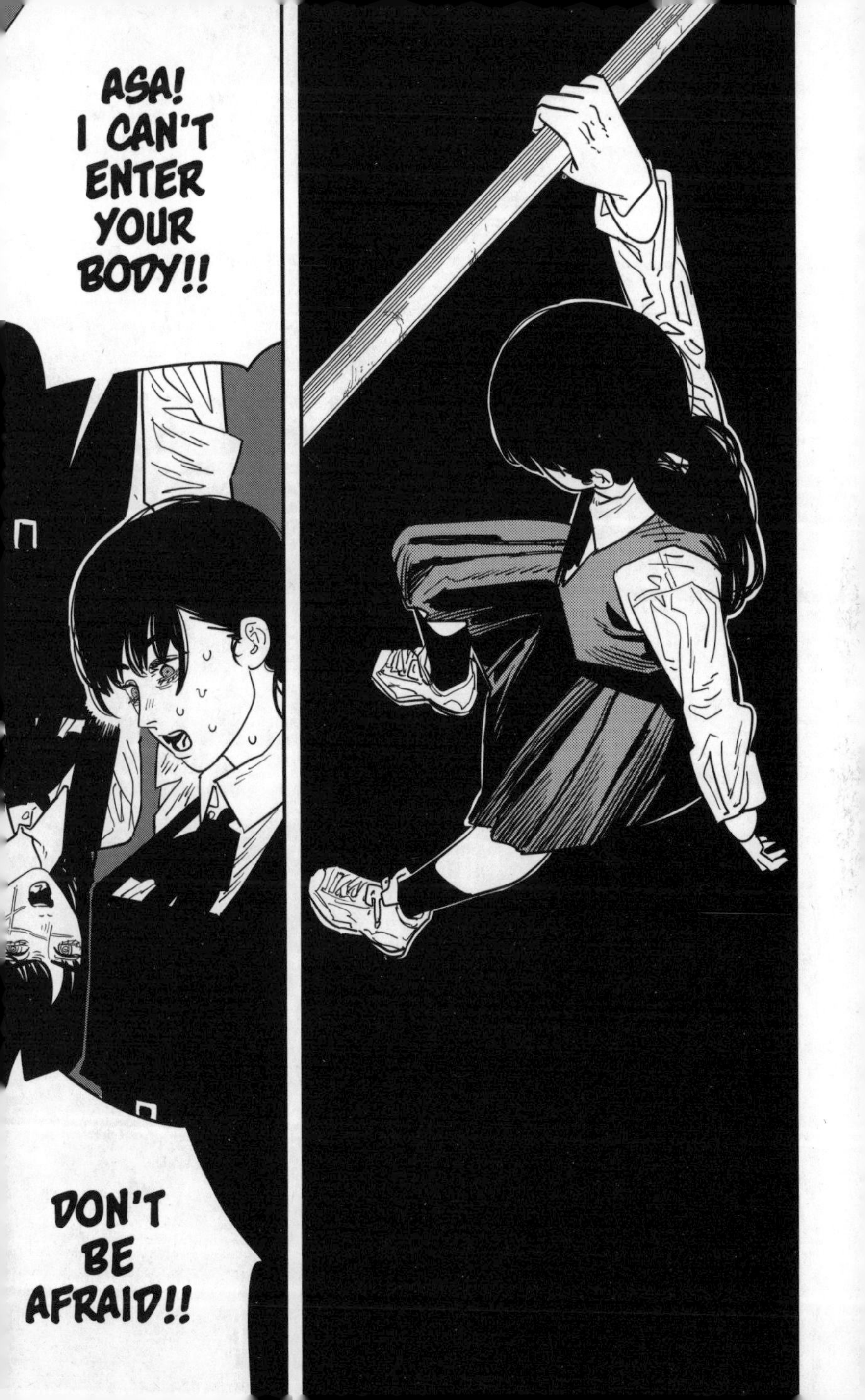
ASA! I CAN'T ENTER YOUR BODY!!
DON'T BE AFRAID!!

Chapter 124: Soup

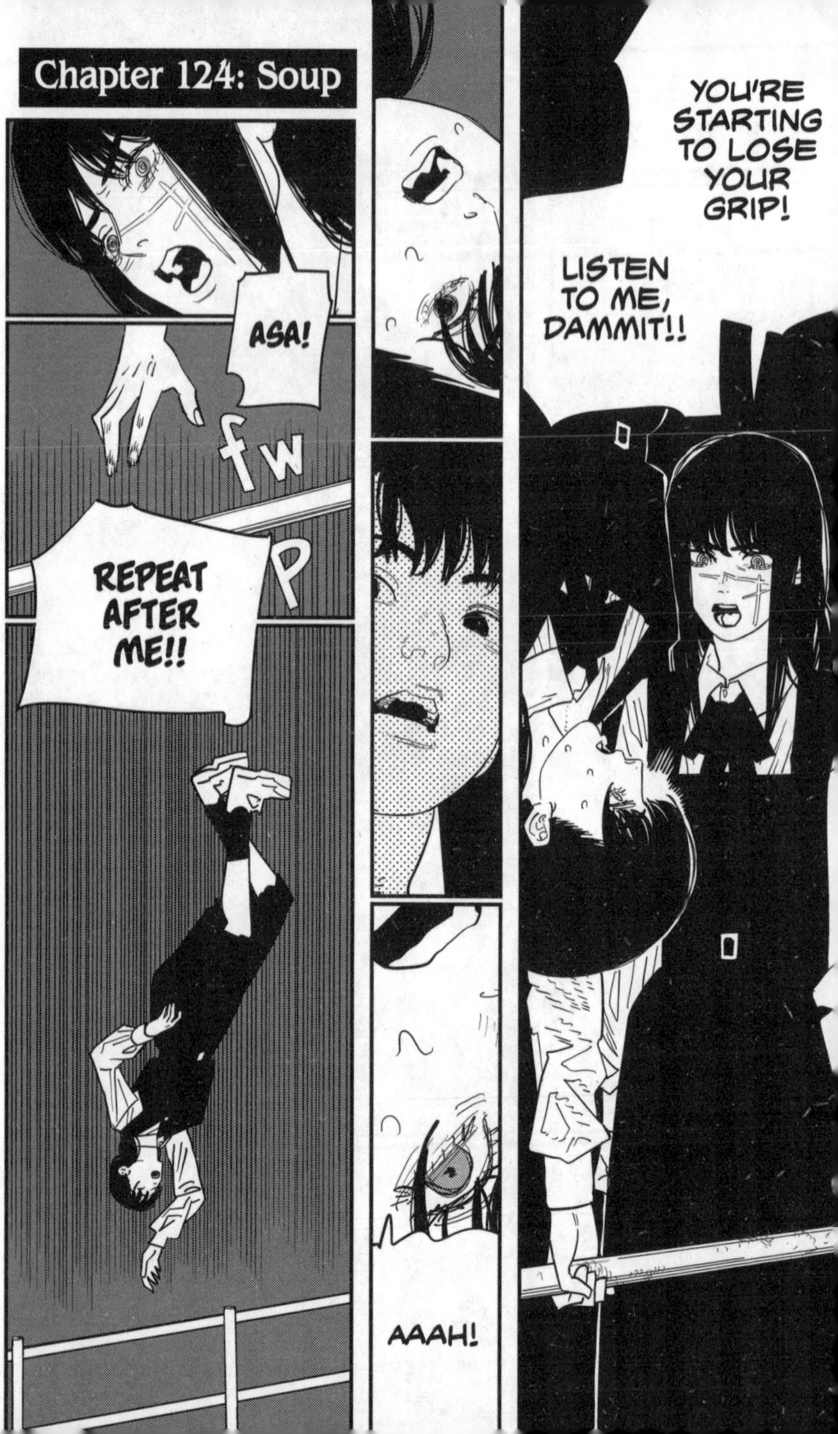
YOU'RE STARTING TO LOSE YOUR GRIP!
LISTEN TO ME, DAMMIT!!
AAAH!
ASA!
fw
P
REPEAT AFTER ME!!

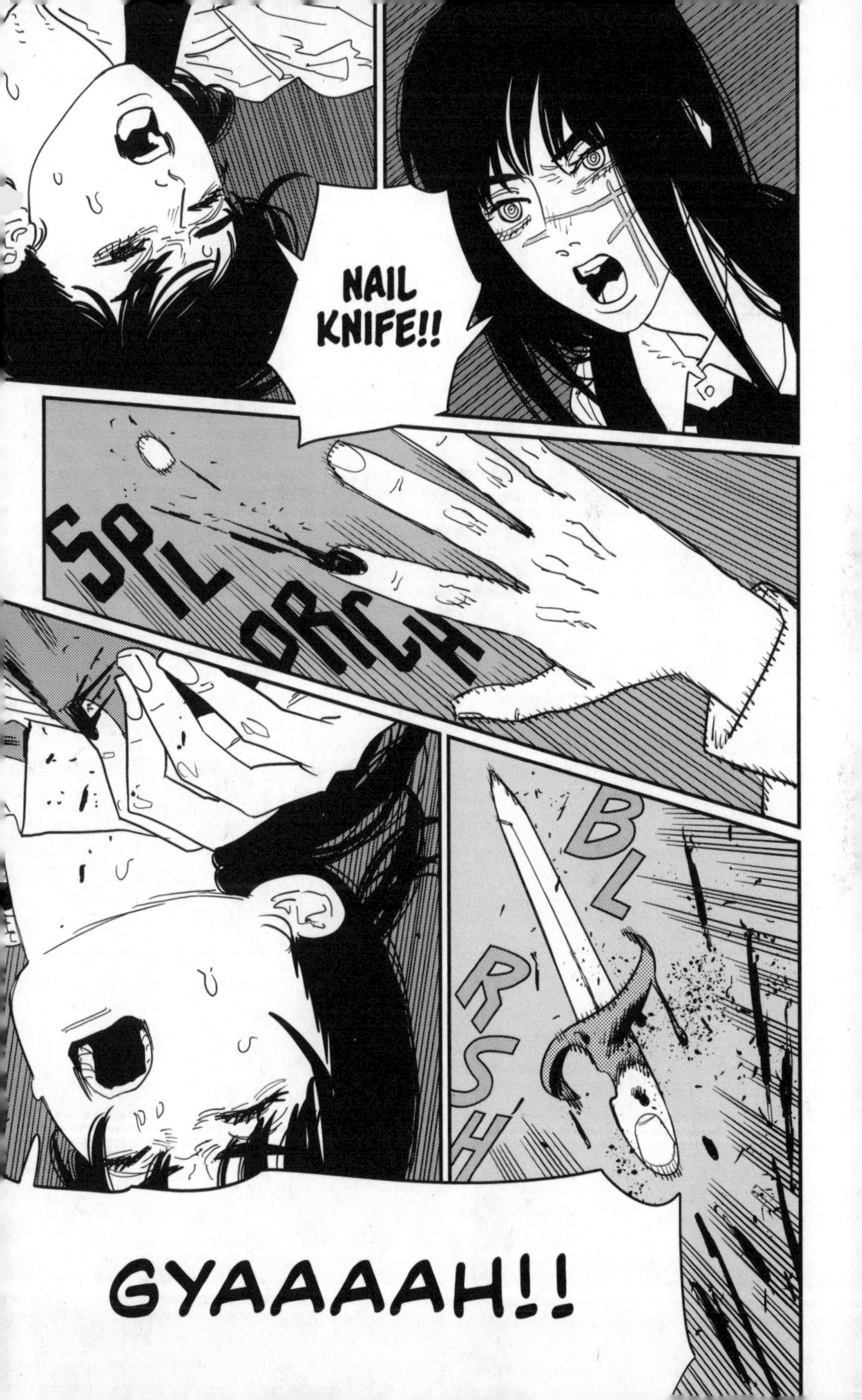
NAIL KNIFE!!
SPLORCH
BLRSH
GYAAAAH!!

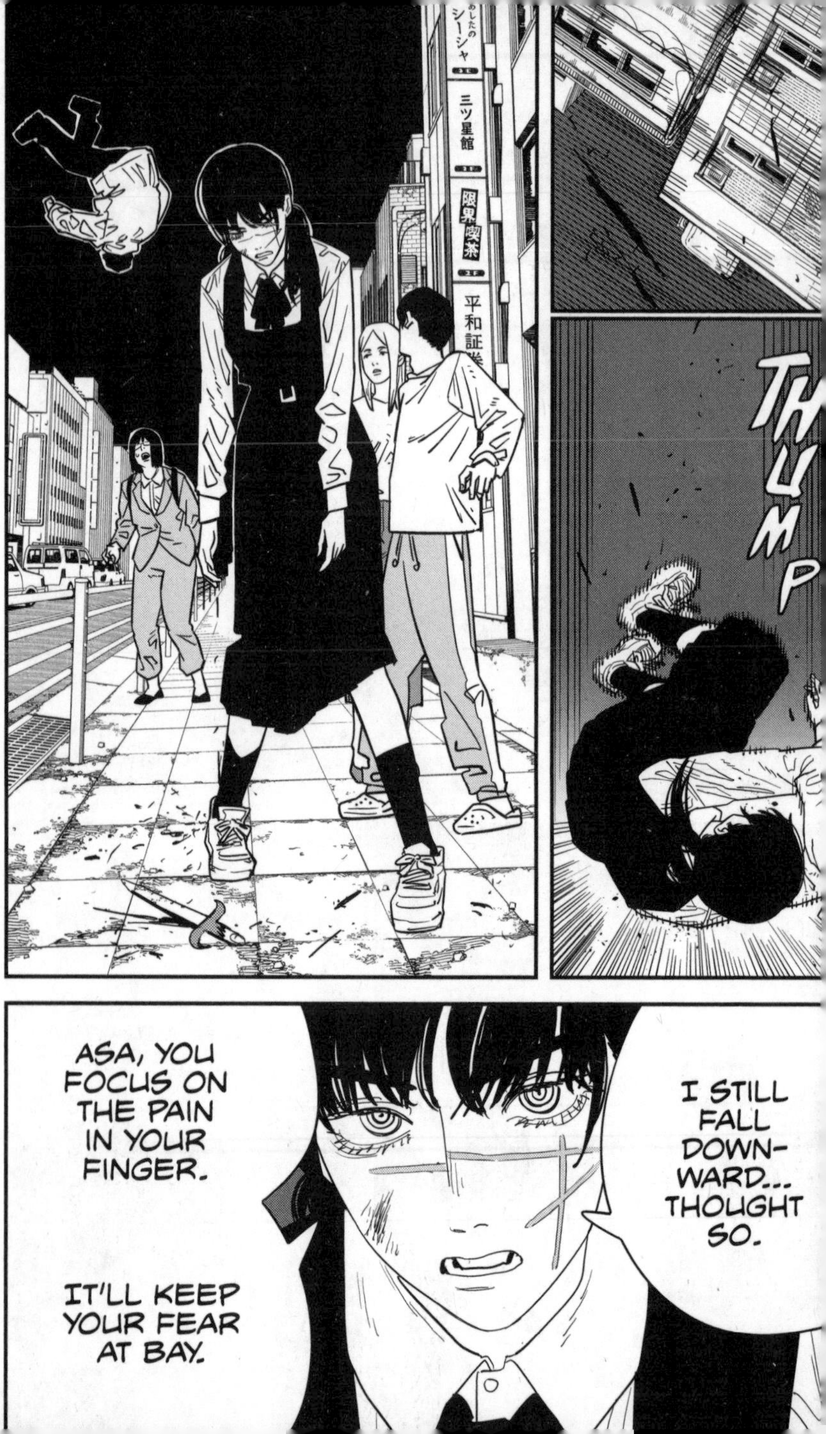
THUMP
あしたのシーシャ
三ツ星館
限界喫茶
I STILL FALL DOWNWARD... THOUGHT SO.
ASA, YOU FOCUS ON THE PAIN IN YOUR FINGER.
IT'LL KEEP YOUR FEAR AT BAY.

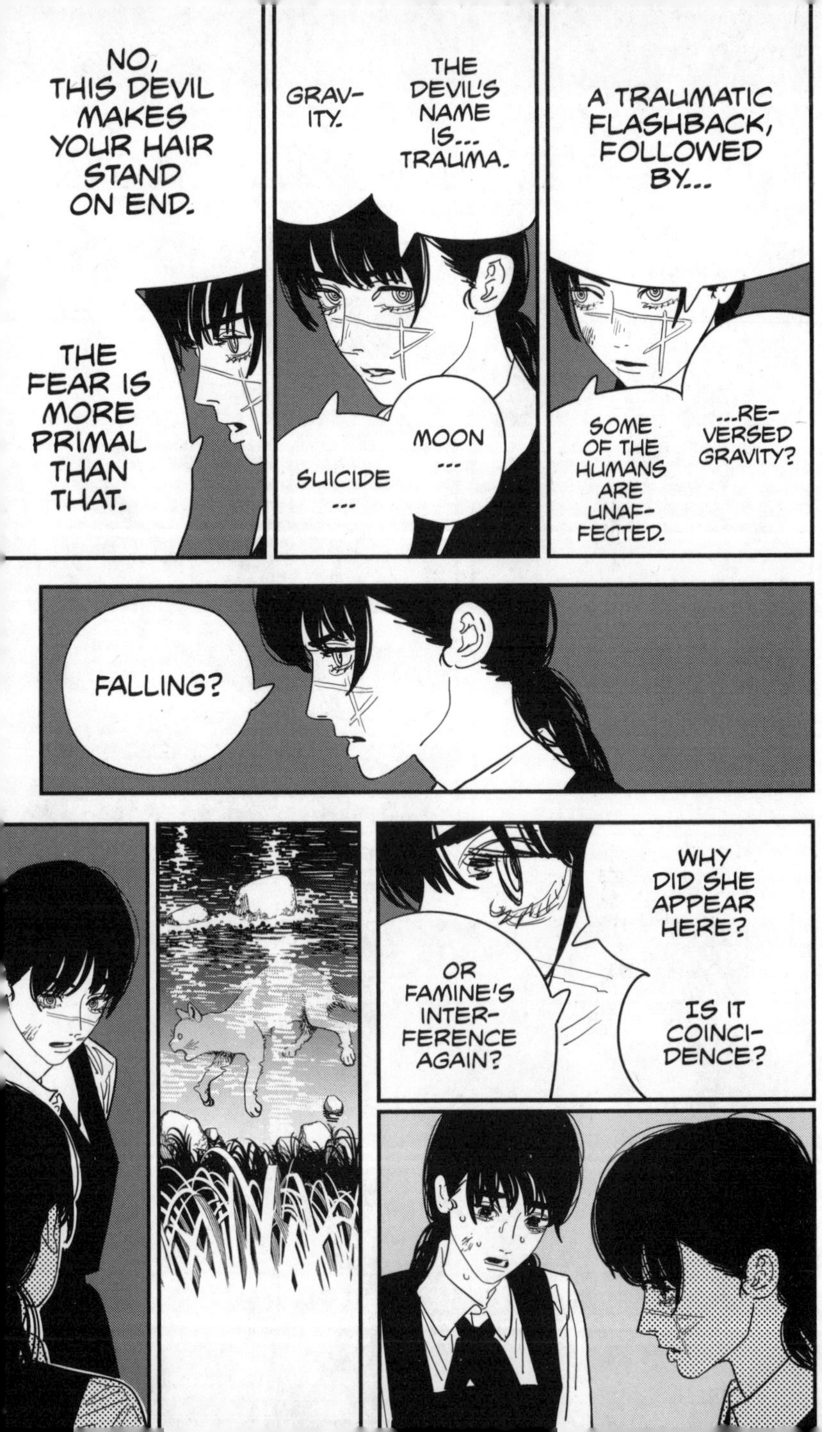
A TRAUMATIC FLASHBACK, FOLLOWED BY...
...REVERSED GRAVITY?
SOME OF THE HUMANS ARE UNAFFECTED.
THE DEVIL'S NAME IS... TRAUMA.
GRAVITY.
MOON...
SUICIDE...
NO, THIS DEVIL MAKES YOUR HAIR STAND ON END.
THE FEAR IS MORE PRIMAL THAN THAT.
FALLING?
WHY DID SHE APPEAR HERE?
IS IT COINCIDENCE?
OR FAMINE'S INTERFERENCE AGAIN?

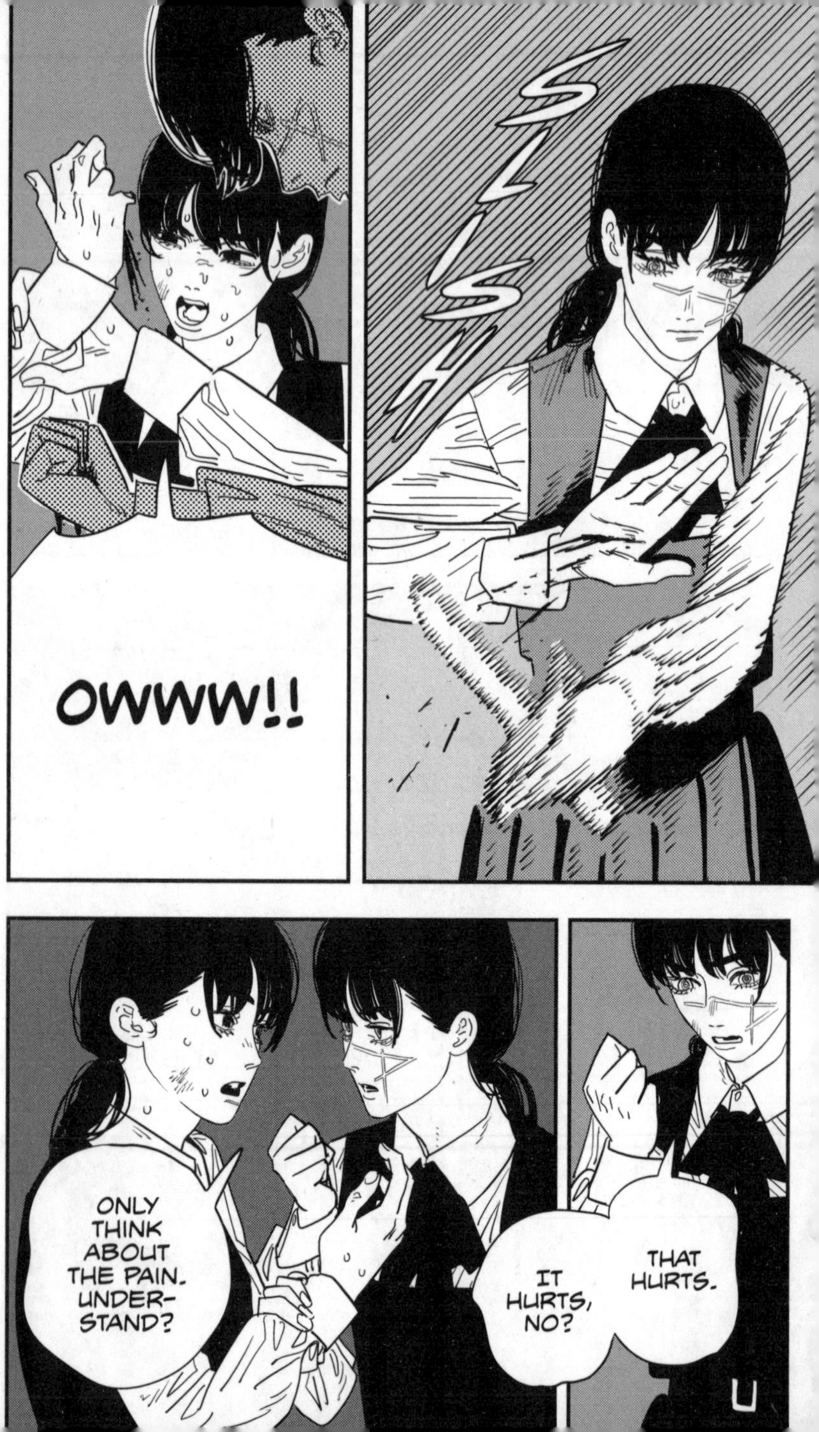
OWWW!!
THAT HURTS.
IT HURTS, NO?
ONLY THINK ABOUT THE PAIN. UNDER-STAND?

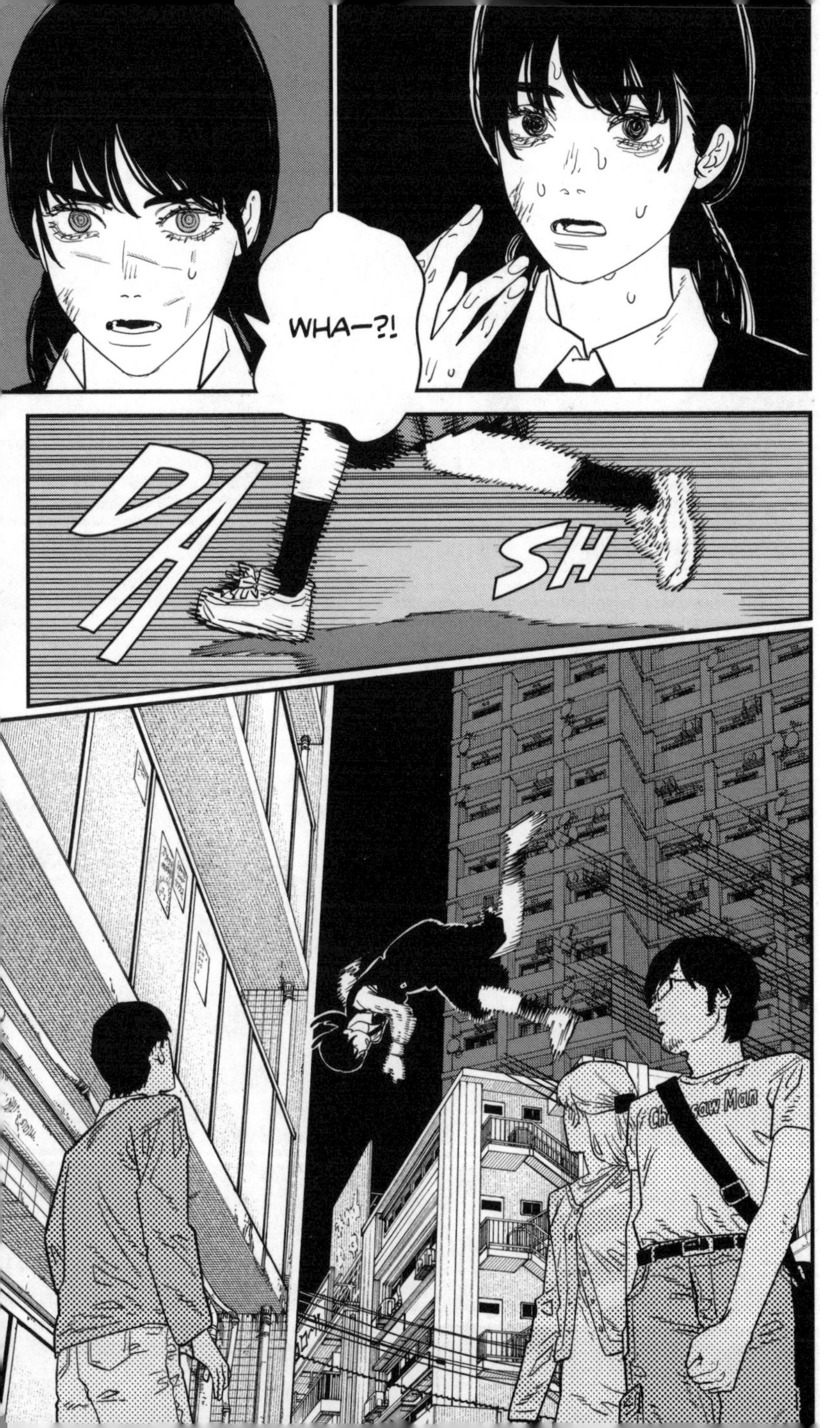
WHA—?!
DASH

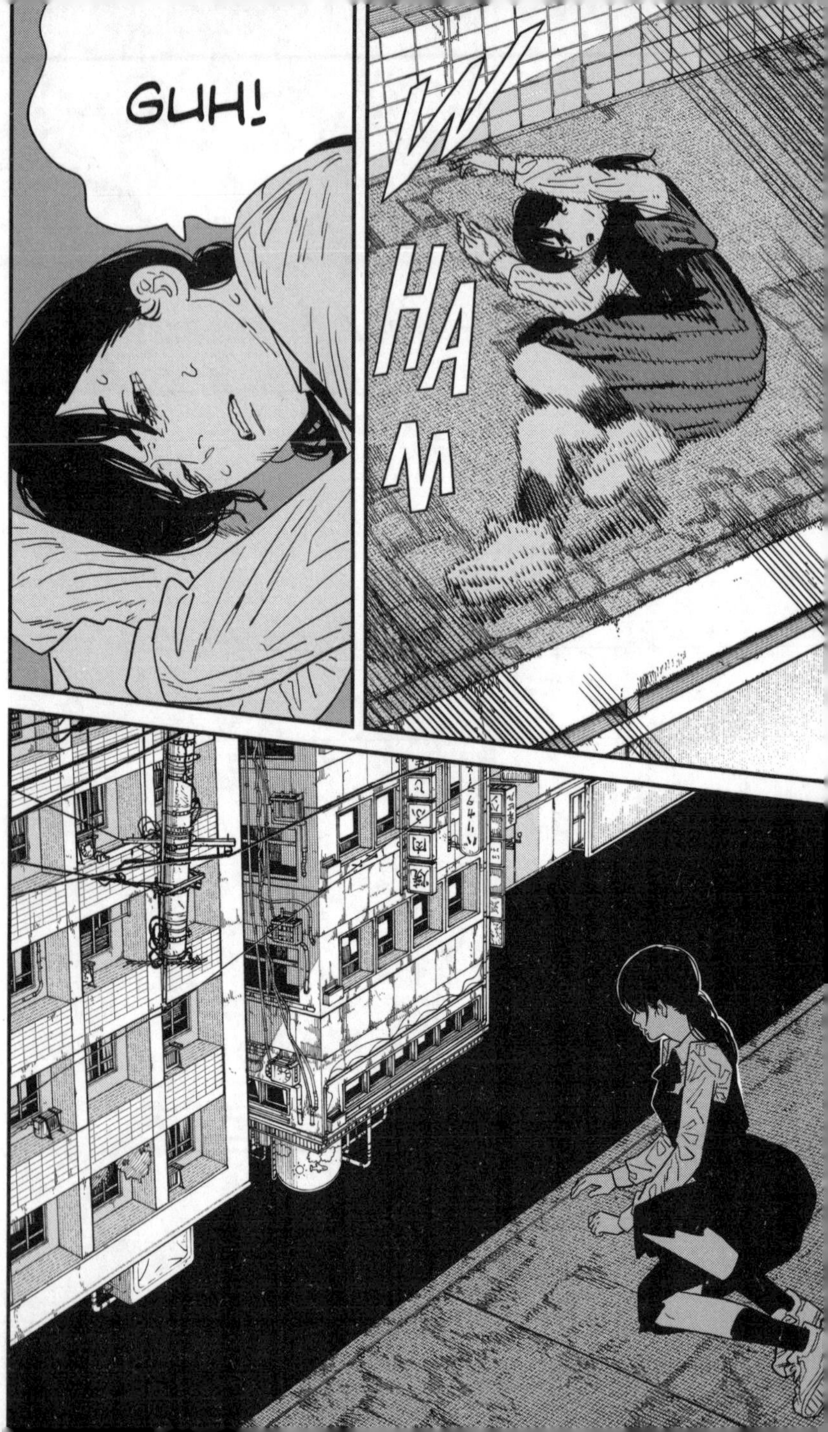
WHAM
GUH!

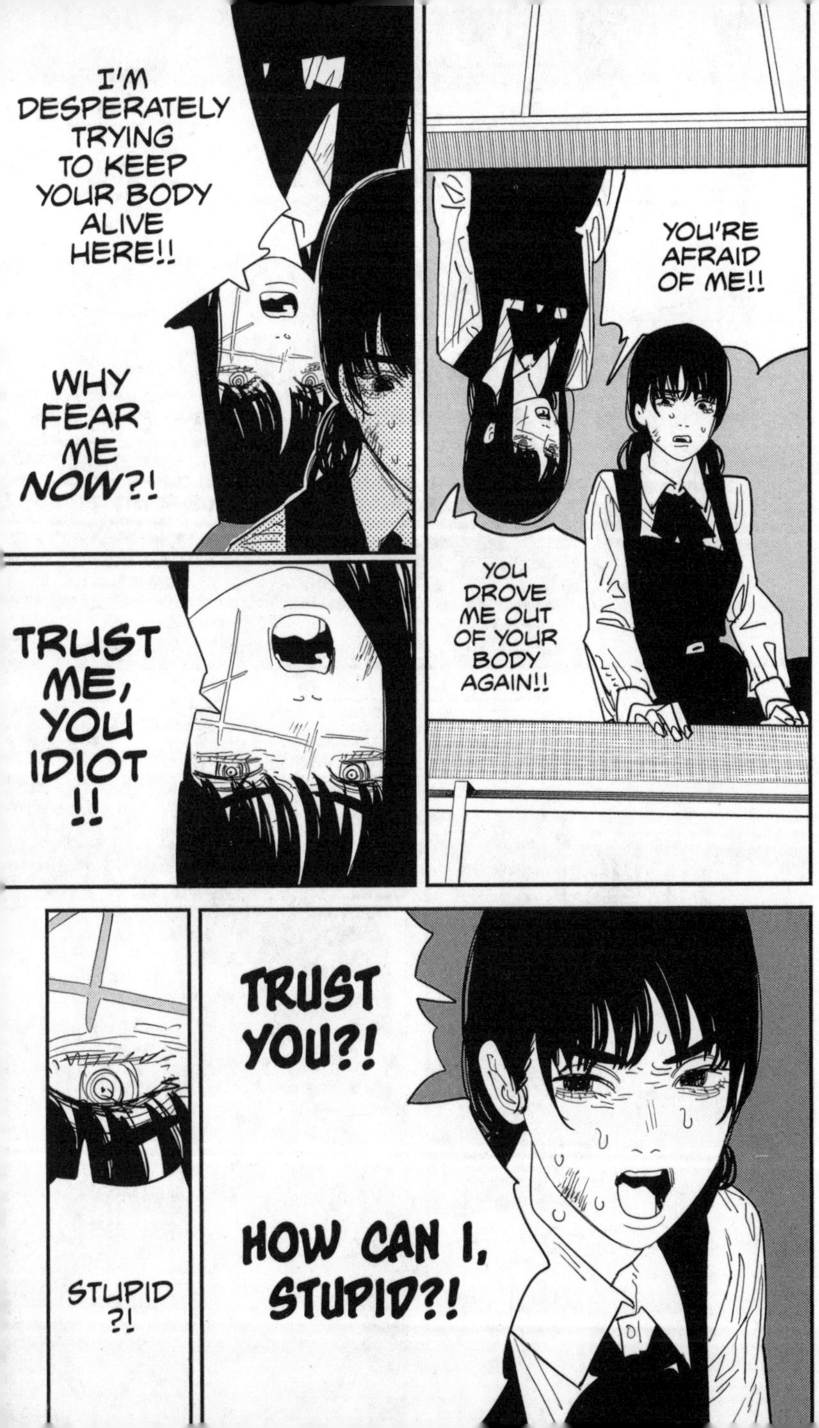
YOU'RE AFRAID OF ME!!
YOU DROVE ME OUT OF YOUR BODY AGAIN!!
I'M DESPERATELY TRYING TO KEEP YOUR BODY ALIVE HERE!!
WHY FEAR ME NOW?!
TRUST ME, YOU IDIOT!!
TRUST YOU?!
HOW CAN I, STUPID?!
STUPID?!

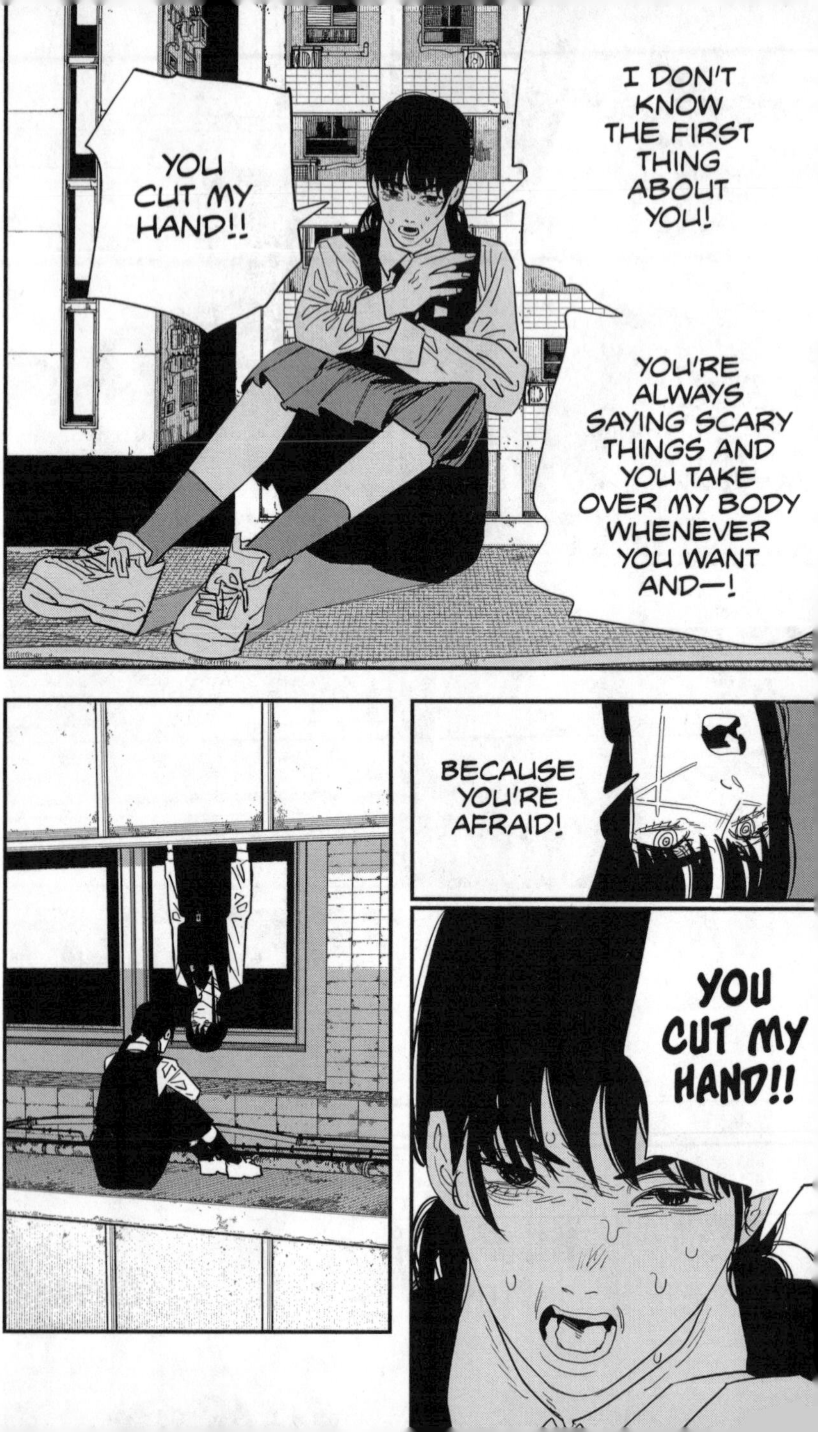
I DON'T KNOW THE FIRST THING ABOUT YOU!
YOU CUT MY HAND!!
YOU'RE ALWAYS SAYING SCARY THINGS AND YOU TAKE OVER MY BODY WHENEVER YOU WANT AND—!
BECAUSE YOU'RE AFRAID!
YOU CUT MY HAND!!

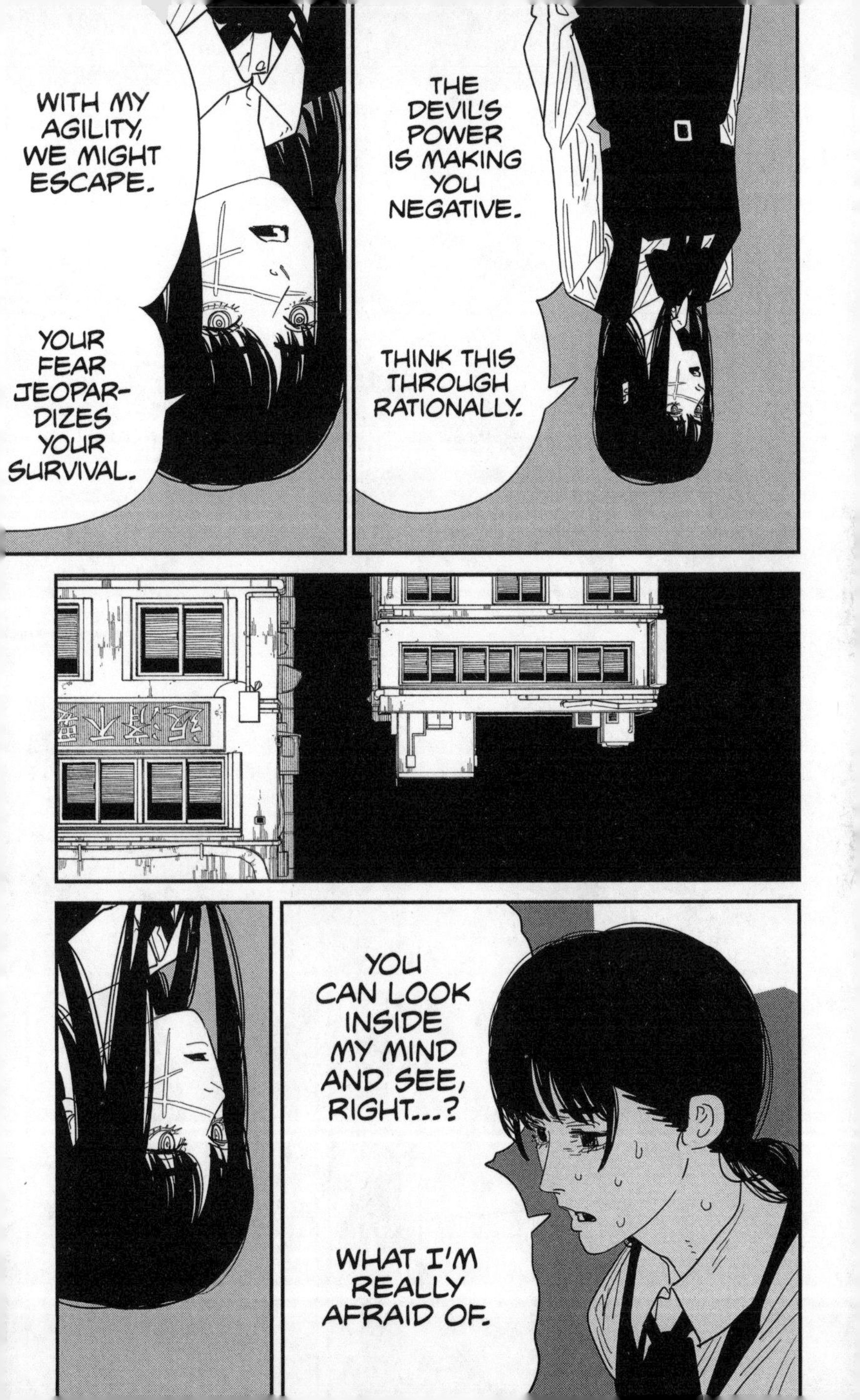
THE DEVIL'S POWER IS MAKING YOU NEGATIVE.
THINK THIS THROUGH RATIONALLY.
WITH MY AGILITY, WE MIGHT ESCAPE.
YOUR FEAR JEOPARDIZES YOUR SURVIVAL.
YOU CAN LOOK INSIDE MY MIND AND SEE, RIGHT...?
WHAT I'M REALLY AFRAID OF.

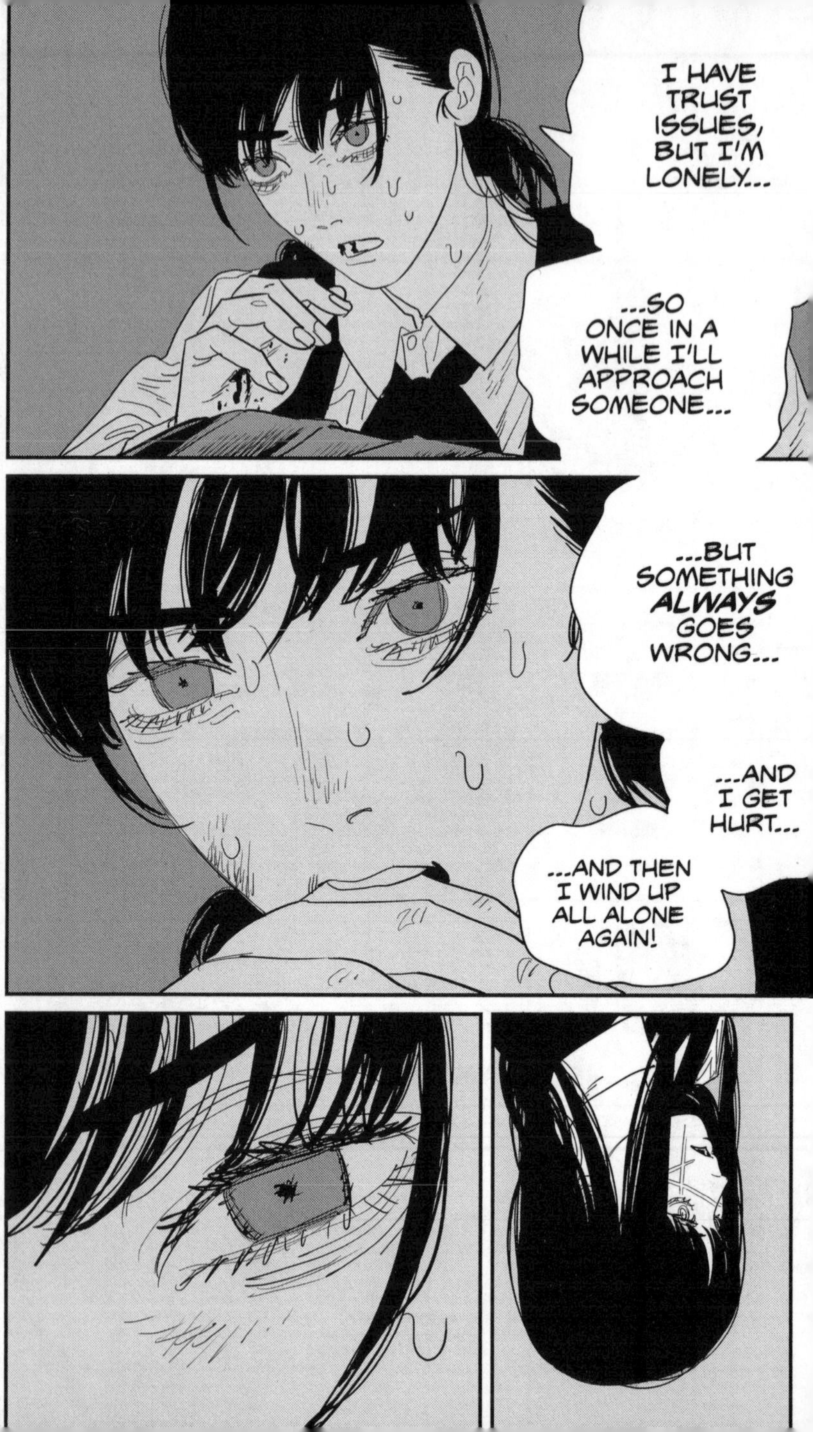
I HAVE TRUST ISSUES, BUT I'M LONELY...
...SO ONCE IN A WHILE I'LL APPROACH SOMEONE...
...BUT SOMETHING ALWAYS GOES WRONG...
...AND I GET HURT...
...AND THEN I WIND UP ALL ALONE AGAIN!

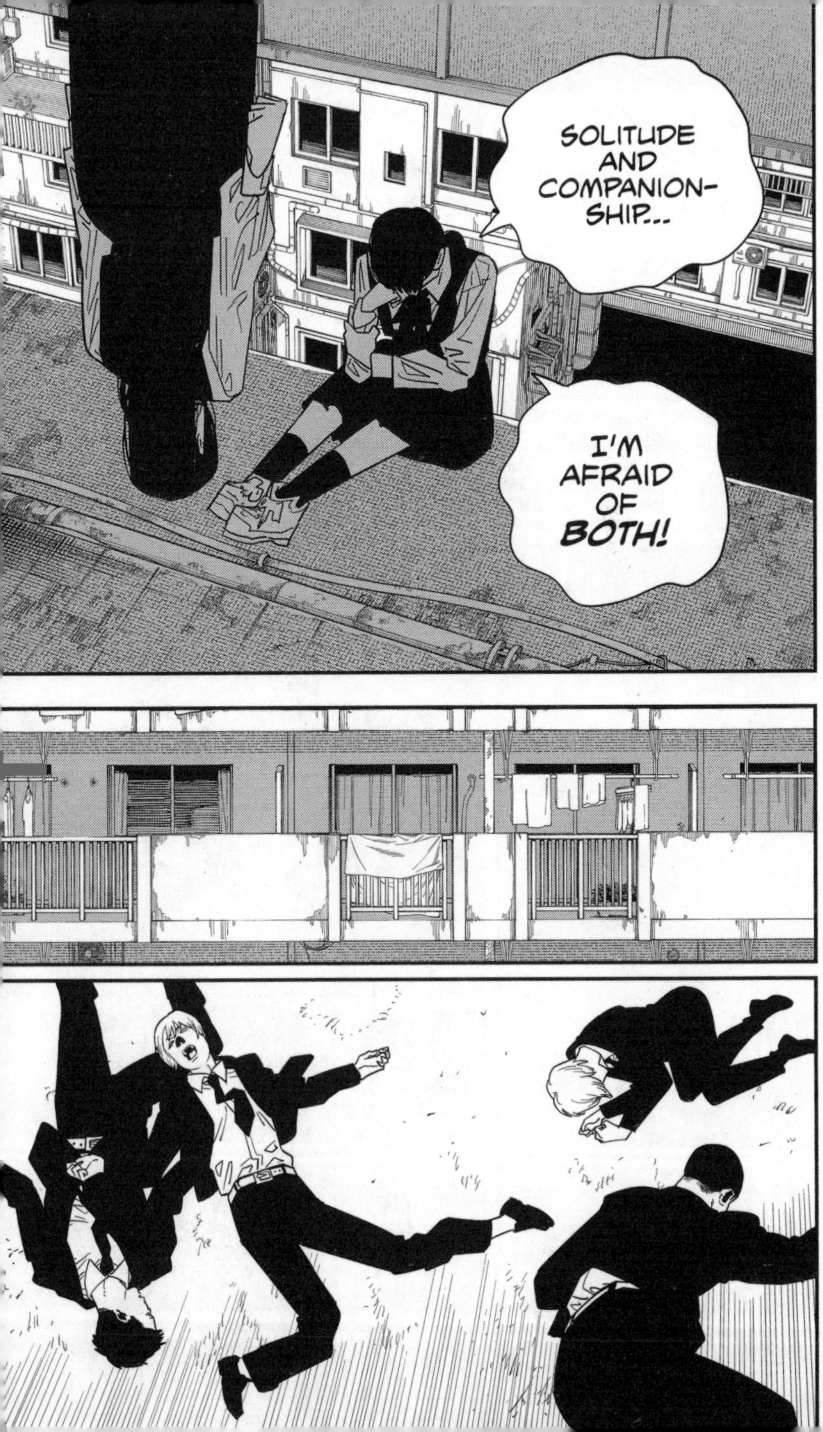
SOLITUDE AND COMPANION-SHIP...
I'M AFRAID OF BOTH!

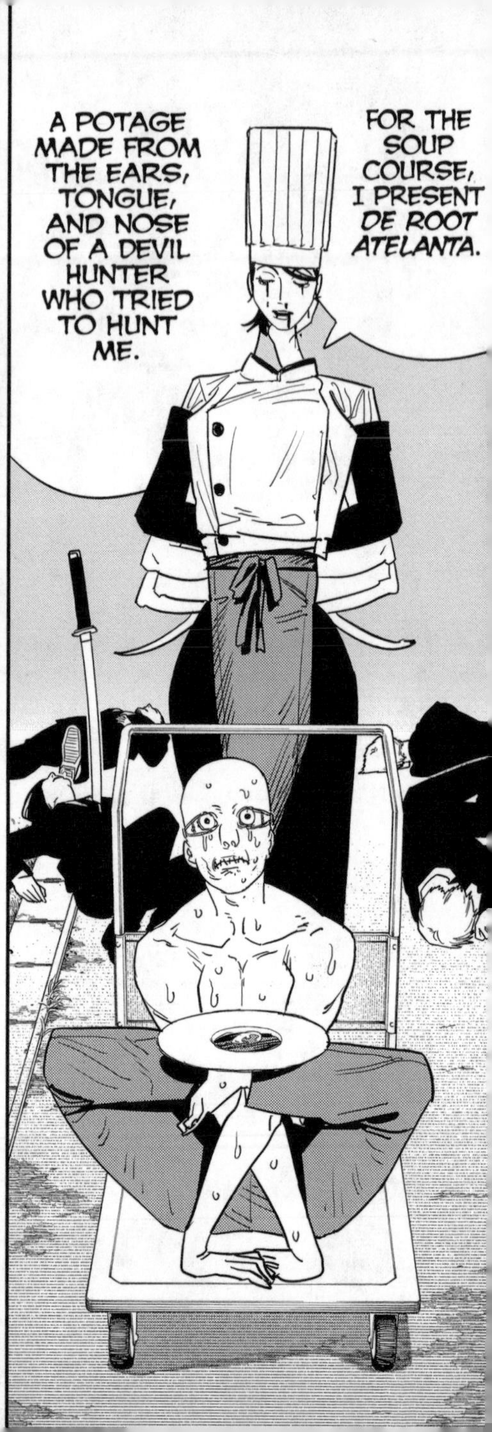
FOR THE SOUP COURSE, I PRESENT *DE ROOT ATELANTA.*
A POTAGE MADE FROM THE EARS, TONGUE, AND NOSE OF A DEVIL HUNTER WHO TRIED TO HUNT ME.
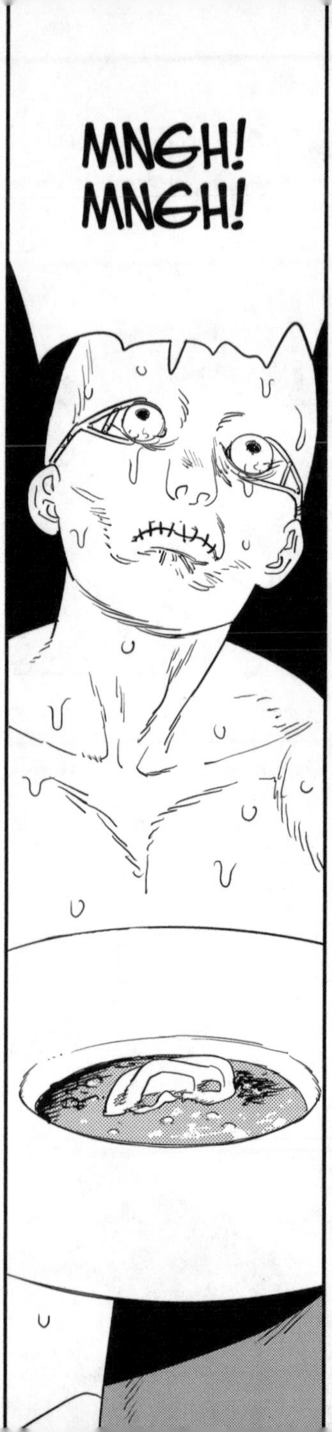
MNGH! MNGH!

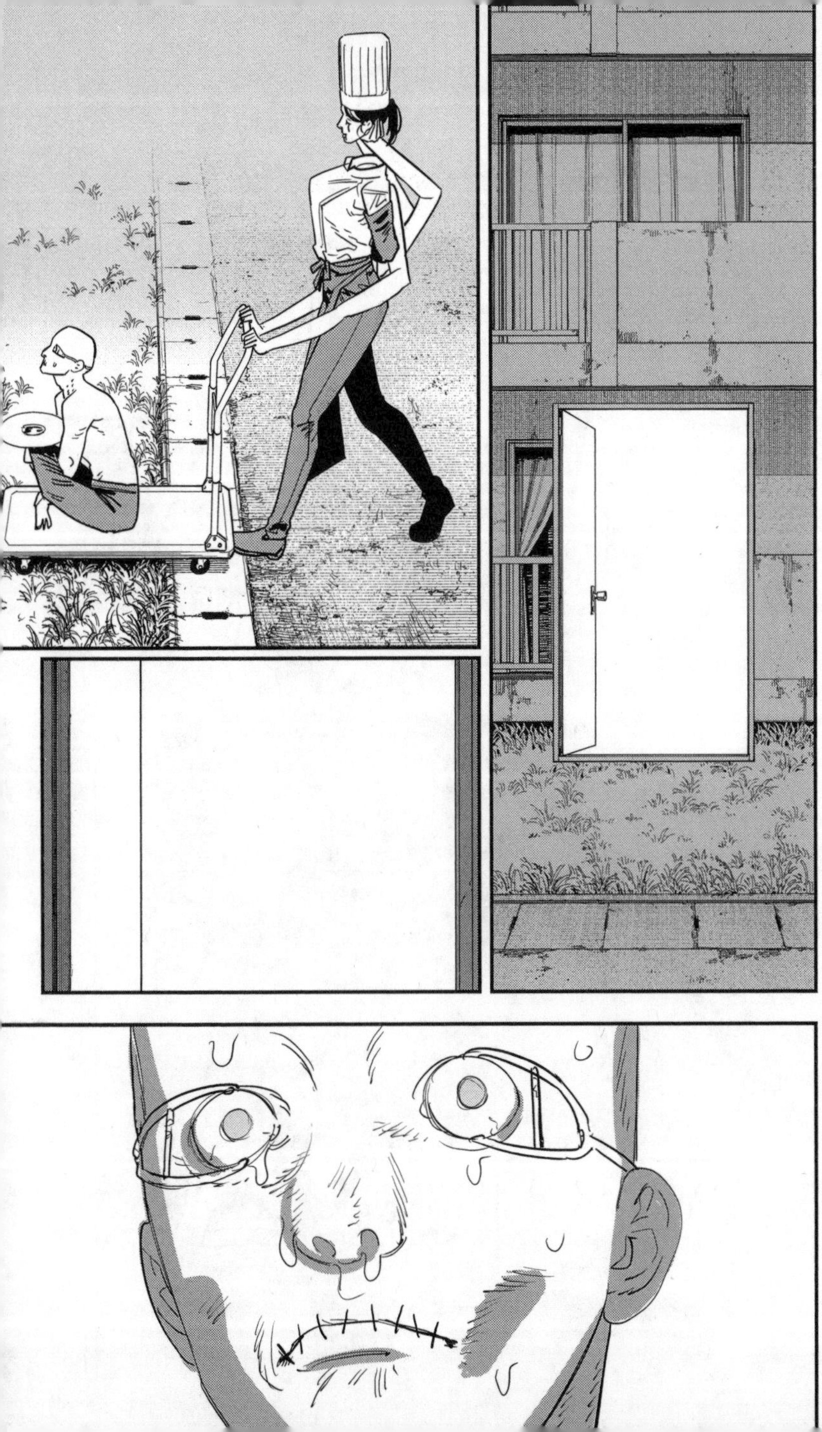

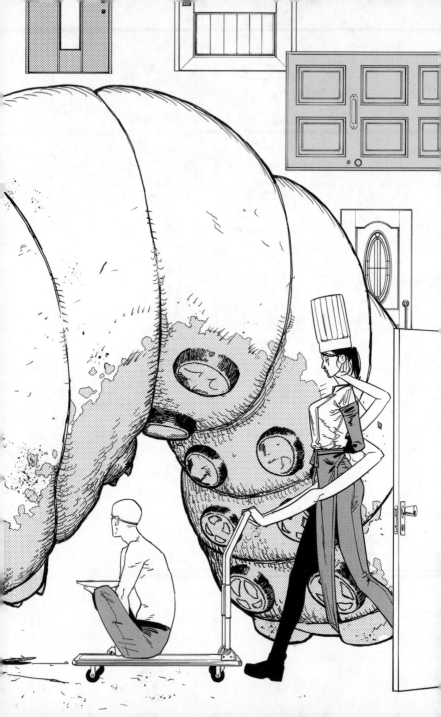

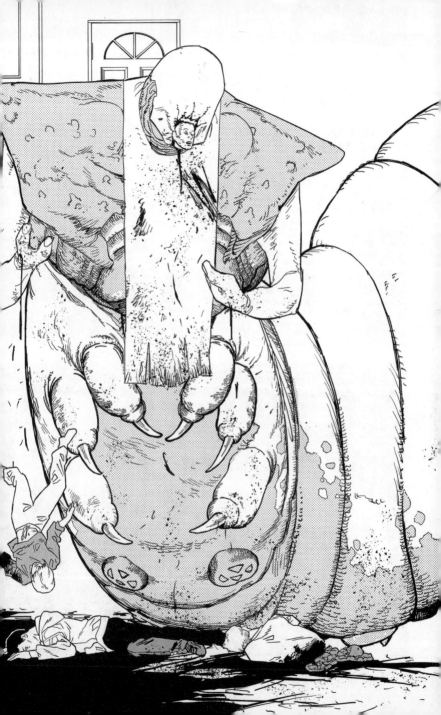

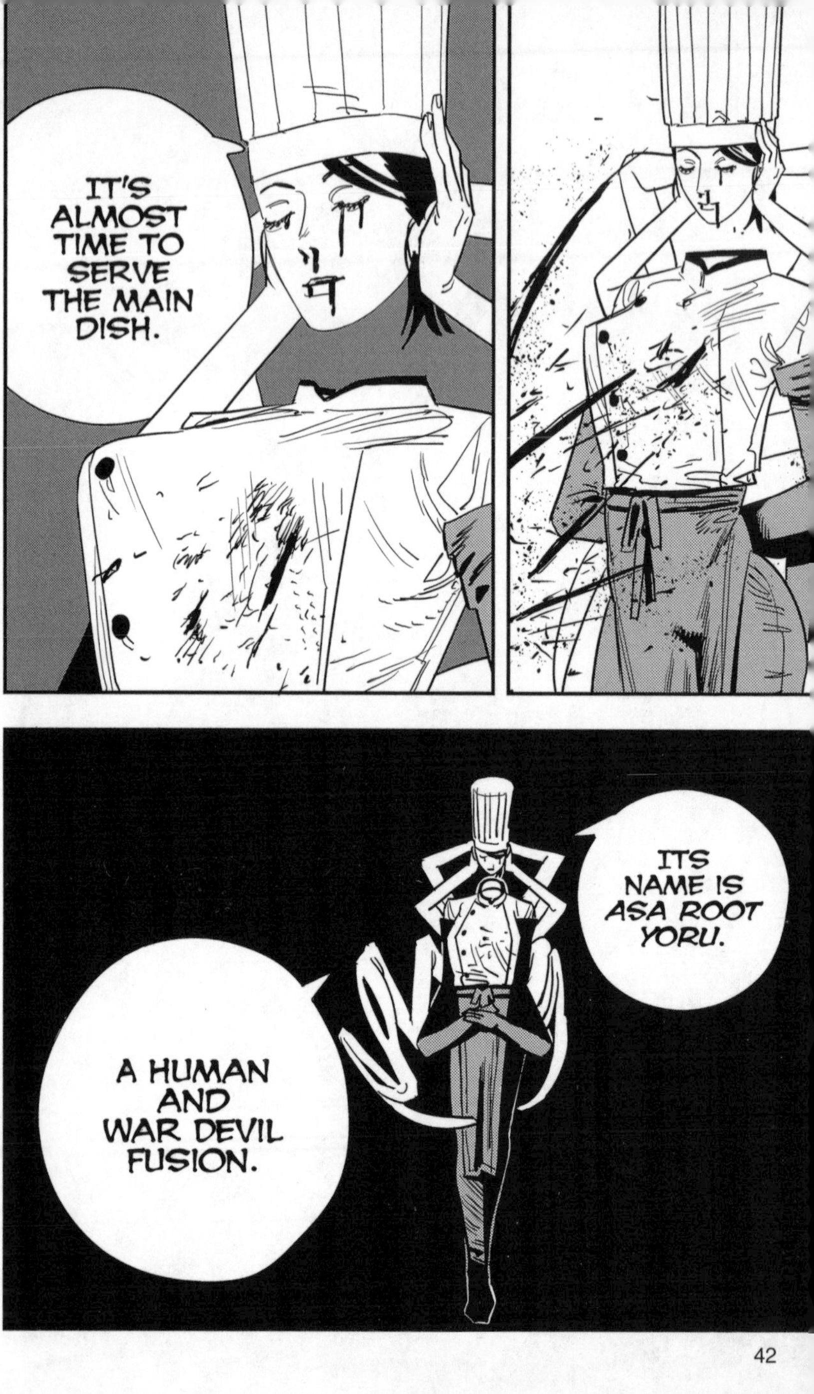
IT'S ALMOST TIME TO SERVE THE MAIN DISH.
ITS NAME IS ASA ROOT YORU.
A HUMAN AND WAR DEVIL FUSION.

Chainsaw man

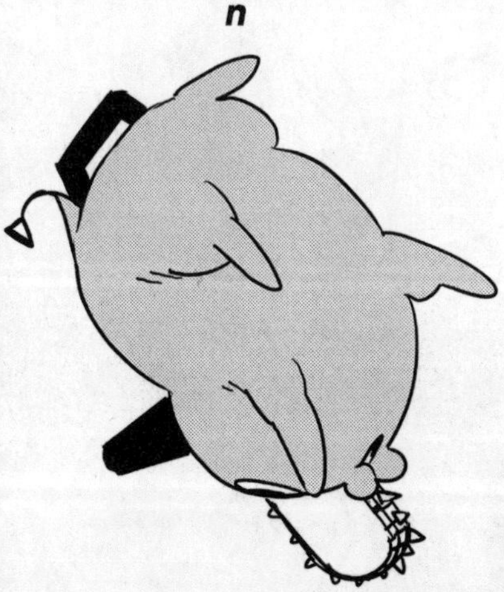

Chapter 125: Apple Thief

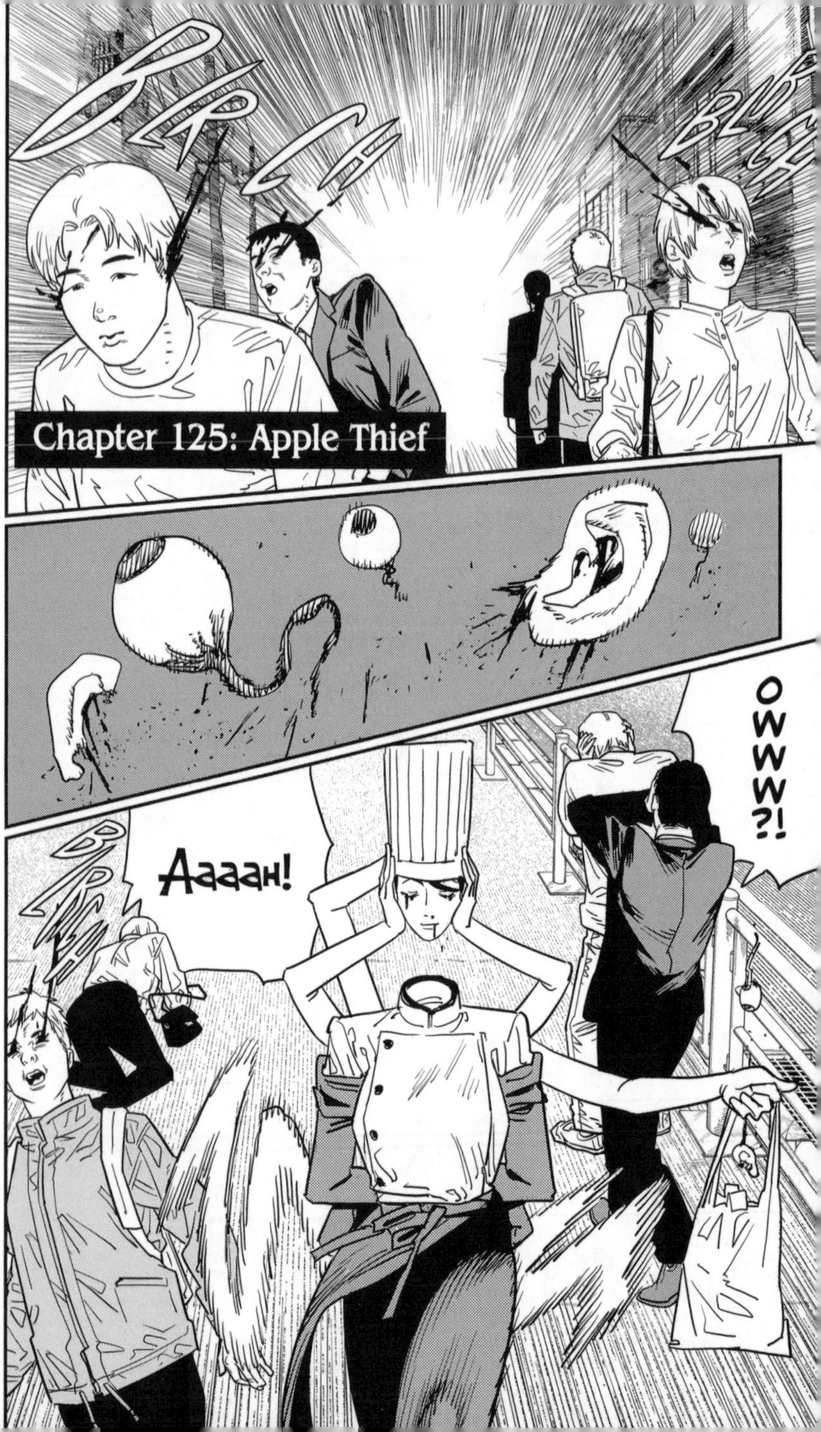
BLRCH
OWWW?!
Aaaah!

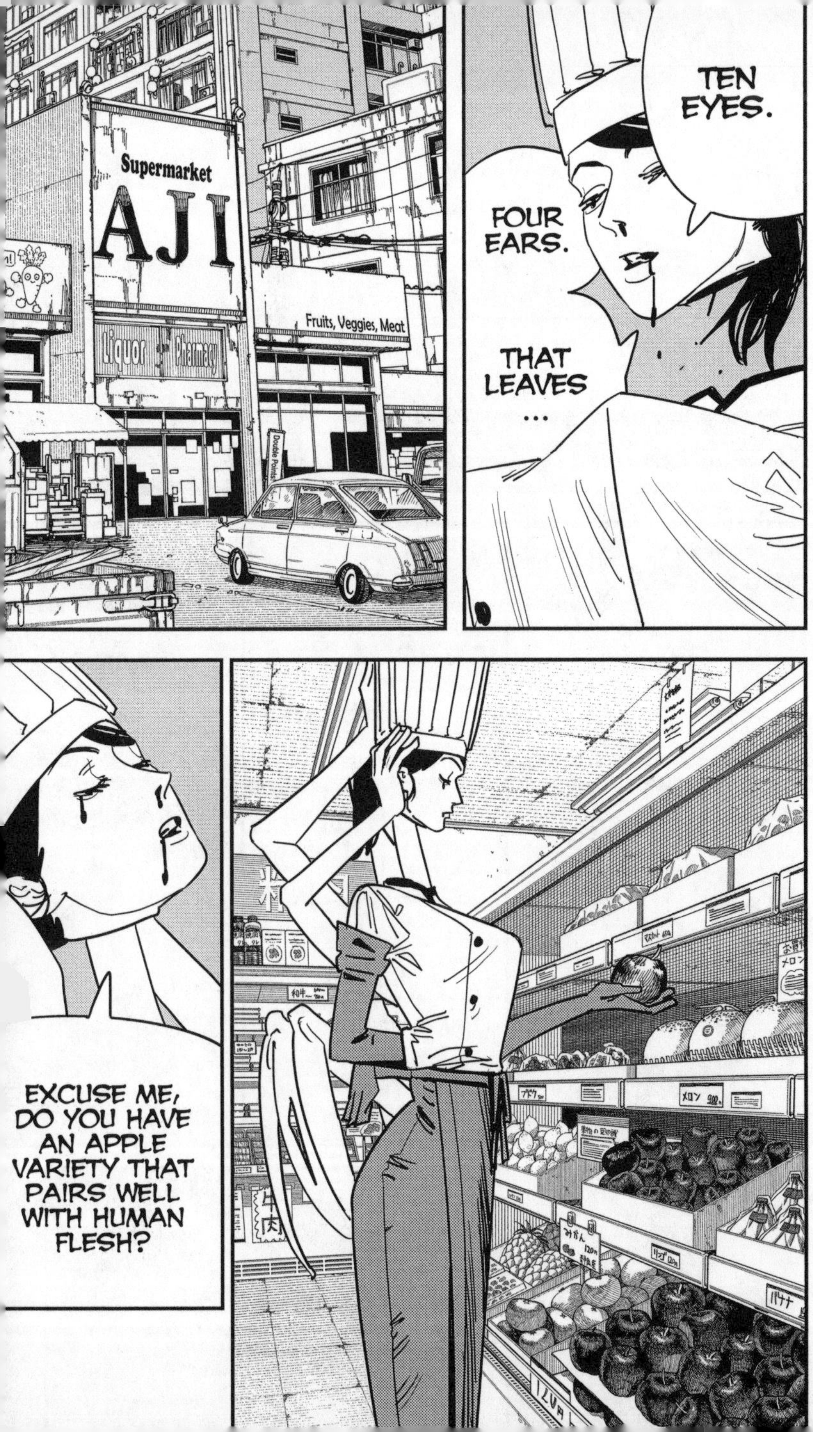

TEN EYES.
FOUR EARS.
THAT LEAVES ...
Supermarket
AJI
Liquor
Pharmacy
Fruits, Veggies, Meat
Double Points!
EXCUSE ME, DO YOU HAVE AN APPLE VARIETY THAT PAIRS WELL WITH HUMAN FLESH?

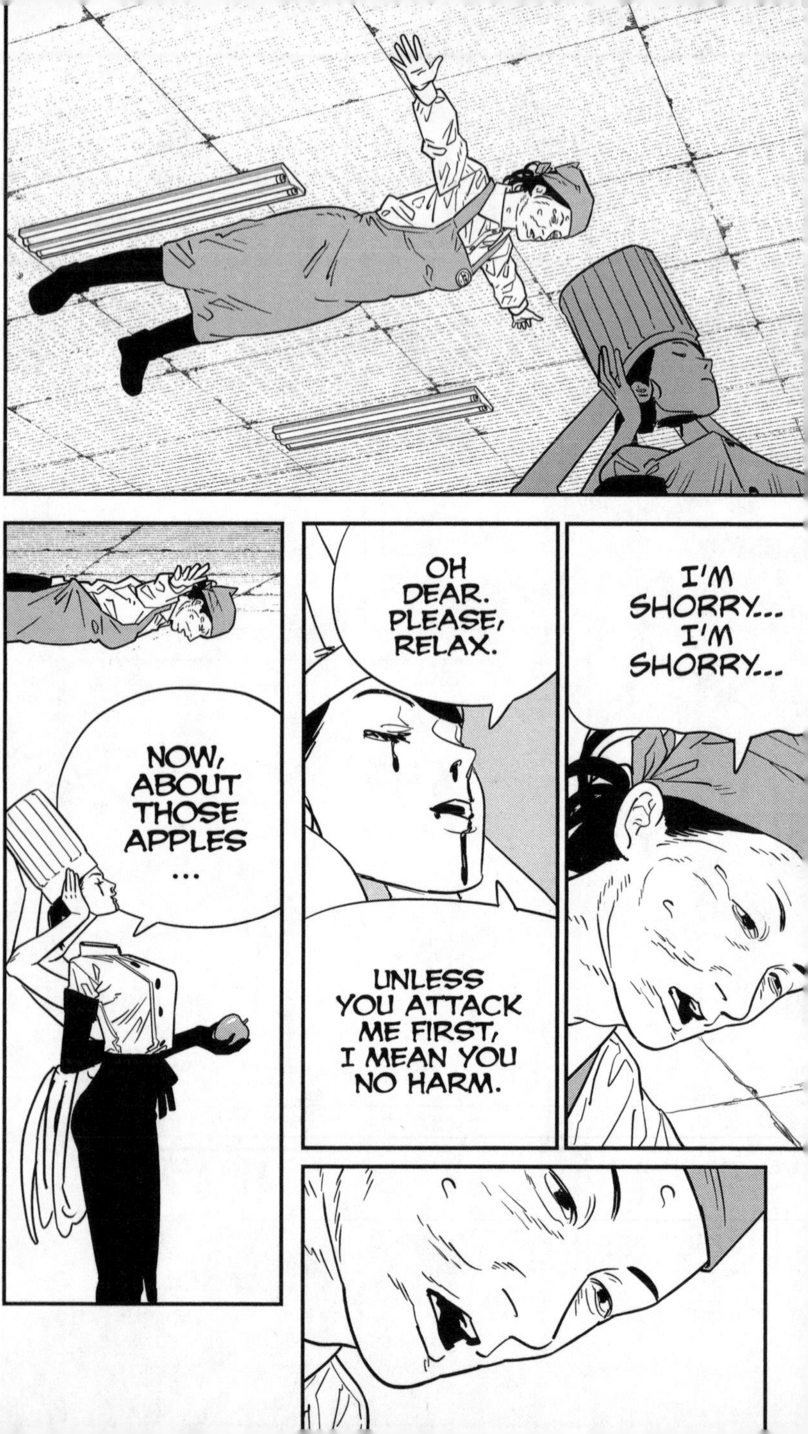
I'M SHORRY... I'M SHORRY...
OH DEAR. PLEASE, RELAX.
UNLESS YOU ATTACK ME FIRST, I MEAN YOU NO HARM.
NOW, ABOUT THOSE APPLES...

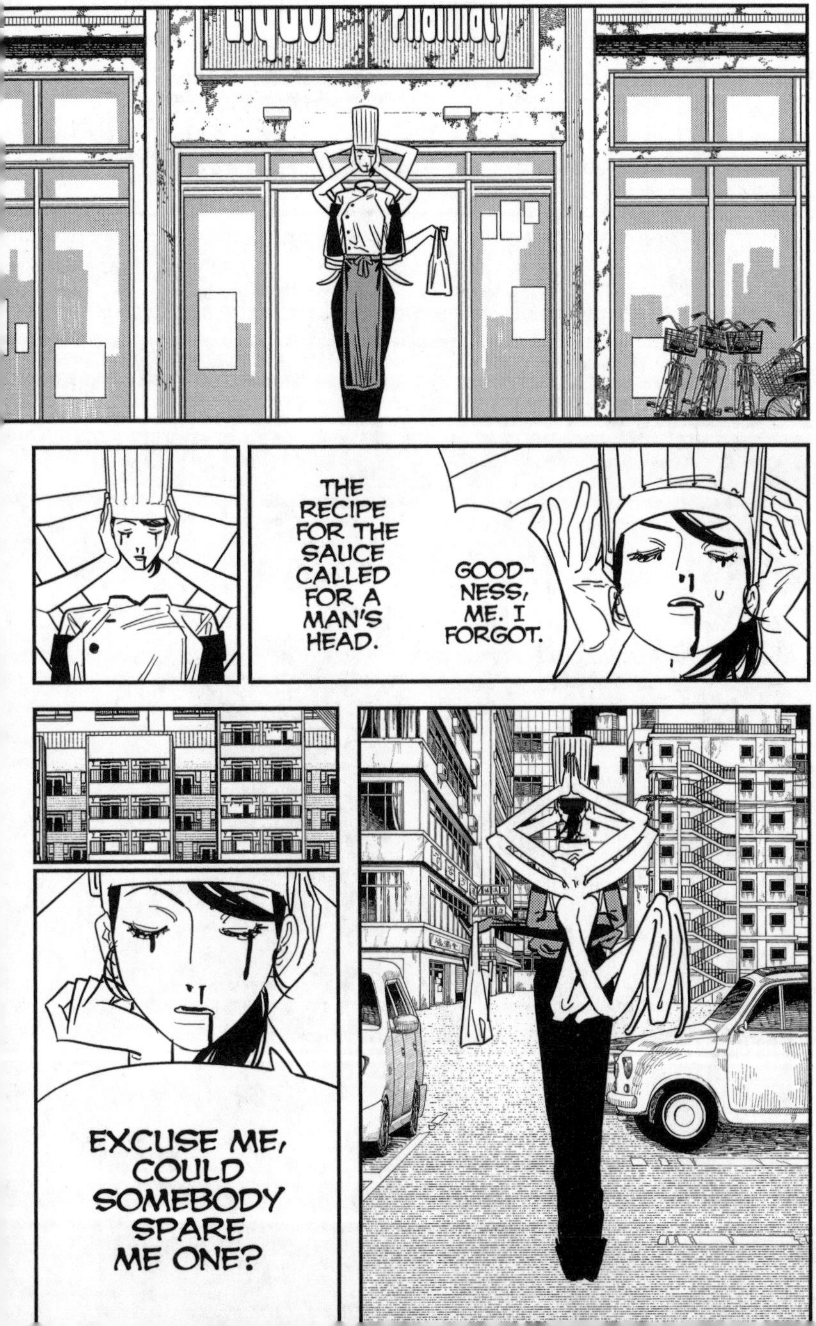
GOOD-NESS, ME. I FORGOT.
THE RECIPE FOR THE SAUCE CALLED FOR A MAN'S HEAD.
EXCUSE ME, COULD SOMEBODY SPARE ME ONE?

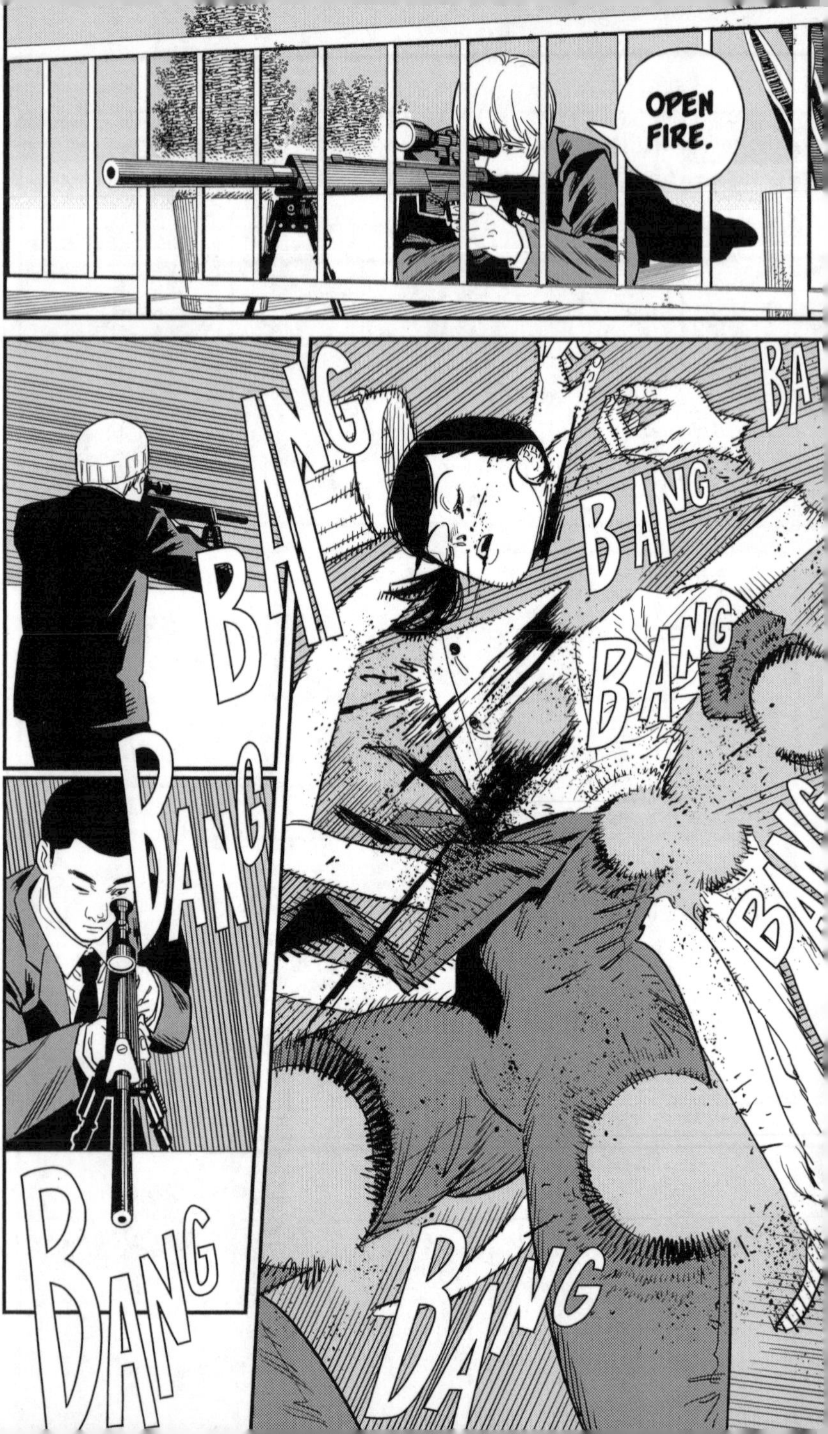

OPEN FIRE.
BANG
BANG
BANG
BANG
BANG
BANG
BANG
BANG

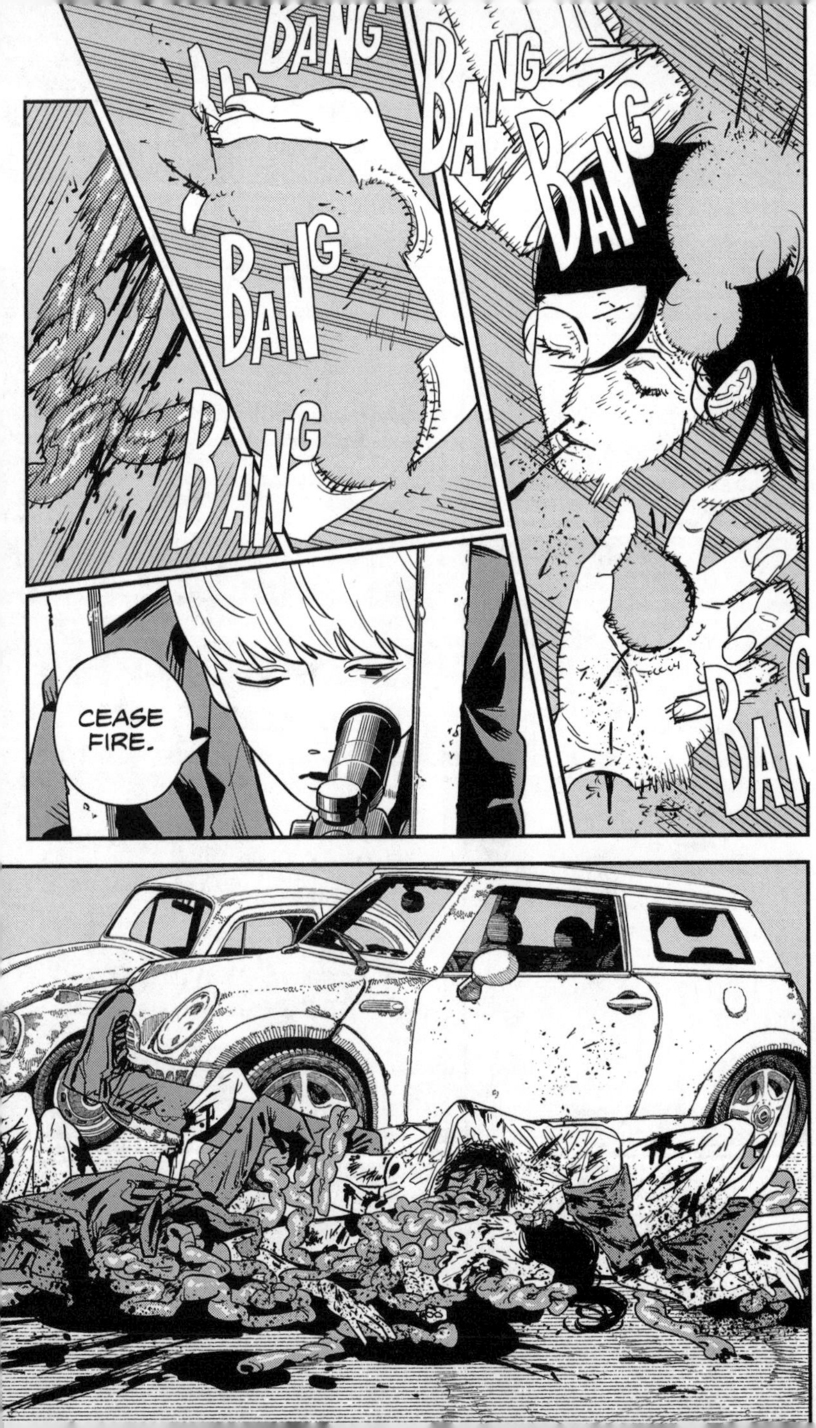
BANG
BANG
BANG
BANG
BANG
BANG
CEASE FIRE.

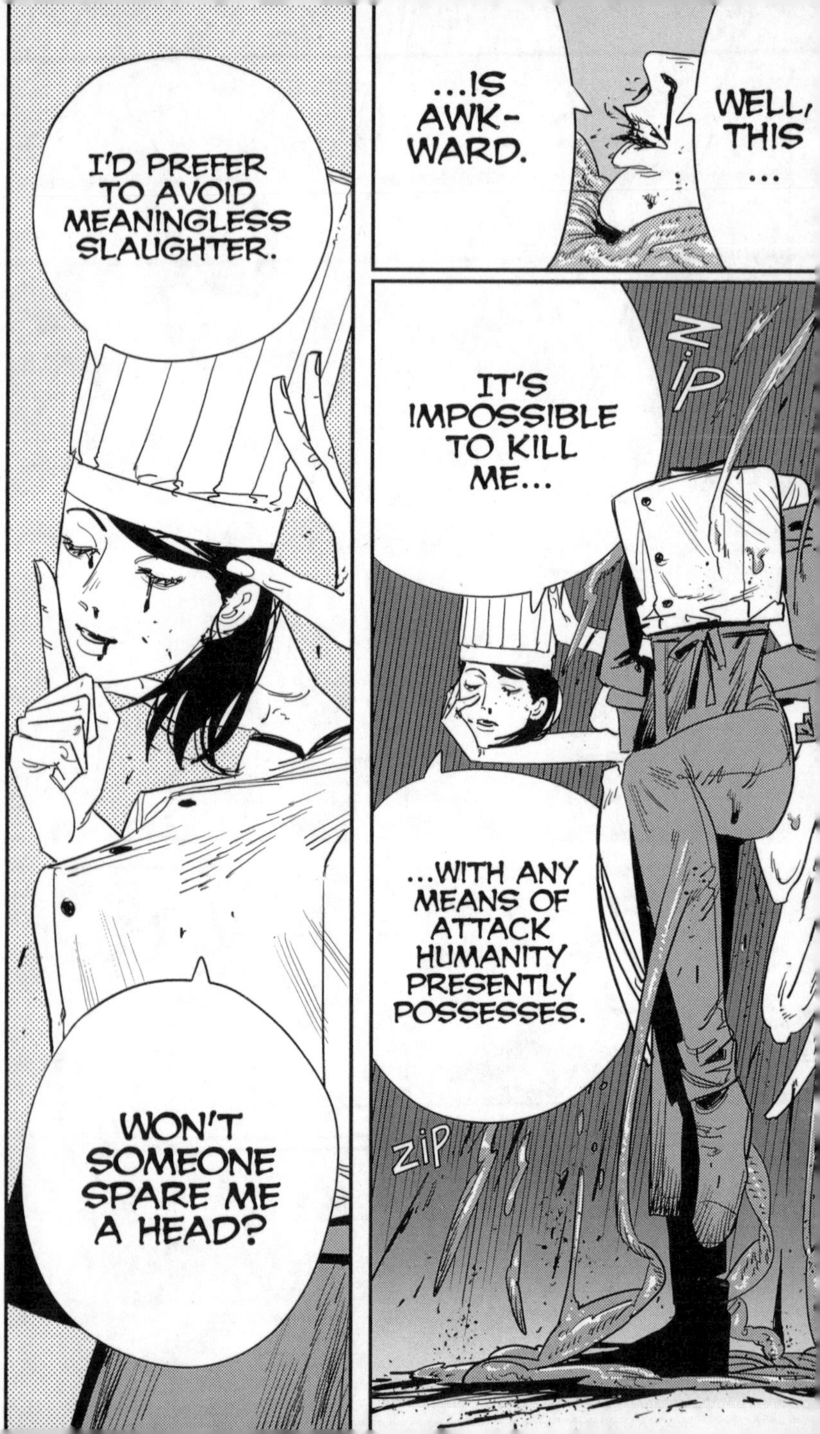
WELL, THIS ...
...IS AWK-WARD.
ZIP
IT'S IMPOSSIBLE TO KILL ME...
...WITH ANY MEANS OF ATTACK HUMANITY PRESENTLY POSSESSES.
ZIP
I'D PREFER TO AVOID MEANINGLESS SLAUGHTER.
WON'T SOMEONE SPARE ME A HEAD?

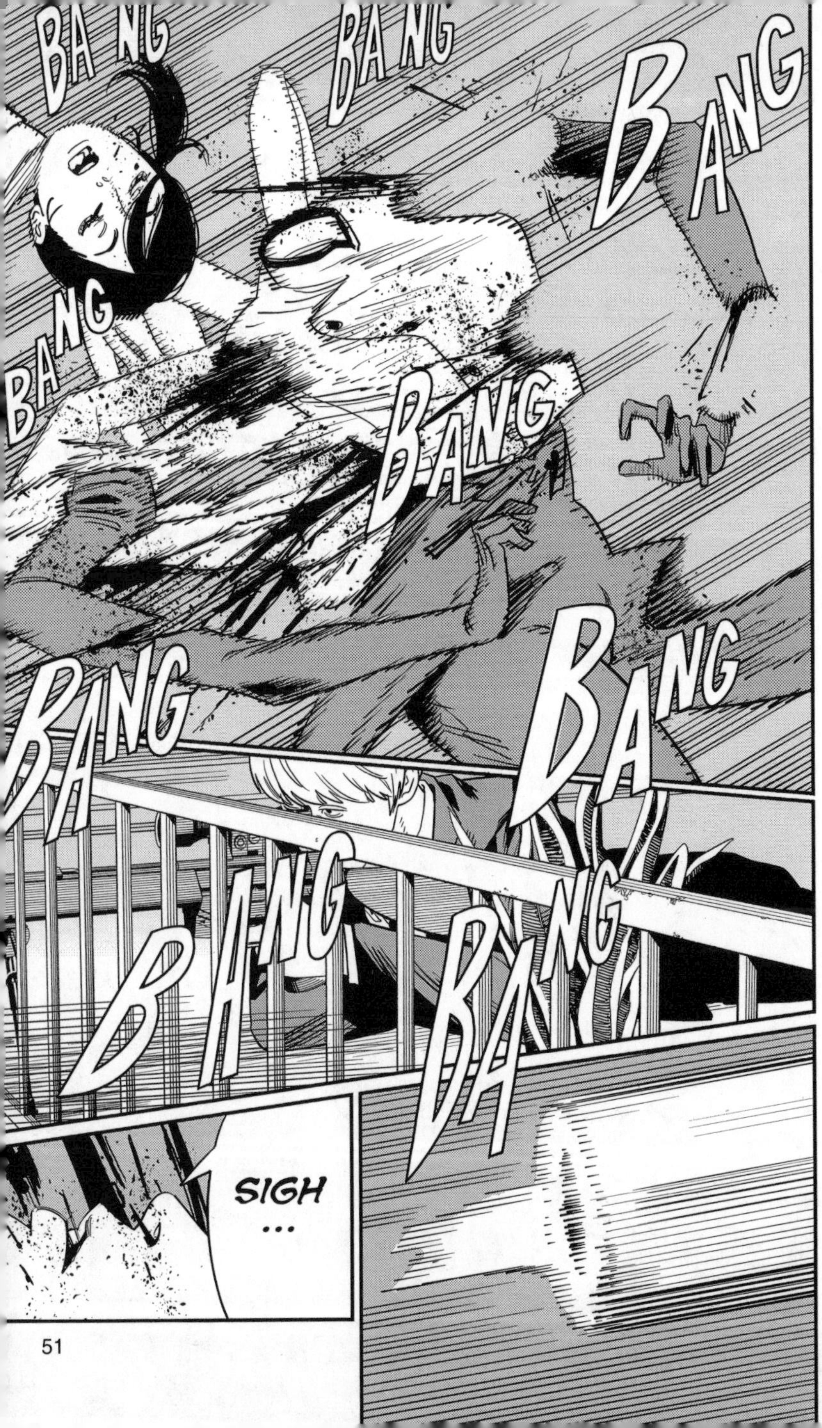
BANG
BANG
BANG
BANG
BANG
BANG
BANG
BANG
BANG
SIGH
...

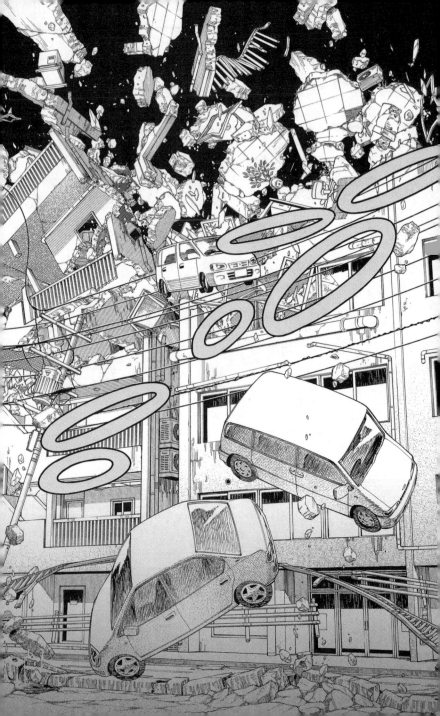

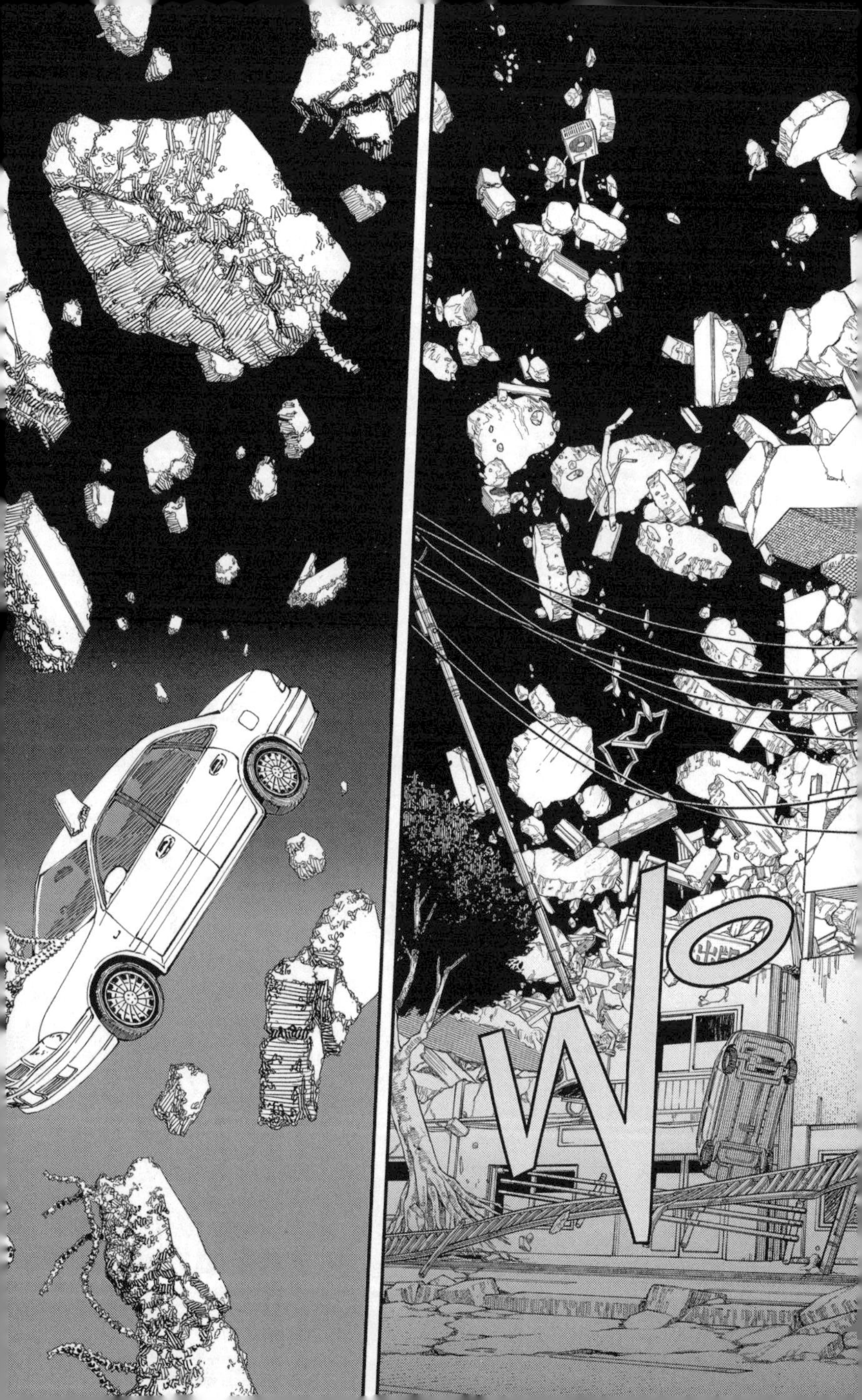
WO

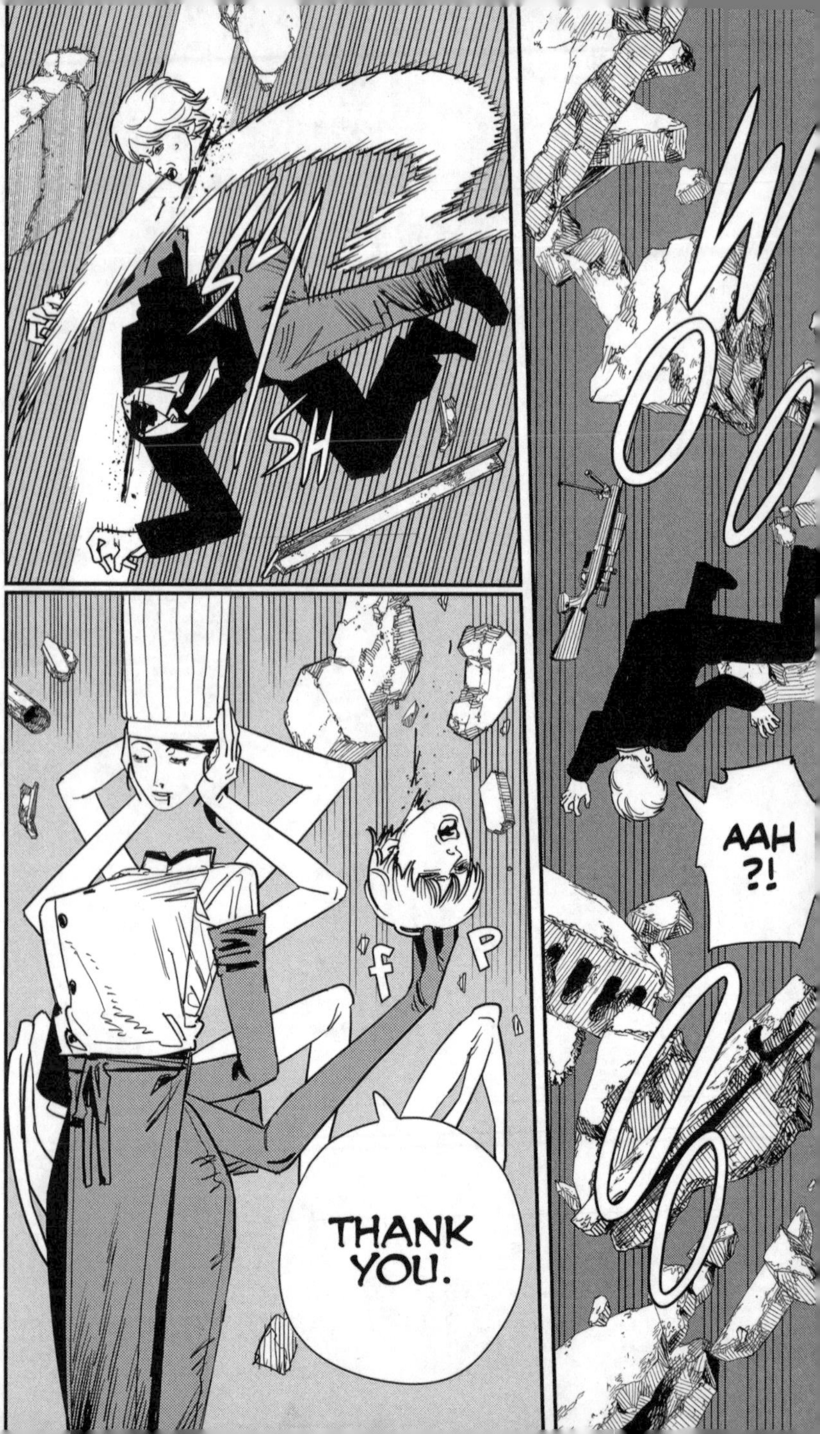
WOOO
AAH ?!
OOO
SH
fP
THANK YOU.

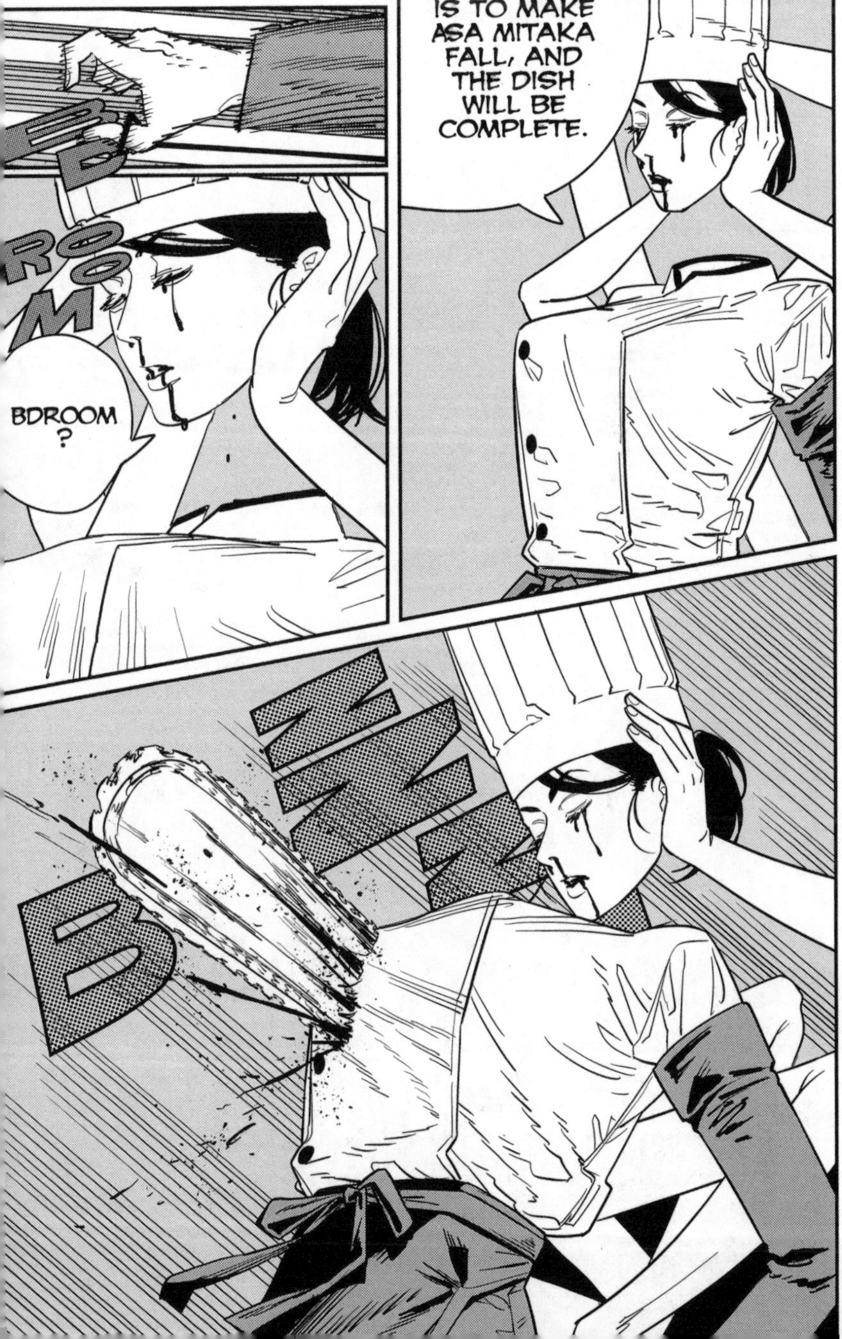
ALL THAT REMAINS IS TO MAKE ASA MITAKA FALL, AND THE DISH WILL BE COMPLETE.
ROOM
BDROOM ?

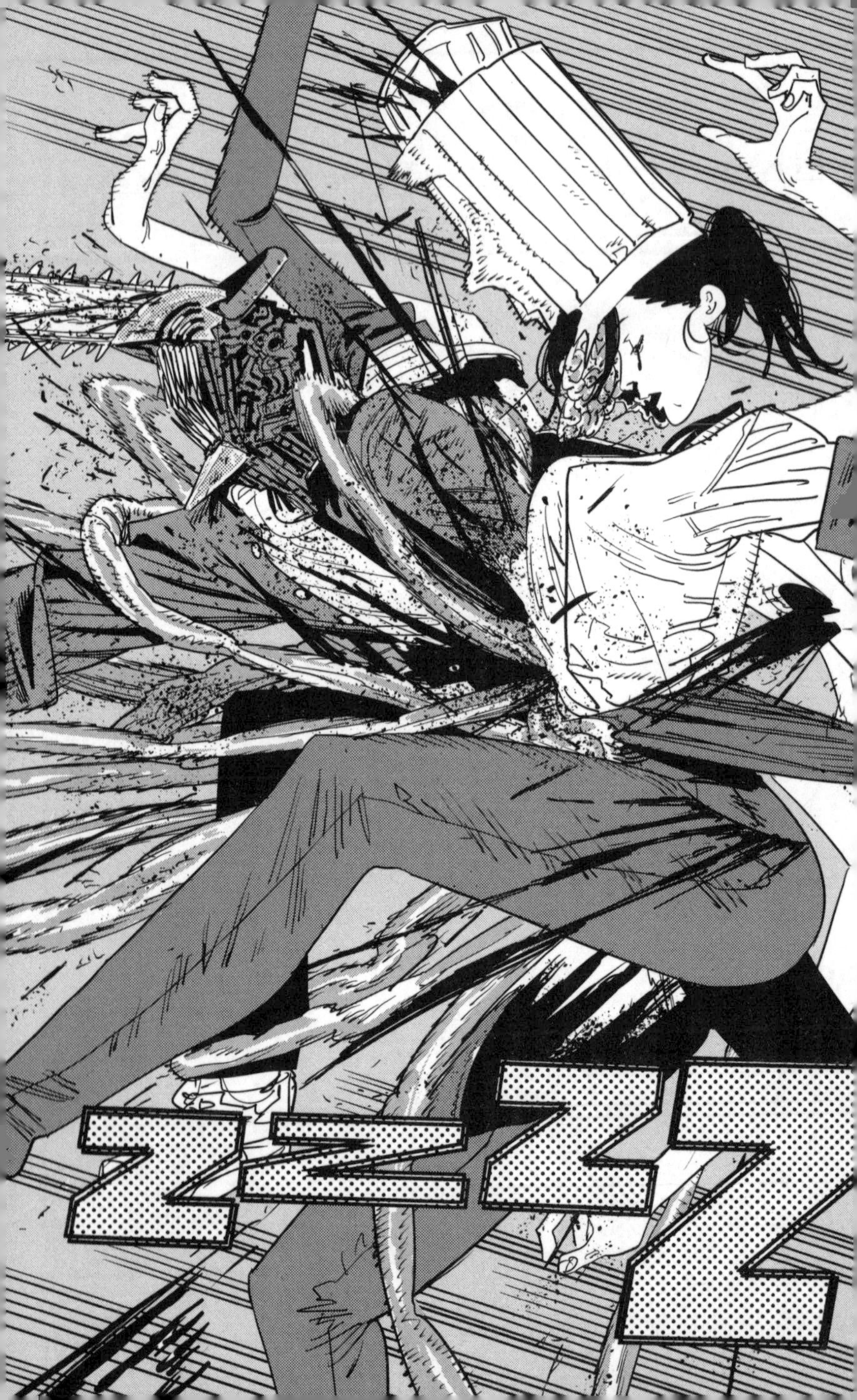
ZZZZ

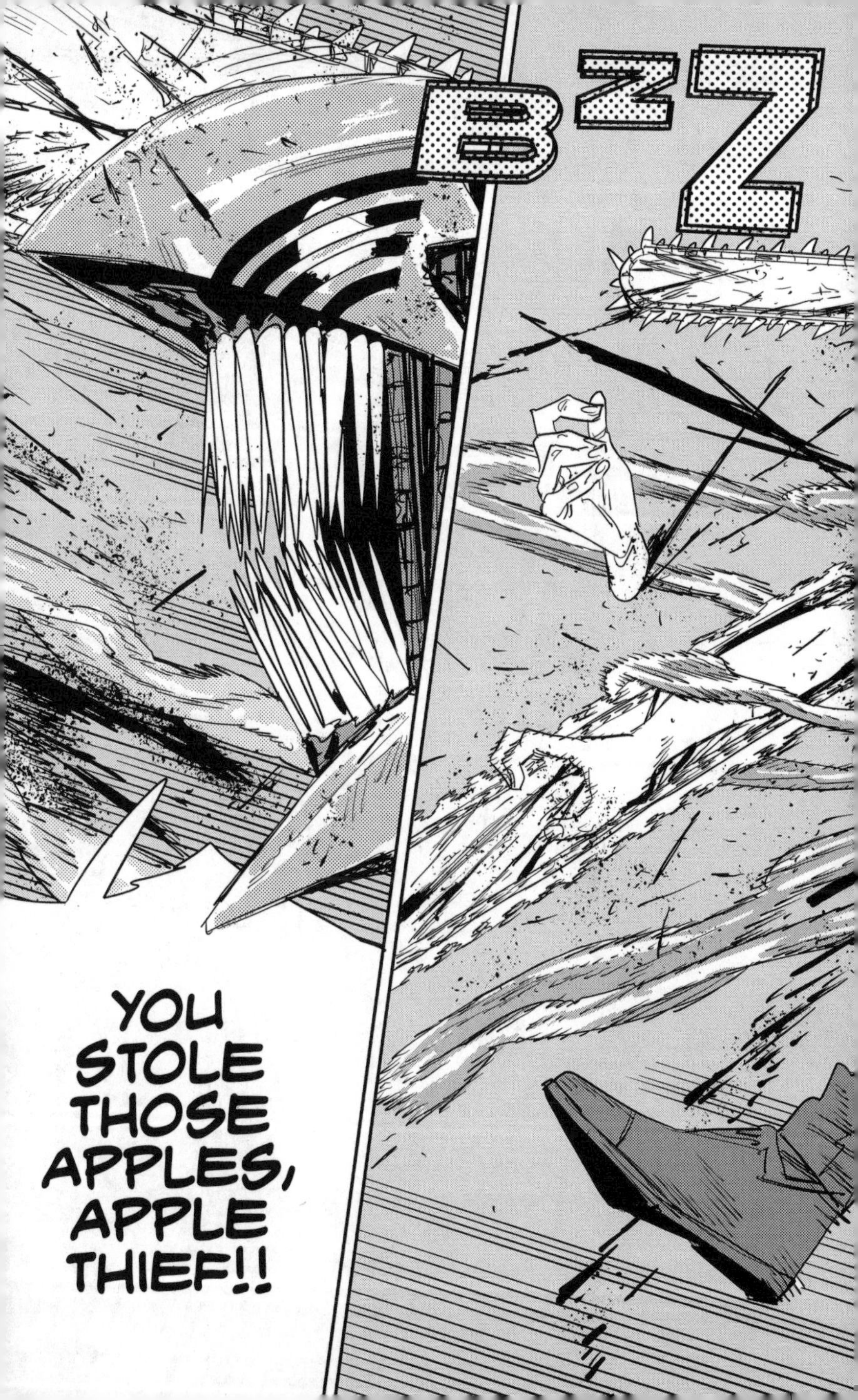
BZZ
YOU STOLE THOSE APPLES, APPLE THIEF!!

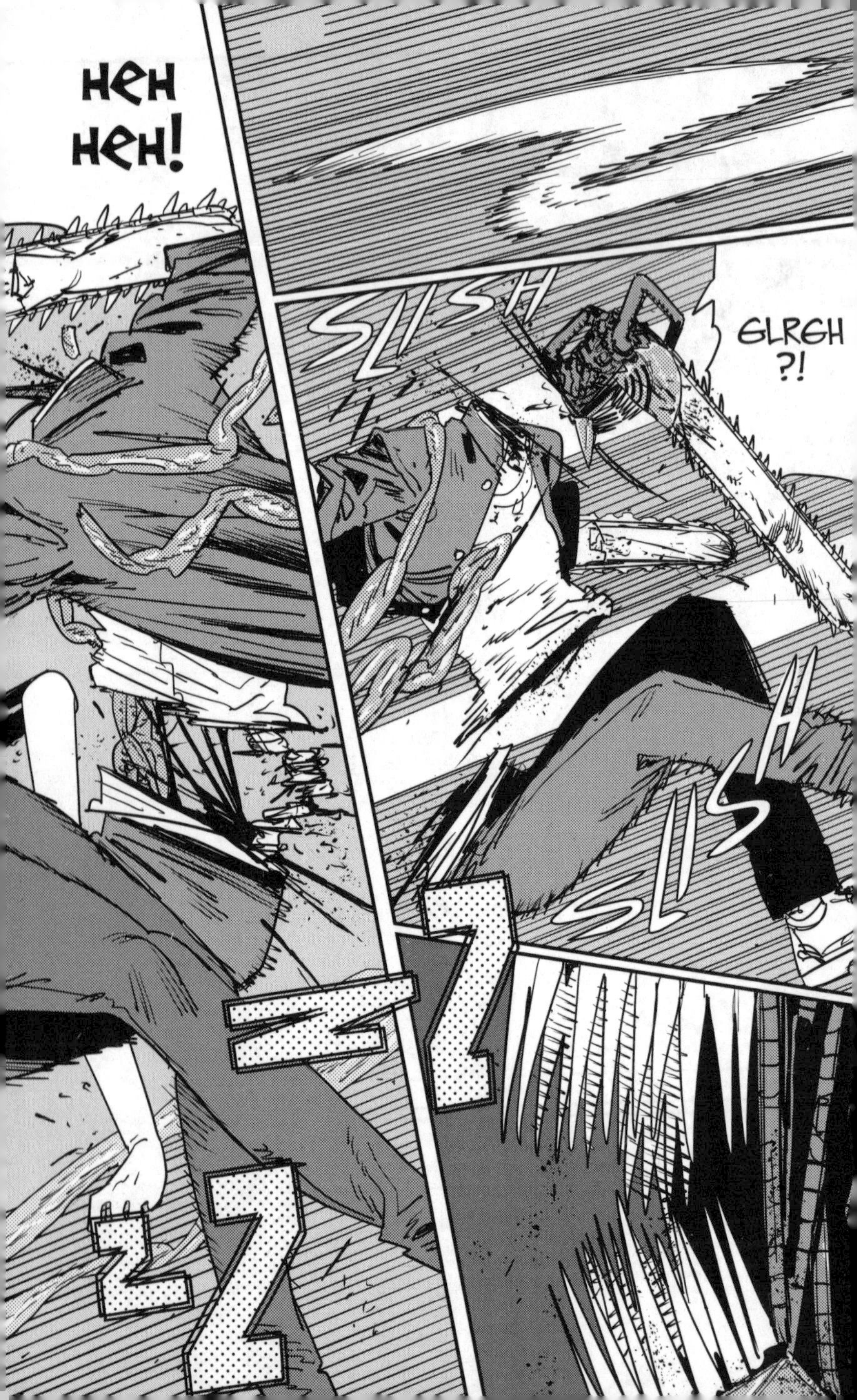

SLISH
GLRGH ?!
SLISH
HEH HEH!

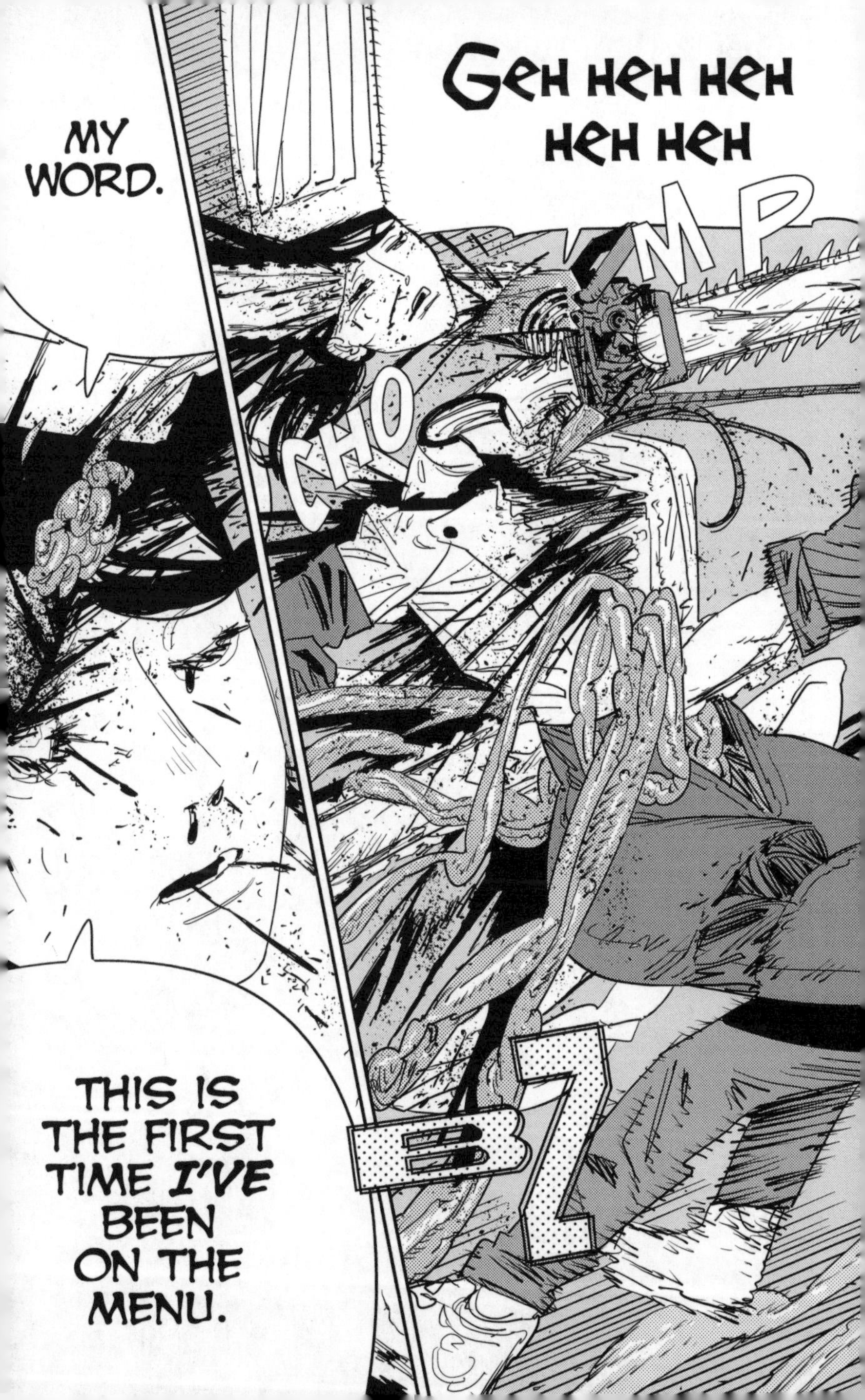
GEH HEH HEH HEH HEH
MP
CHO
BZ
MY WORD.
THIS IS THE FIRST TIME I'VE BEEN ON THE MENU.

Chapter 126: Food Fight

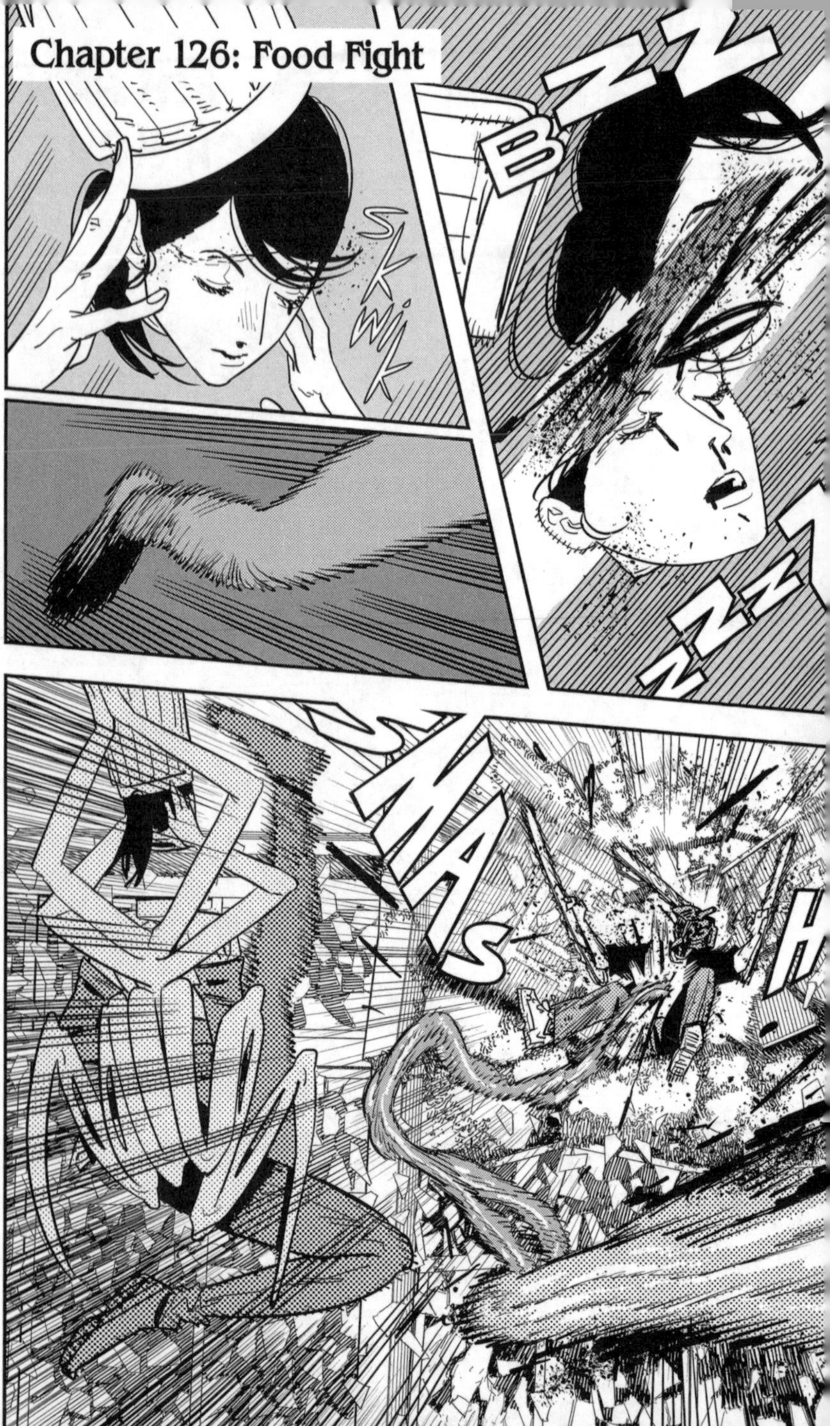
BZZN
SKWIK
SMASH

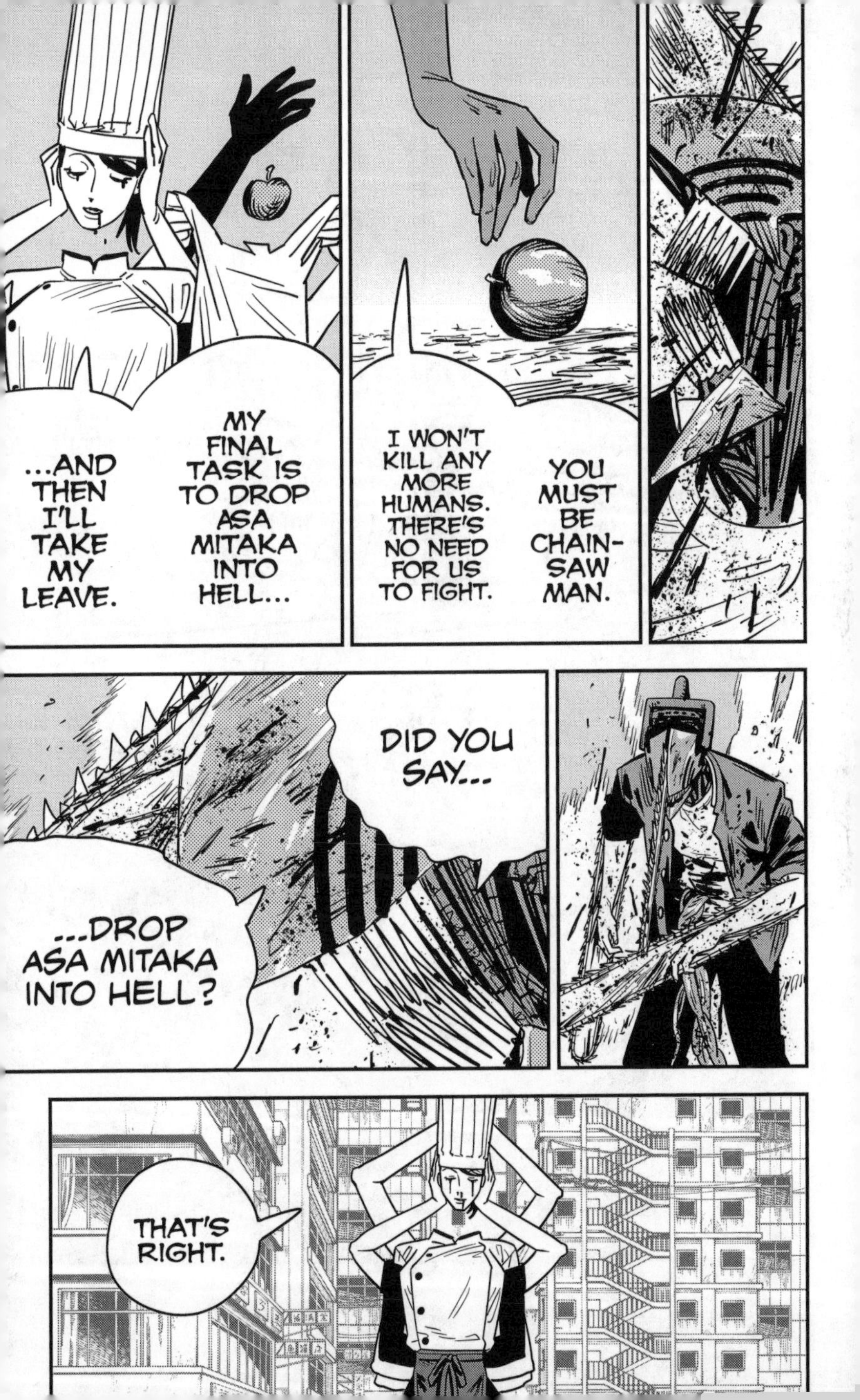
YOU MUST BE CHAIN-SAW MAN.
I WON'T KILL ANY MORE HUMANS. THERE'S NO NEED FOR US TO FIGHT.
MY FINAL TASK IS TO DROP ASA MITAKA INTO HELL...
...AND THEN I'LL TAKE MY LEAVE.
DID YOU SAY...
...DROP ASA MITAKA INTO HELL?
THAT'S RIGHT.

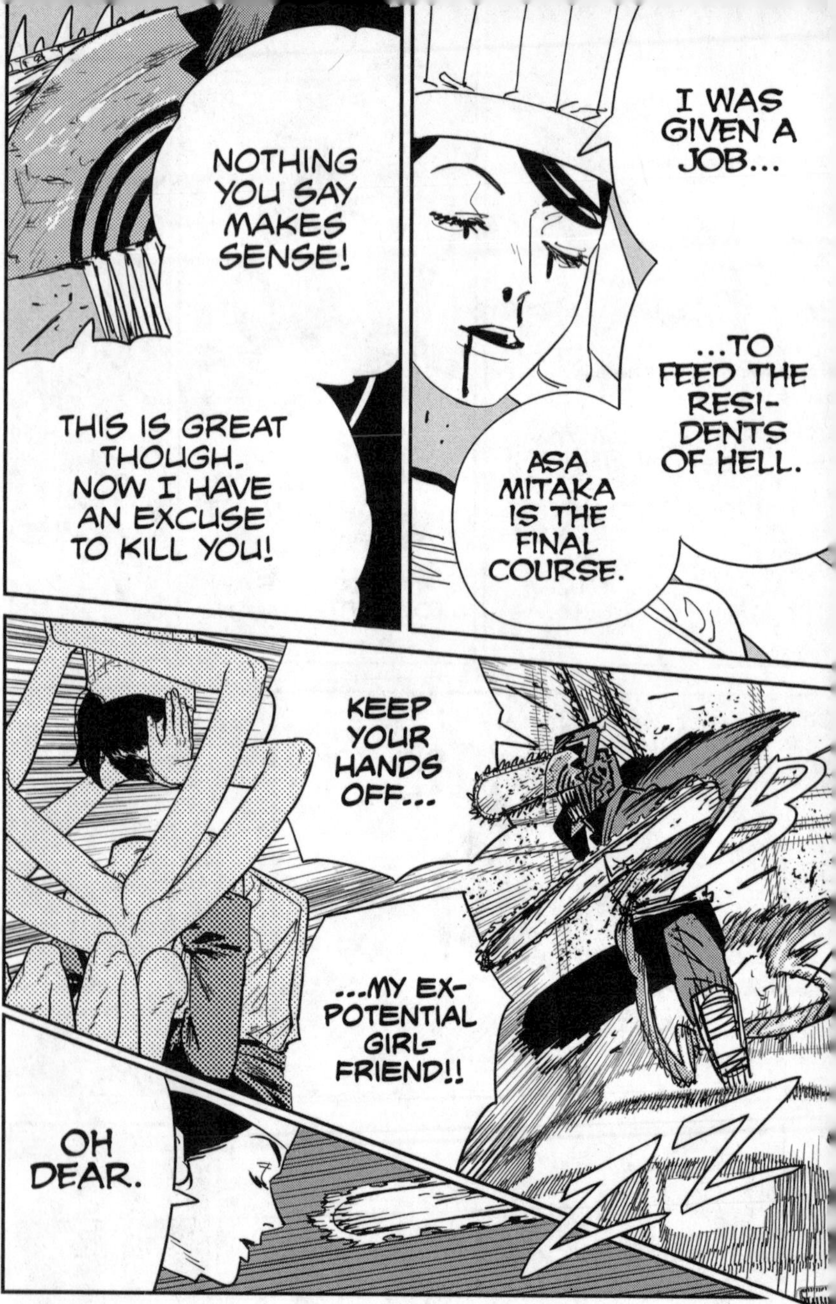
I WAS GIVEN A JOB...
...TO FEED THE RESI-DENTS OF HELL.
ASA MITAKA IS THE FINAL COURSE.
NOTHING YOU SAY MAKES SENSE!
THIS IS GREAT THOUGH. NOW I HAVE AN EXCUSE TO KILL YOU!
KEEP YOUR HANDS OFF...
...MY EX-POTENTIAL GIRL-FRIEND!!
OH DEAR.

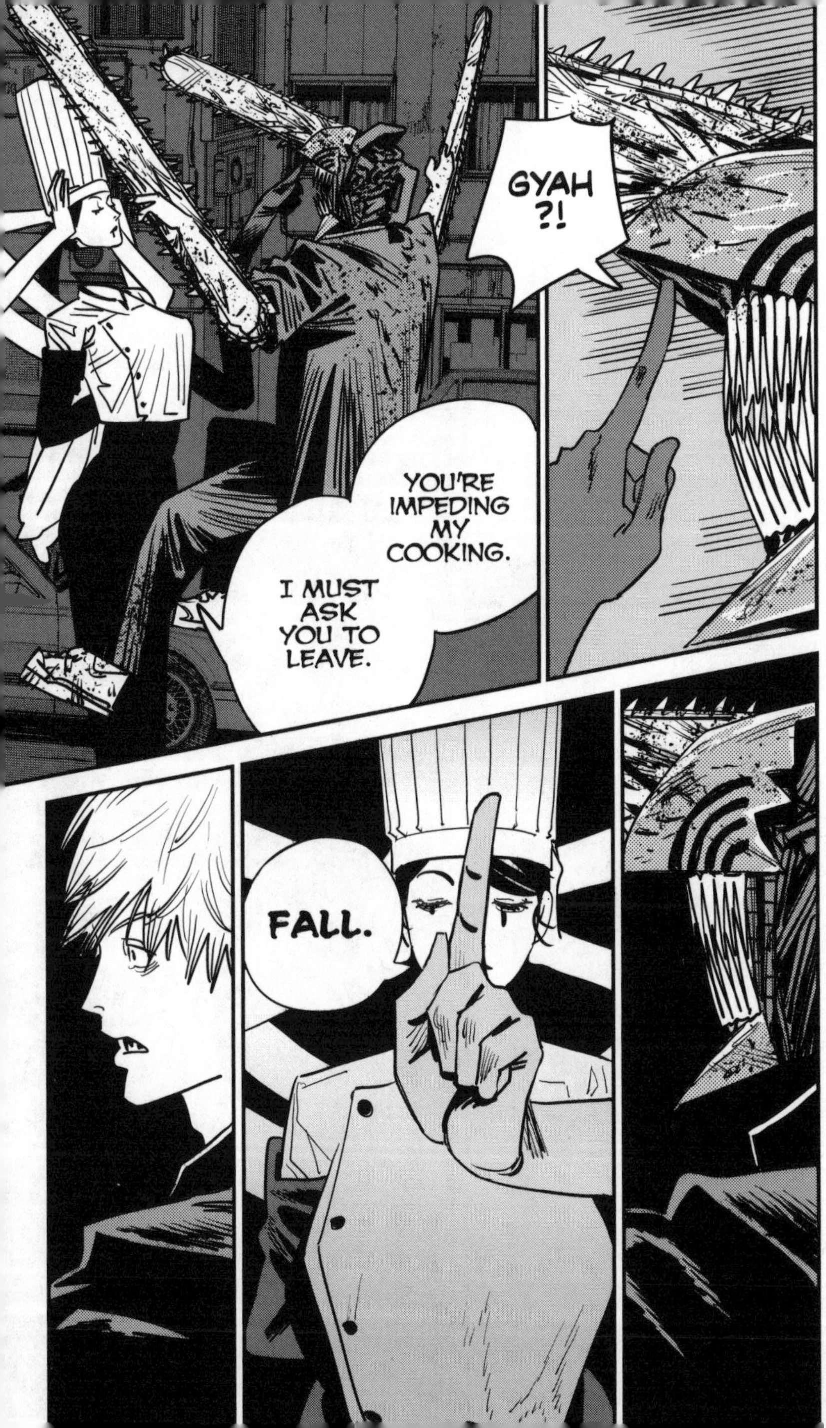
GYAH ?!
YOU'RE IMPEDING MY COOKING.
I MUST ASK YOU TO LEAVE.
FALL.

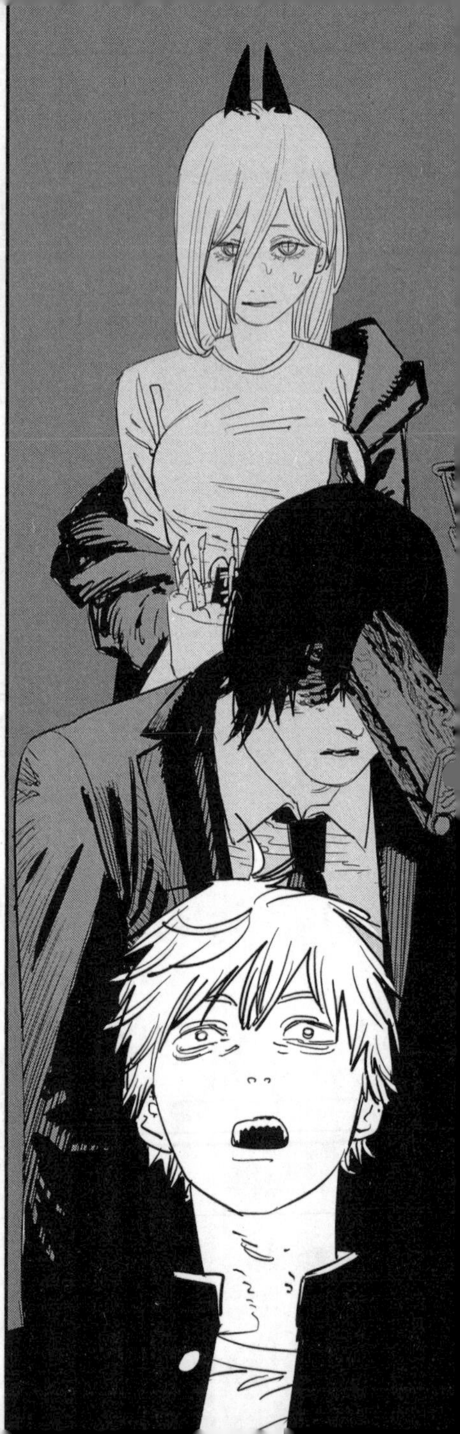

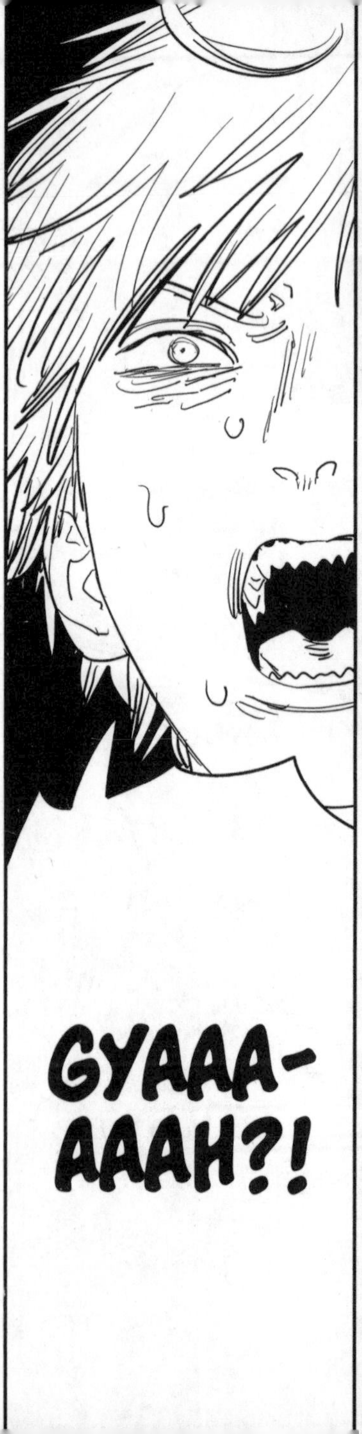
GYAAA-
AAAH?!

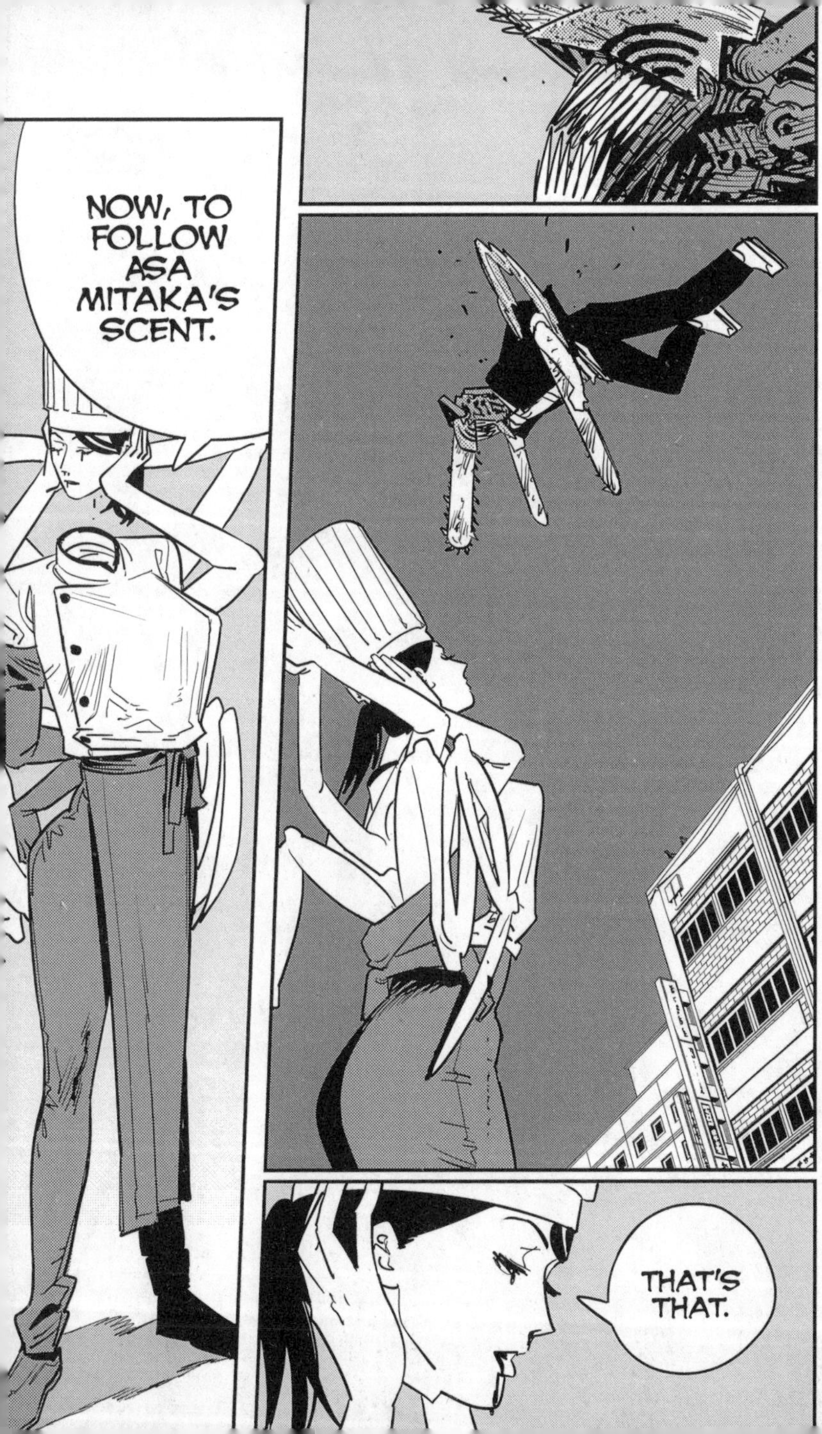
THAT'S THAT.
NOW, TO FOLLOW ASA MITAKA'S SCENT.

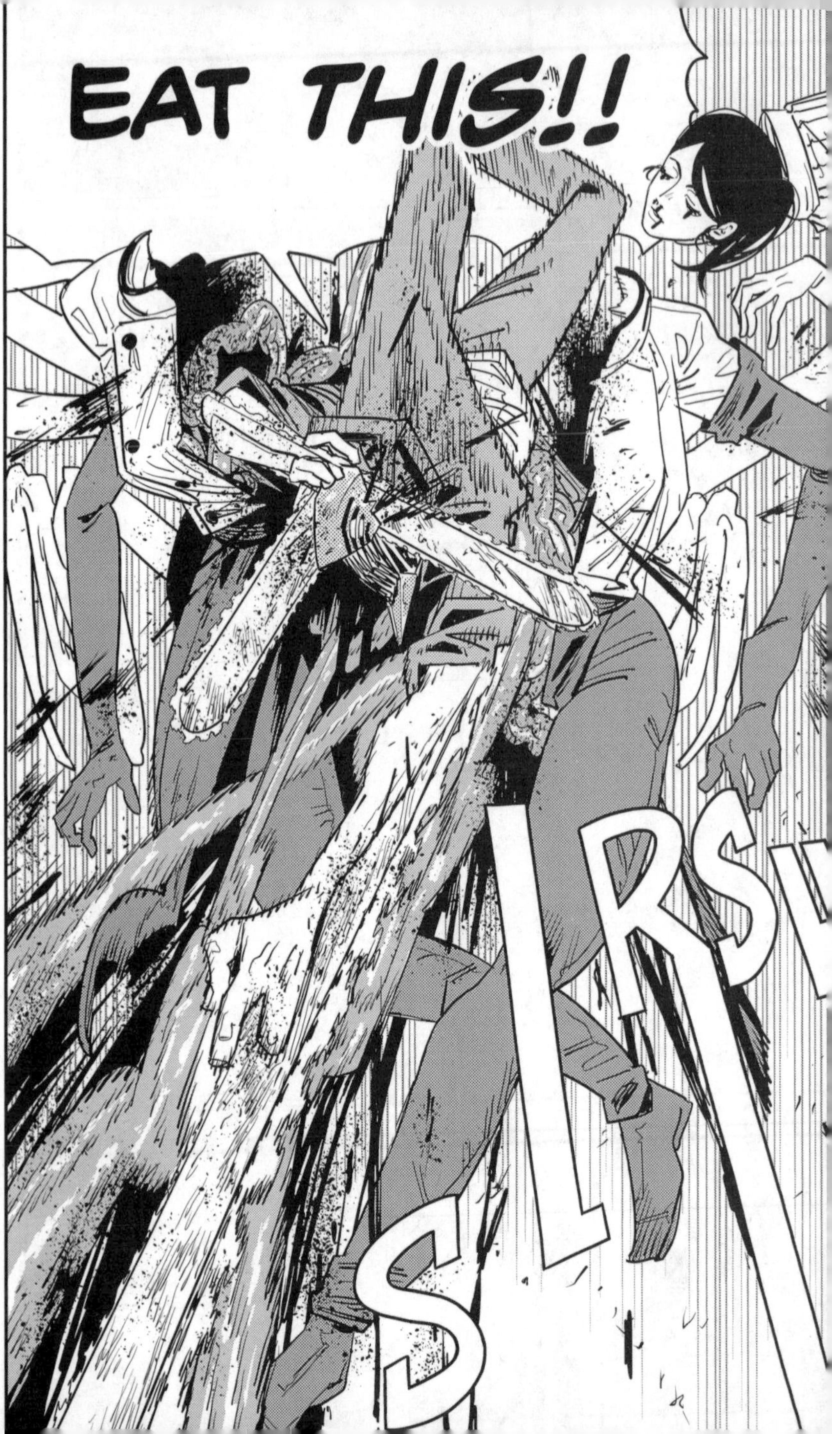
EAT THIS!!
SLRS

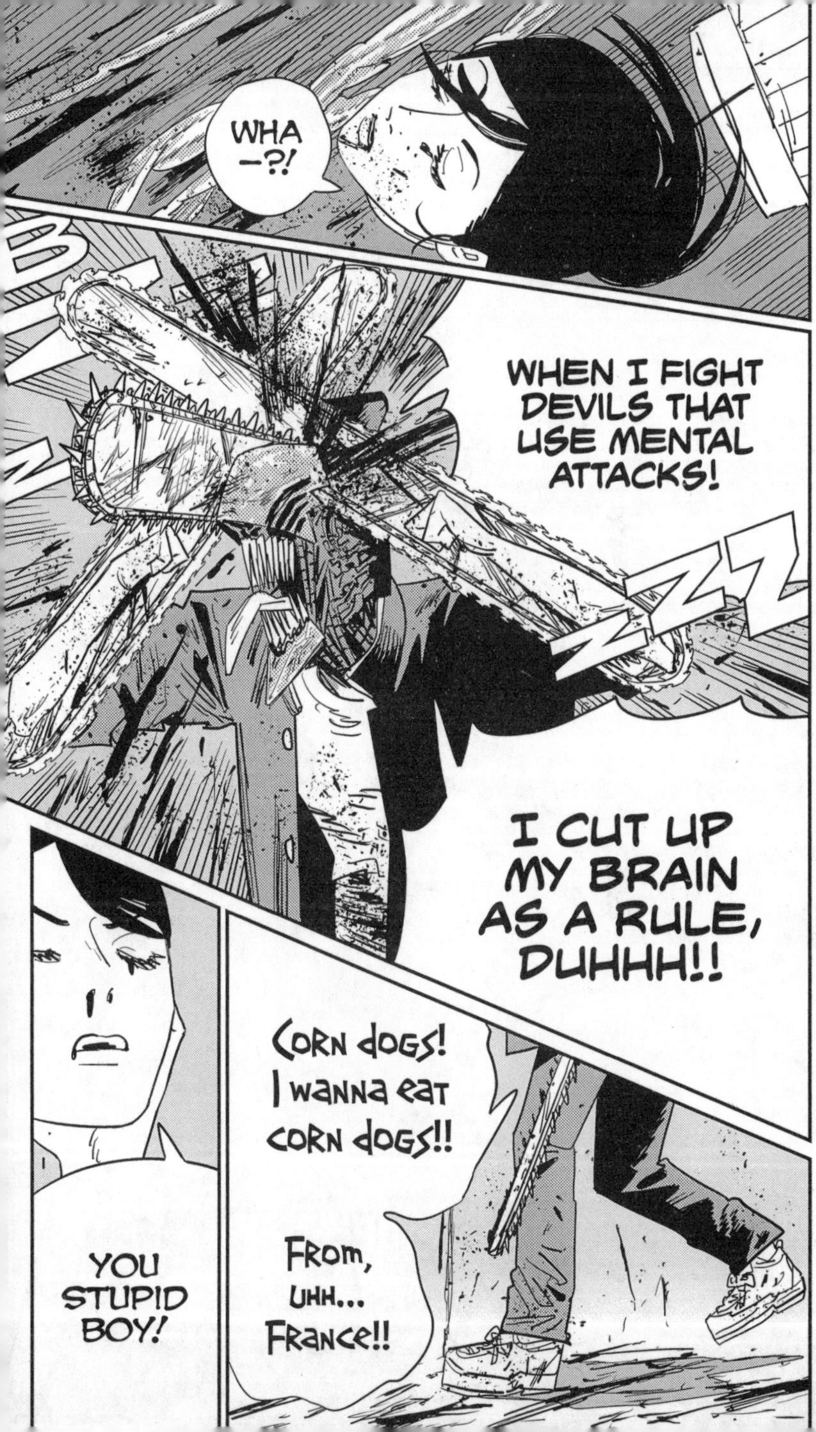
WHA—?!
ZZZ
WHEN I FIGHT DEVILS THAT USE MENTAL ATTACKS!
I CUT UP MY BRAIN AS A RULE, DUHHH!!
Corn dogs! I wanna eat corn dogs!!
From, uhh... France!!
YOU STUPID BOY!

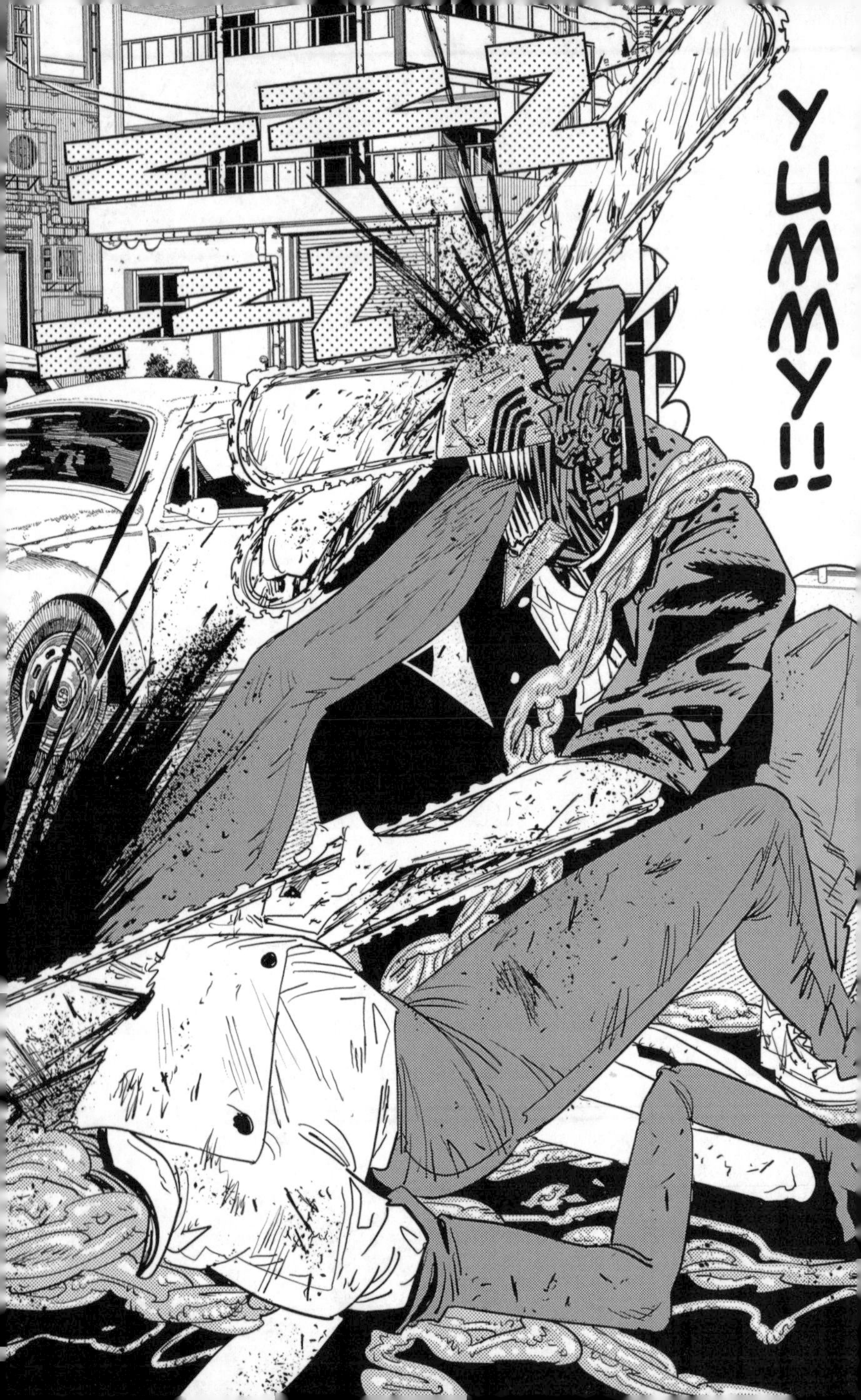
YUMMY!!

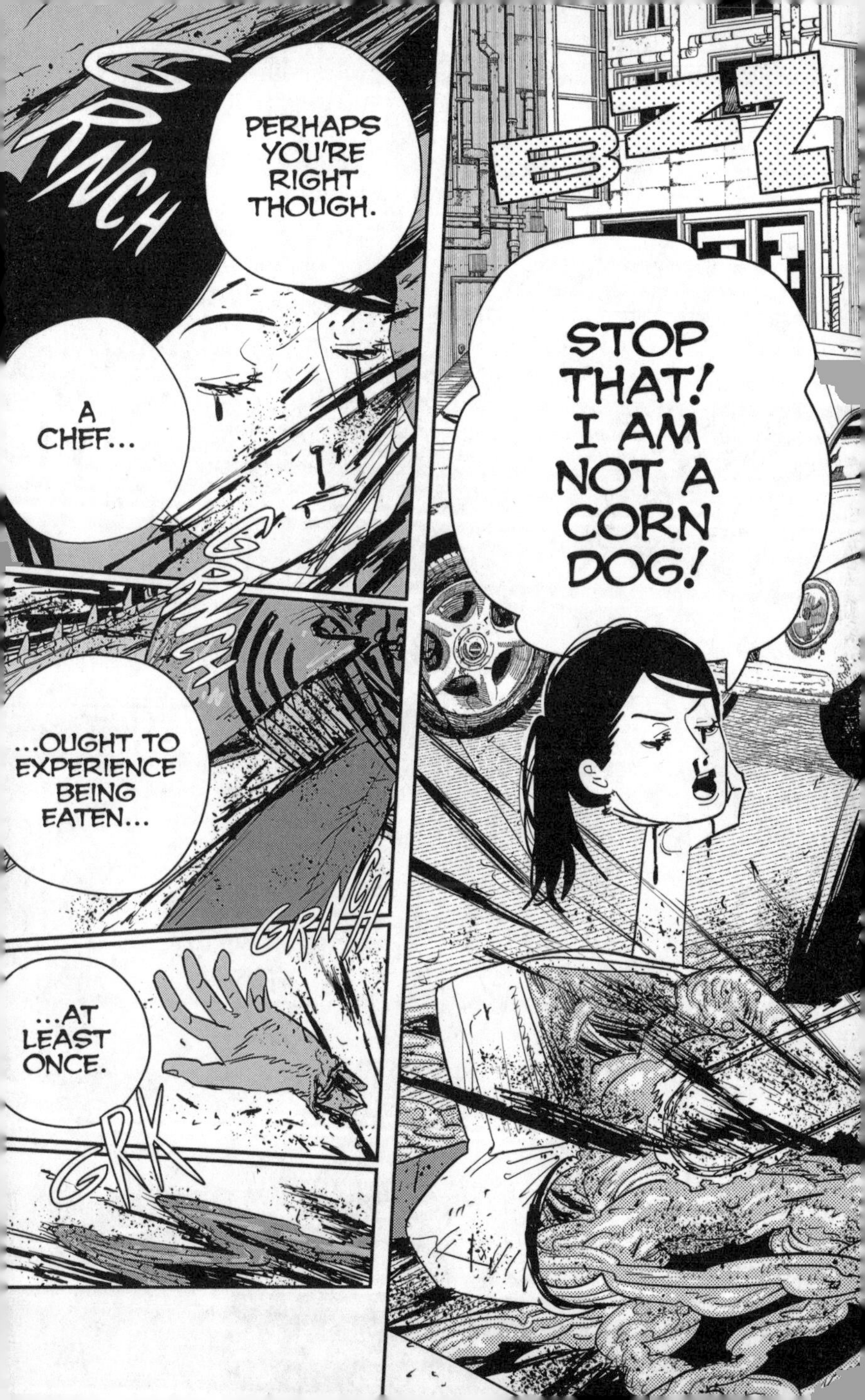
BZZ
STOP THAT! I AM NOT A CORN DOG!
GRNCH
PERHAPS YOU'RE RIGHT THOUGH.
A CHEF...
GRNCH
...OUGHT TO EXPERIENCE BEING EATEN...
GRNCH
...AT LEAST ONCE.
GRK

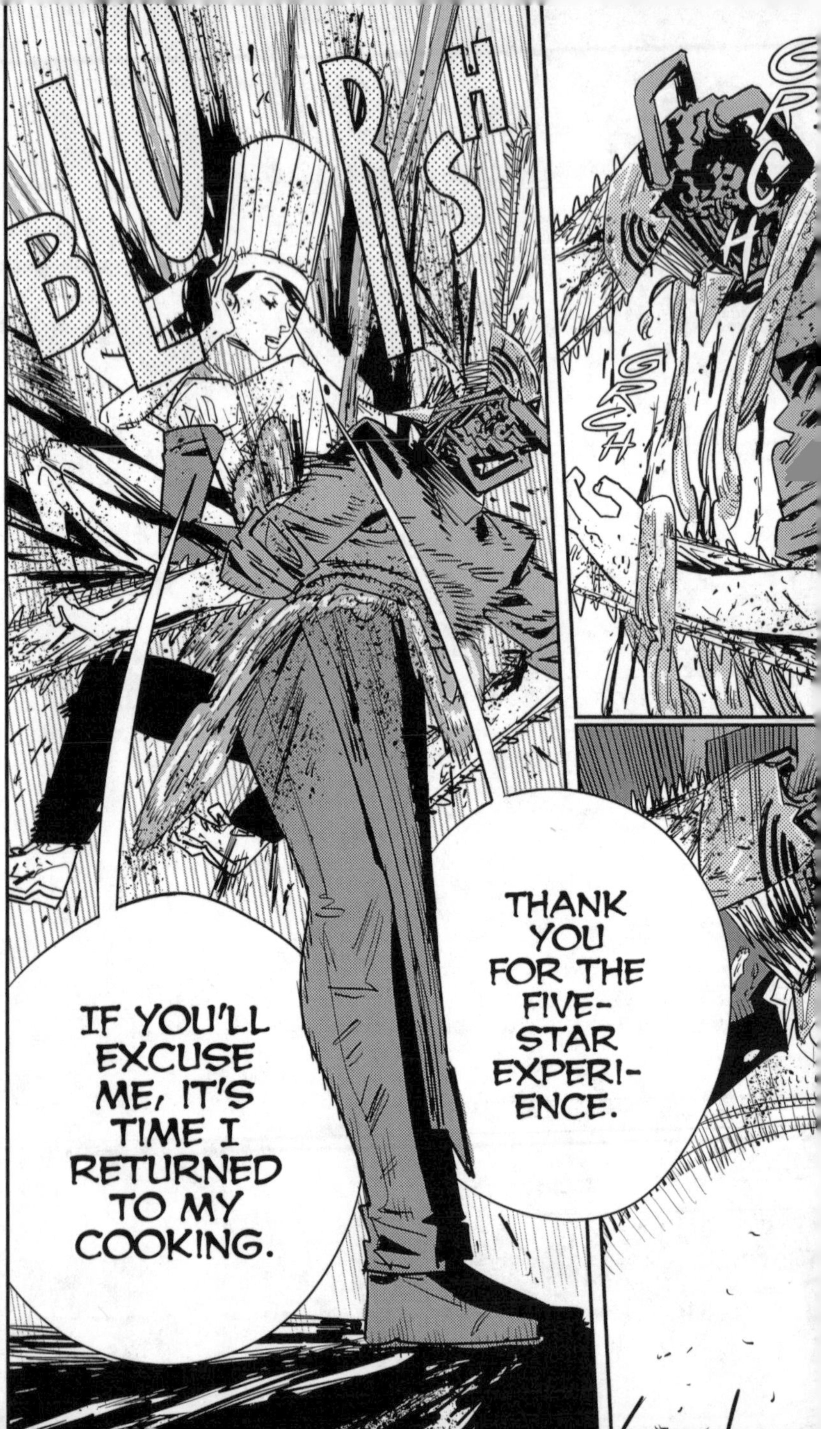
GRCH
GRCH
BLURSH
THANK YOU FOR THE FIVE-STAR EXPERIENCE.
IF YOU'LL EXCUSE ME, IT'S TIME I RETURNED TO MY COOKING.

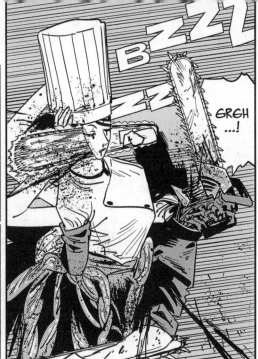

BZZZ

ZZZ

GRGH
...!

SPLRT

fliK

YIPE!

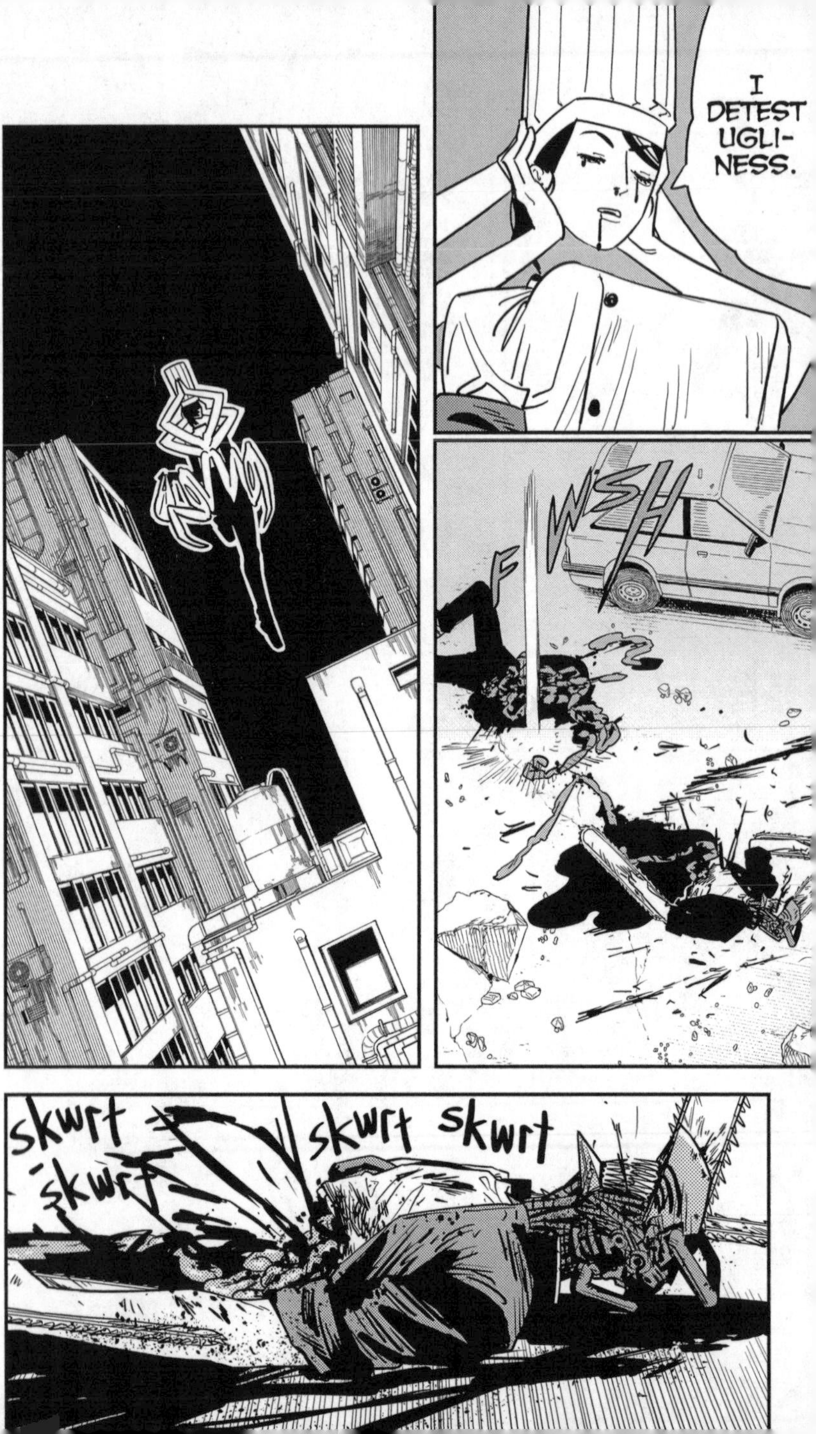
I DETEST UGLINESS.
FWSH
skwrt
skwrt
skwrt
skwrt

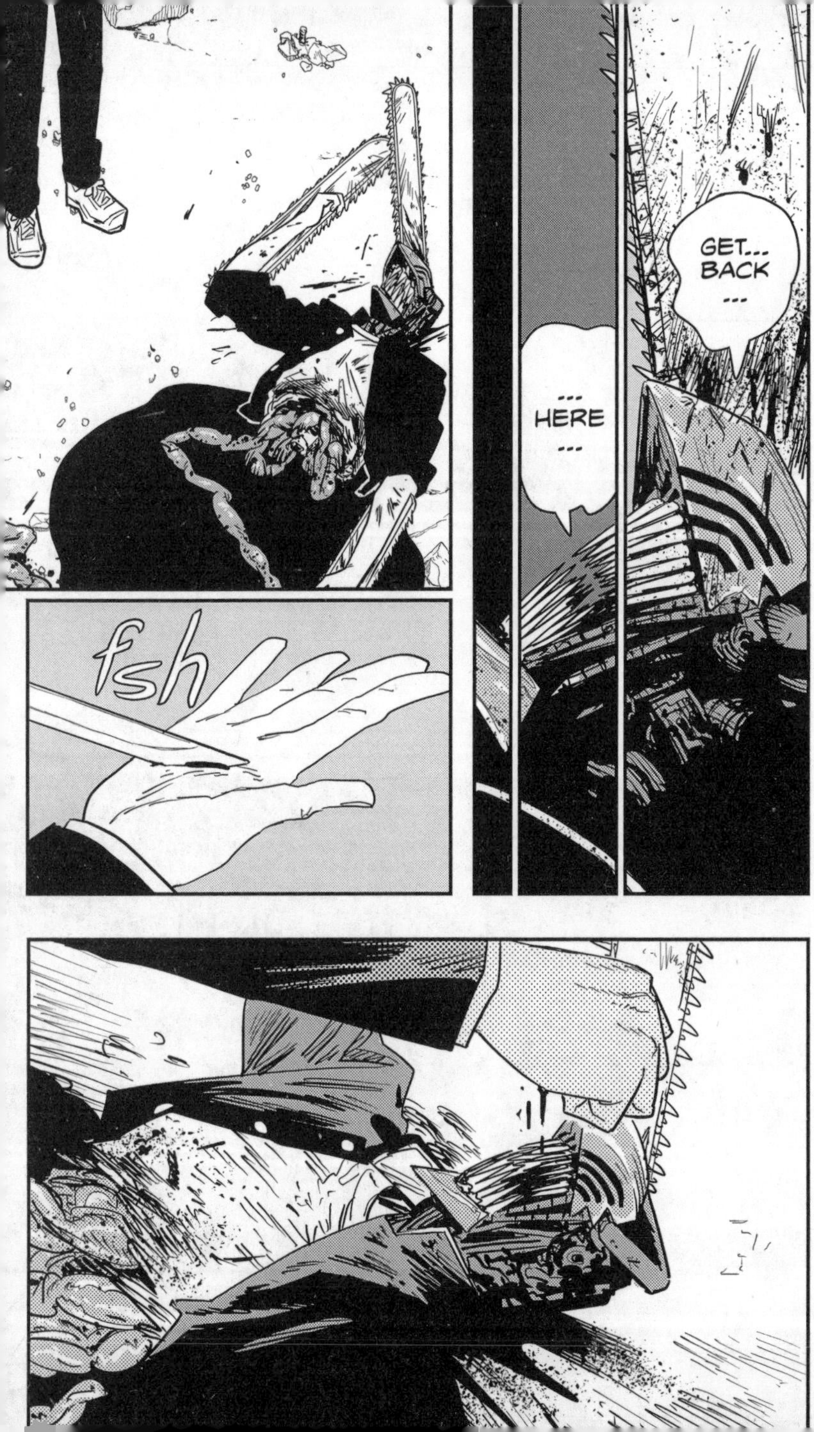
GET... BACK ...
... HERE ...
fsh

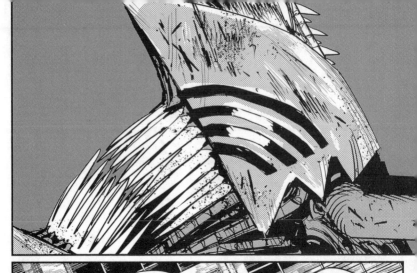

...CHAINSAW MAN.

I STILL NEED YOU TO FIGHT...

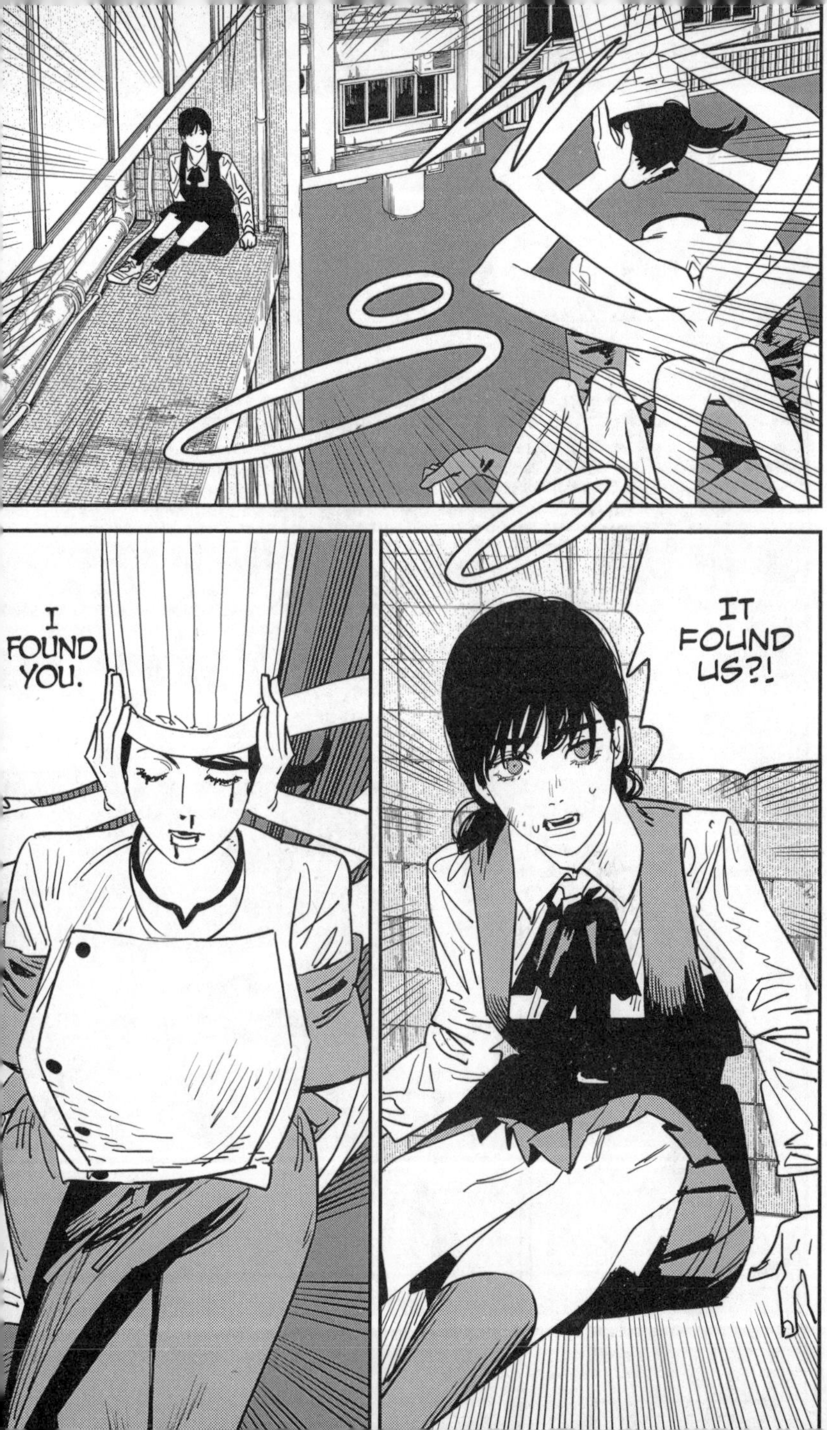
IT FOUND US?!
I FOUND YOU.

Chapter 127: Save the Asa

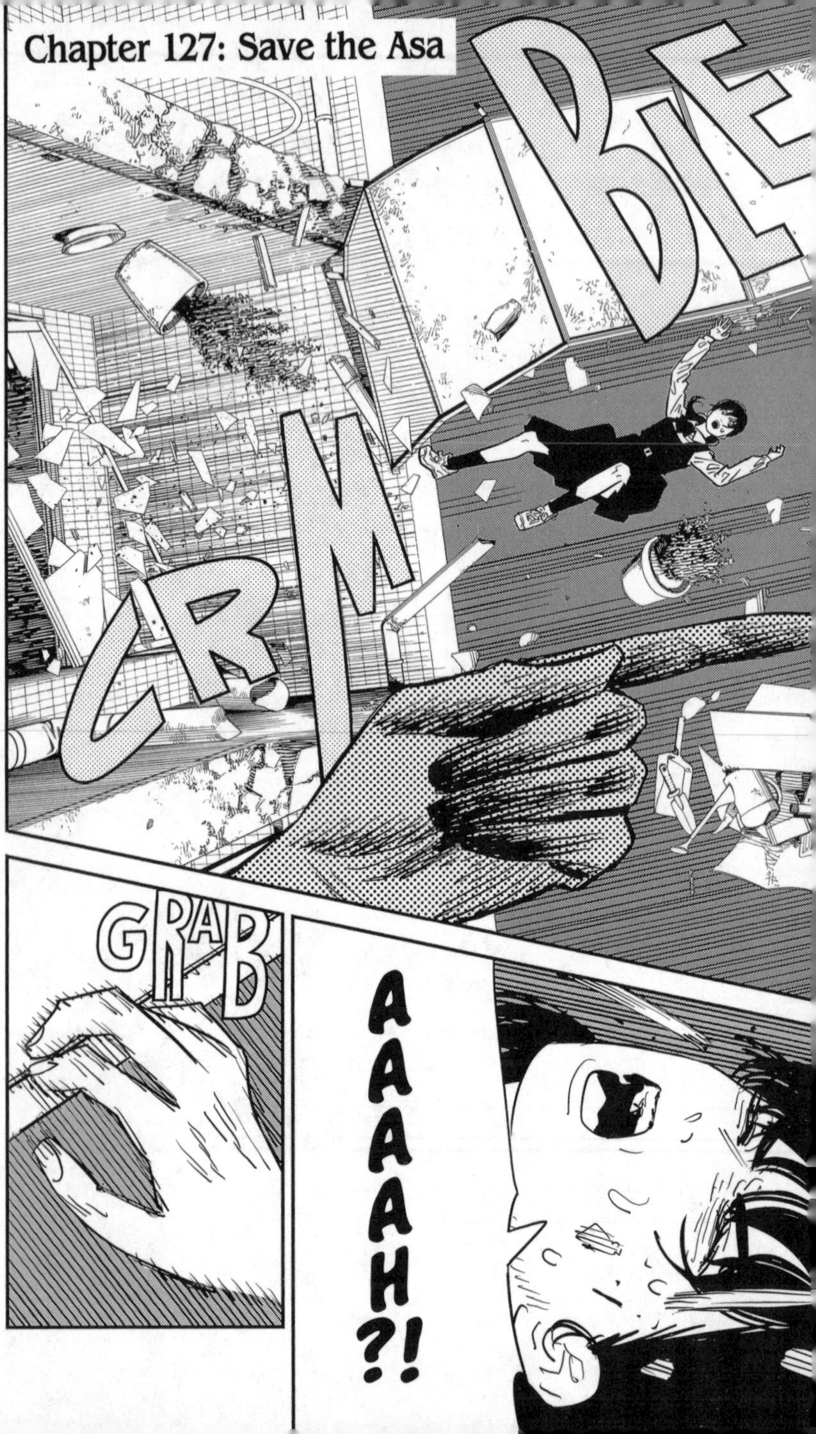
BLE
CRM
AAAAAH?!
GRAB

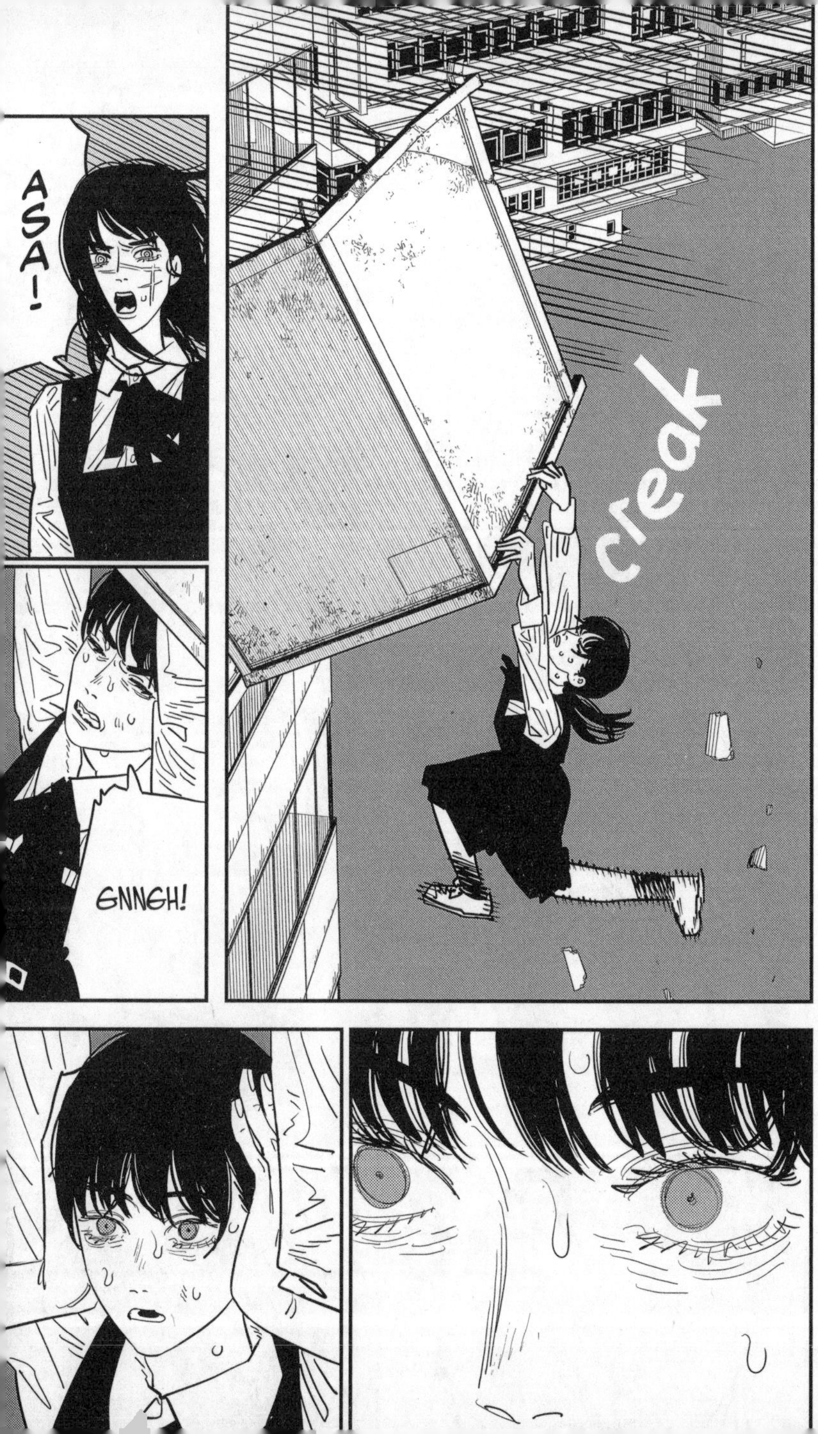
creak
ASA!
GNNGH!

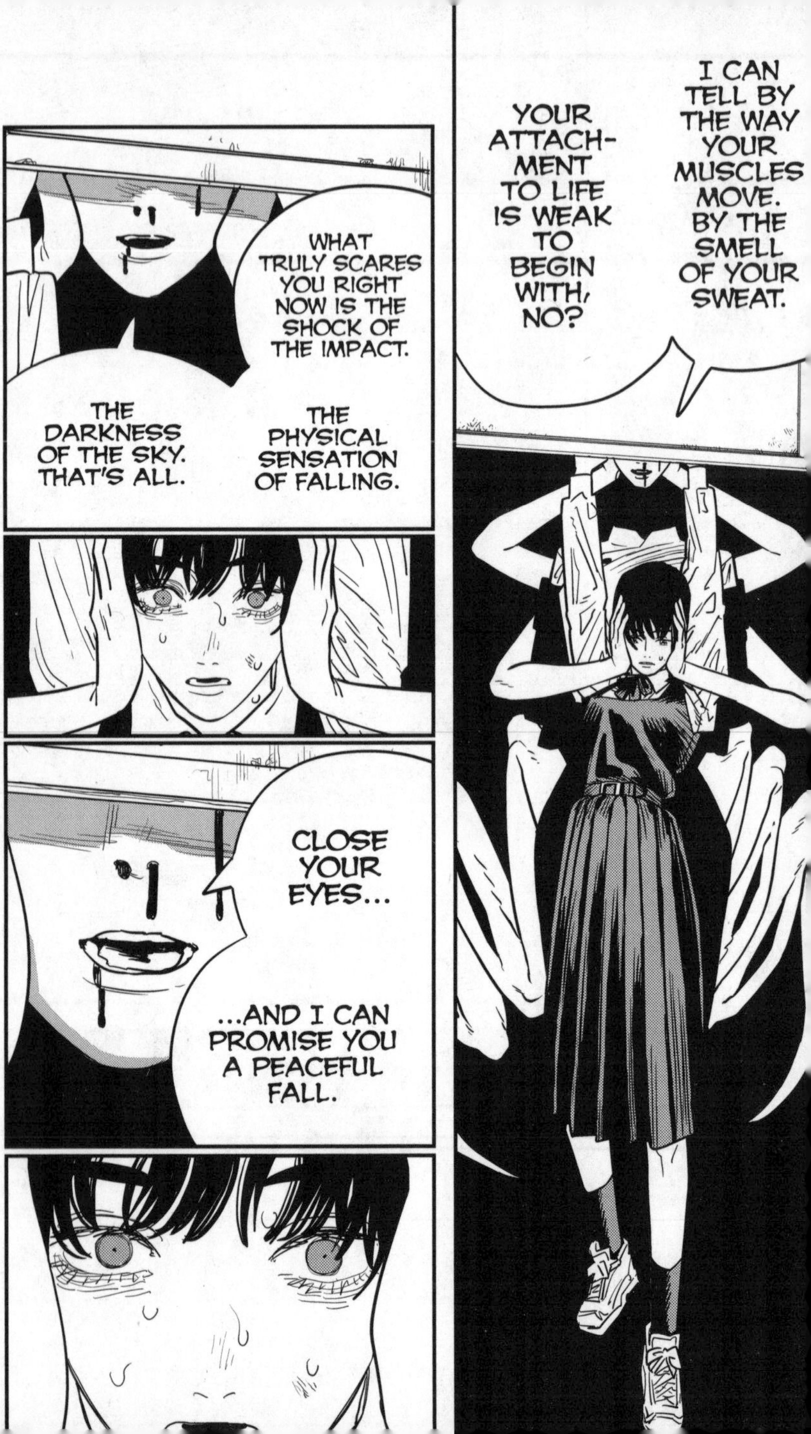
I CAN TELL BY THE WAY YOUR MUSCLES MOVE. BY THE SMELL OF YOUR SWEAT.
YOUR ATTACHMENT TO LIFE IS WEAK TO BEGIN WITH, NO?
WHAT TRULY SCARES YOU RIGHT NOW IS THE SHOCK OF THE IMPACT.
THE PHYSICAL SENSATION OF FALLING.
THE DARKNESS OF THE SKY. THAT'S ALL.
CLOSE YOUR EYES...
...AND I CAN PROMISE YOU A PEACEFUL FALL.

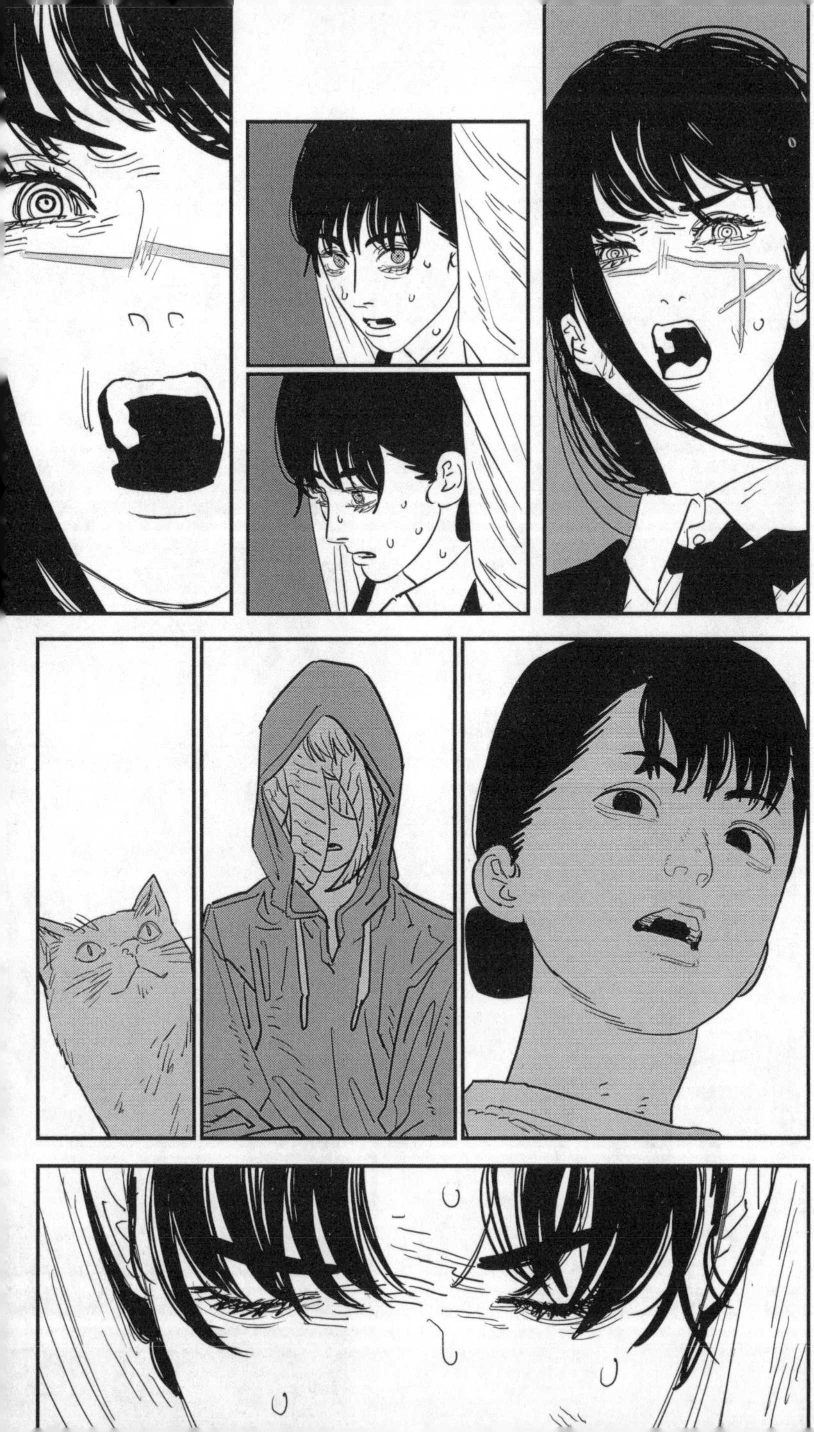

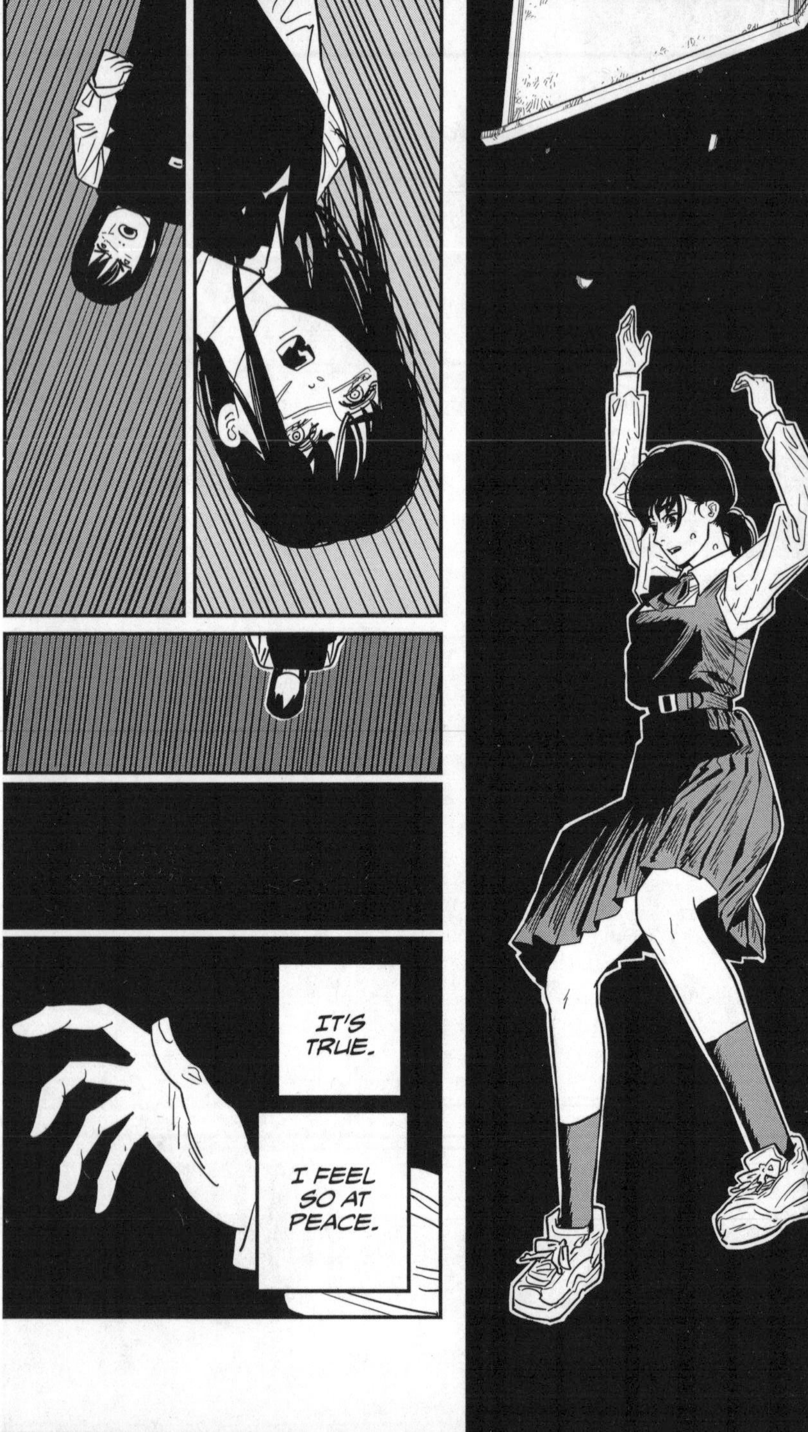
IT'S TRUE.
I FEEL SO AT PEACE.

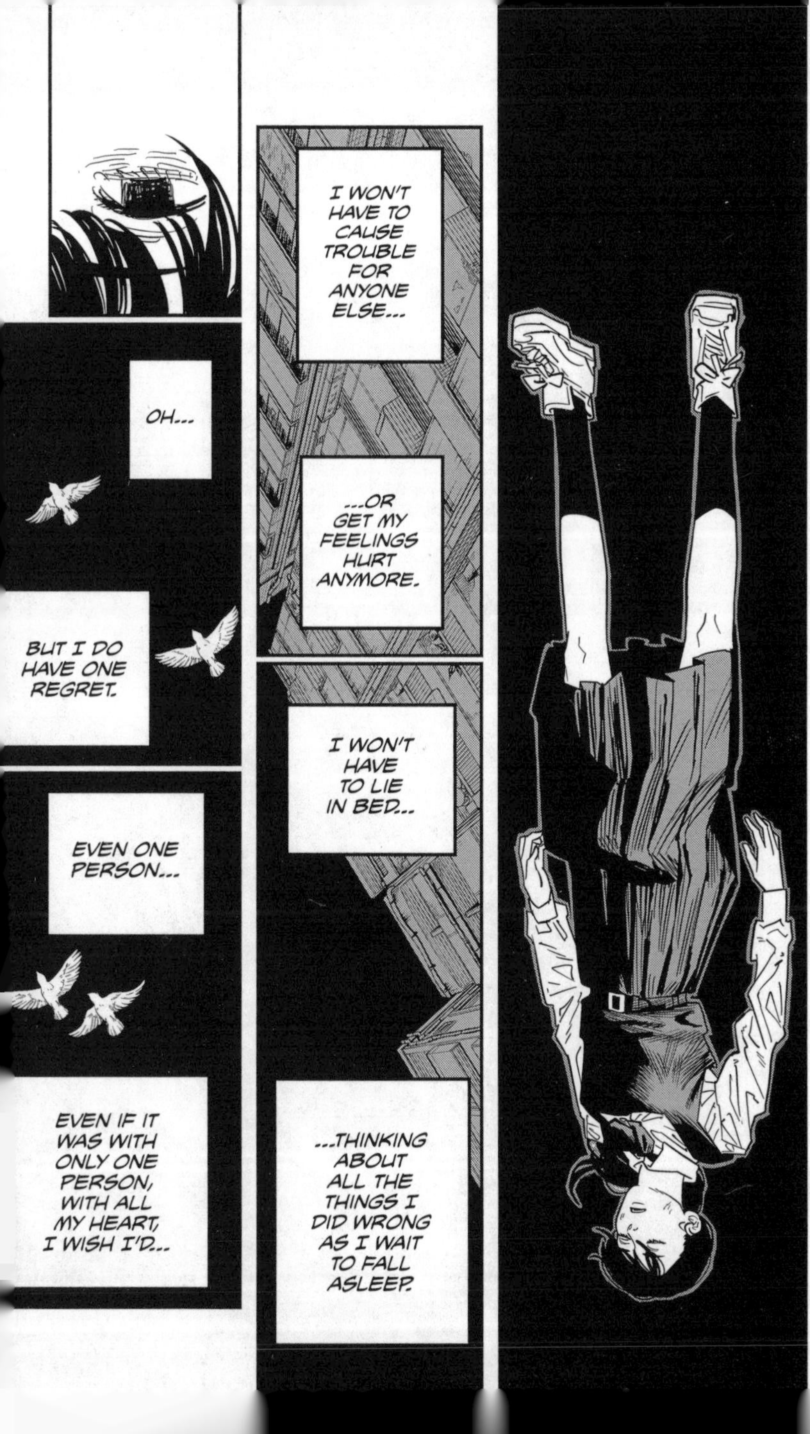
I WON'T HAVE TO CAUSE TROUBLE FOR ANYONE ELSE...
...OR GET MY FEELINGS HURT ANYMORE.
I WON'T HAVE TO LIE IN BED...
...THINKING ABOUT ALL THE THINGS I DID WRONG AS I WAIT TO FALL ASLEEP.
OH...
BUT I DO HAVE ONE REGRET.
EVEN ONE PERSON...
EVEN IF IT WAS WITH ONLY ONE PERSON, WITH ALL MY HEART, I WISH I'D...

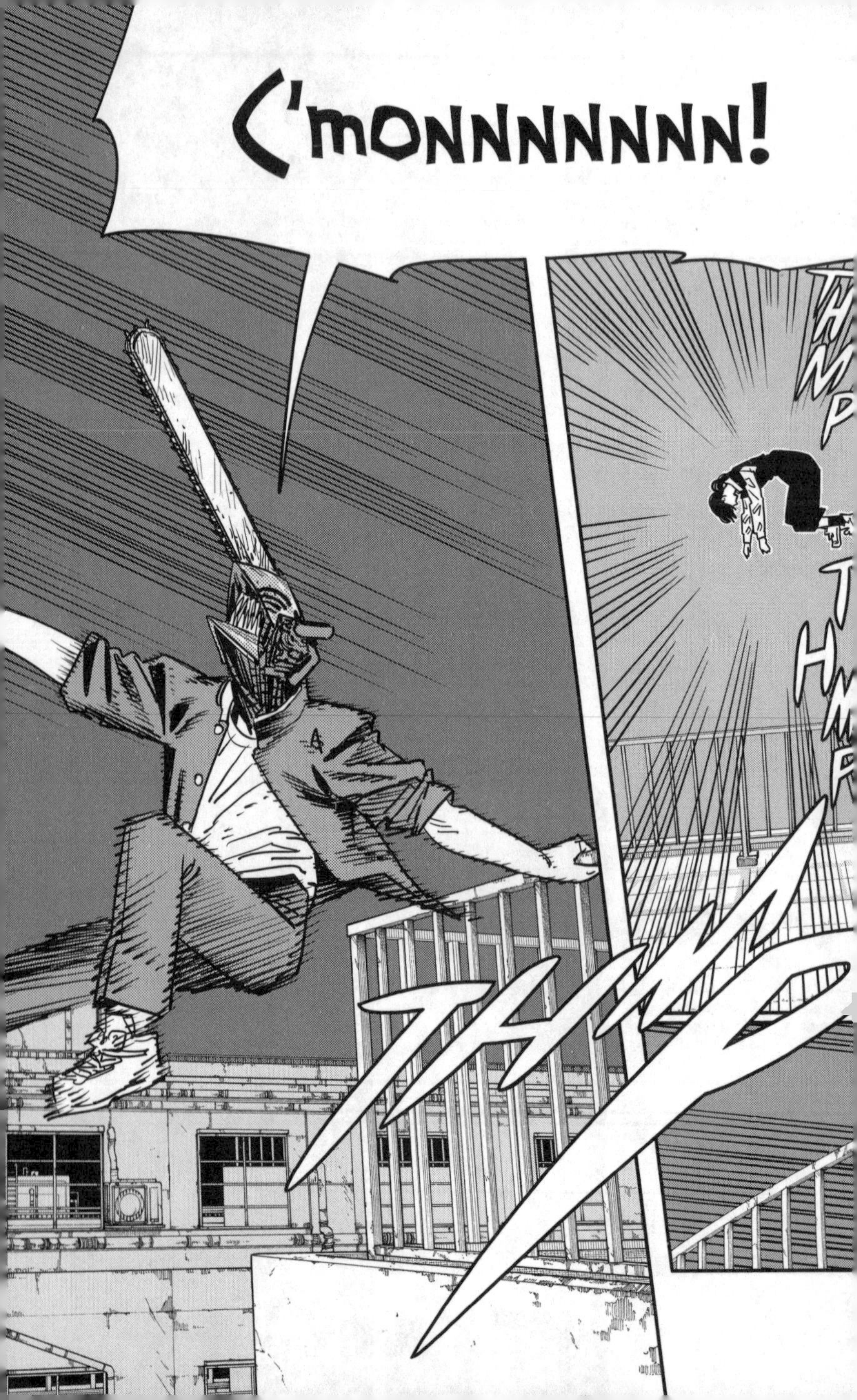
C'MONNNNNNN!
THMP
THMP
THWD

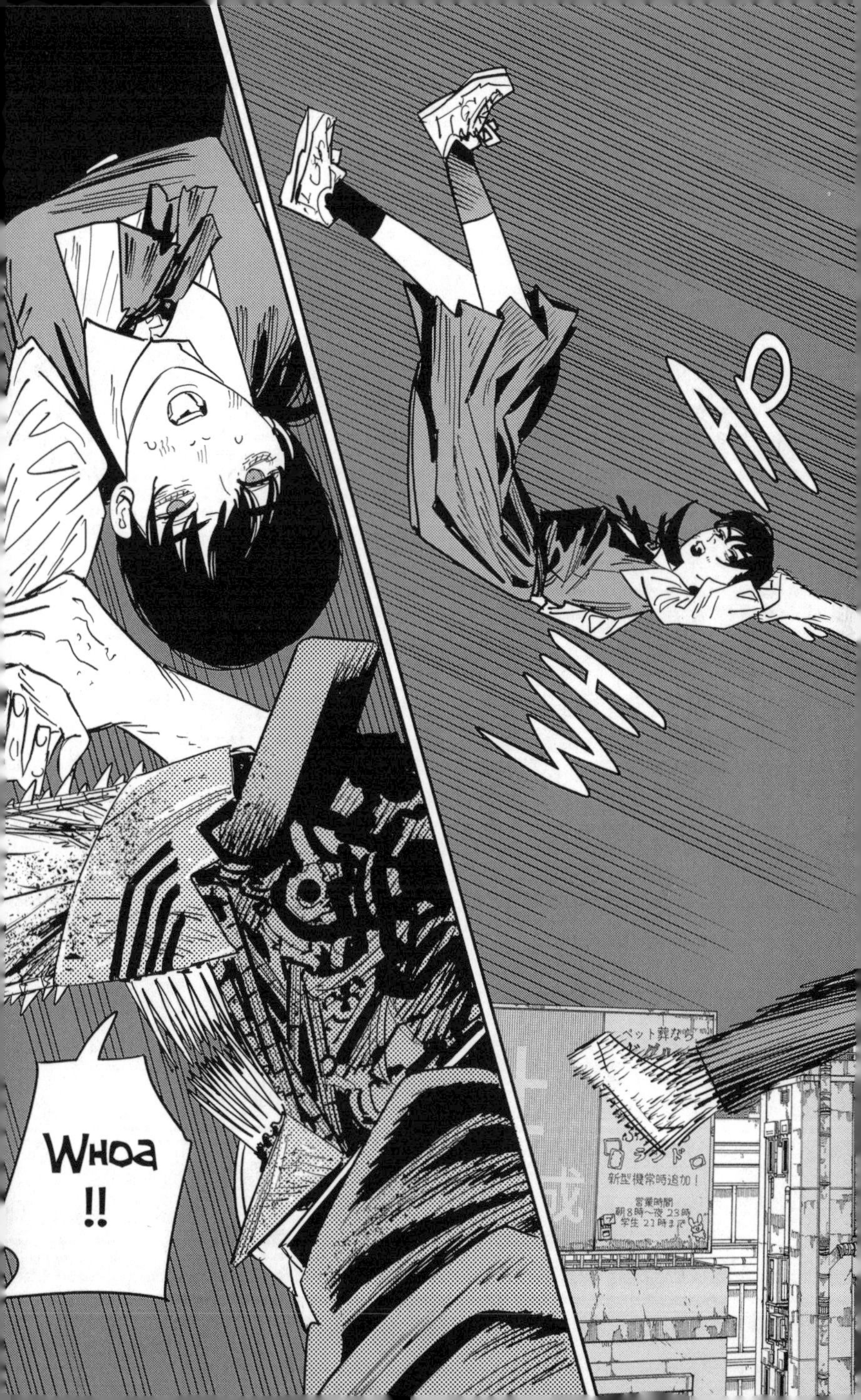
WHAP
ペット葬なら
新型機常時追加！
営業時間
朝8時～夜23時
学生21時まで
Whoa!!

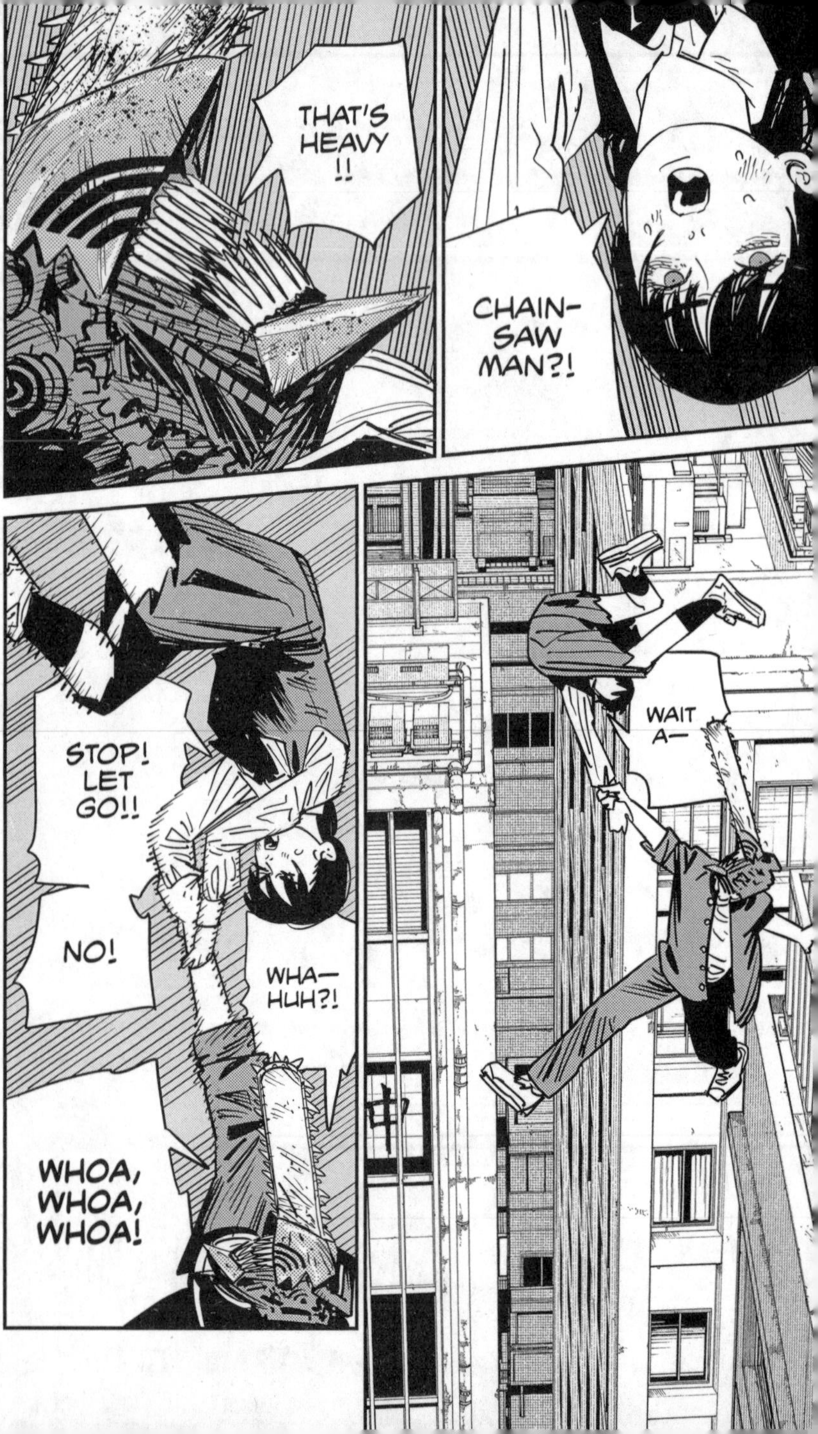
CHAIN-SAW MAN?!
THAT'S HEAVY !!
WAIT A—
STOP! LET GO!!
WHA—HUH?!
NO!
WHOA, WHOA, WHOA!

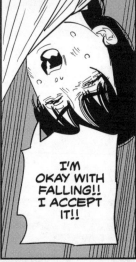

I'M OKAY WITH FALLING!! I ACCEPT IT!!
ARE YOU NUTS?!
LIFE IS NOTHING BUT PAIN!!
GETTING MADE INTO A FOOL, GETTING YOUR EXPEC-TATIONS UP ONLY TO BE LET DOWN!
ISN'T IT?!
WELL, YEAH, BUT, LIKE...!
WHOA—AH?!

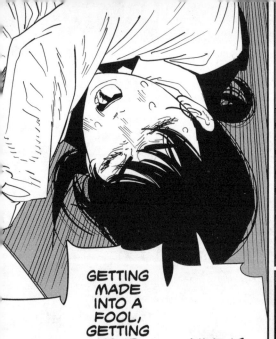

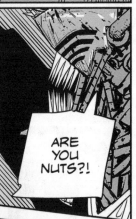

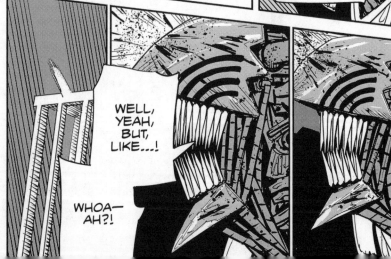

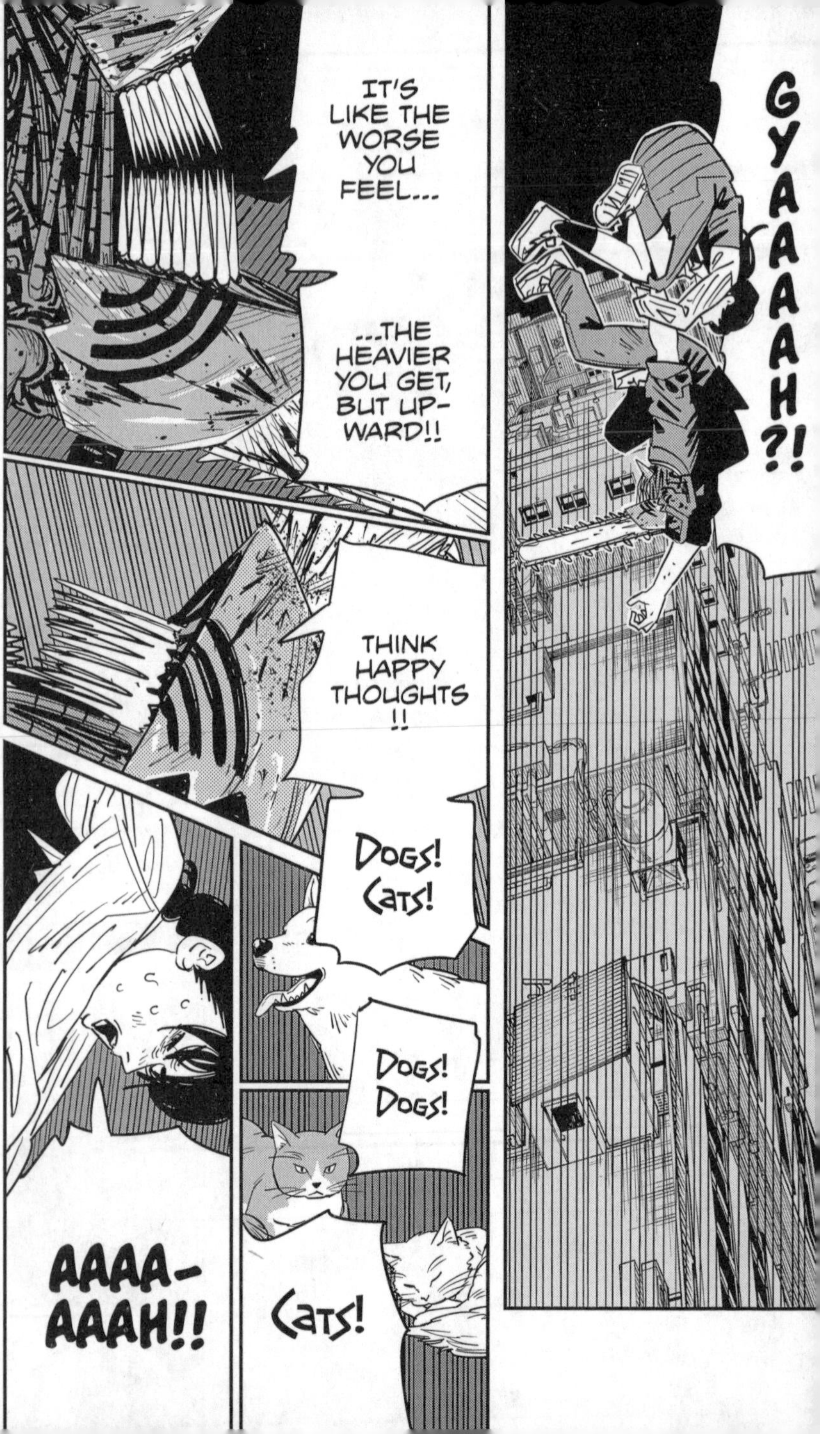
GYAAAAH?!
IT'S LIKE THE WORSE YOU FEEL...
...THE HEAVIER YOU GET, BUT UP-WARD!!
THINK HAPPY THOUGHTS!!
DOGS! CATS!
DOGS! DOGS!
CATS!
AAAA-AAAH!!

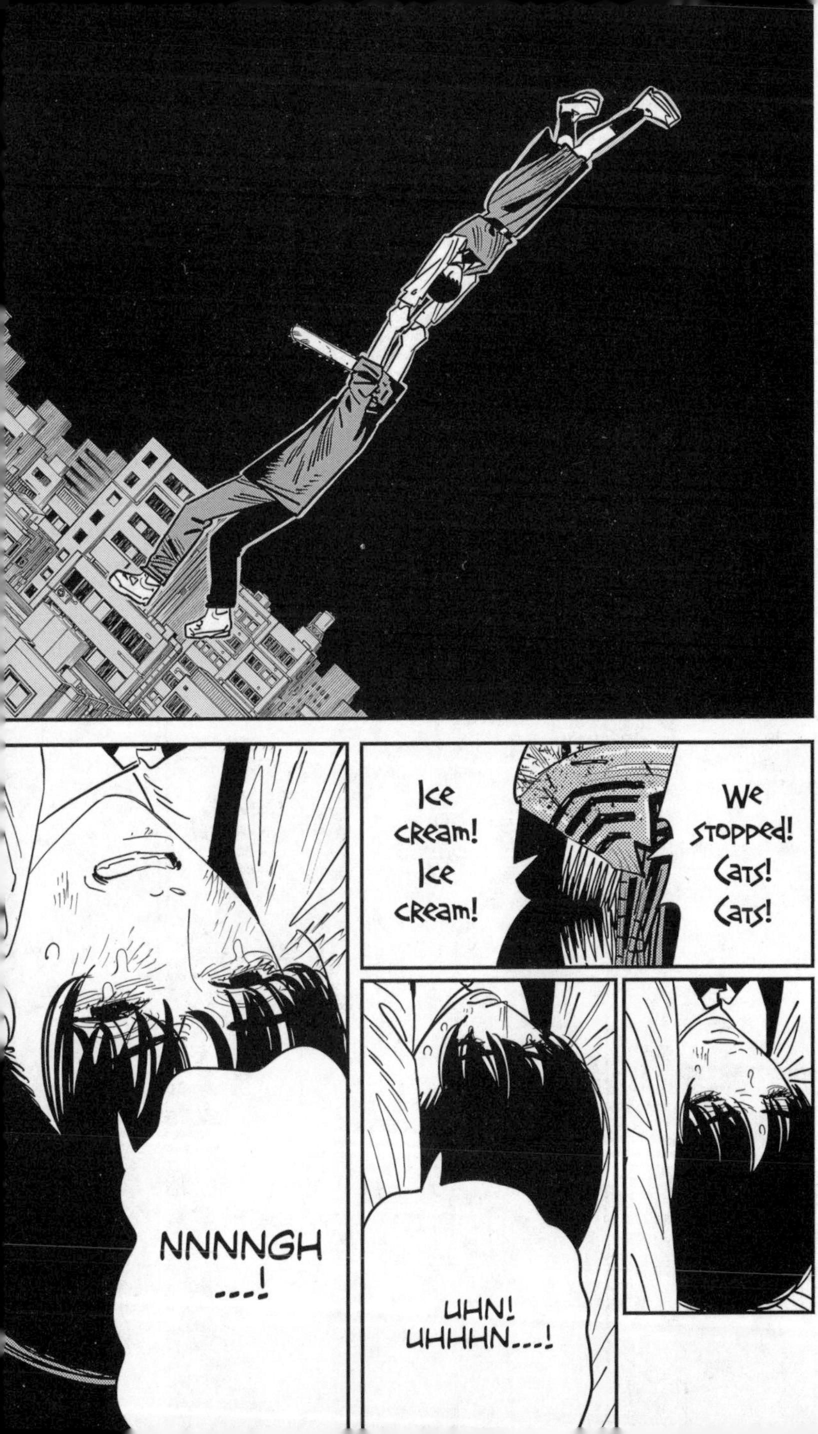
We stopped! Cats! Cats!
Ice cream! Ice cream!
UHN! UHHHN...!
NNNNGH ...!

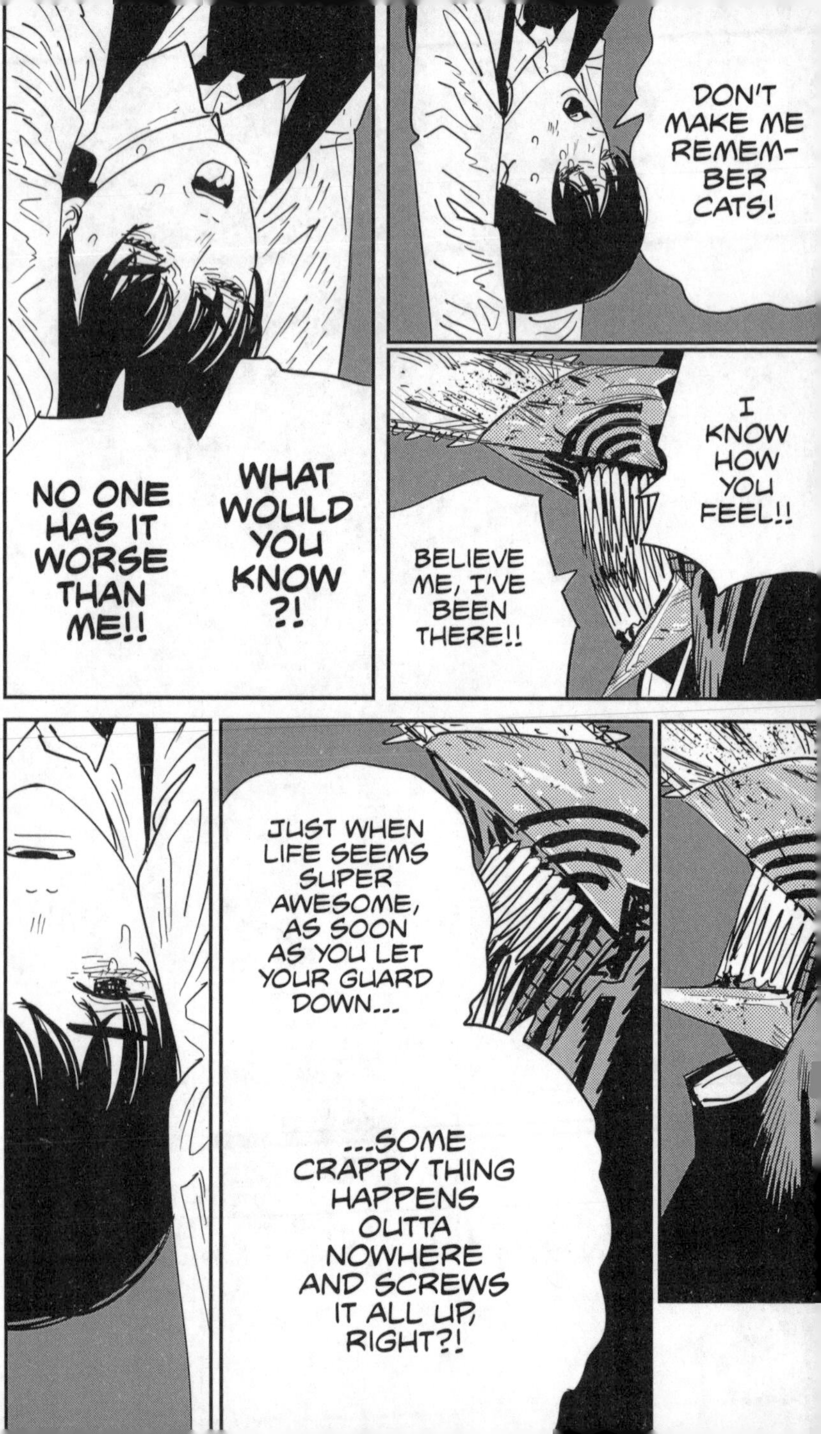
DON'T MAKE ME REMEM-BER CATS!
I KNOW HOW YOU FEEL!!
BELIEVE ME, I'VE BEEN THERE!!
WHAT WOULD YOU KNOW ?!
NO ONE HAS IT WORSE THAN ME!!
JUST WHEN LIFE SEEMS SUPER AWESOME, AS SOON AS YOU LET YOUR GUARD DOWN...
...SOME CRAPPY THING HAPPENS OUTTA NOWHERE AND SCREWS IT ALL UP, RIGHT?!

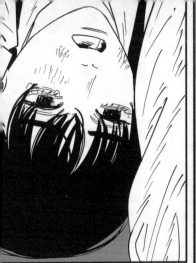

YOU KNOW LIFE ISN'T **ALL** BAD...

...BUT DAY IN AND DAY OUT, ALL YOU CAN REMEMBER IS THE BAD STUFF...

...AND THE DISASTERS KEEP PILIN' UP LIKE A HAMBURGER MADE OF CRAP, RIGHT?

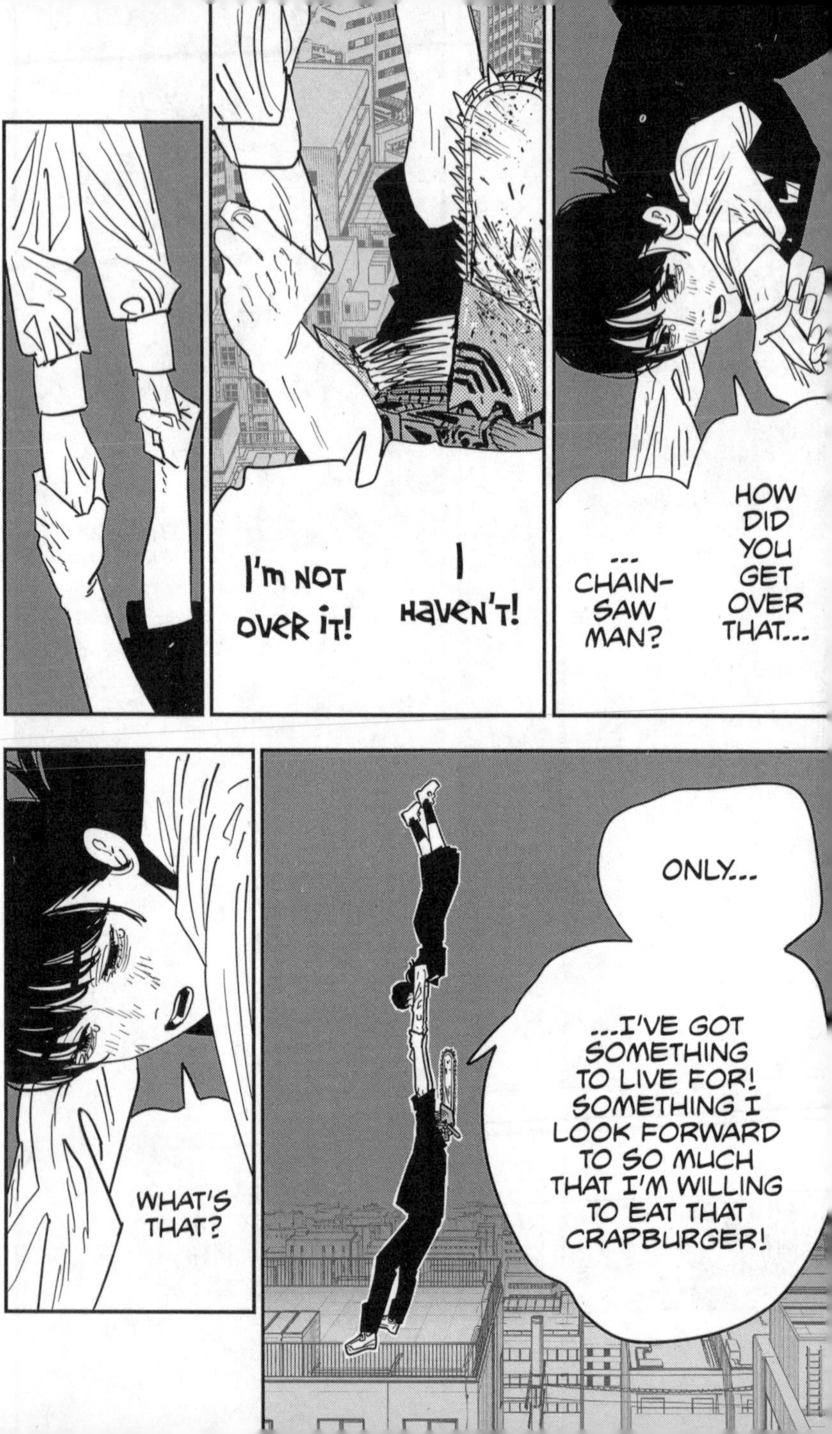
HOW DID YOU GET OVER THAT...
...CHAIN-SAW MAN?
I HAVEN'T!
I'M NOT OVER IT!
ONLY...
...I'VE GOT SOMETHING TO LIVE FOR! SOMETHING I LOOK FORWARD TO SO MUCH THAT I'M WILLING TO EAT THAT CRAPBURGER!
WHAT'S THAT?

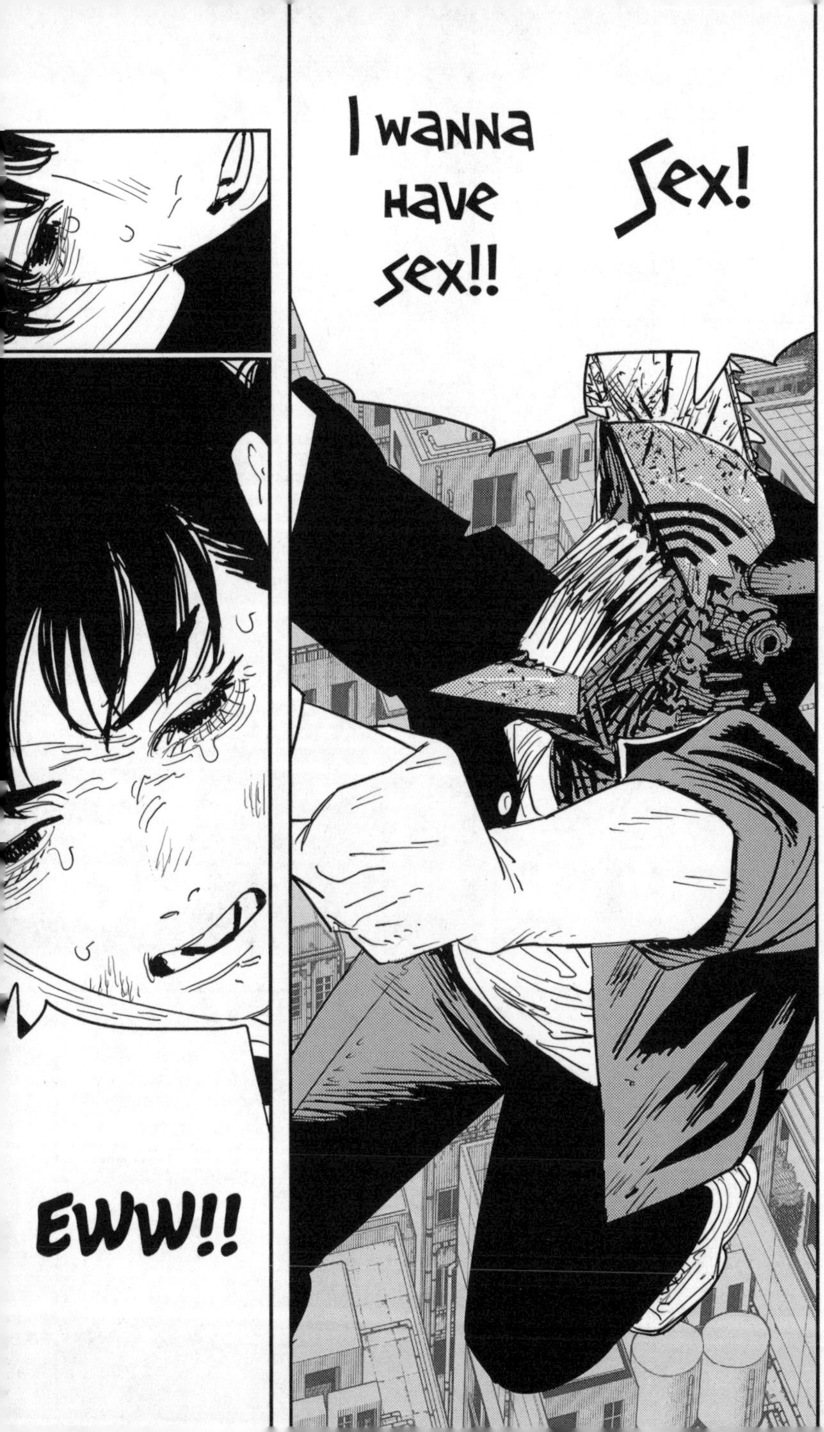
I wanna have sex!!
Sex!
EWW!!

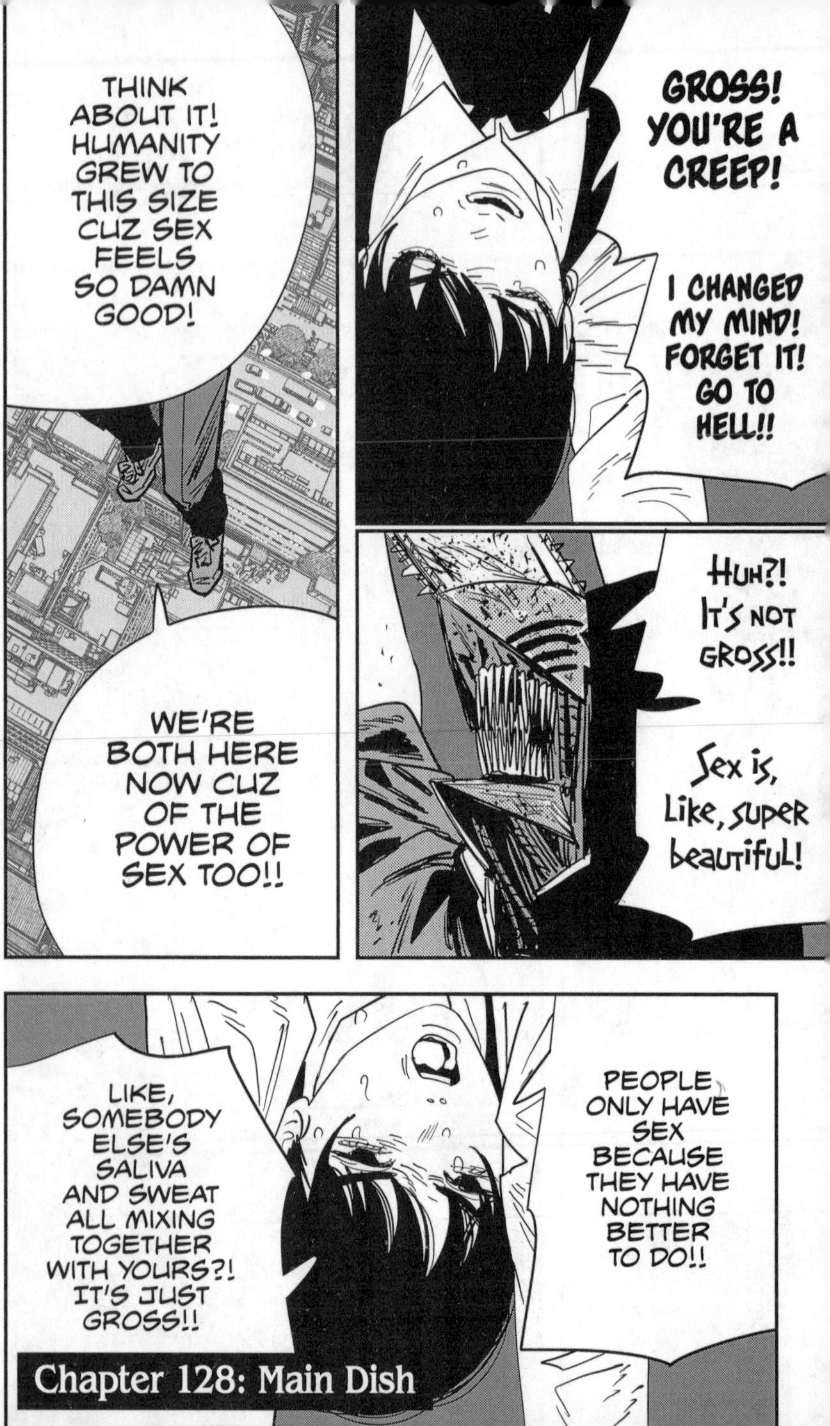
GROSS! YOU'RE A CREEP!
I CHANGED MY MIND! FORGET IT! GO TO HELL!!
HUH?! IT'S NOT GROSS!!
Sex is, Like, super beautiful!
THINK ABOUT IT! HUMANITY GREW TO THIS SIZE CUZ SEX FEELS SO DAMN GOOD!
WE'RE BOTH HERE NOW CUZ OF THE POWER OF SEX TOO!!
PEOPLE ONLY HAVE SEX BECAUSE THEY HAVE NOTHING BETTER TO DO!!
LIKE, SOMEBODY ELSE'S SALIVA AND SWEAT ALL MIXING TOGETHER WITH YOURS?! IT'S JUST GROSS!!
Chapter 128: Main Dish

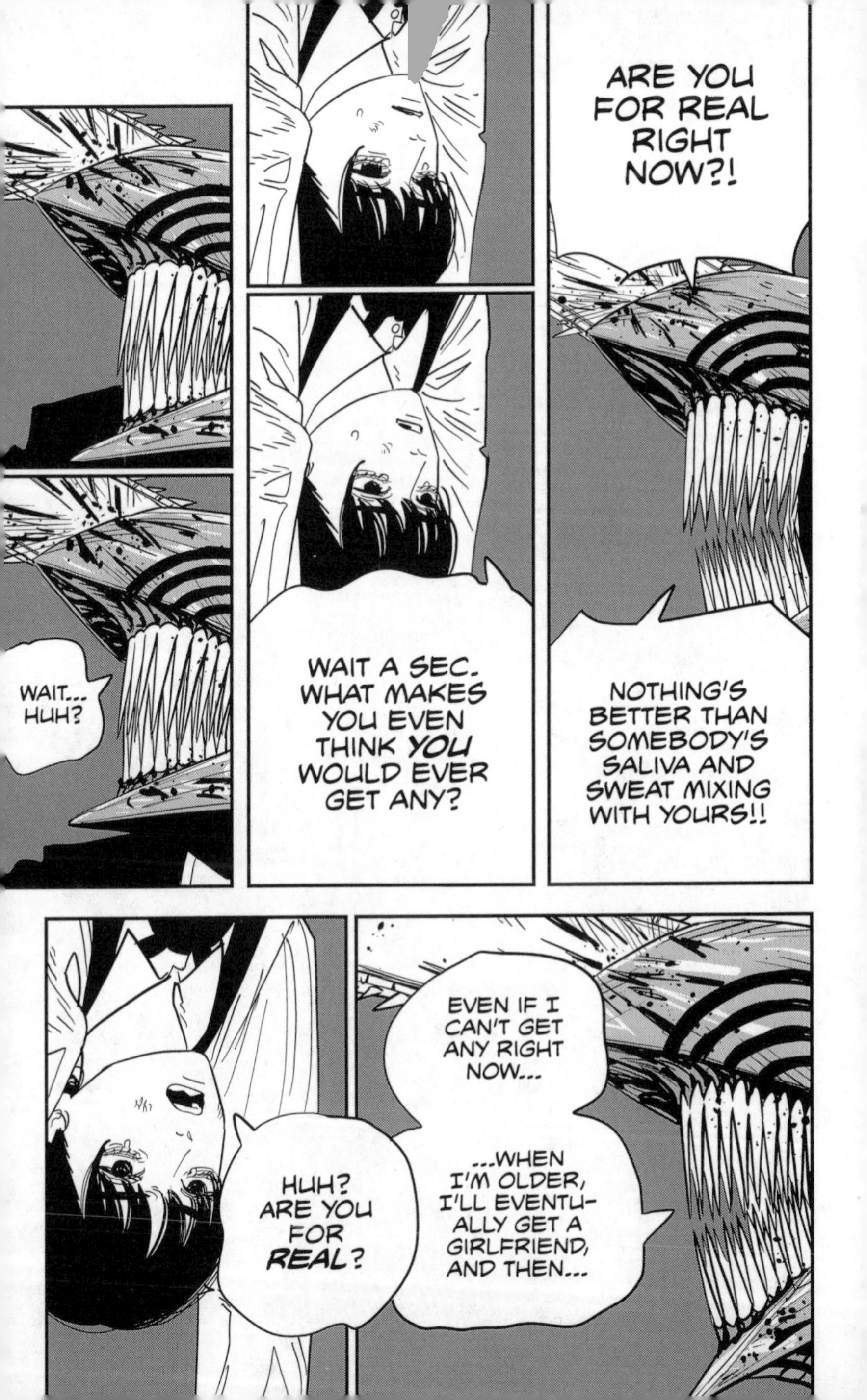
ARE YOU FOR REAL RIGHT NOW?!
NOTHING'S BETTER THAN SOMEBODY'S SALIVA AND SWEAT MIXING WITH YOURS!!
WAIT A SEC. WHAT MAKES YOU EVEN THINK *YOU* WOULD EVER GET ANY?
WAIT... HUH?
EVEN IF I CAN'T GET ANY RIGHT NOW...
...WHEN I'M OLDER, I'LL EVENTU-ALLY GET A GIRLFRIEND, AND THEN...
HUH? ARE YOU FOR *REAL*?

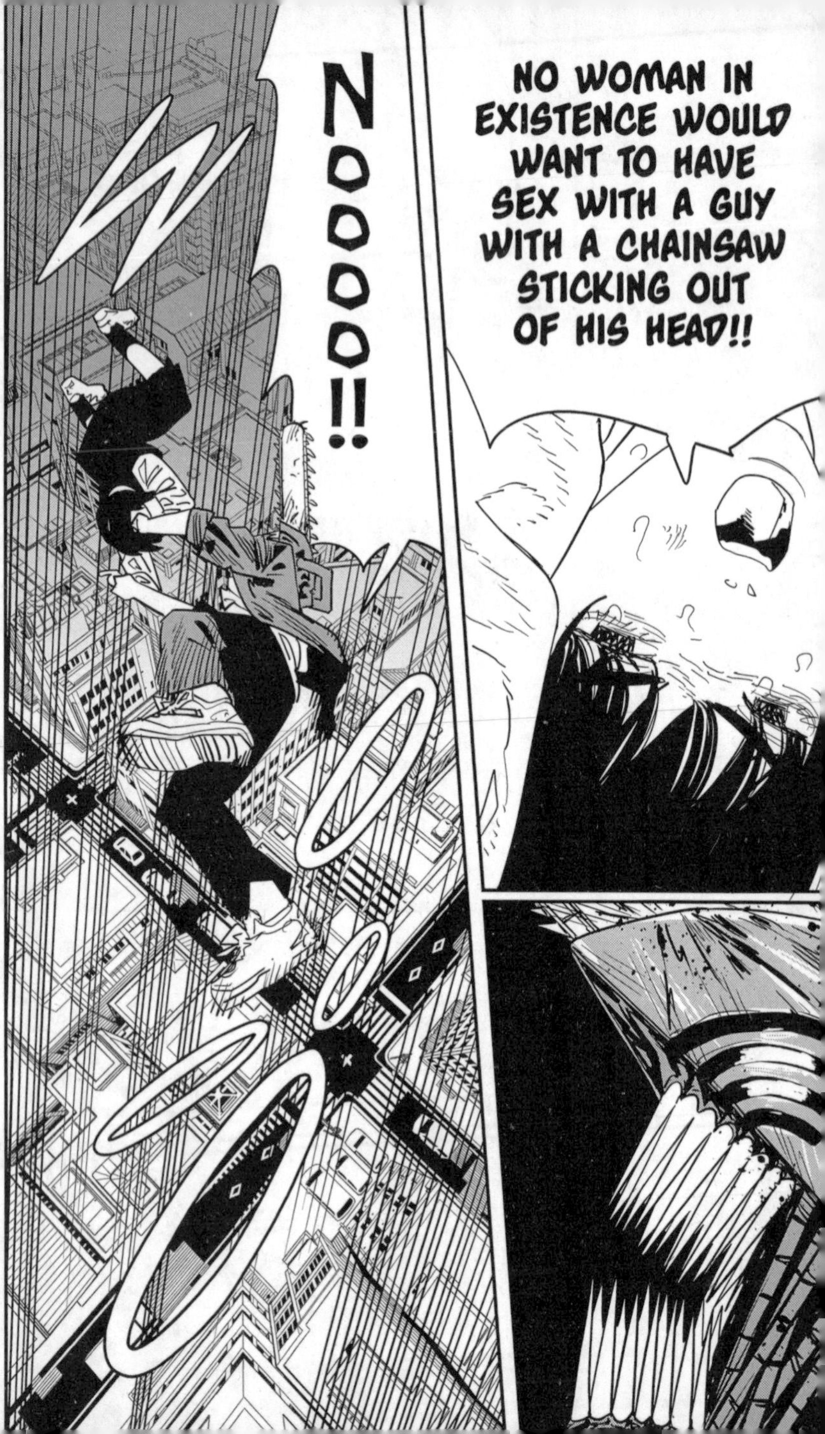
NO WOMAN IN EXISTENCE WOULD WANT TO HAVE SEX WITH A GUY WITH A CHAINSAW STICKING OUT OF HIS HEAD!!
NOOOO!!

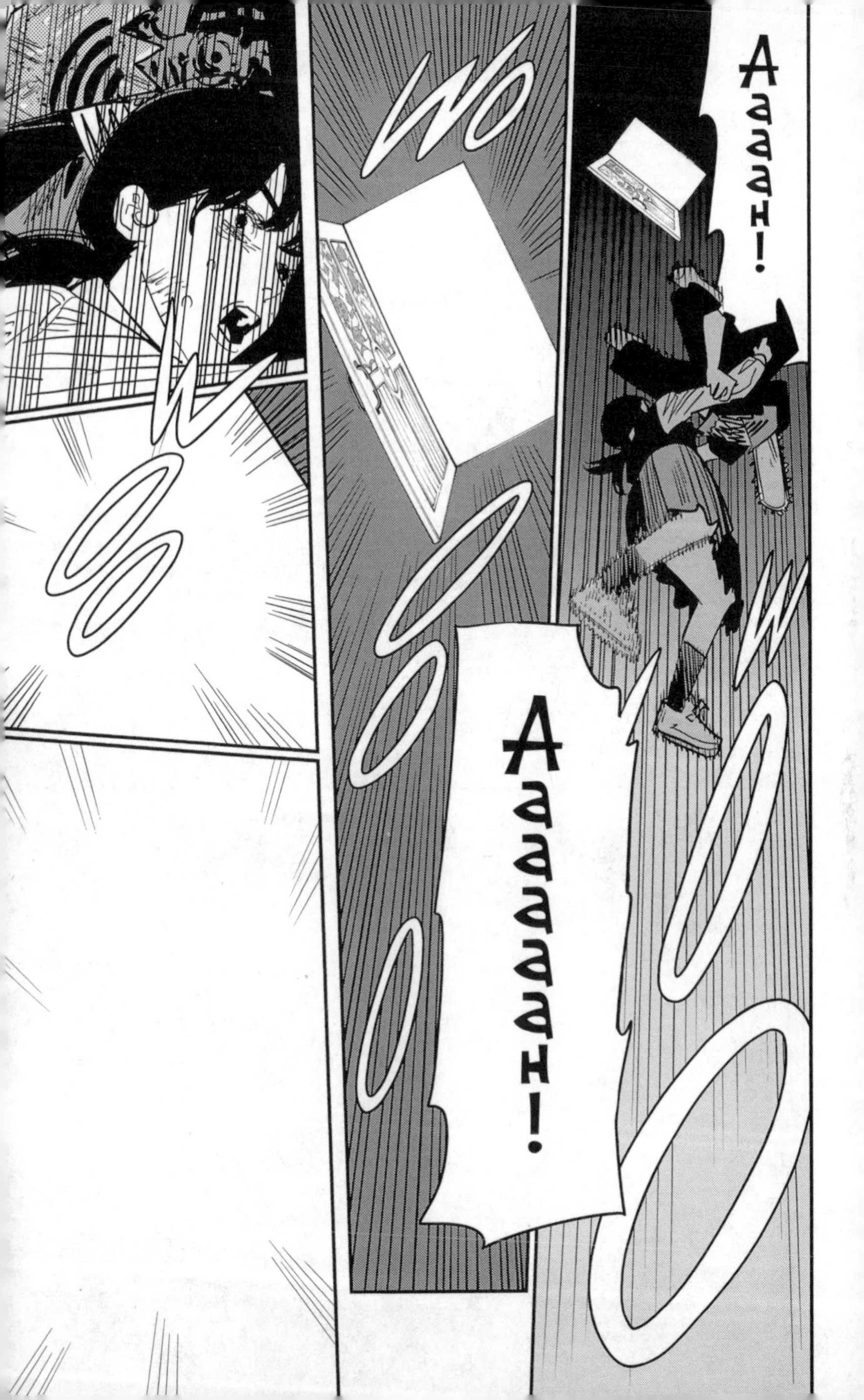
Aaaaah!
Aaaaaaah!

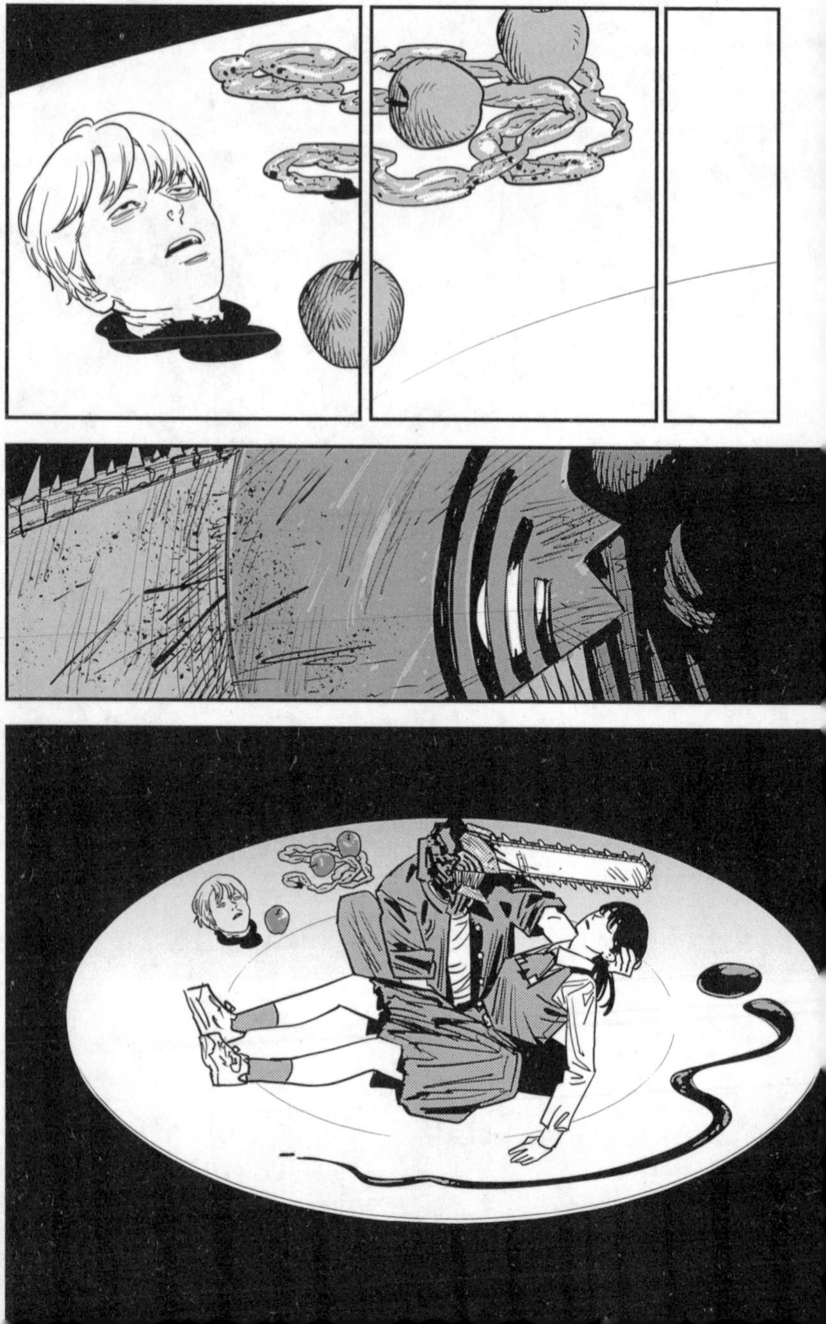

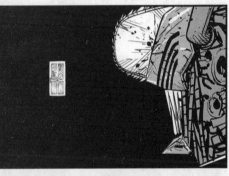

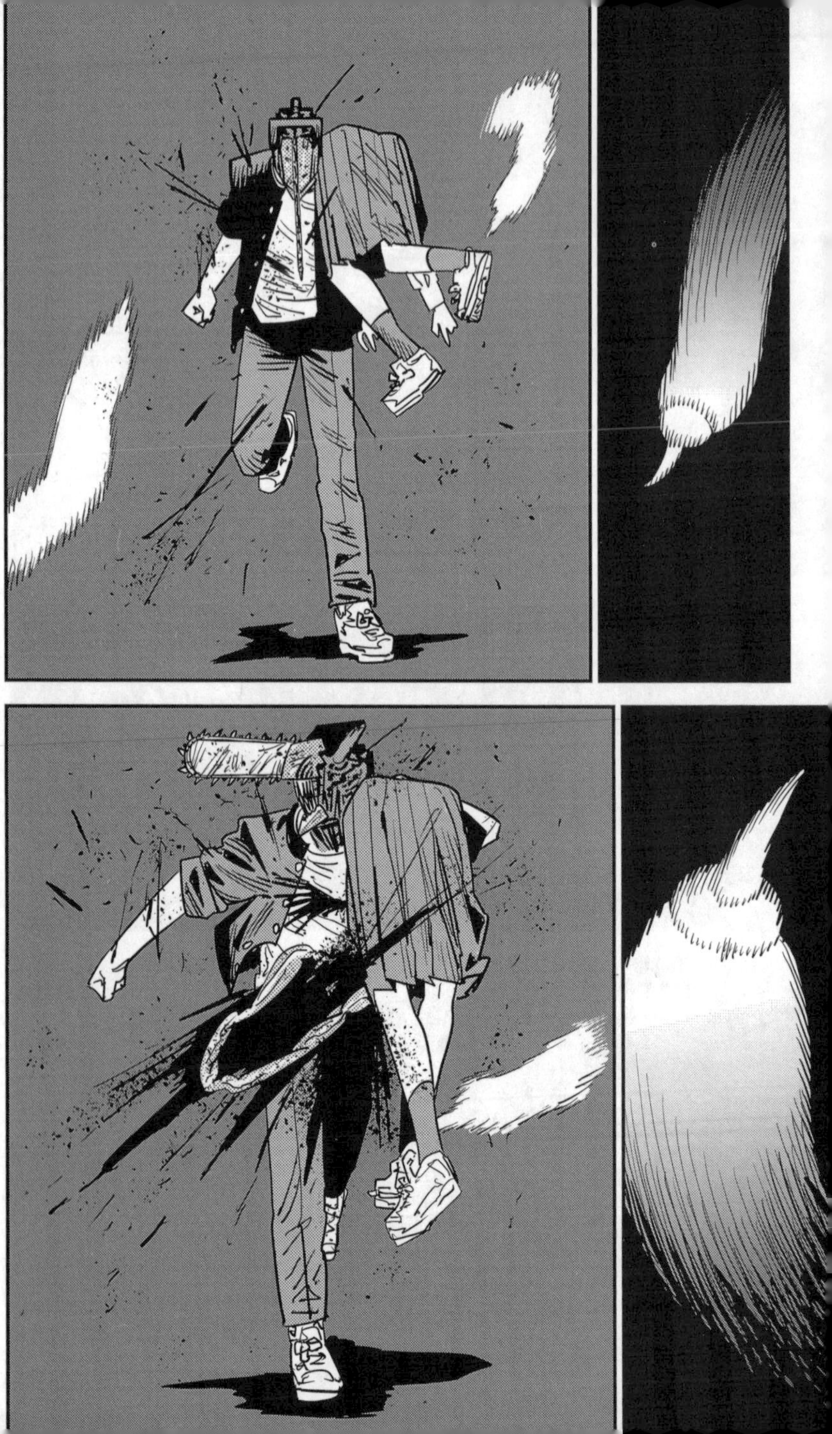

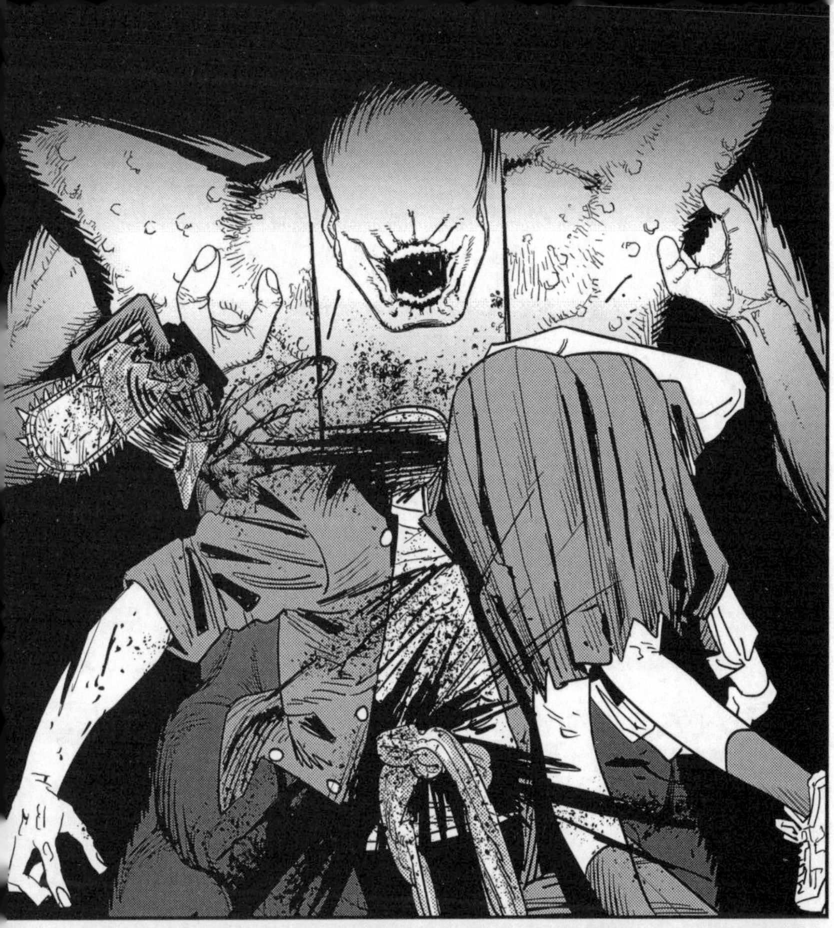

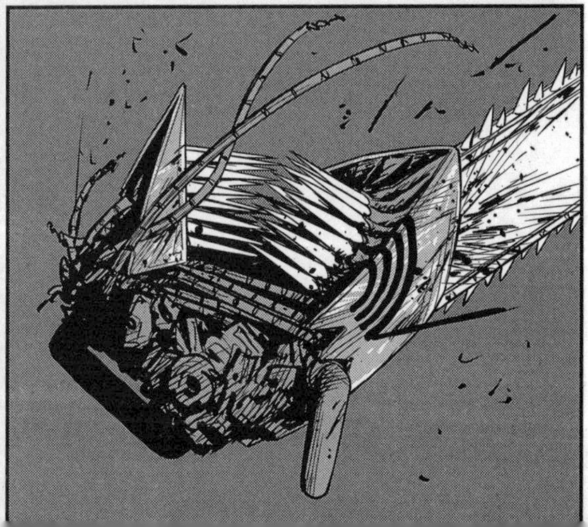

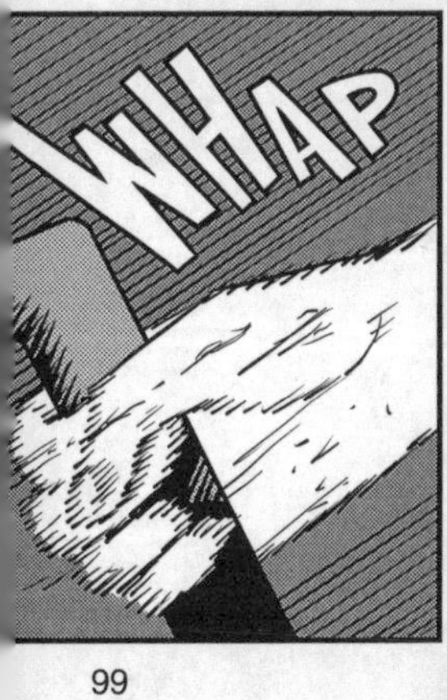
WHAP

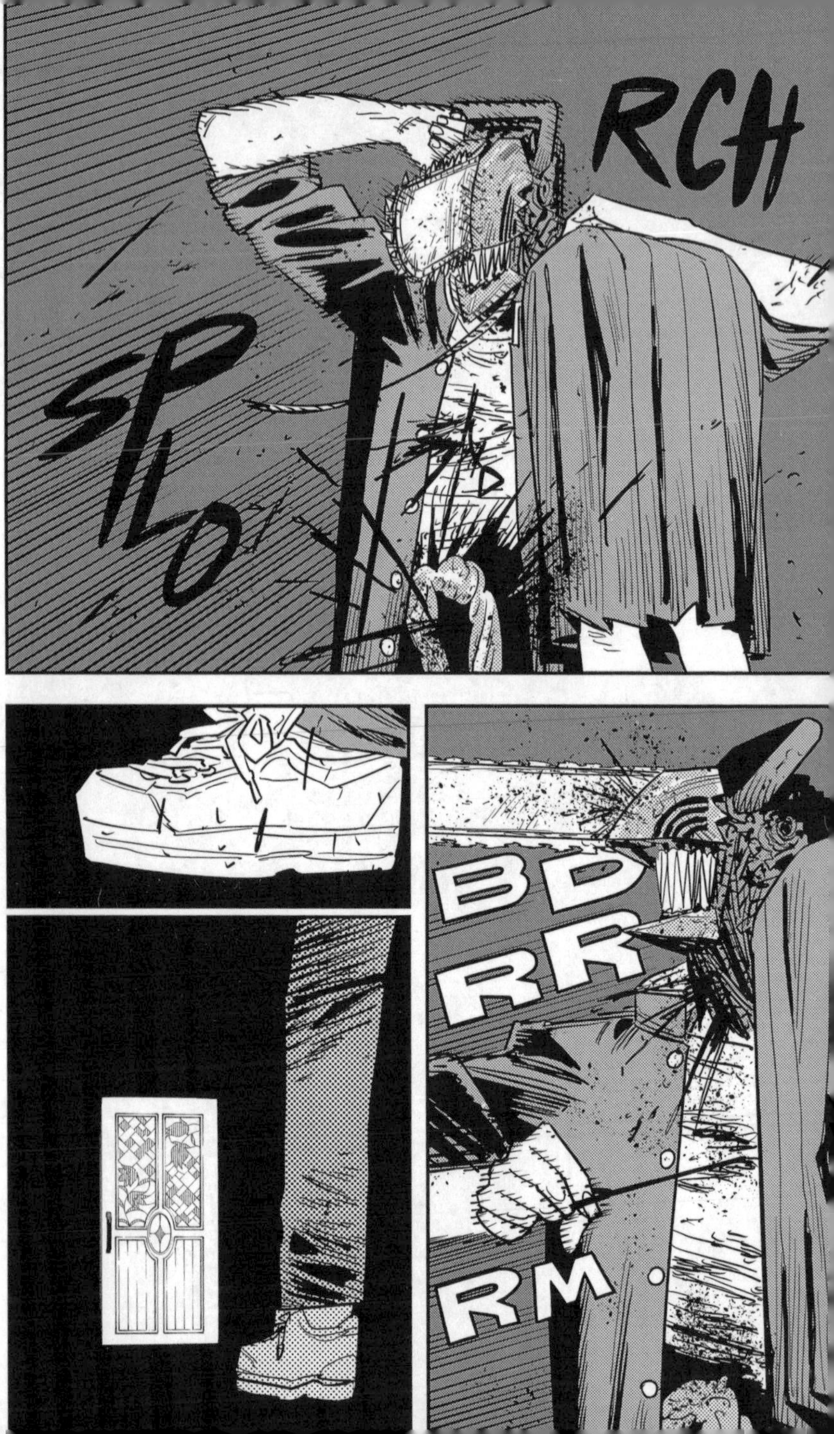
RCH
SPLO
BD
RR
RM

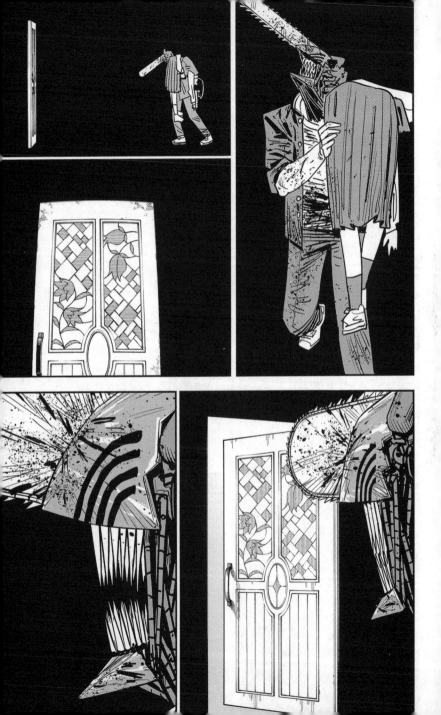

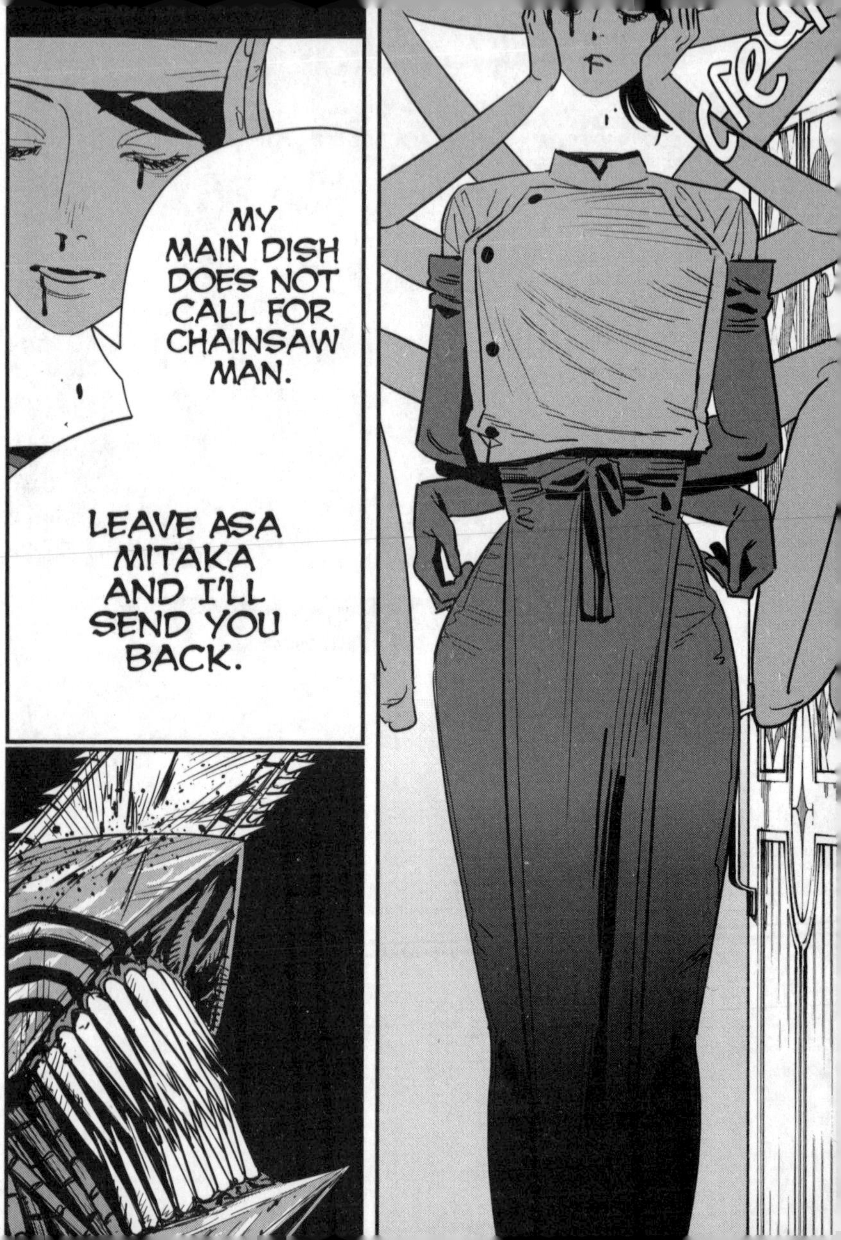
MY MAIN DISH DOES NOT CALL FOR CHAINSAW MAN.
LEAVE ASA MITAKA AND I'LL SEND YOU BACK.

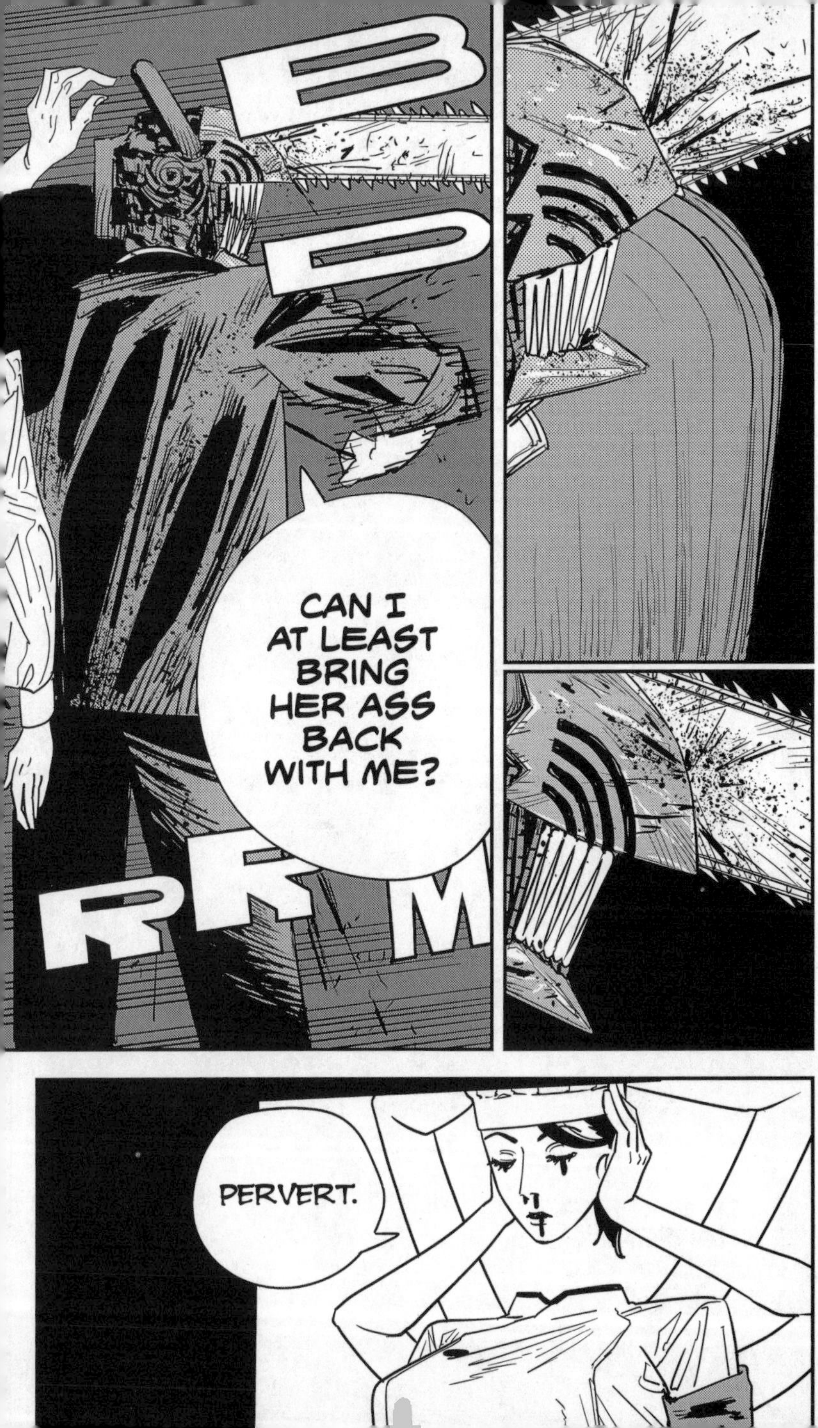
CAN I AT LEAST BRING HER ASS BACK WITH ME?
PERVERT.

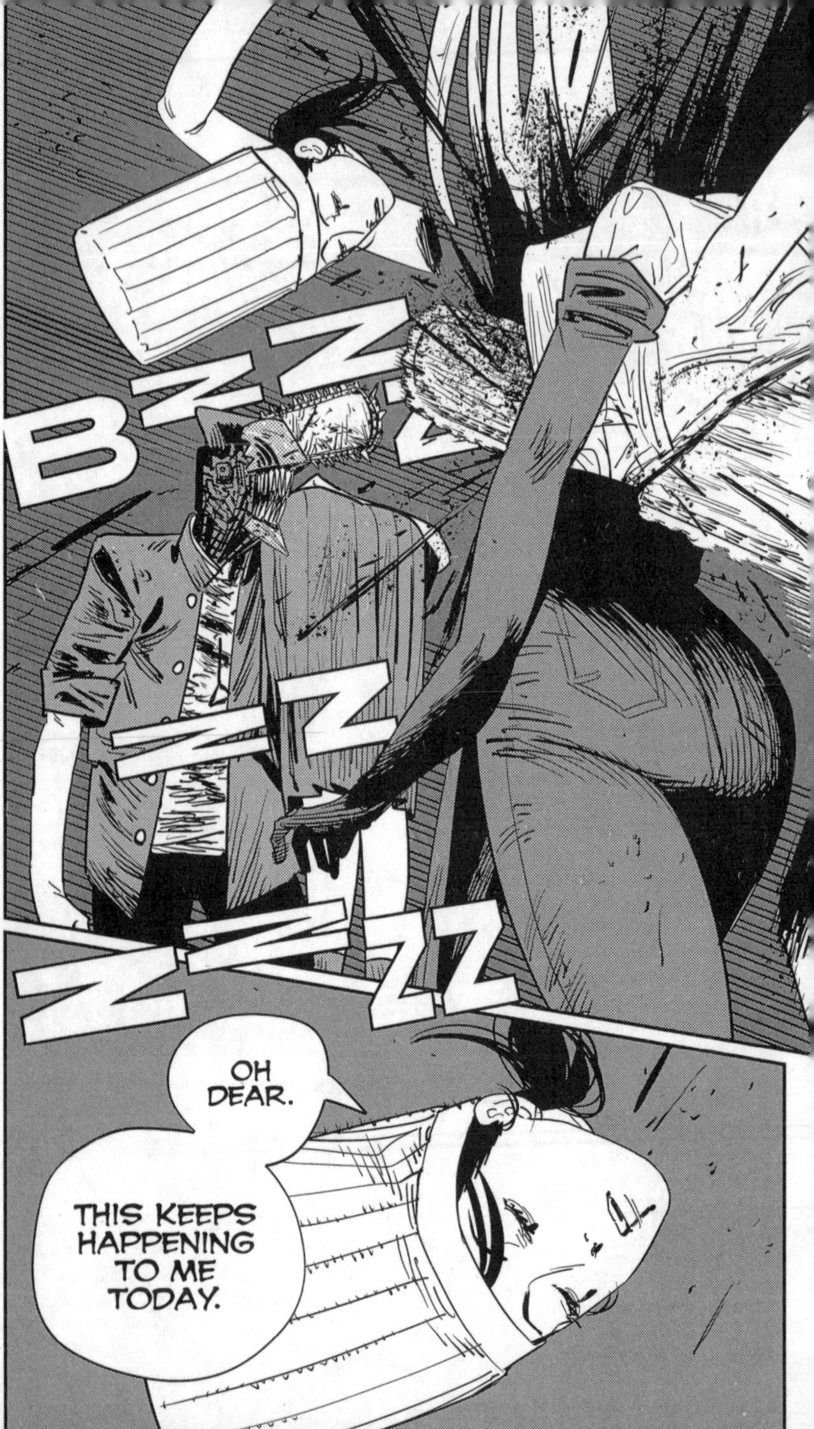
BZZZ
ZZ
ZZZZZ
OH DEAR.
THIS KEEPS HAPPENING TO ME TODAY.

THE FALLING DEVIL HAS NO TOLERANCE FOR DINERS WHO LEAVE THEIR FOOD UNFINISHED.

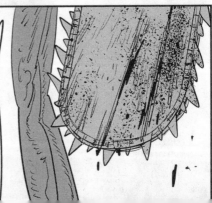

THEY'LL DESPERATELY TRY TO DEVOUR ASA MITAKA, LEST THEY BE KILLED BY THE FALLING DEVIL.

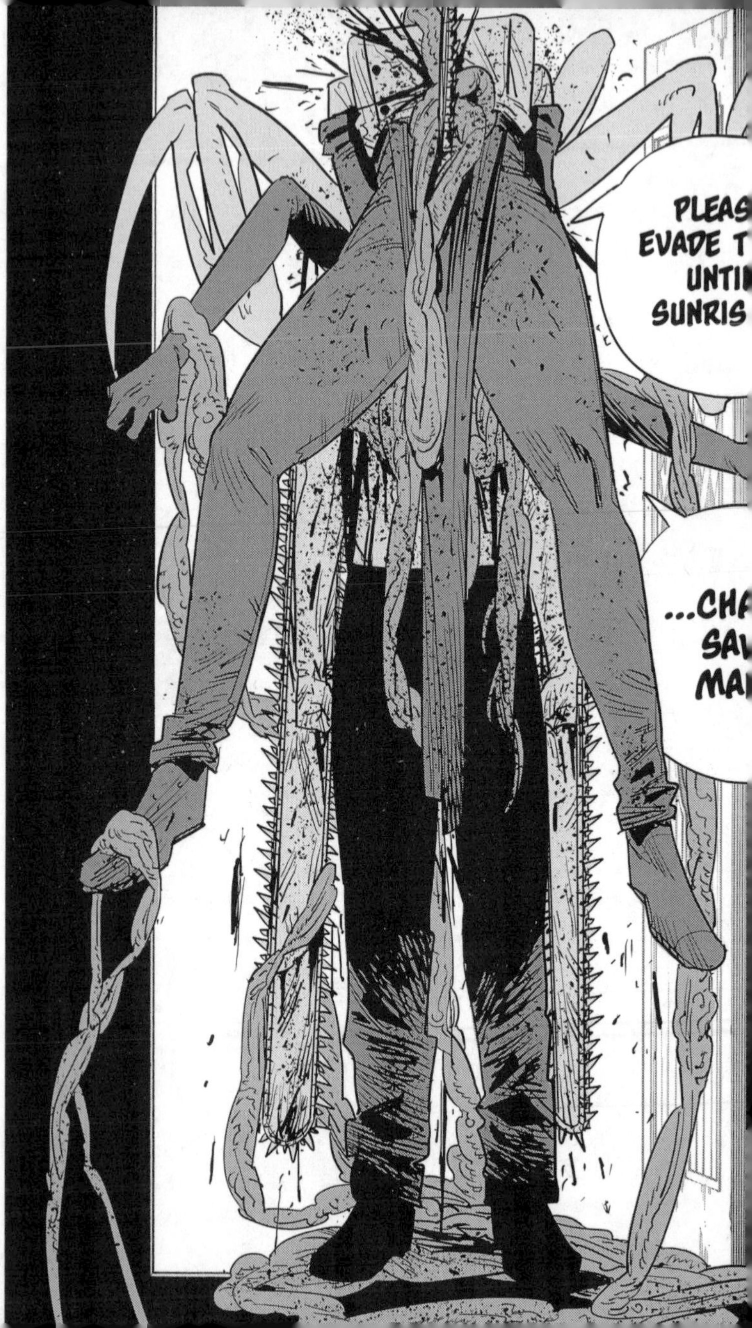
PLEAS EVADE T UNTI SUNRIS
...CHA SA MA

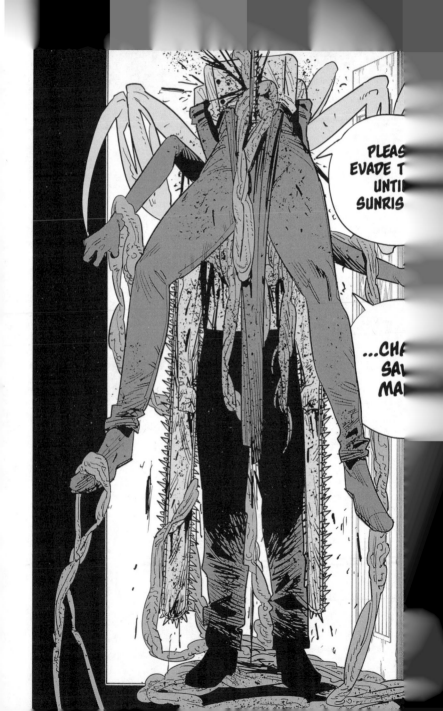

Chain saw man

Chapter 129: Save Me, Chainsaw Man

TWO...
...CHAIN-SAW MANS?

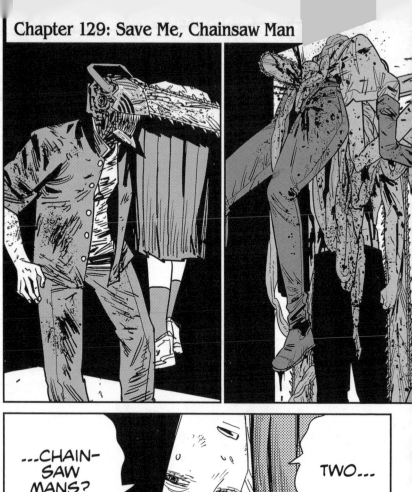

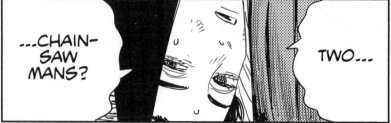

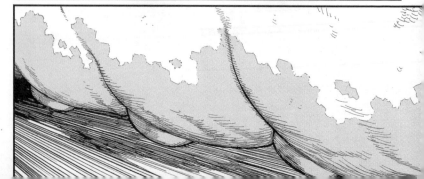

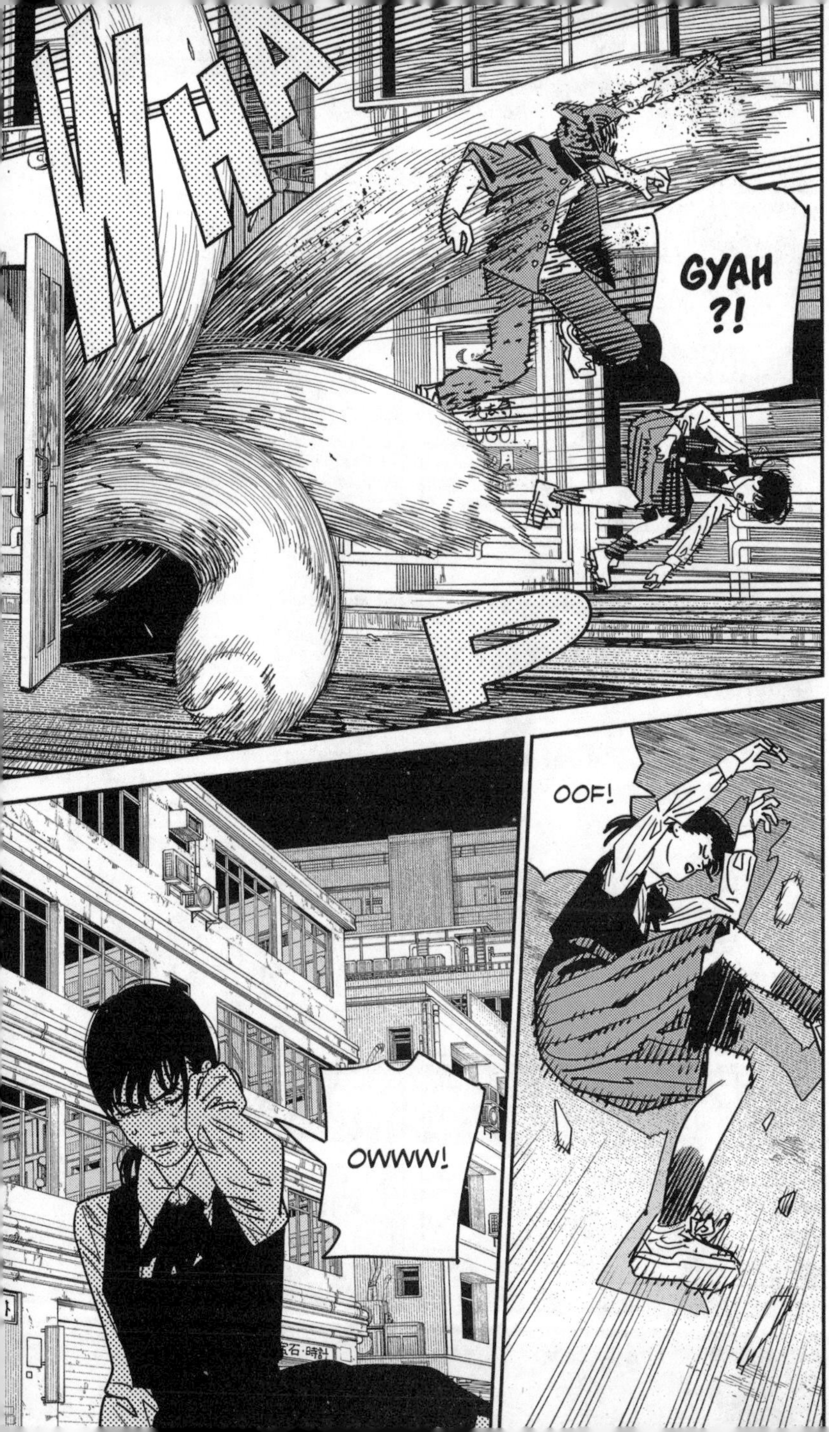
GYAH ?!
WHAP
OOF!
OWWW!

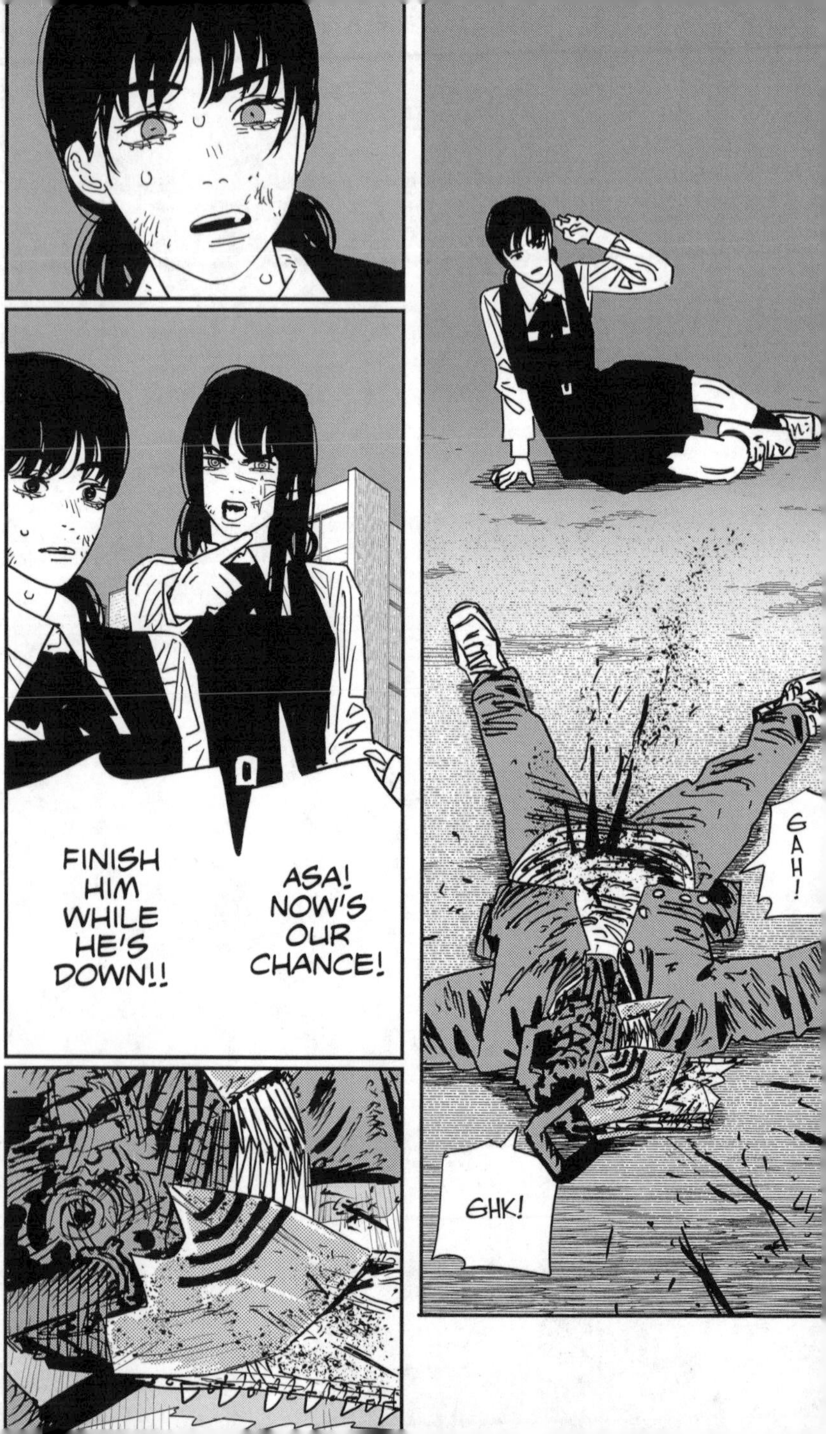
GAH!
GHK!
ASA! NOW'S OUR CHANCE!
FINISH HIM WHILE HE'S DOWN!!

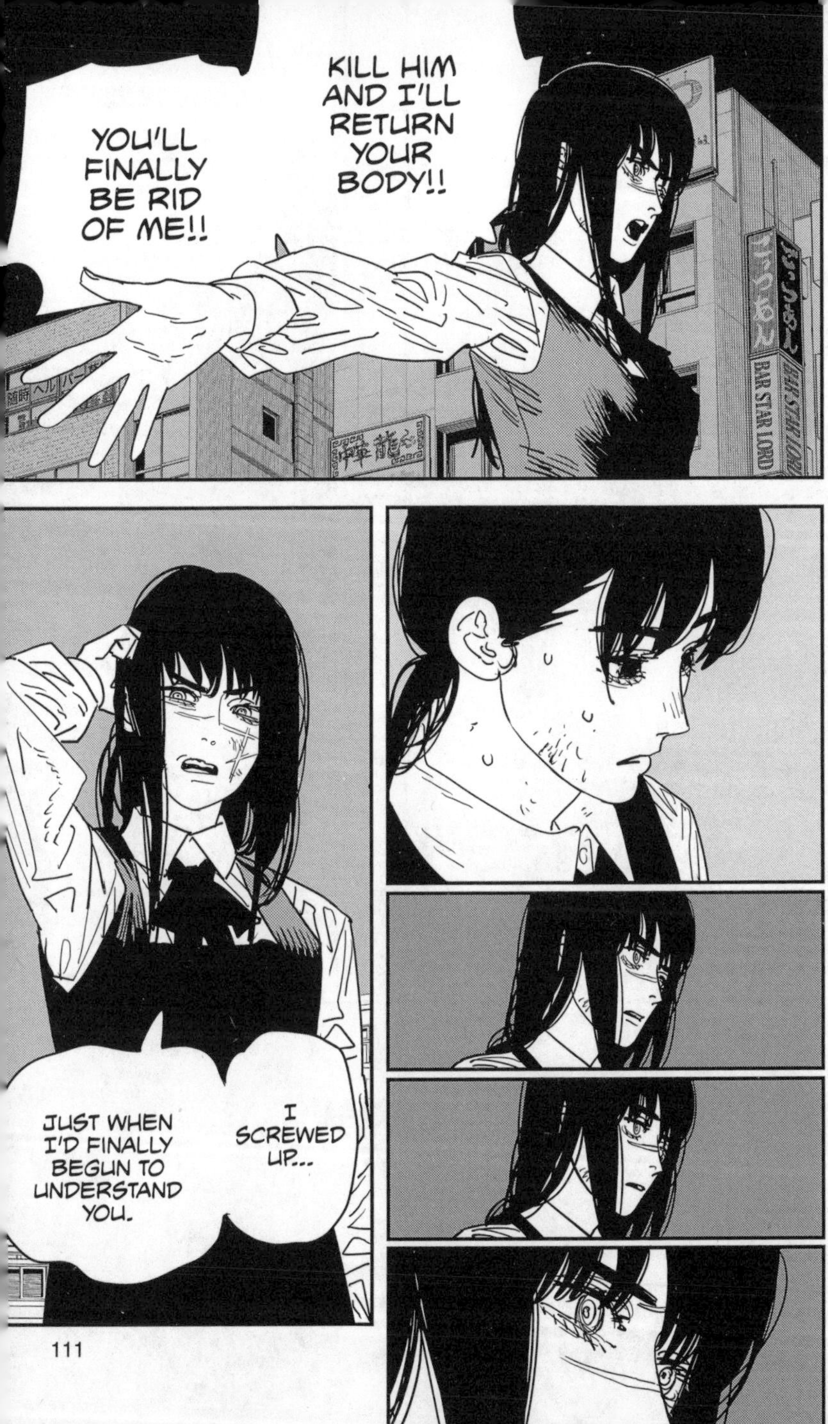
KILL HIM AND I'LL RETURN YOUR BODY!!
YOU'LL FINALLY BE RID OF ME!!
BAR STAR LORD
BAR STAR LORD
I SCREWED UP...
JUST WHEN I'D FINALLY BEGUN TO UNDERSTAND YOU.

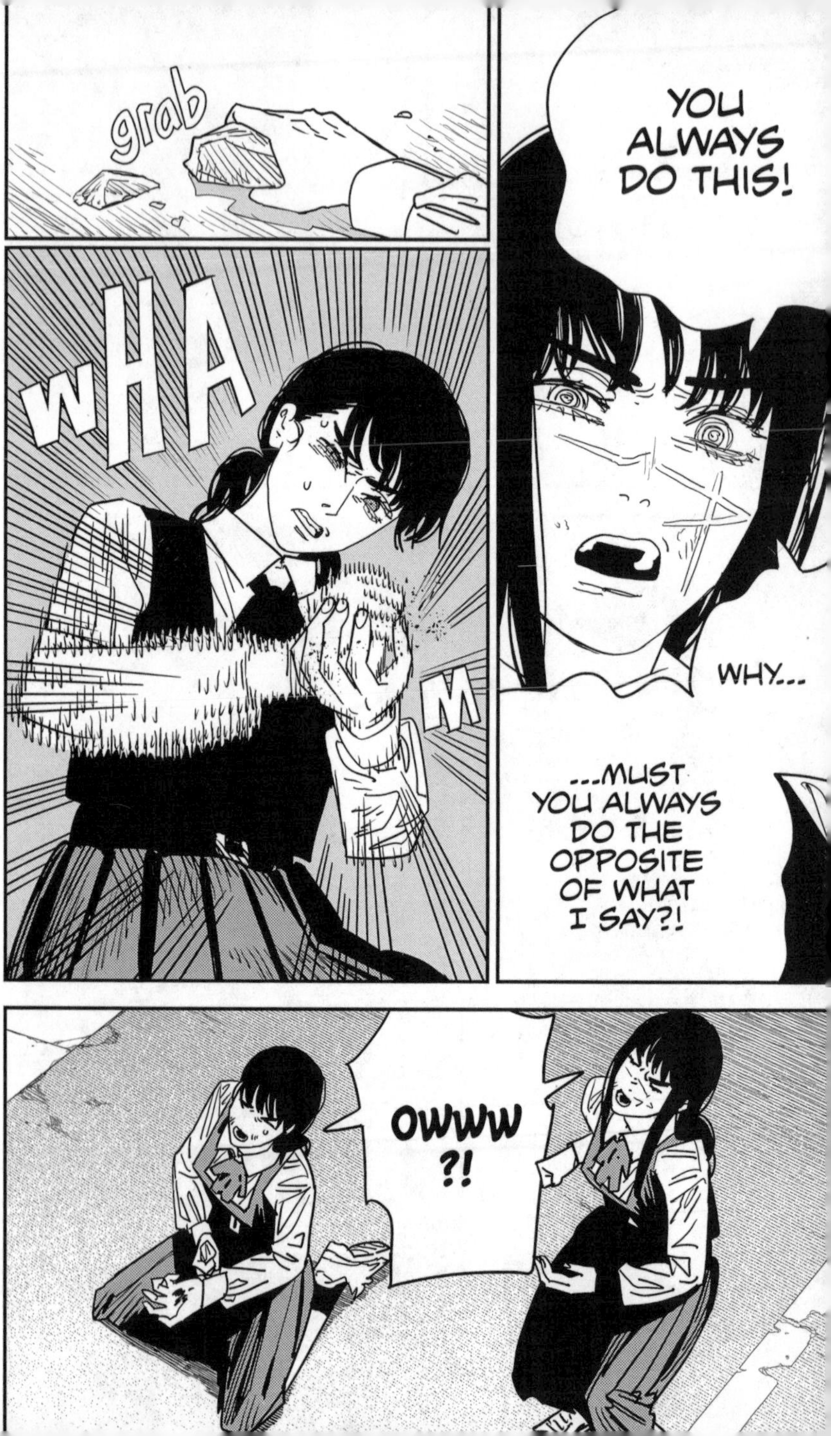
YOU ALWAYS DO THIS!
WHY...
...MUST YOU ALWAYS DO THE OPPOSITE OF WHAT I SAY?!
grab
wHAM
OWWW ?!

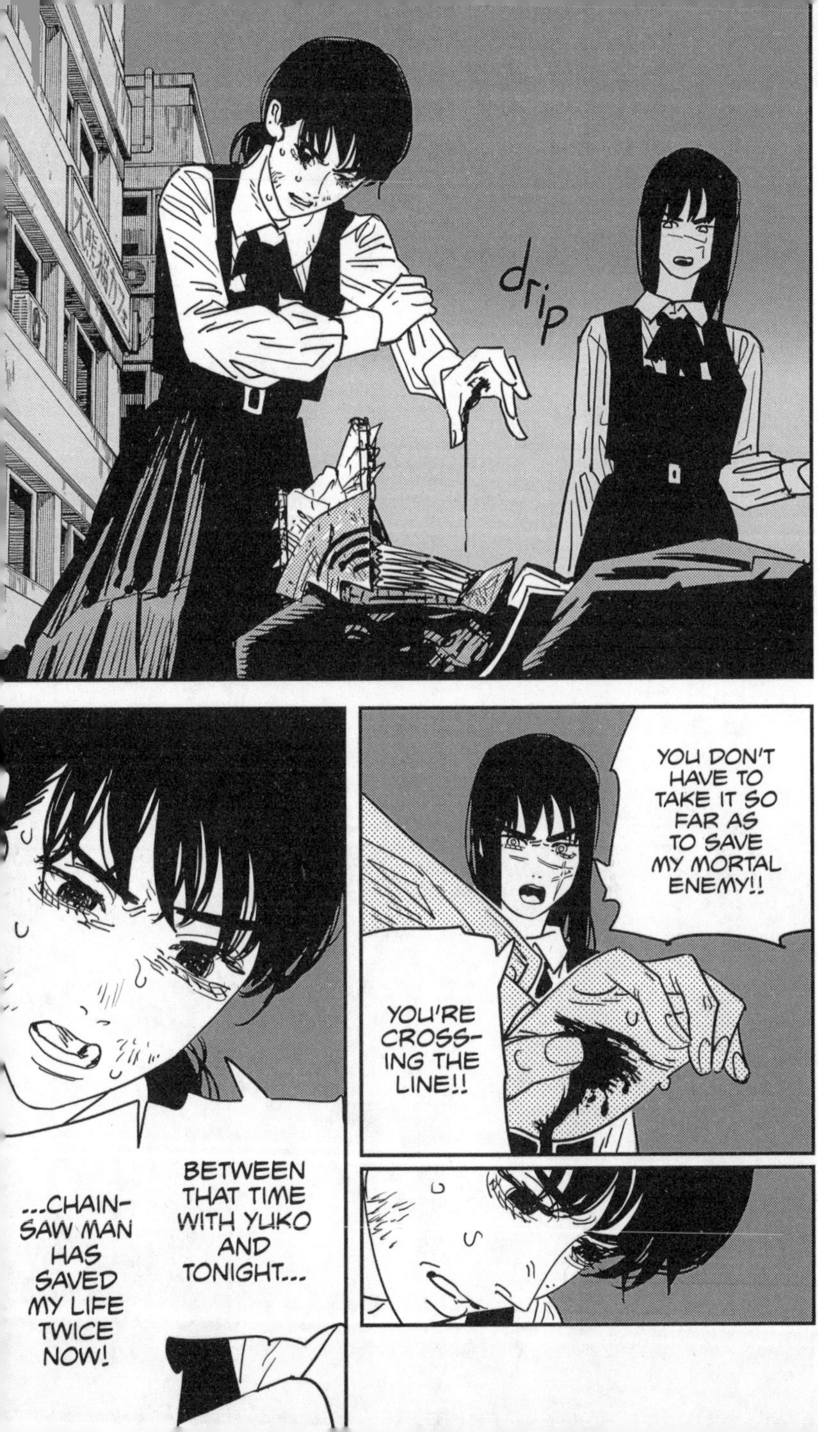
drip
YOU DON'T HAVE TO TAKE IT SO FAR AS TO SAVE MY MORTAL ENEMY!!
YOU'RE CROSS-ING THE LINE!!
BETWEEN THAT TIME WITH YUKO AND TONIGHT...
...CHAIN-SAW MAN HAS SAVED MY LIFE TWICE NOW!

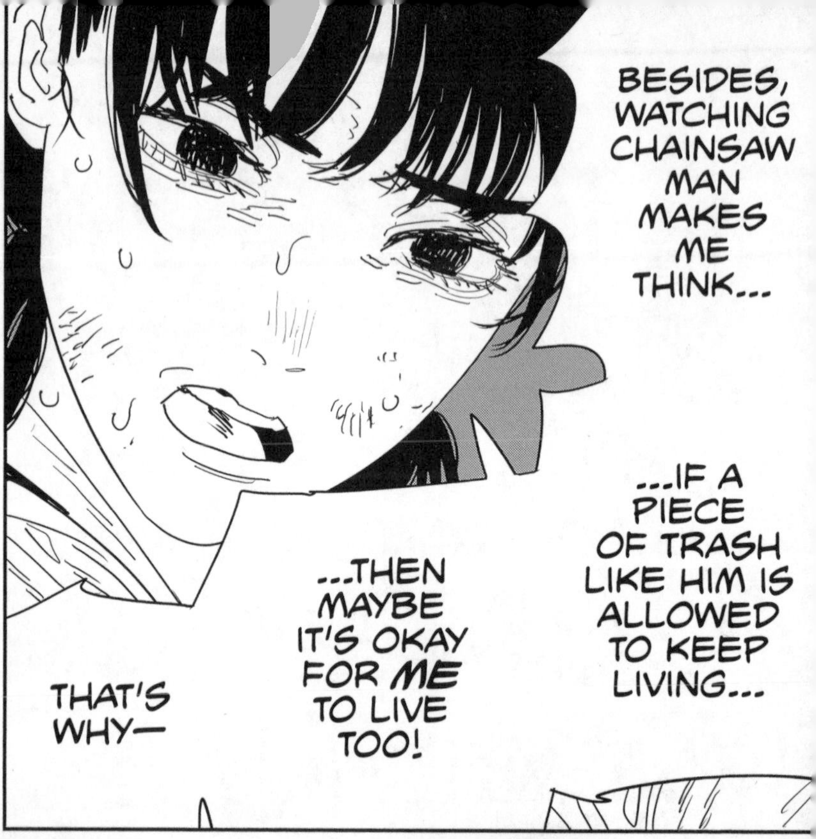
BESIDES, WATCHING CHAINSAW MAN MAKES ME THINK...
...IF A PIECE OF TRASH LIKE HIM IS ALLOWED TO KEEP LIVING...
...THEN MAYBE IT'S OKAY FOR *ME* TO LIVE TOO!
THAT'S WHY—
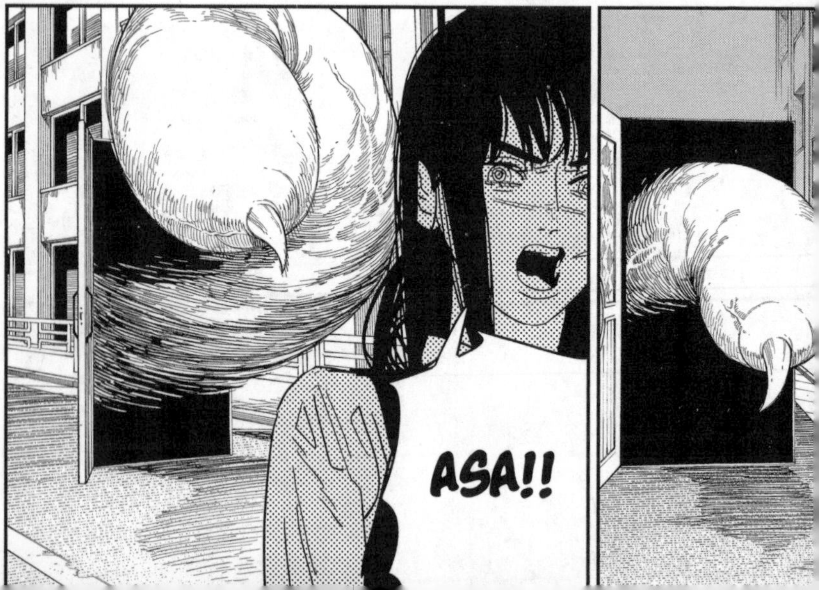
ASA!!

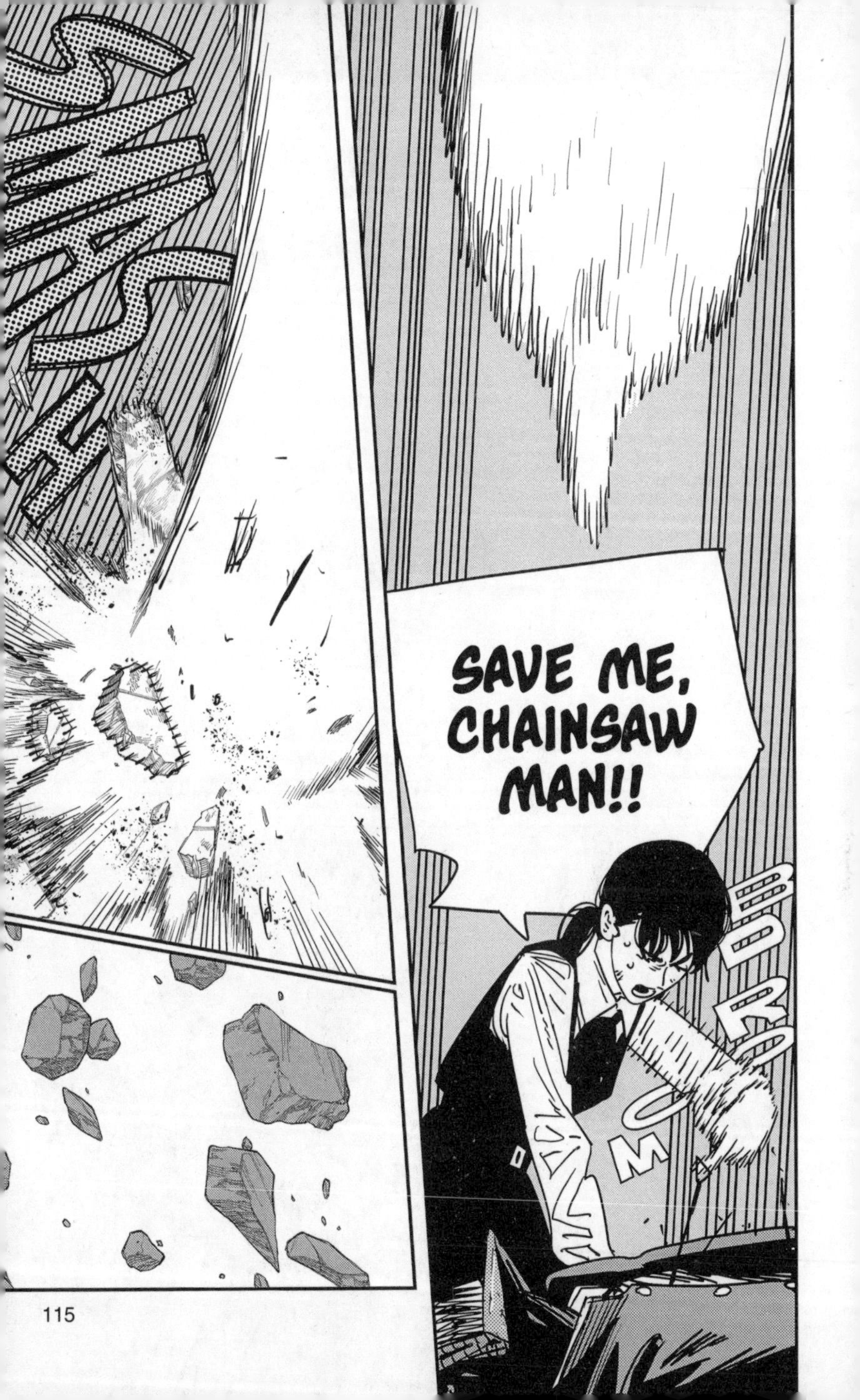
SAVE ME, CHAINSAW MAN!!

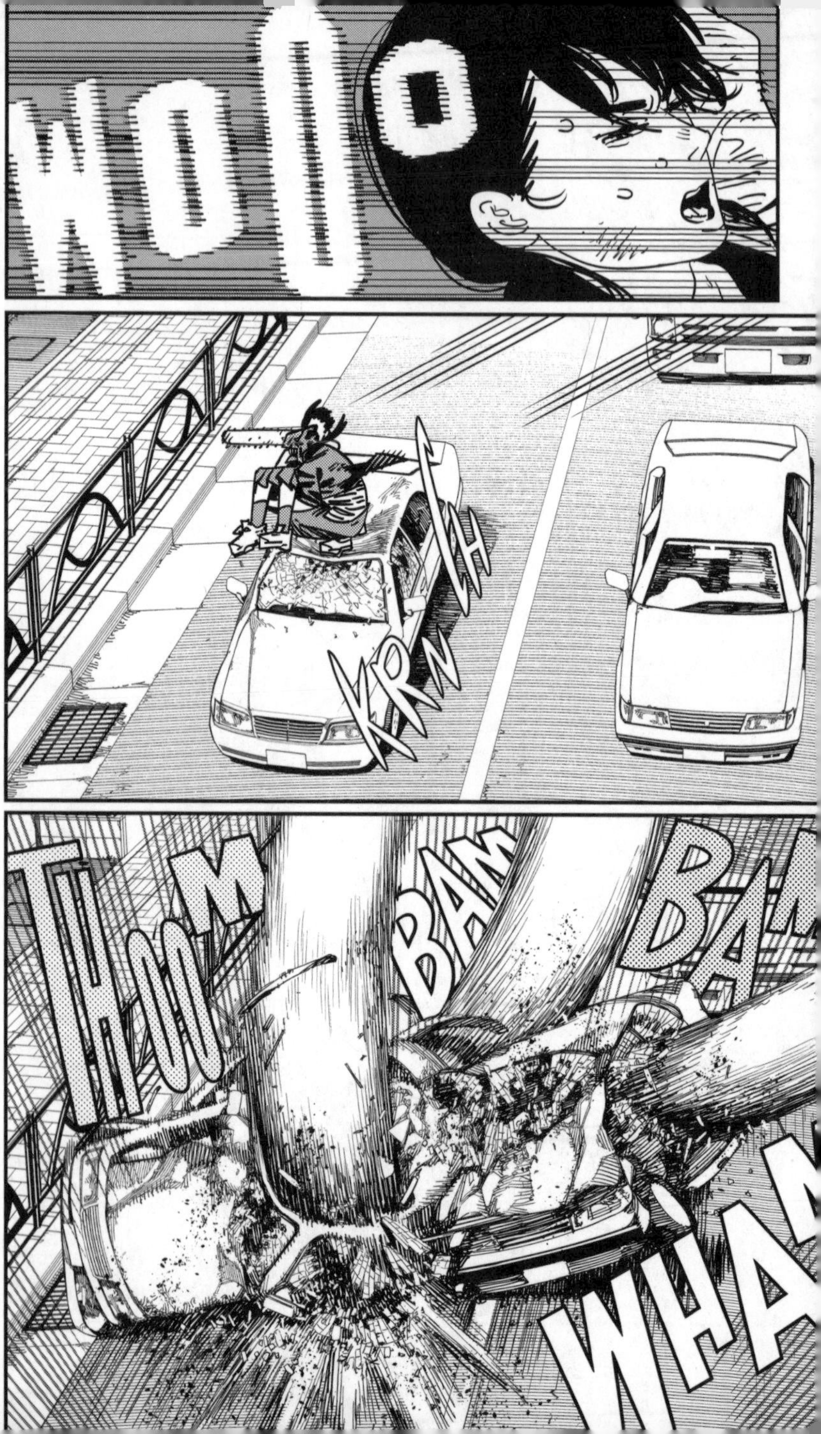
WHOOO
KRNCH
BAM
BAM
THOOM
WHA

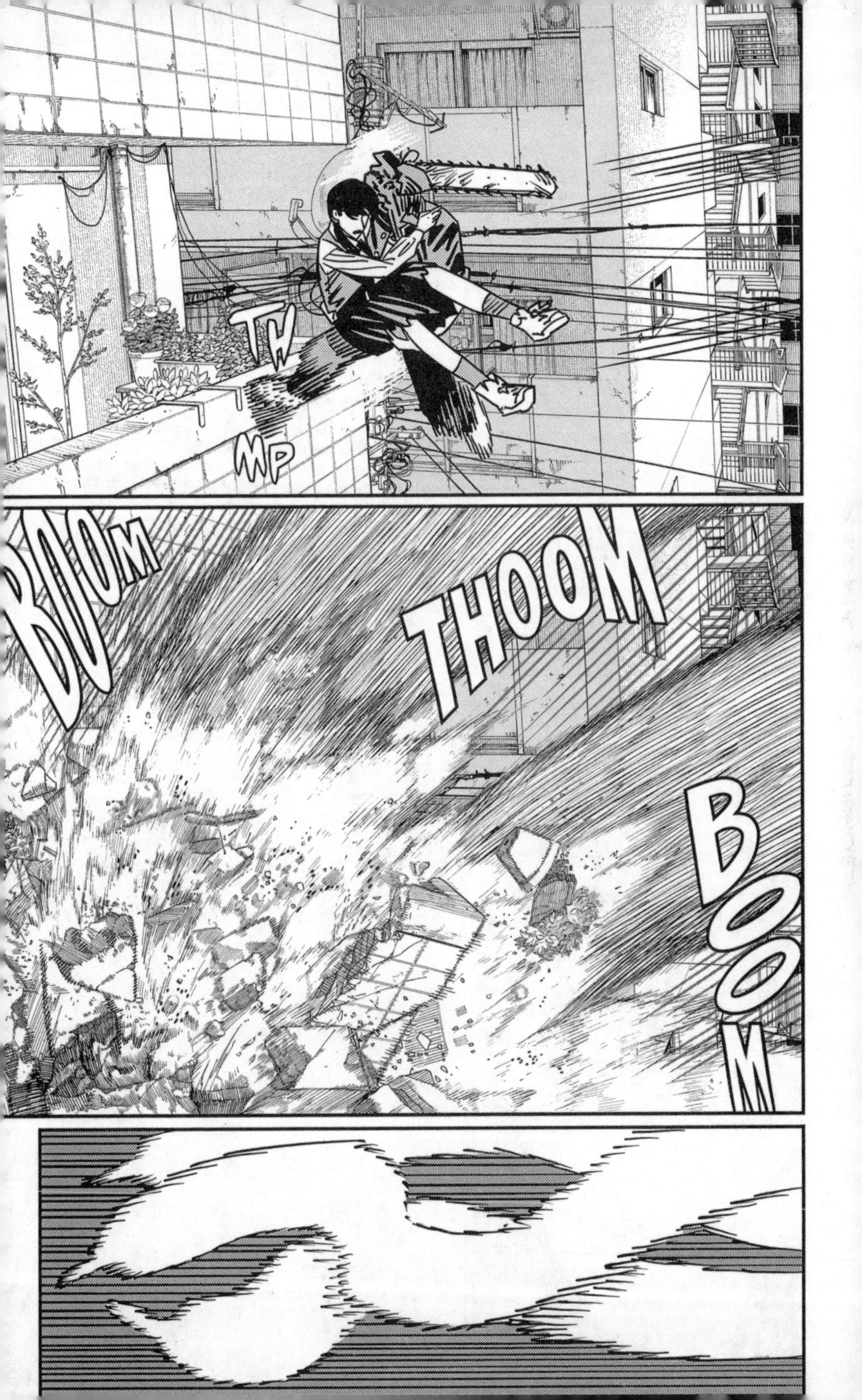
THUMP
THOOM
BOOOM
BOOM

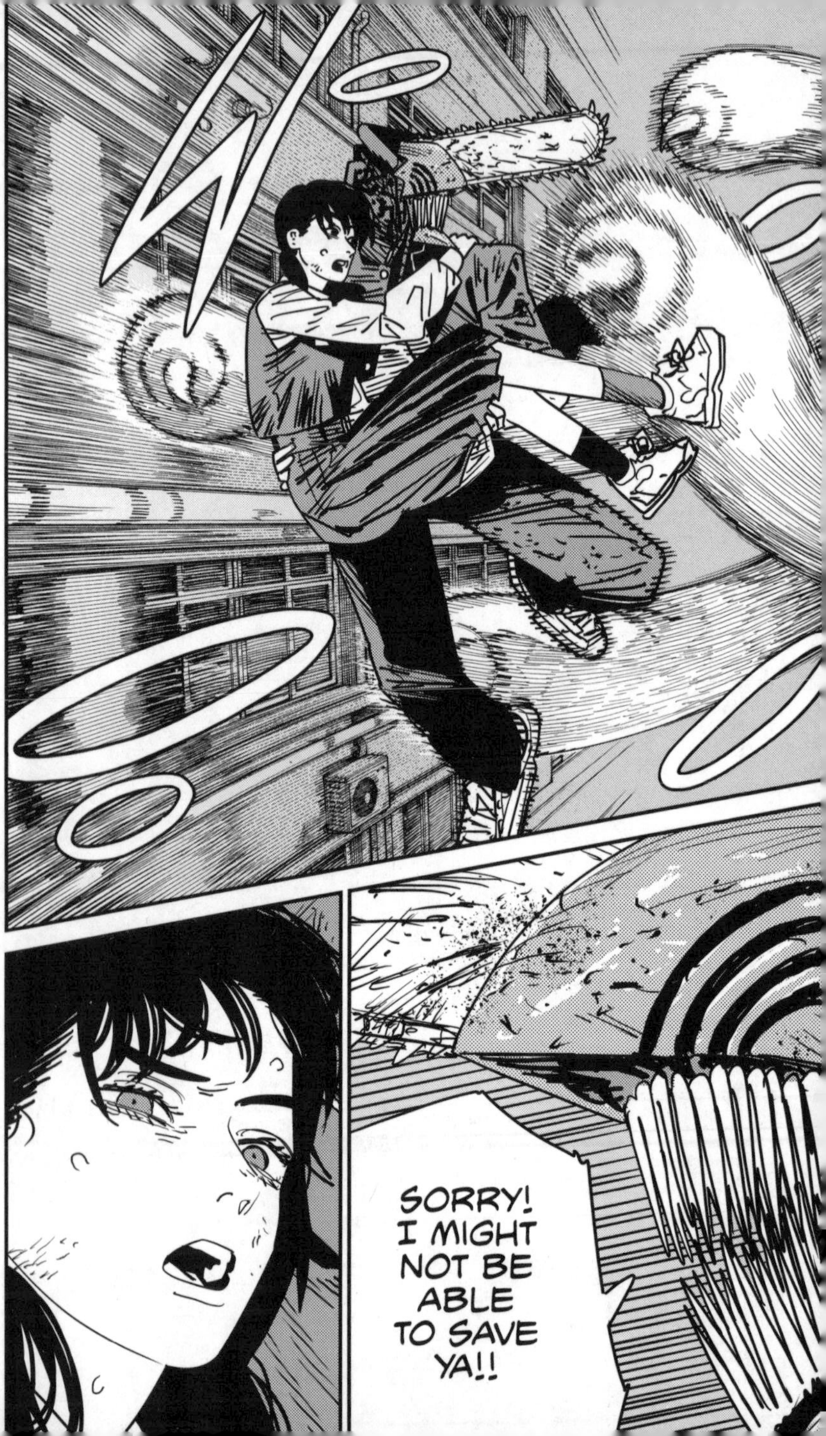
SORRY! I MIGHT NOT BE ABLE TO SAVE YA!!

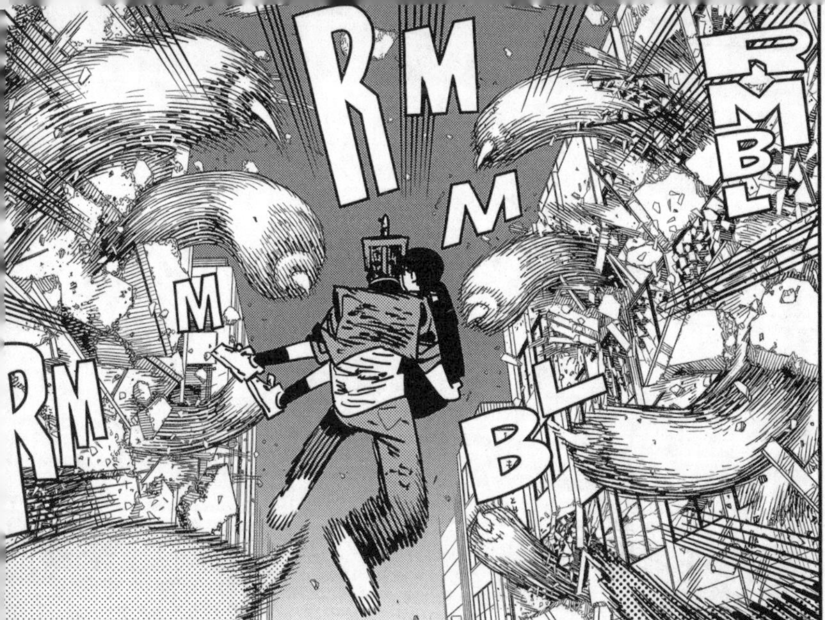
RMBL
RMMBL
RMM
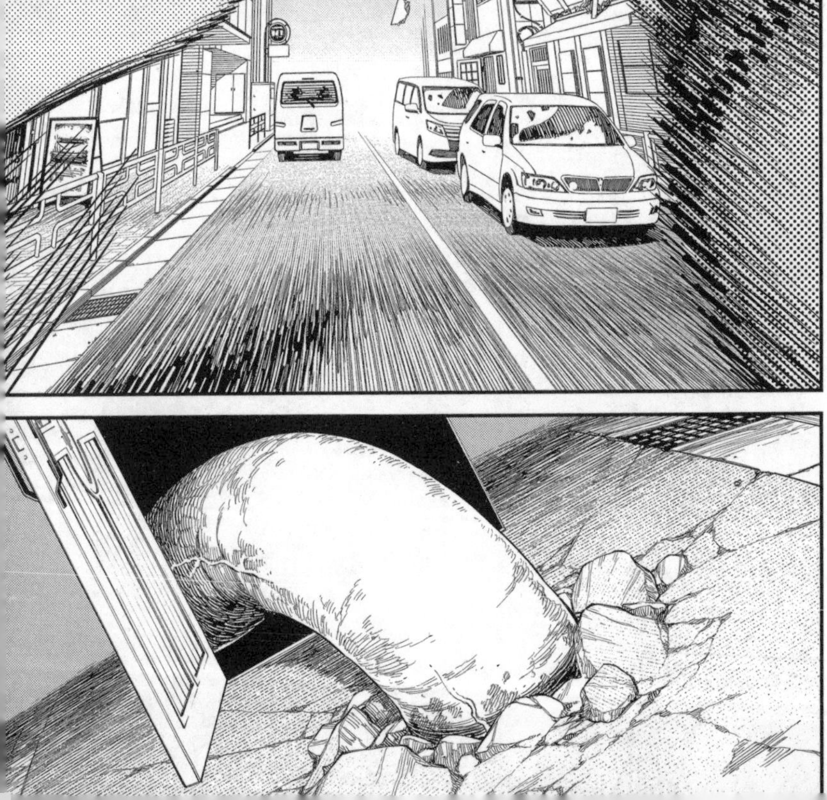

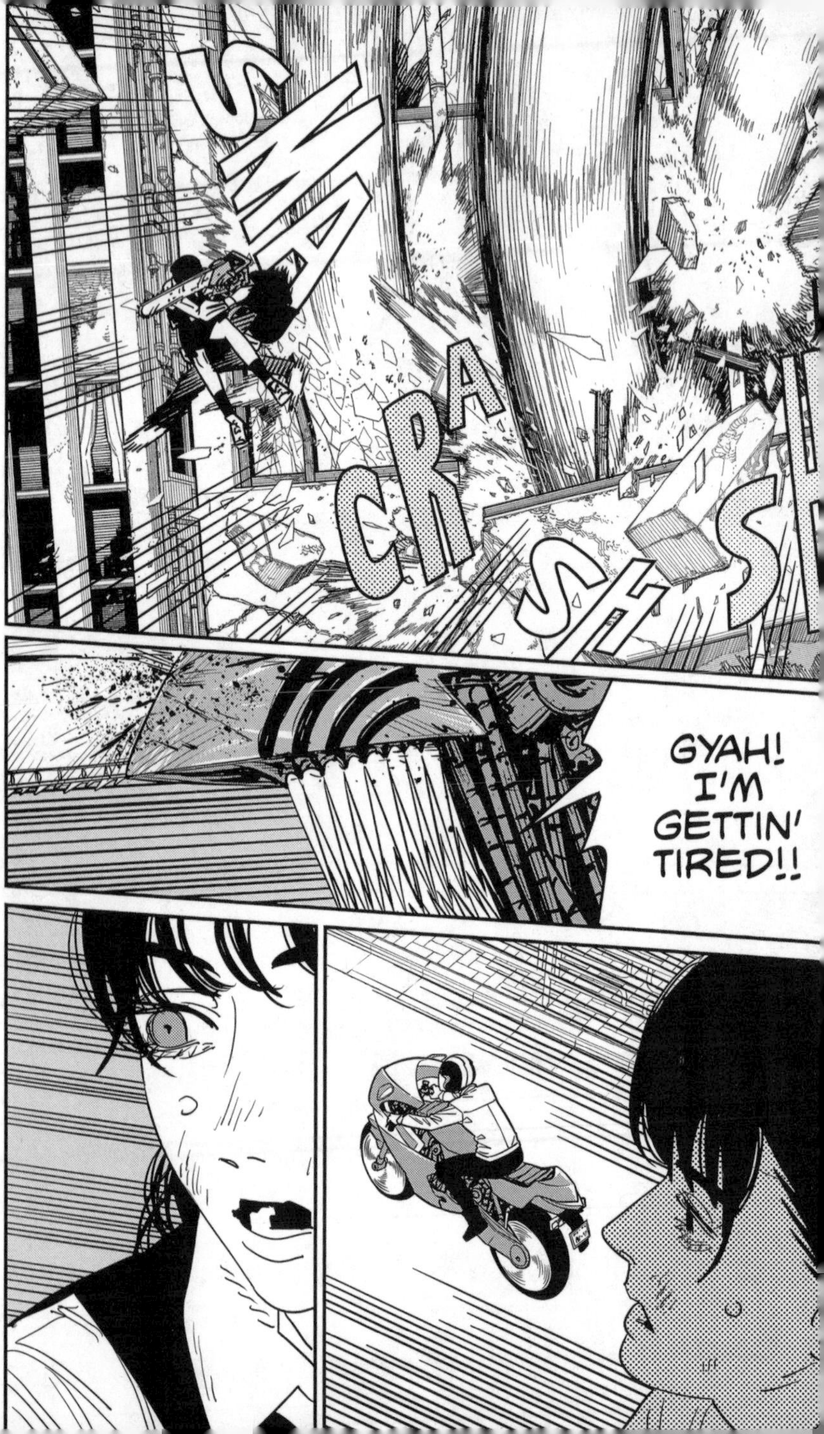
SMASH
CRASH
CRASH
GYAH! I'M GETTIN' TIRED!!

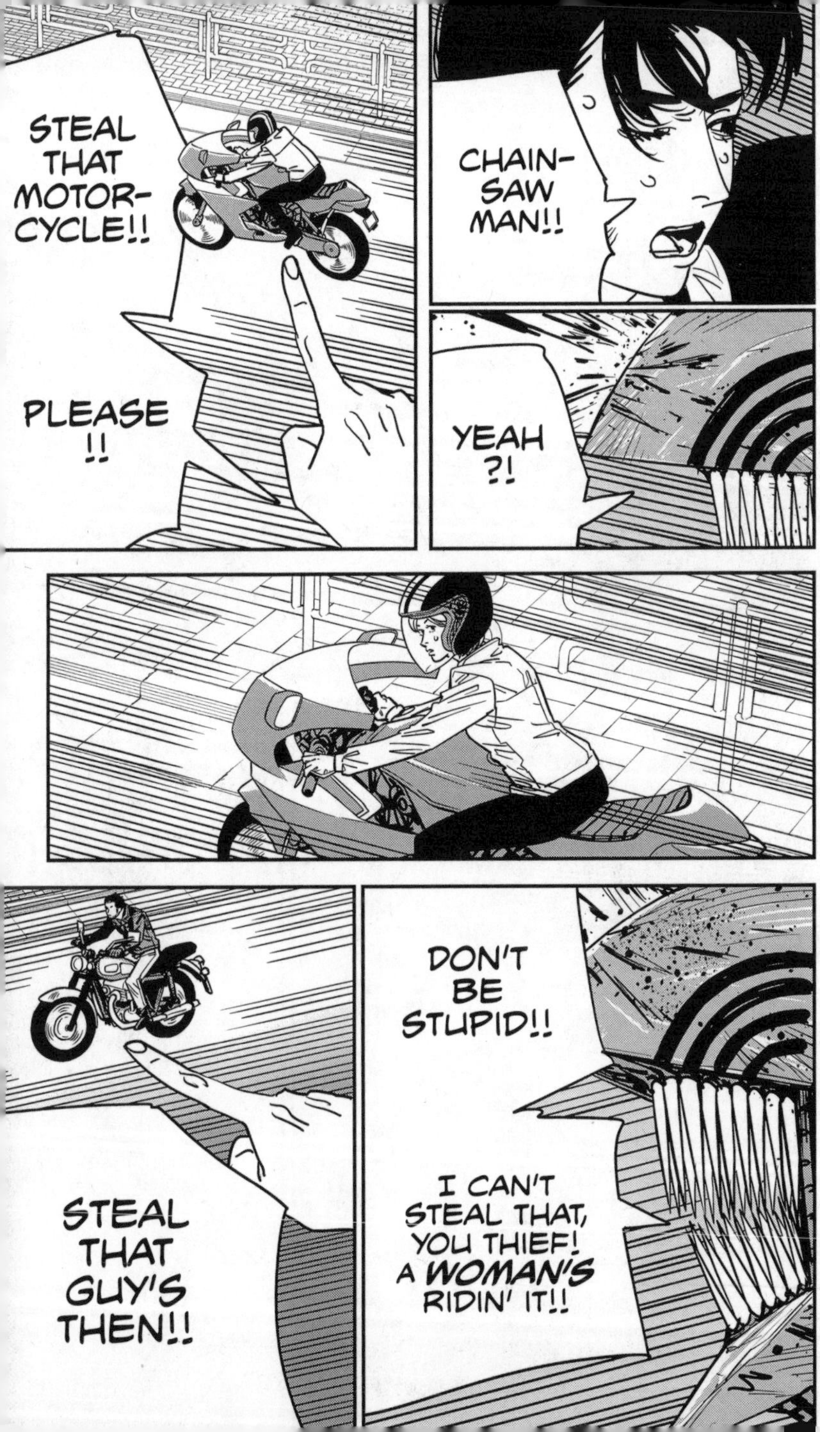

CHAIN-SAW MAN!!
YEAH ?!
STEAL THAT MOTOR-CYCLE!!
PLEASE !!
DON'T BE STUPID!!
I CAN'T STEAL THAT, YOU THIEF! A *WOMAN'S* RIDIN' IT!!
STEAL THAT GUY'S THEN!!

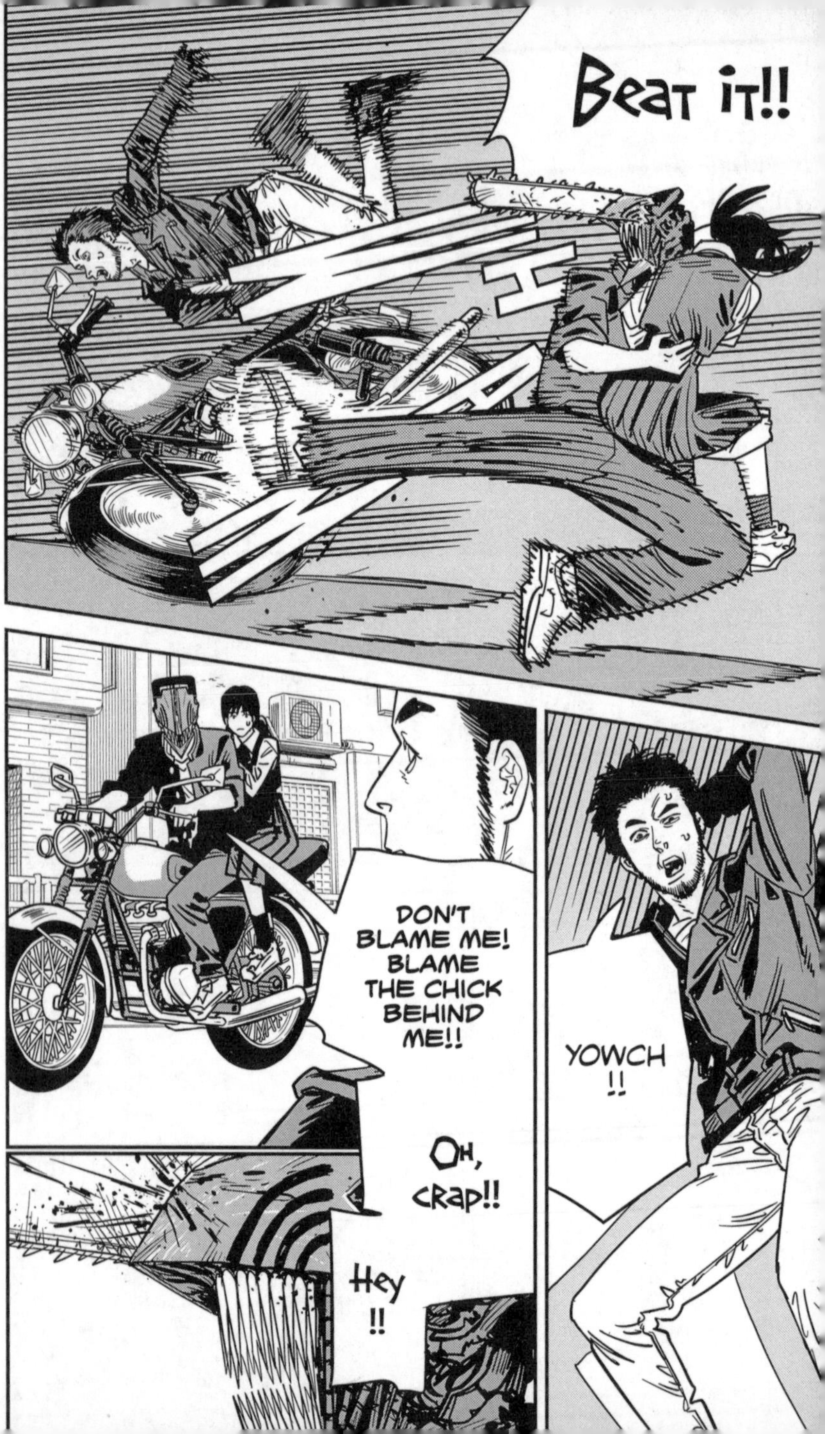
Beat it!!
YOWCH!!
DON'T BLAME ME! BLAME THE CHICK BEHIND ME!!
Oh, crap!!
Hey!!

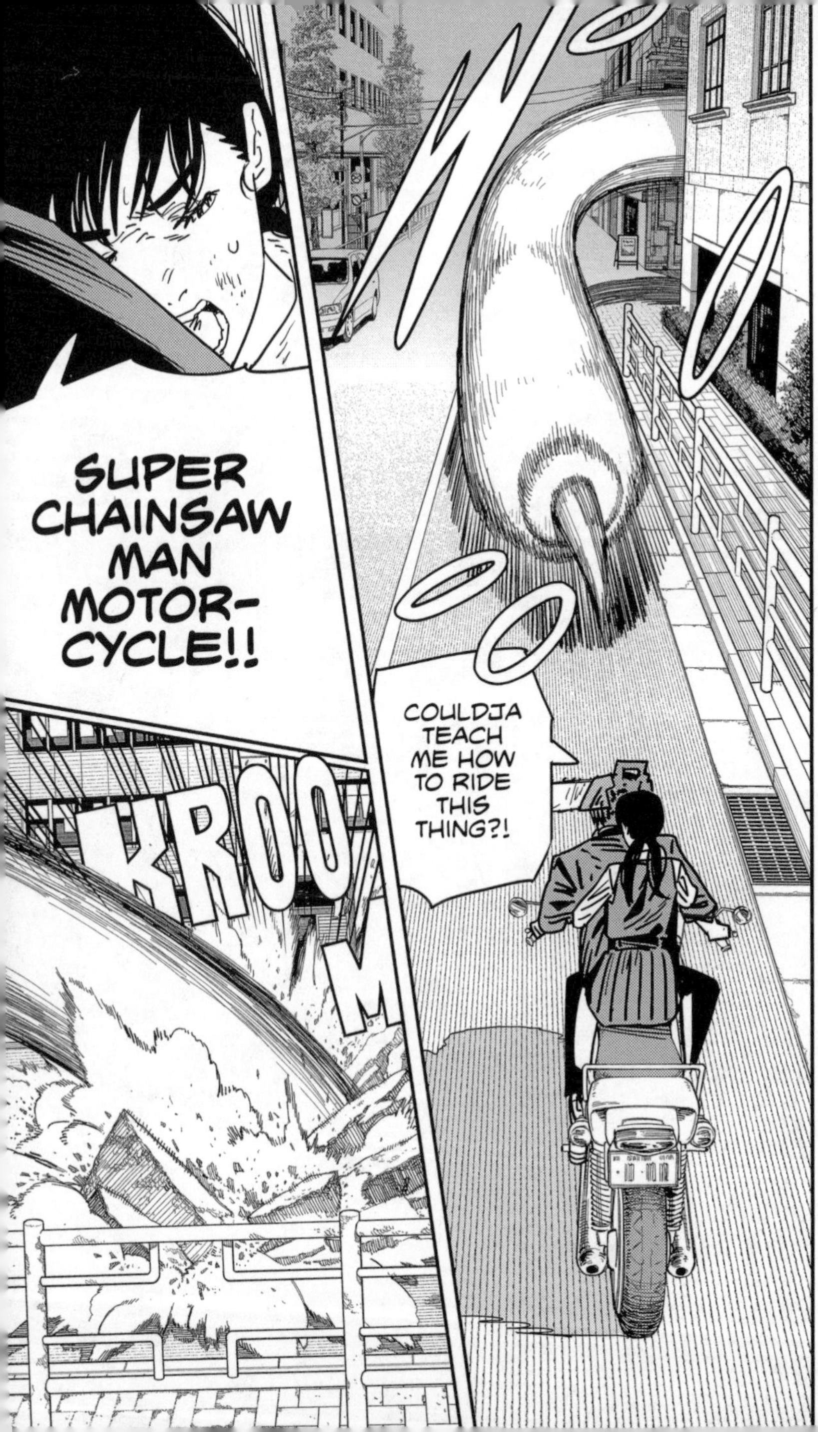
COULDJA TEACH ME HOW TO RIDE THIS THING?!
SUPER CHAINSAW MAN MOTOR-CYCLE!!
KROOOM

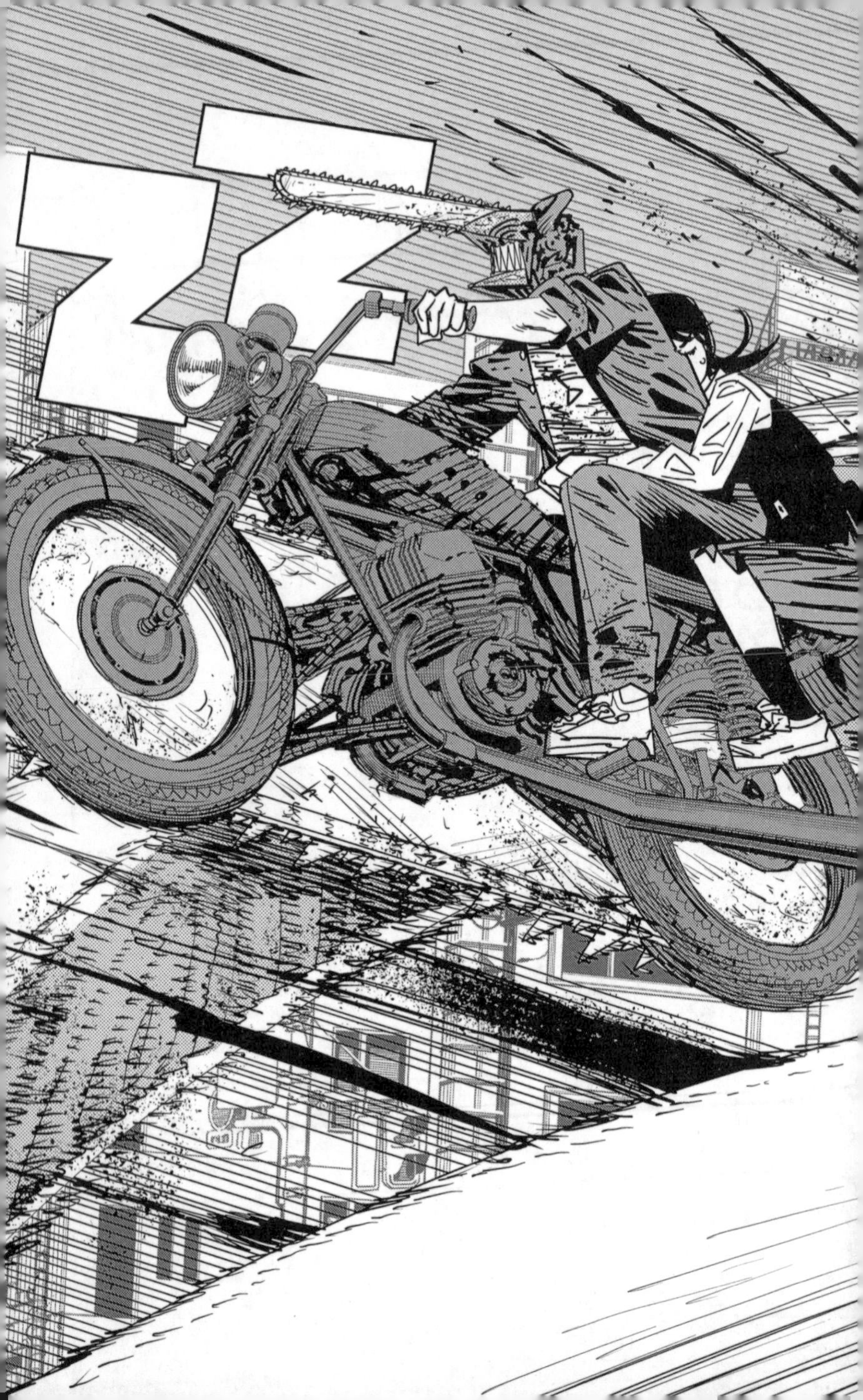
ZZ

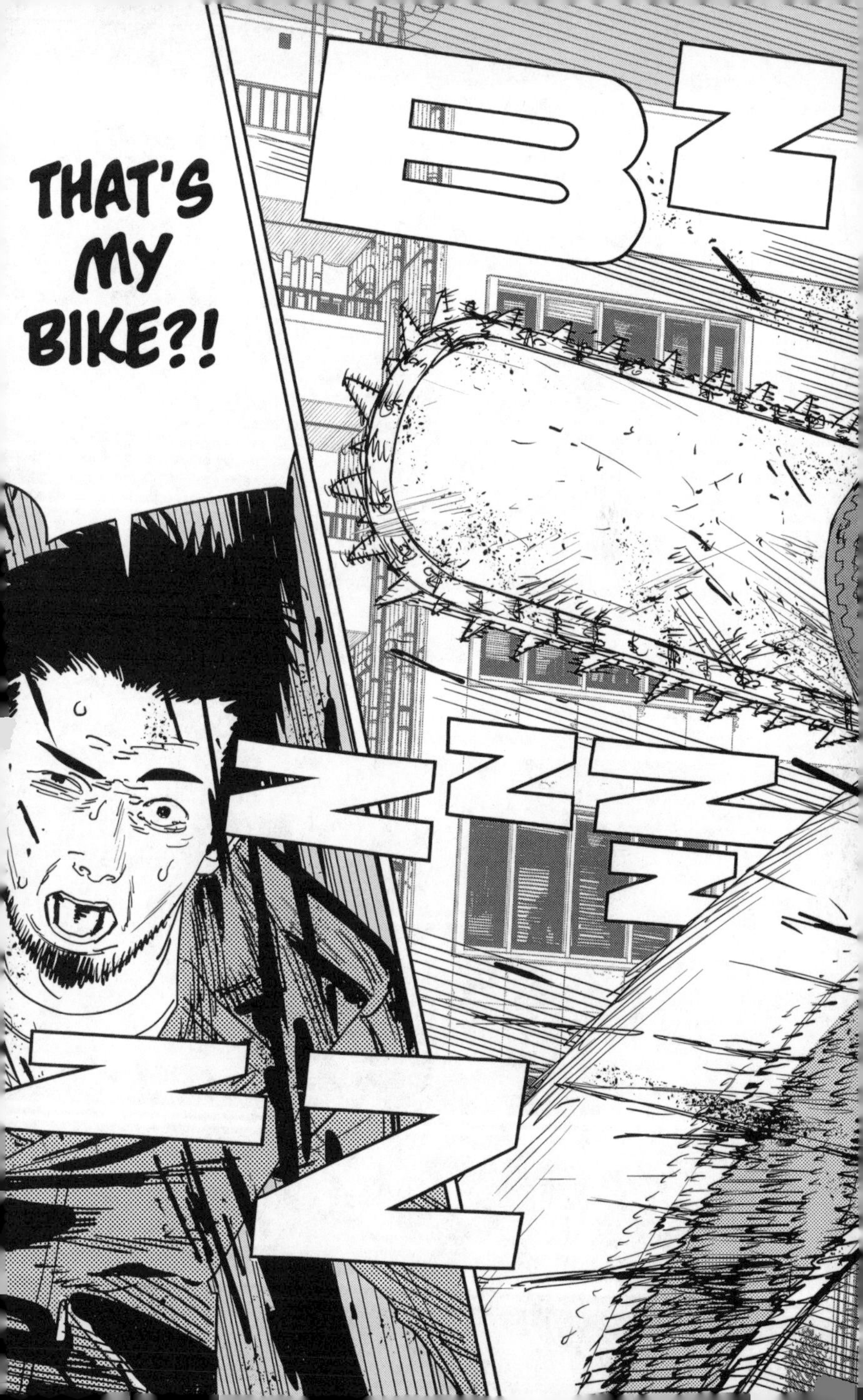
THAT'S MY BIKE?!
BZ
ZZZ
Z
ZZ

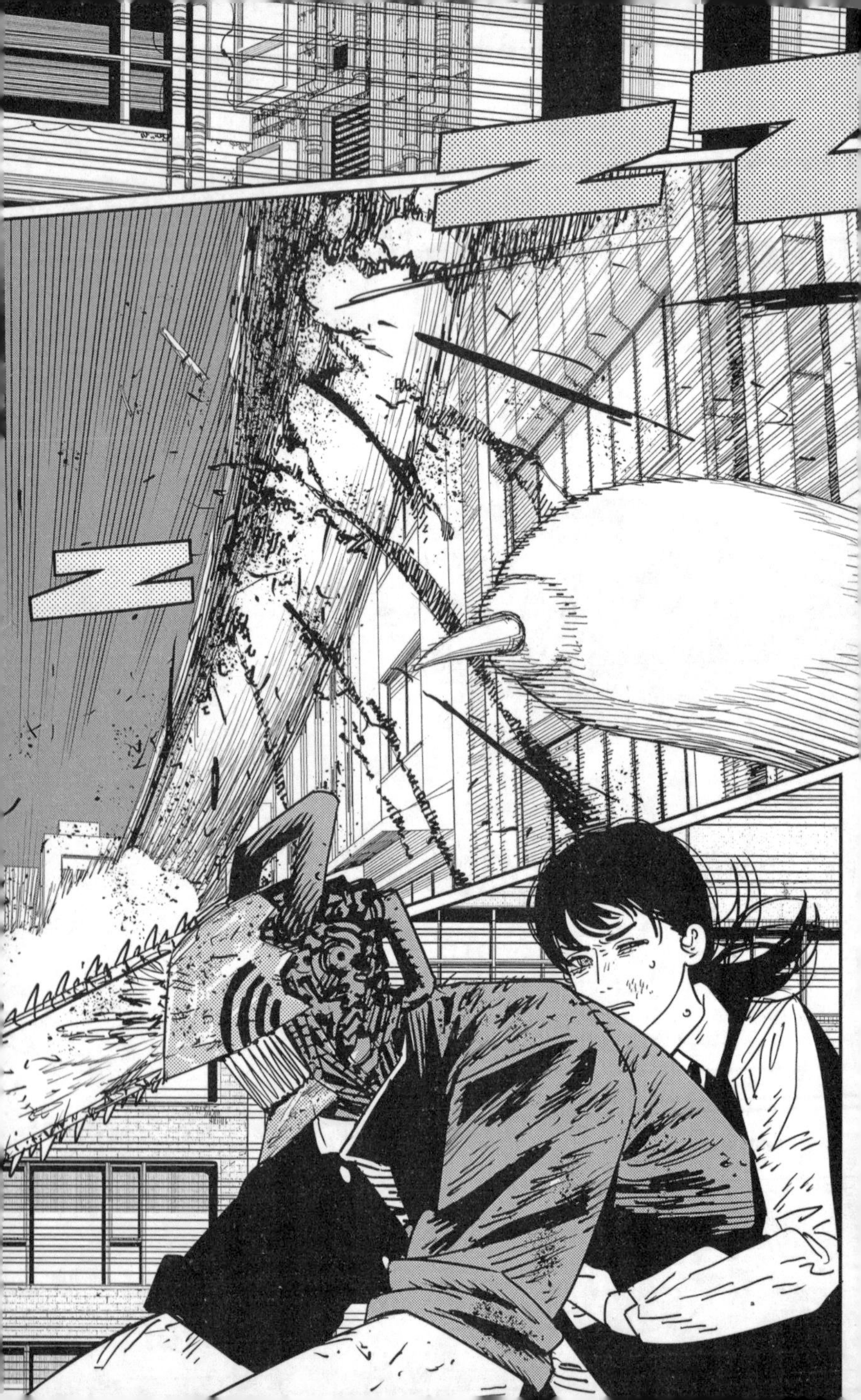

Chapter 130: Kill Building

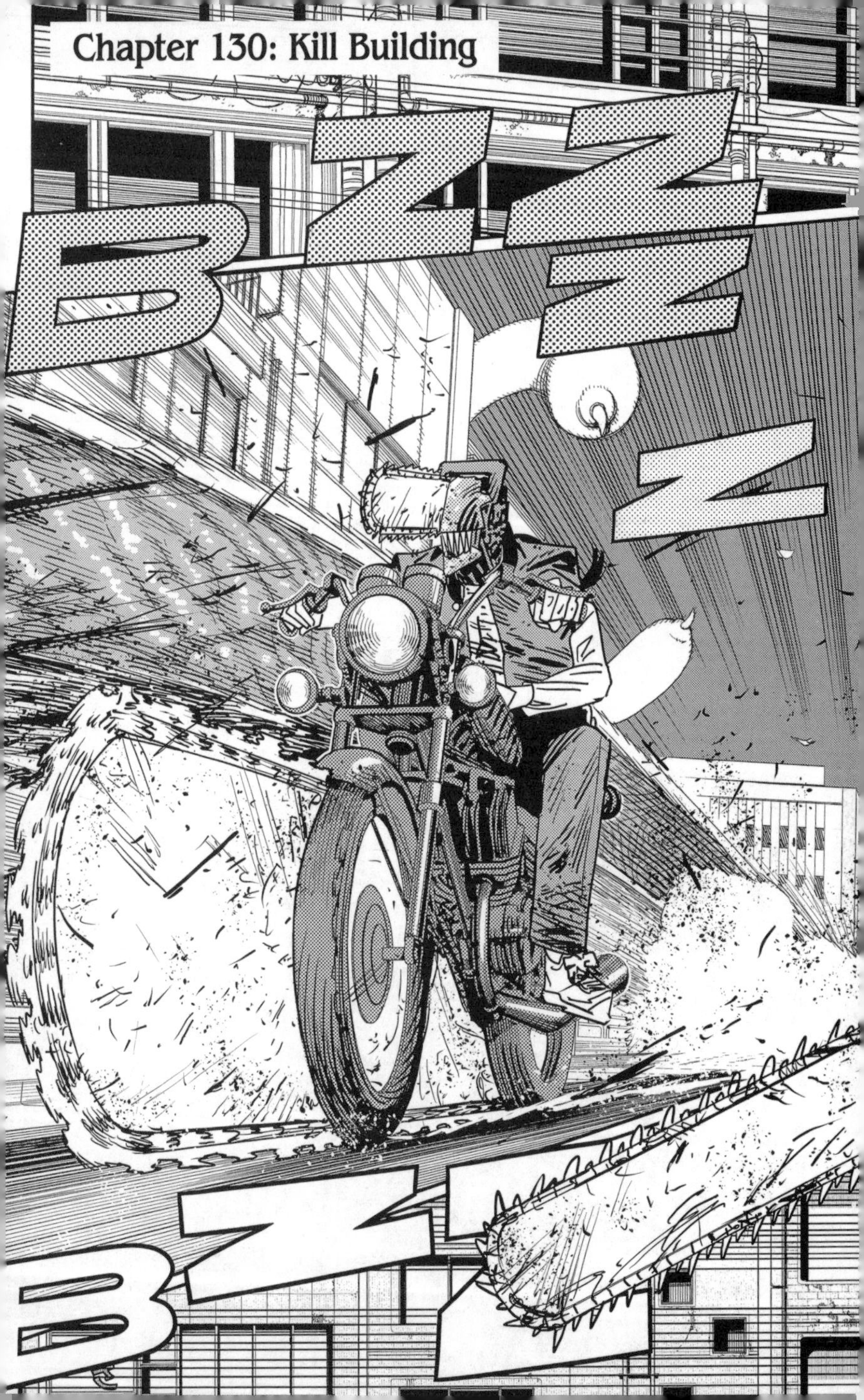
BZZN
BZZ

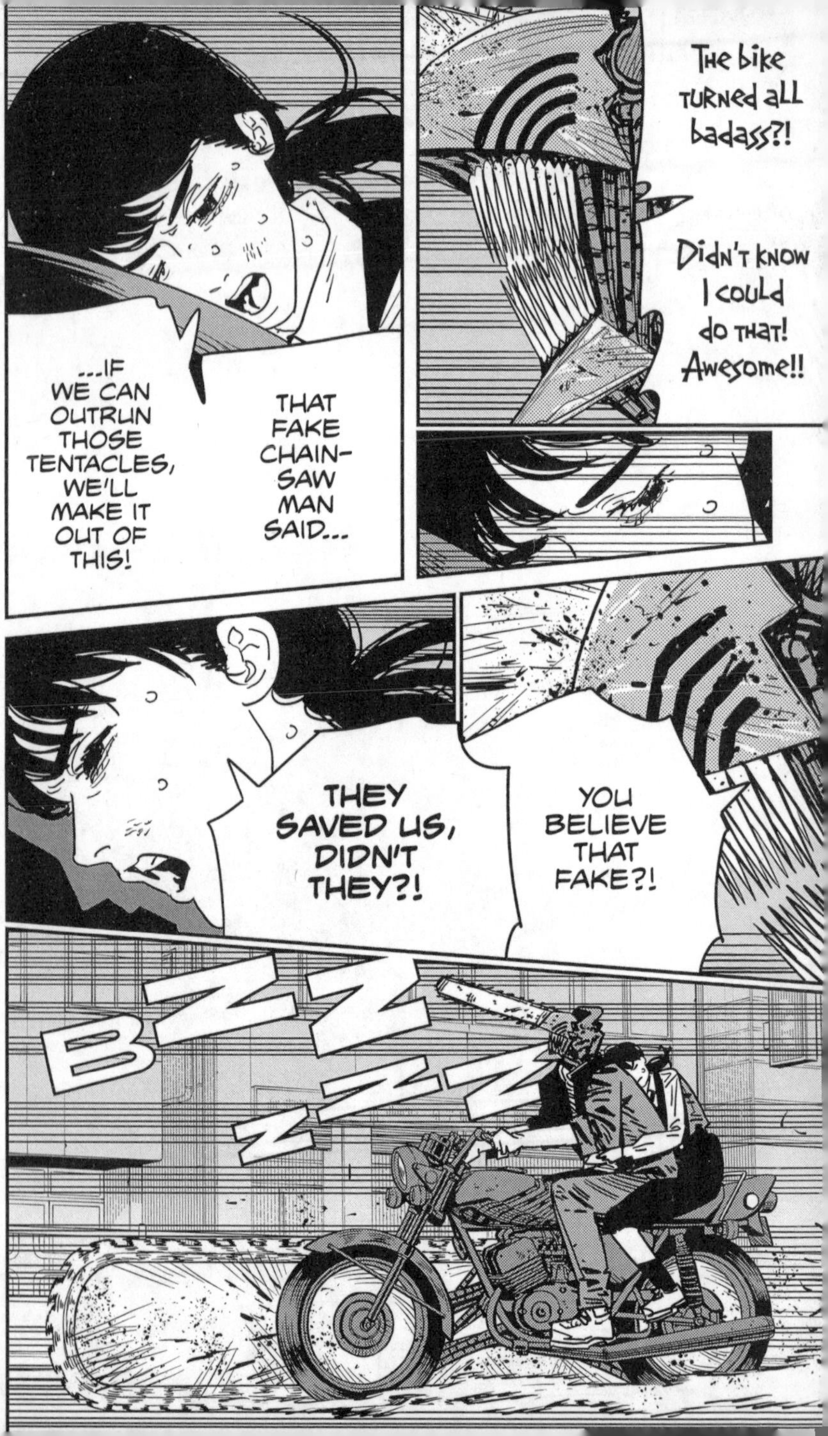
The bike turned all badass?!
Didn't know I could do that! Awesome!!
THAT FAKE CHAIN-SAW MAN SAID...
...IF WE CAN OUTRUN THOSE TENTACLES, WE'LL MAKE IT OUT OF THIS!
YOU BELIEVE THAT FAKE?!
THEY SAVED US, DIDN'T THEY?!
BZZZZZ

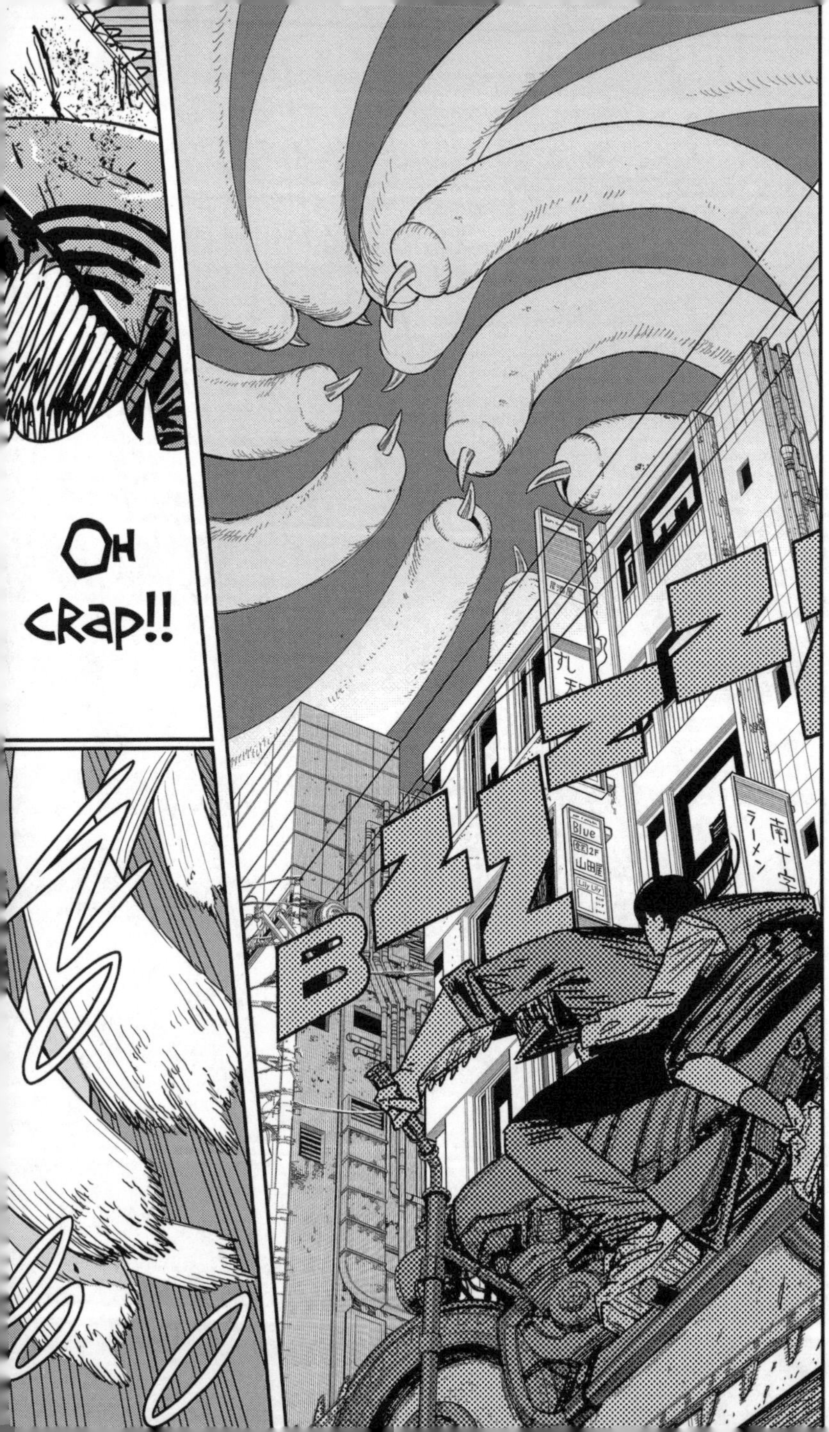
BZZZZ
すし
Blue
2F
山田屋
Lily Lily
南十字
ラーメン
OH CRAP!!

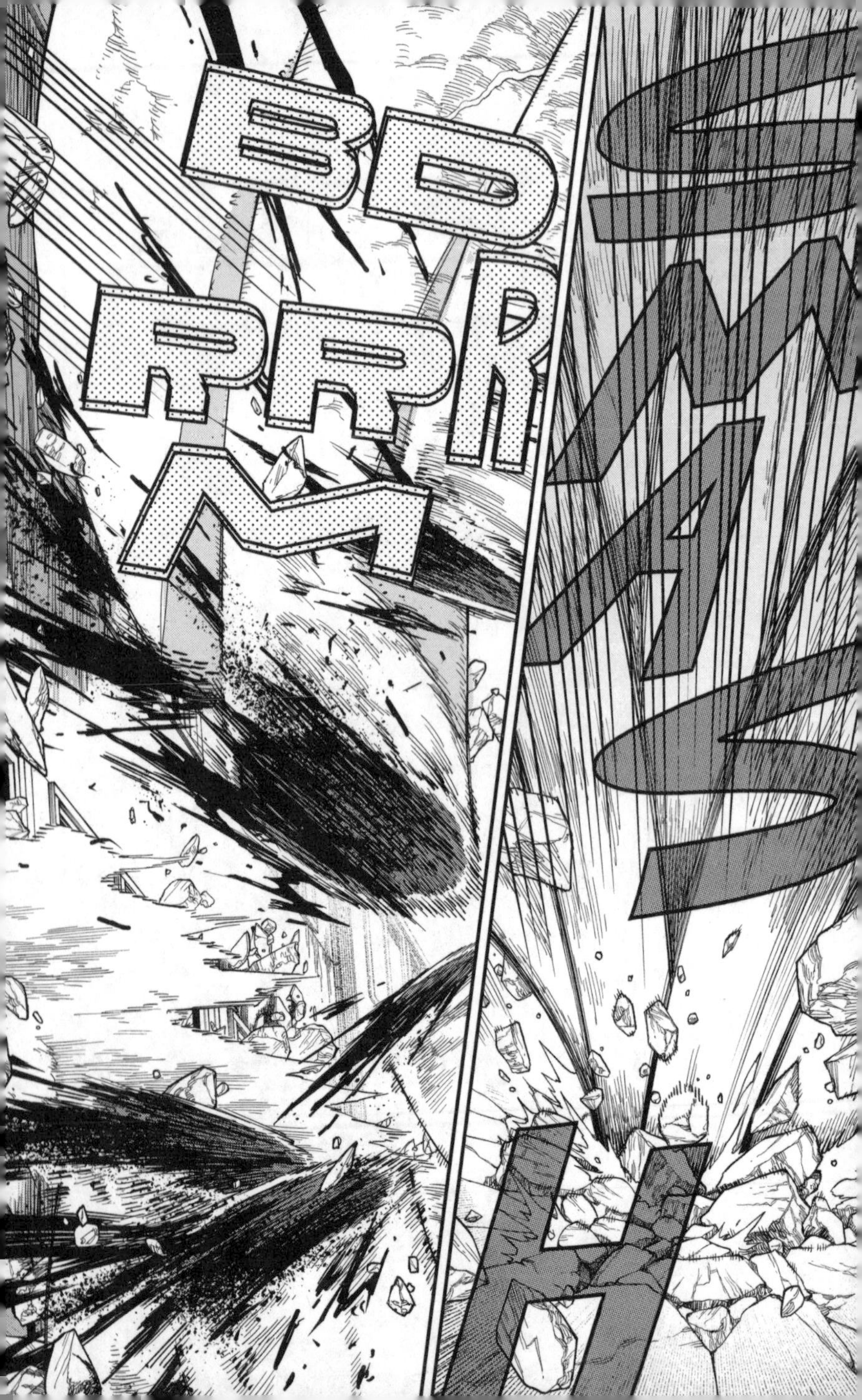
SMASH
BDRRRM

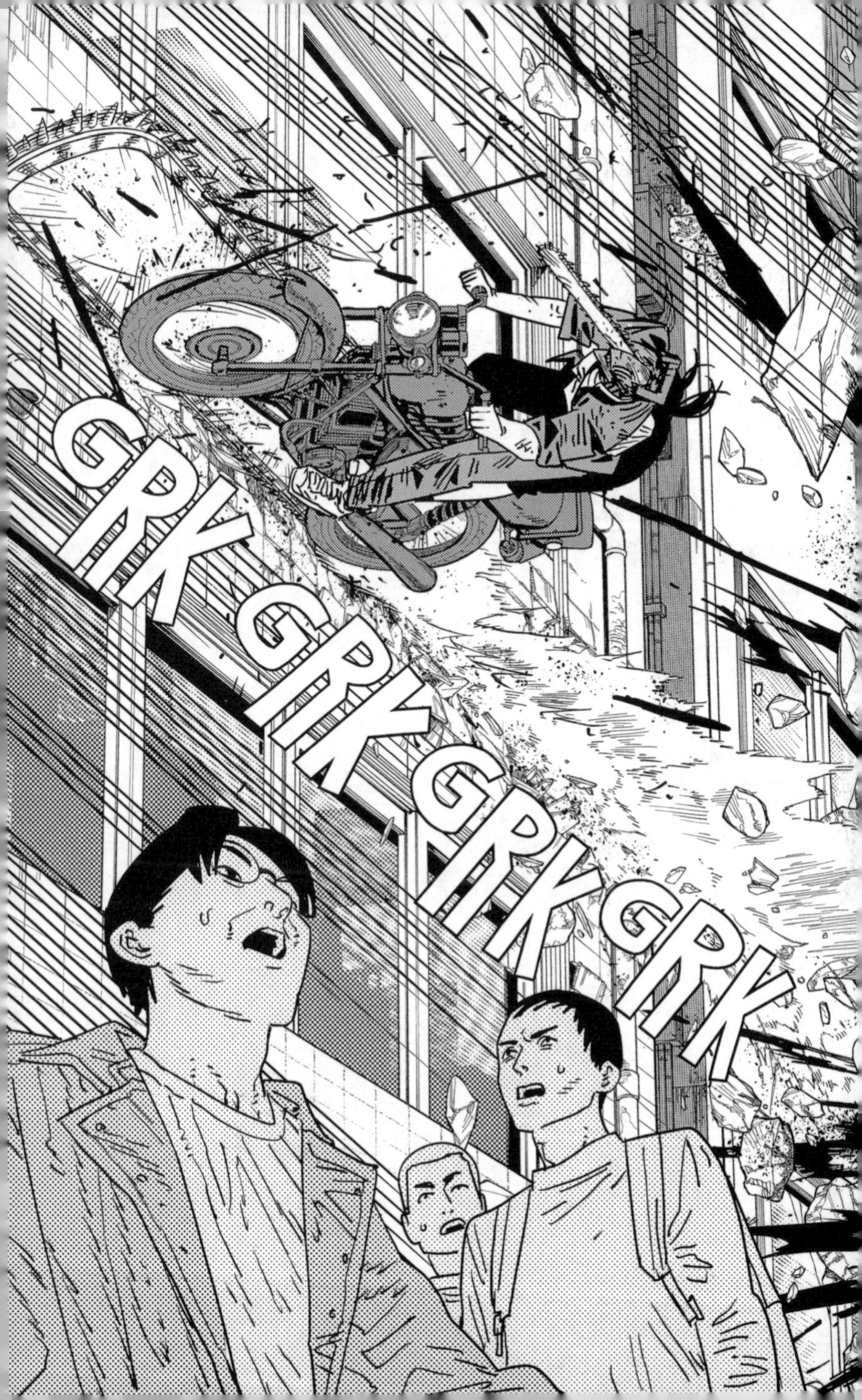
GRK GRK GRK GRK

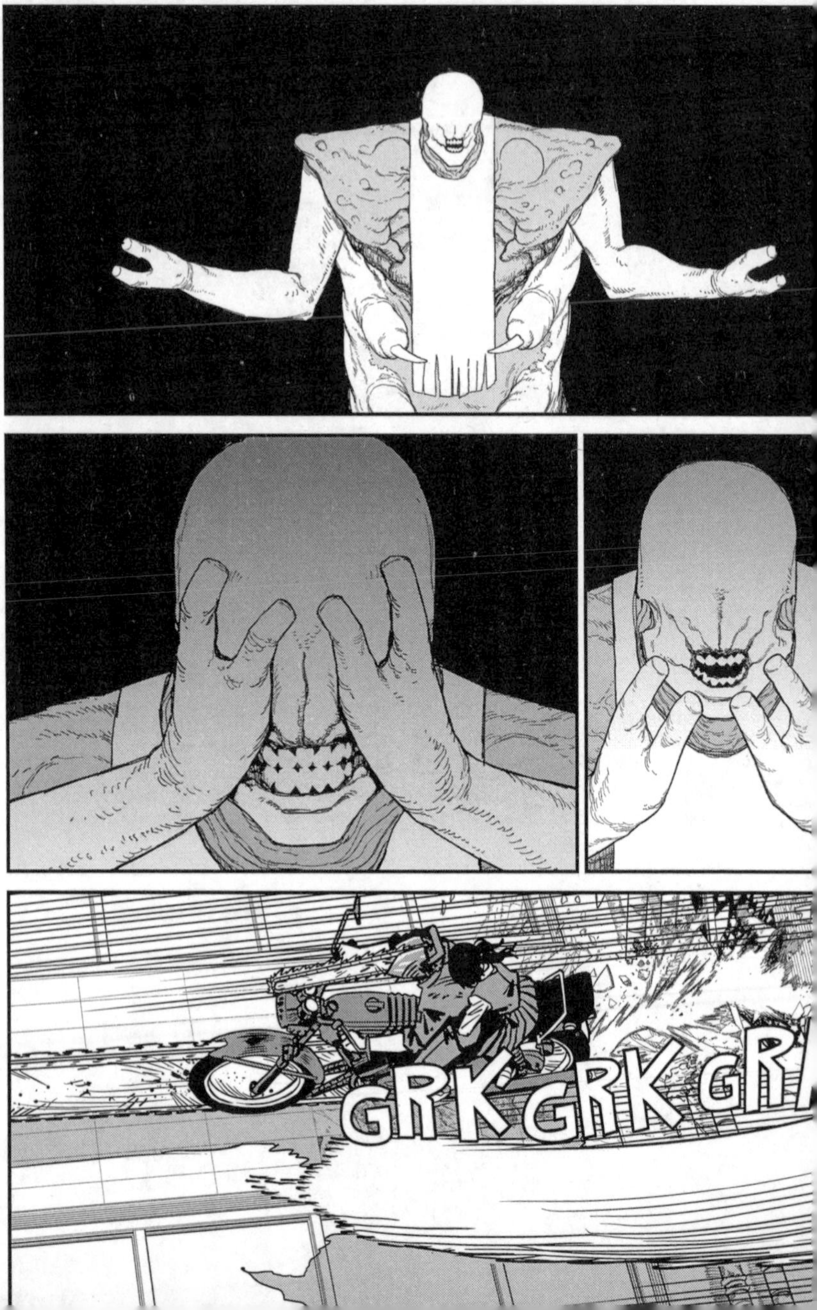
GRK GRK GR

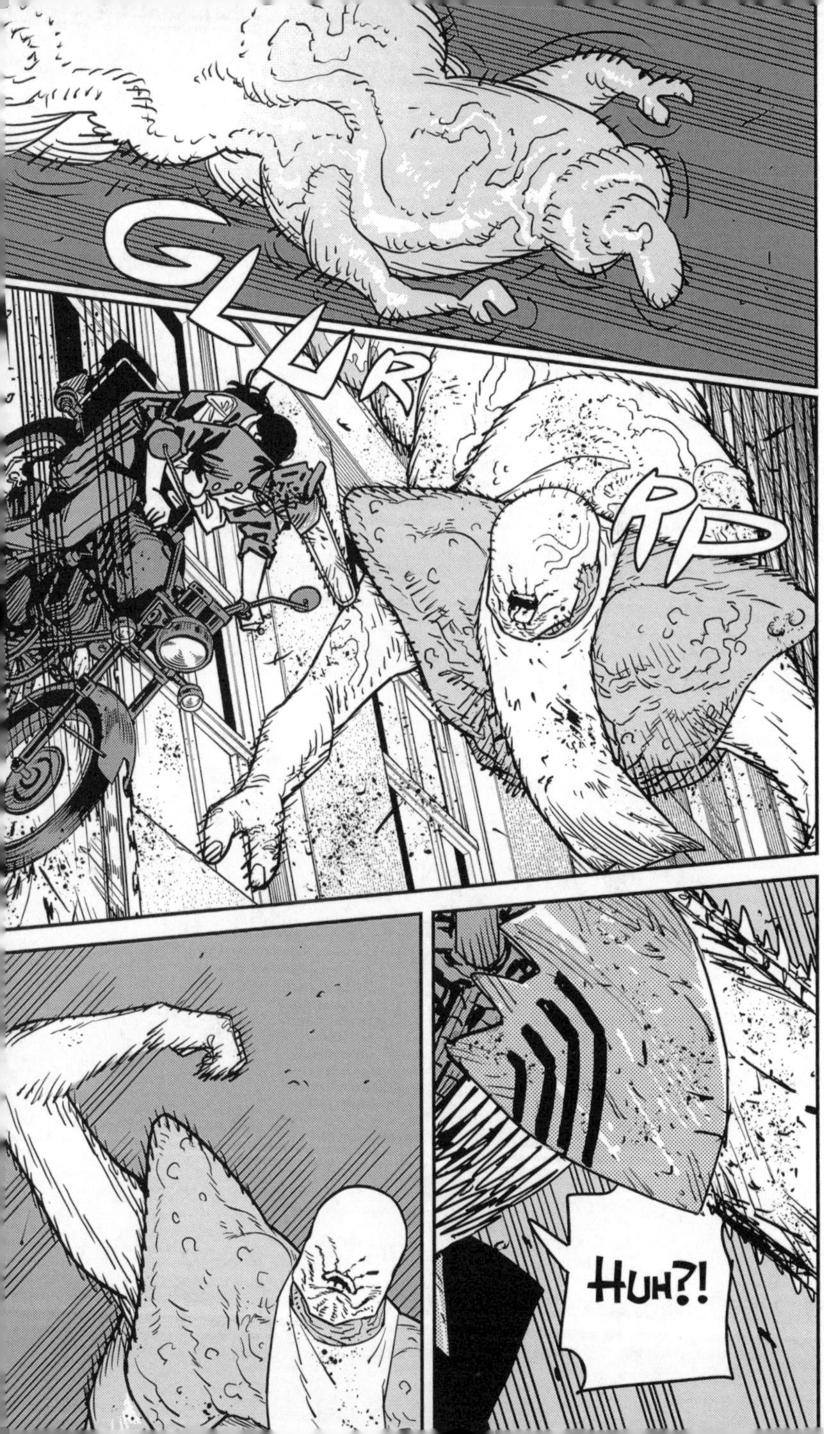
GLURP
HUH?!

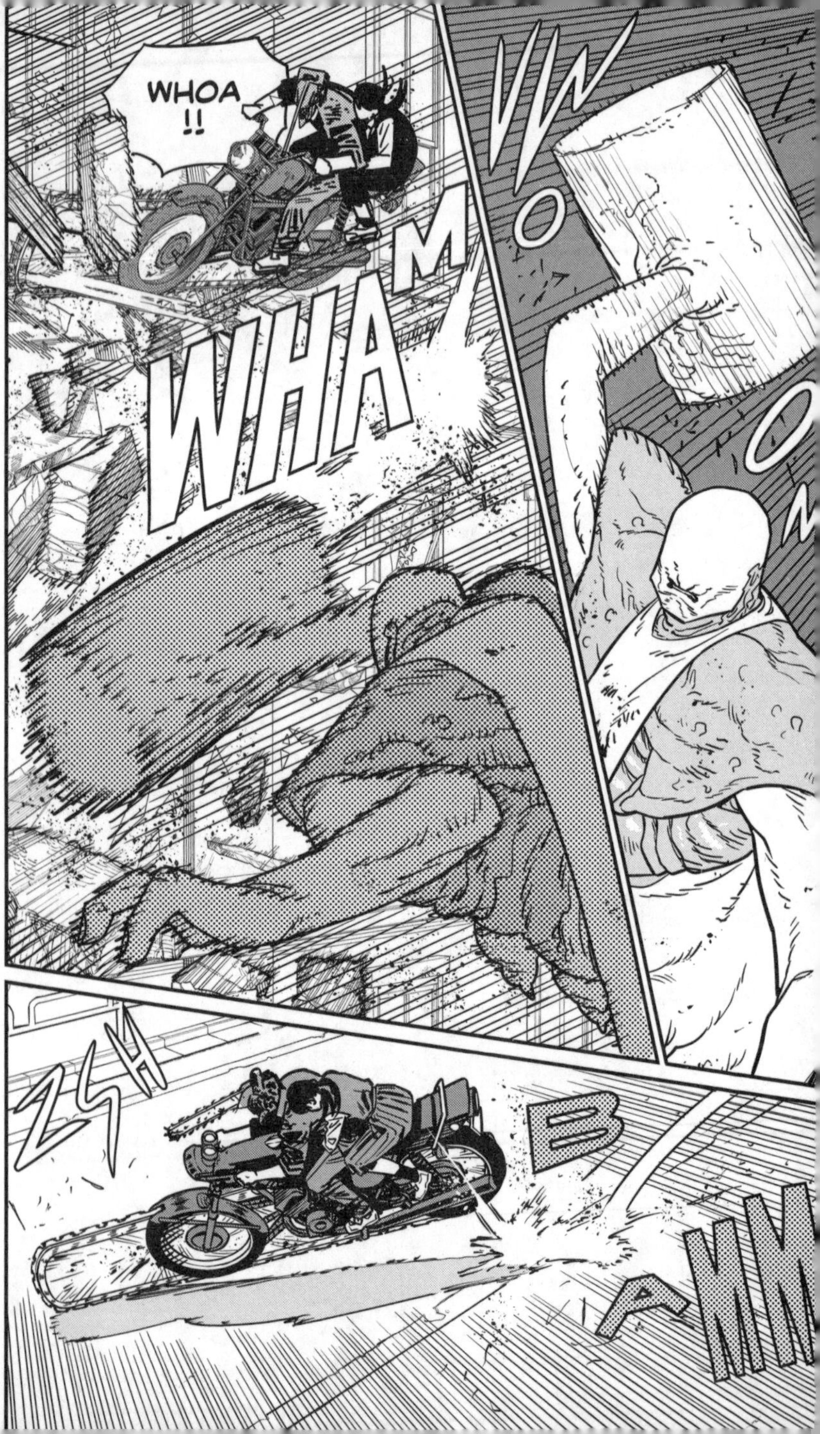
VWOO
WHOA !!
WHAM
BAMM
ZSH

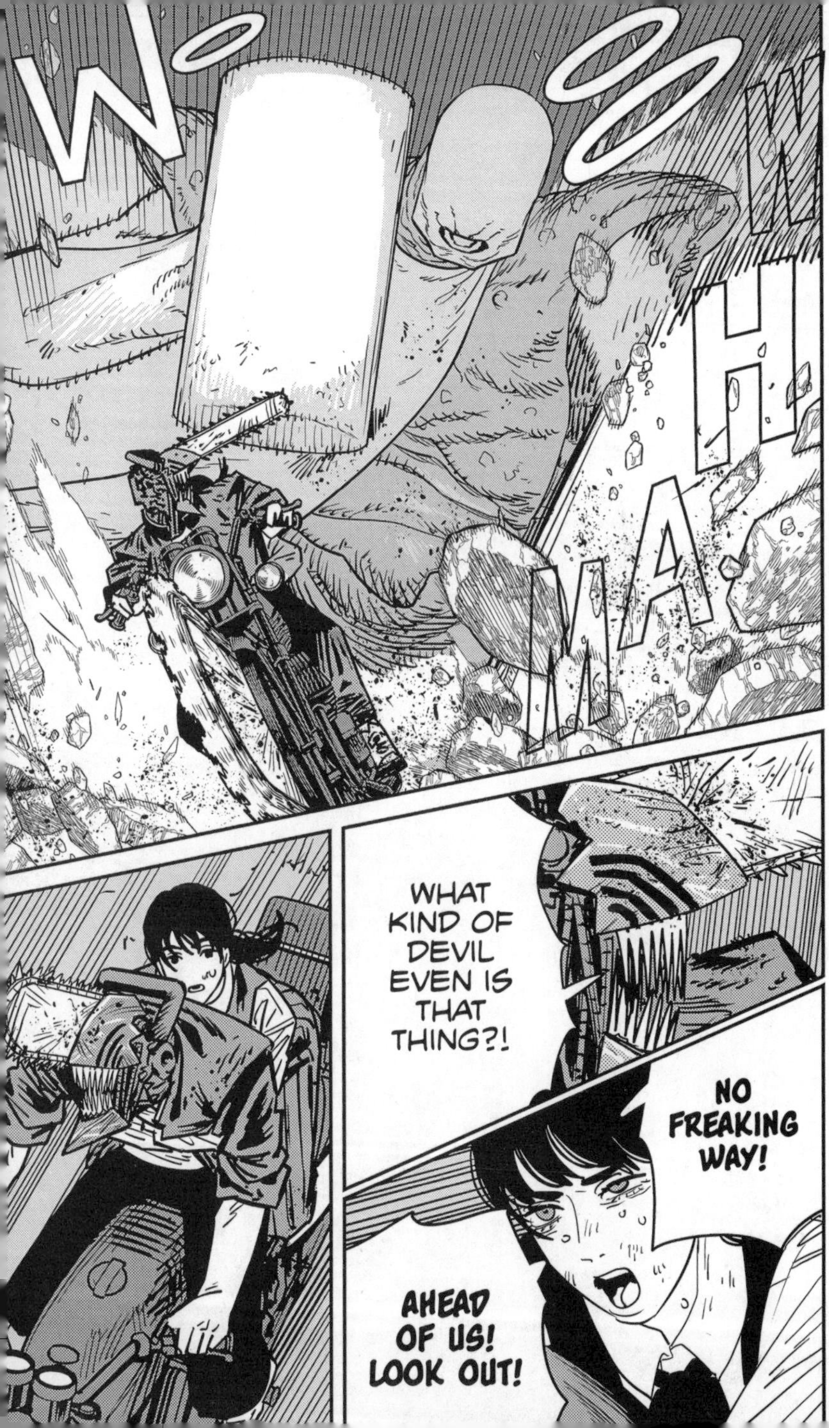
WOOW
HMA
WHAT KIND OF DEVIL EVEN IS THAT THING?!
NO FREAKING WAY!
AHEAD OF US! LOOK OUT!

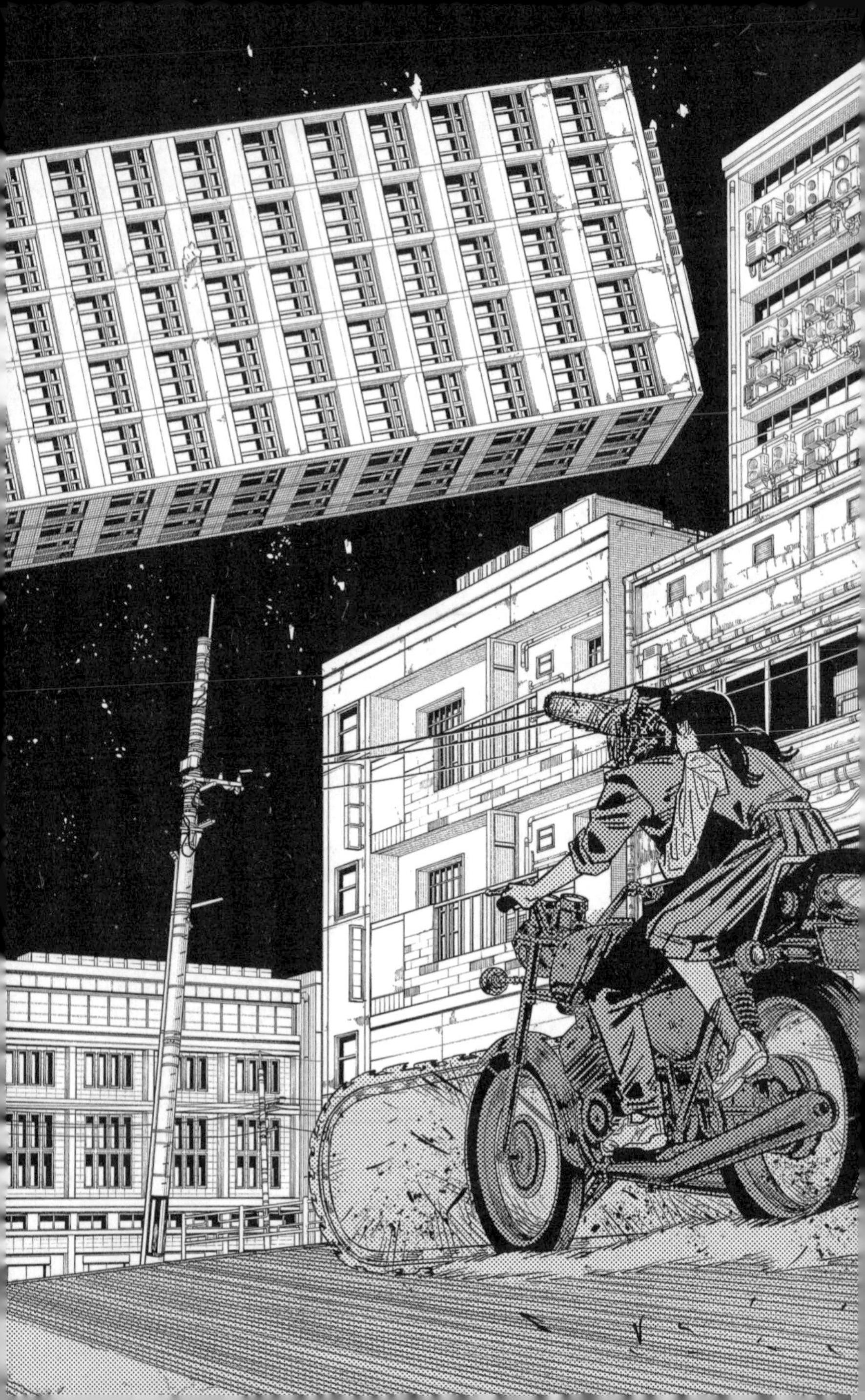

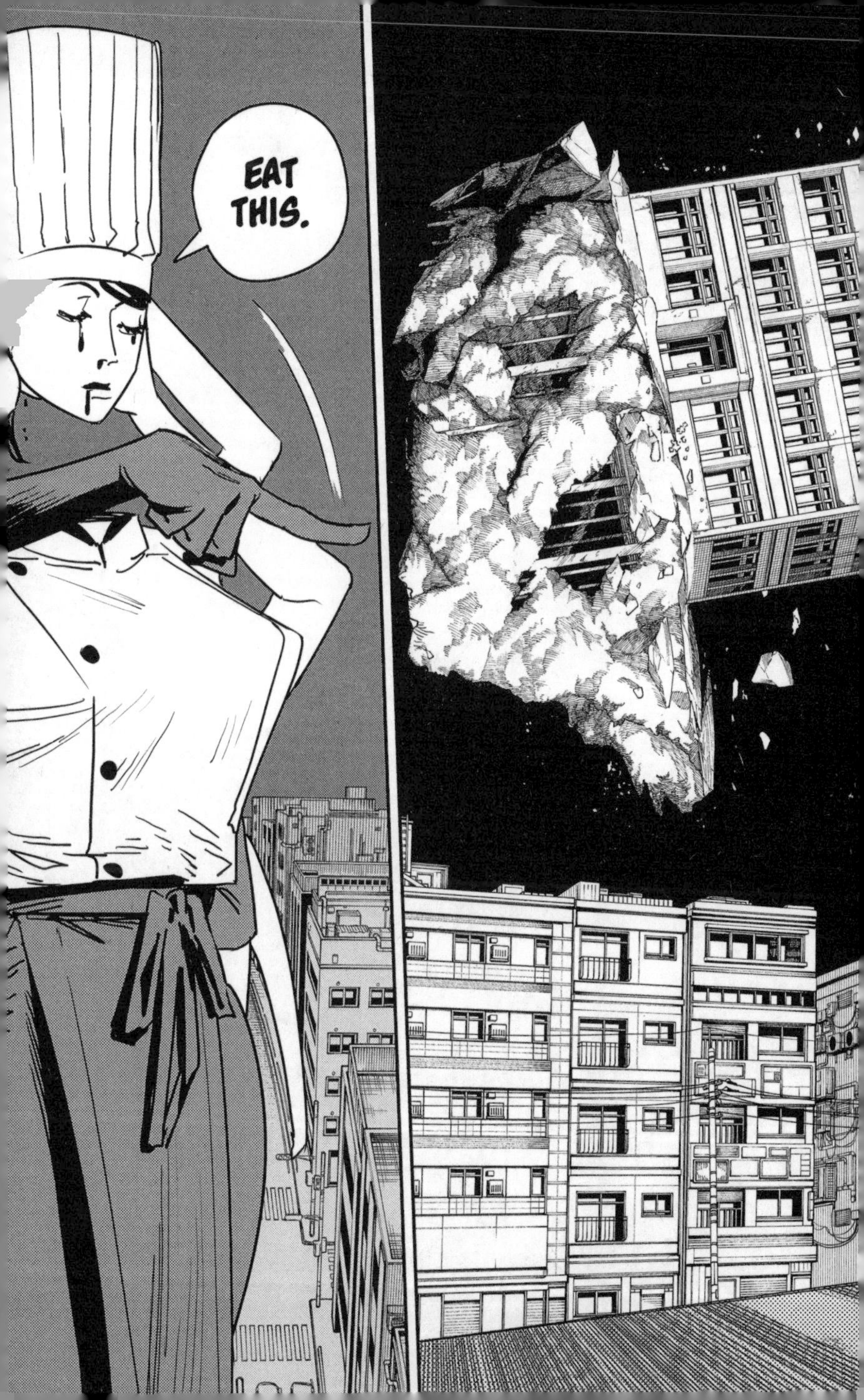
EAT THIS.

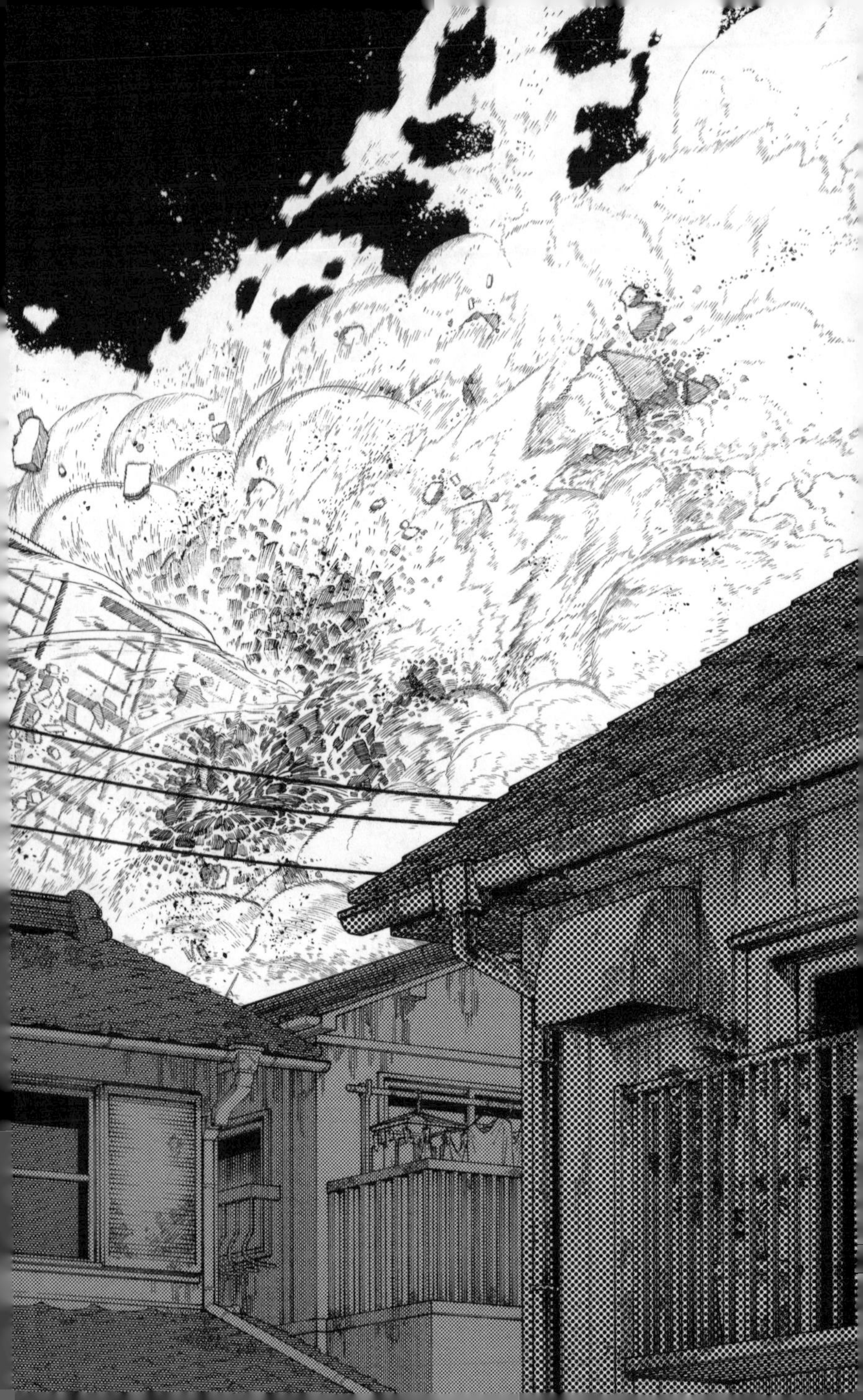

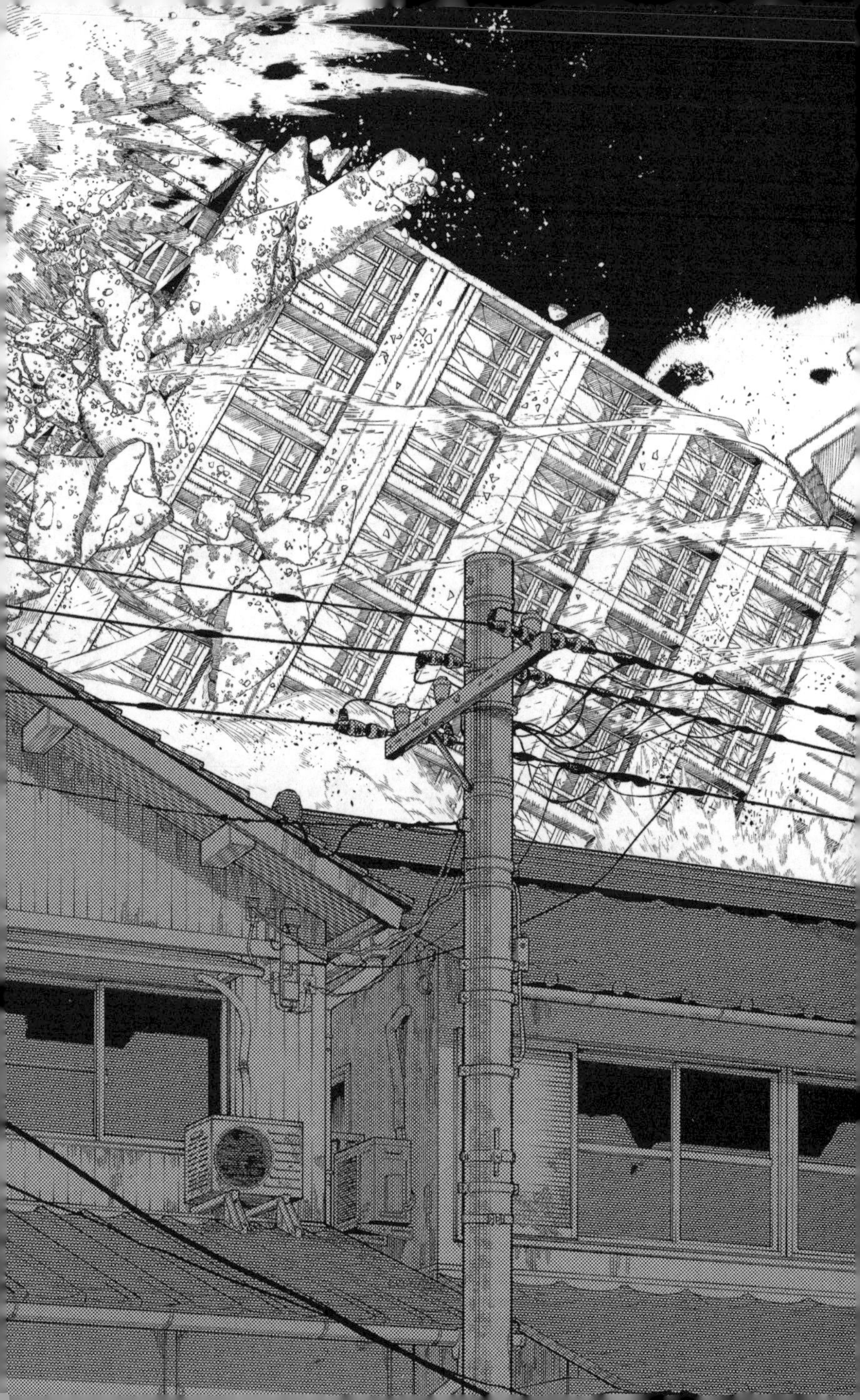

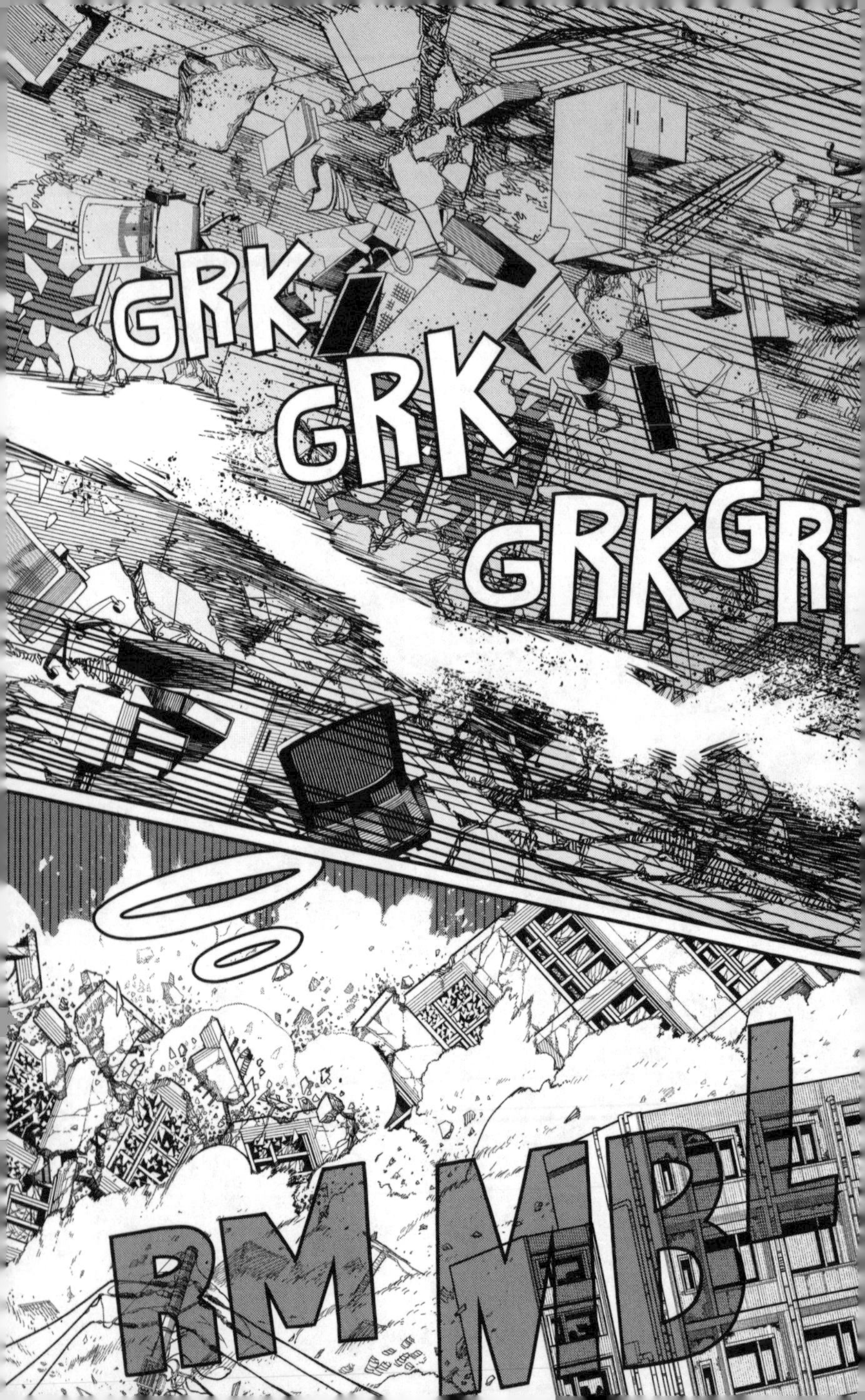
GRK
GRK
GRK
GR
RMMBL

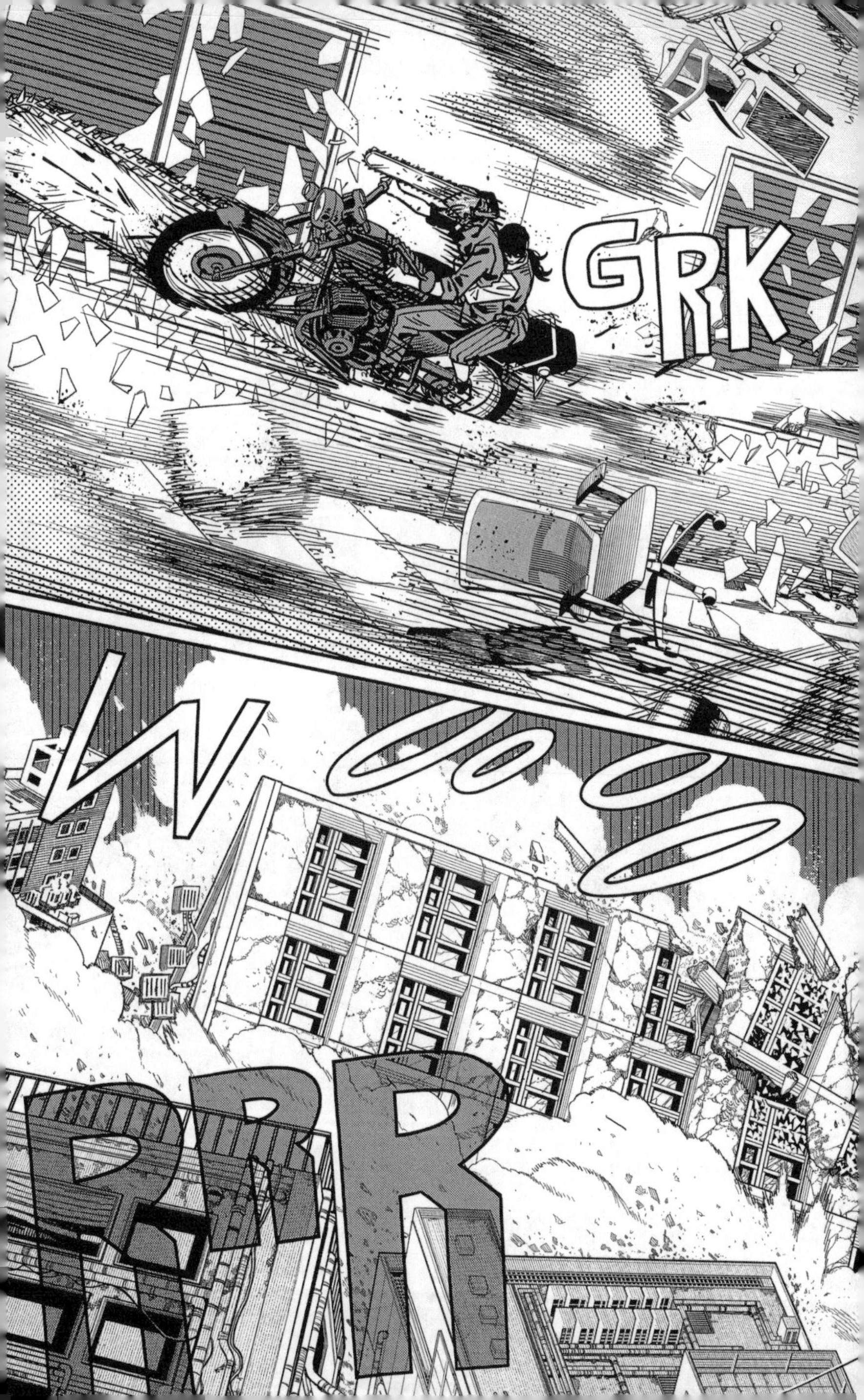
GRK
WOOOO
RRR

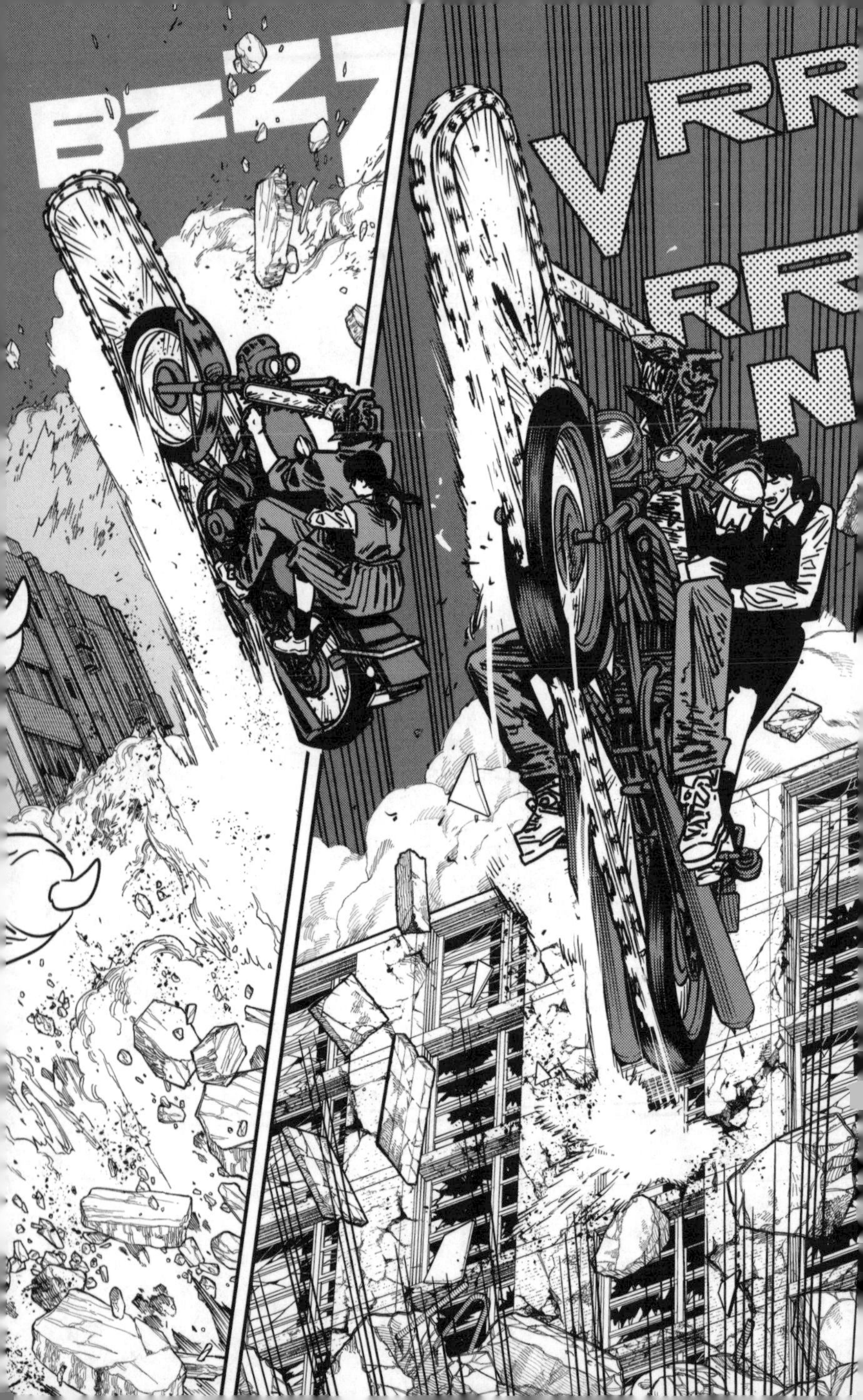
VRR
VRR
N
BZZZ

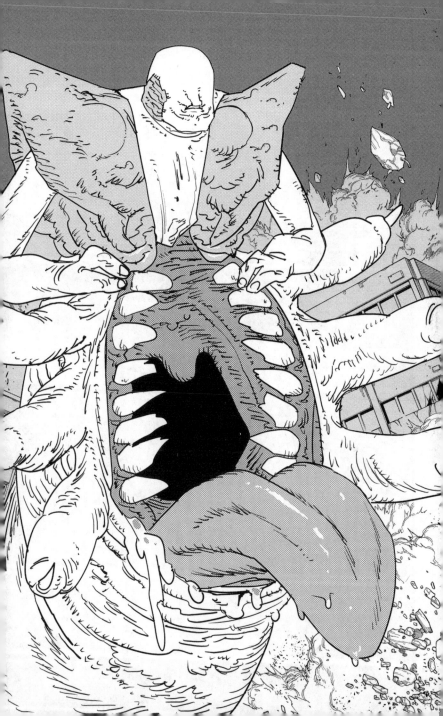

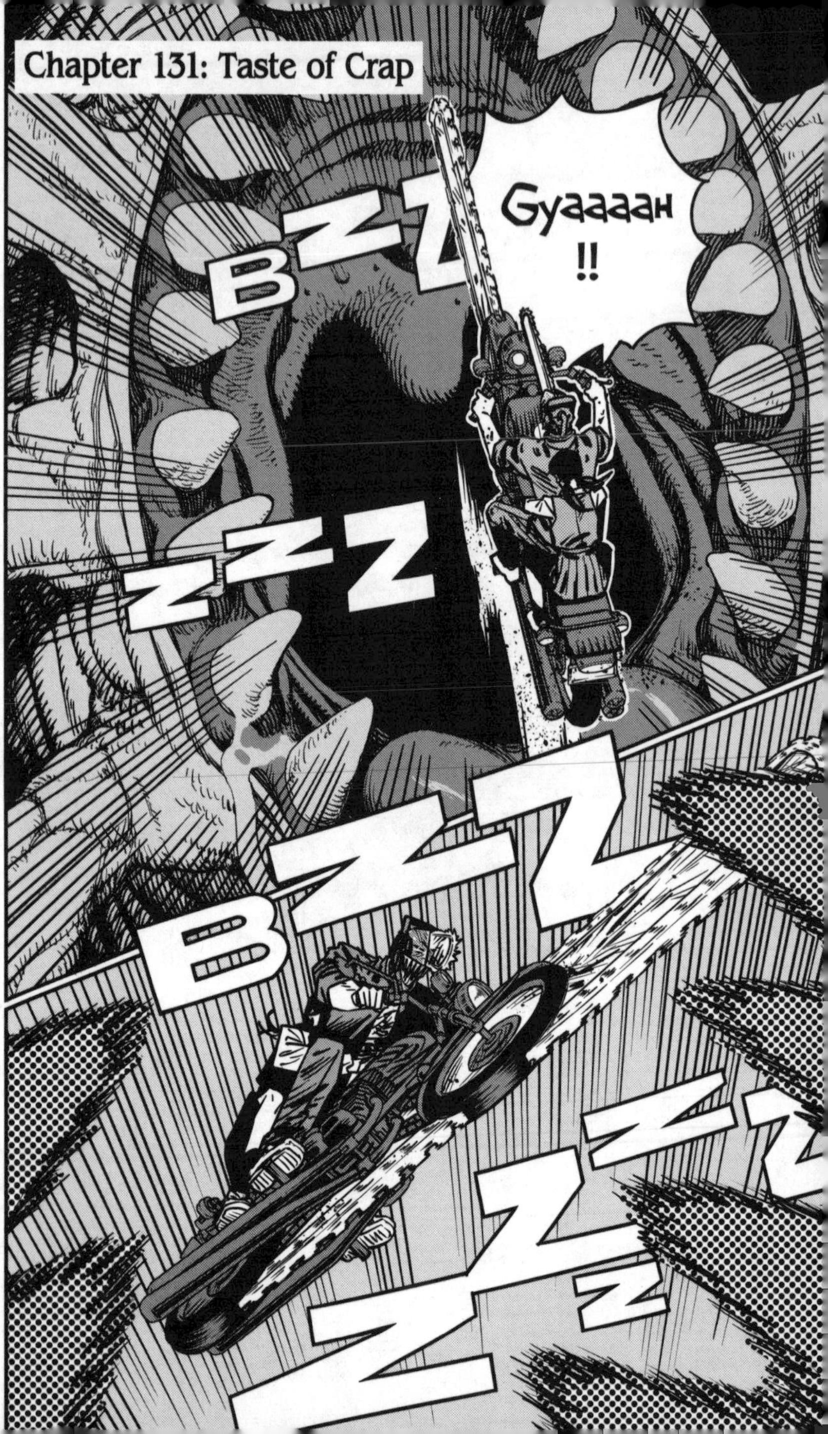
Chapter 131: Taste of Crap
Gyaaaaah !!
BZZZ
ZZZ
BZZZ
ZZZZZ

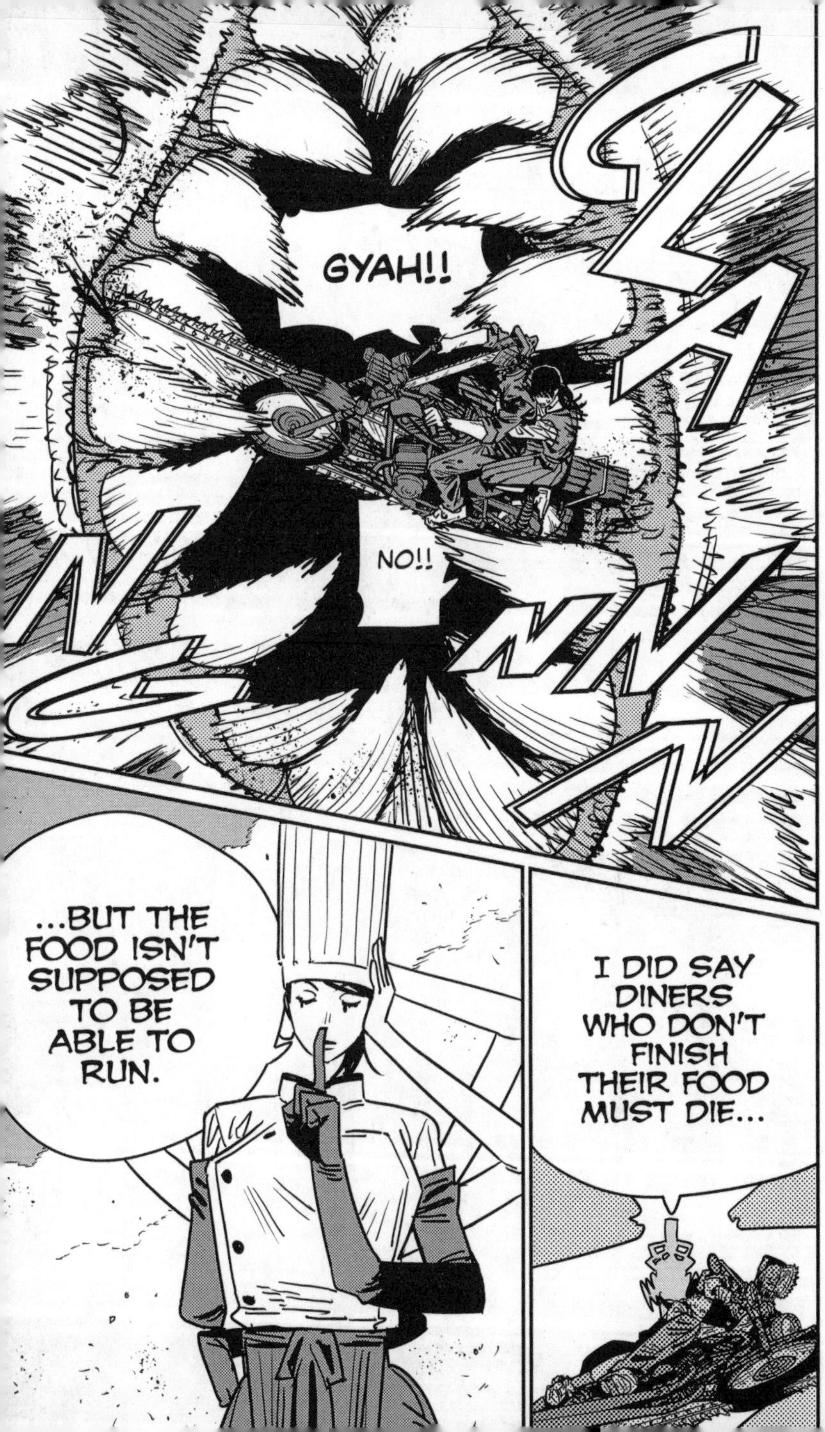
GYAH!!
NO!!
I DID SAY DINERS WHO DON'T FINISH THEIR FOOD MUST DIE...
...BUT THE FOOD ISN'T SUPPOSED TO BE ABLE TO RUN.

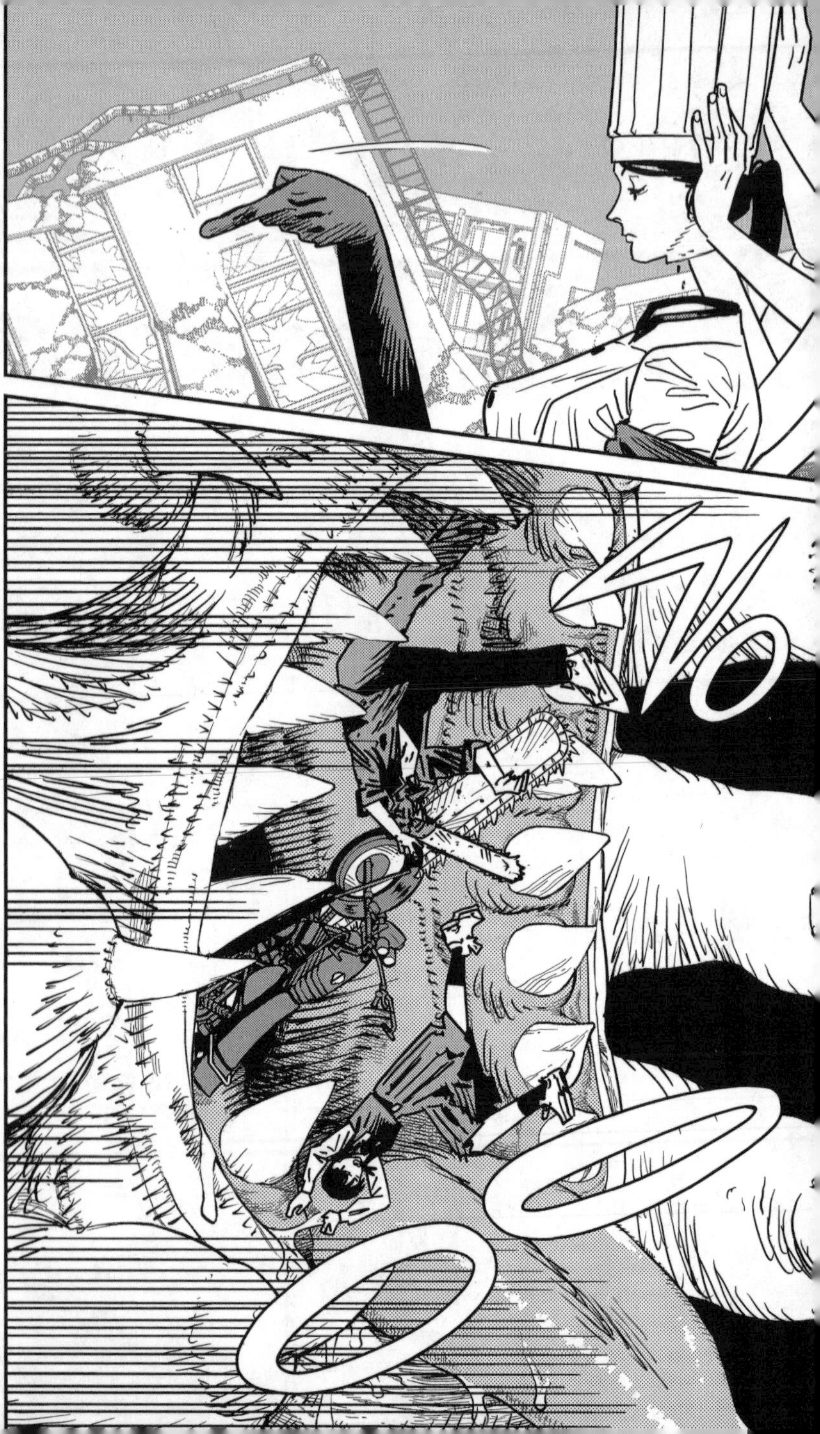

HOW
IS THE
TASTE...

...OF
HUMAN
STEEPED
IN FEAR?

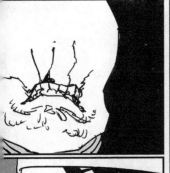

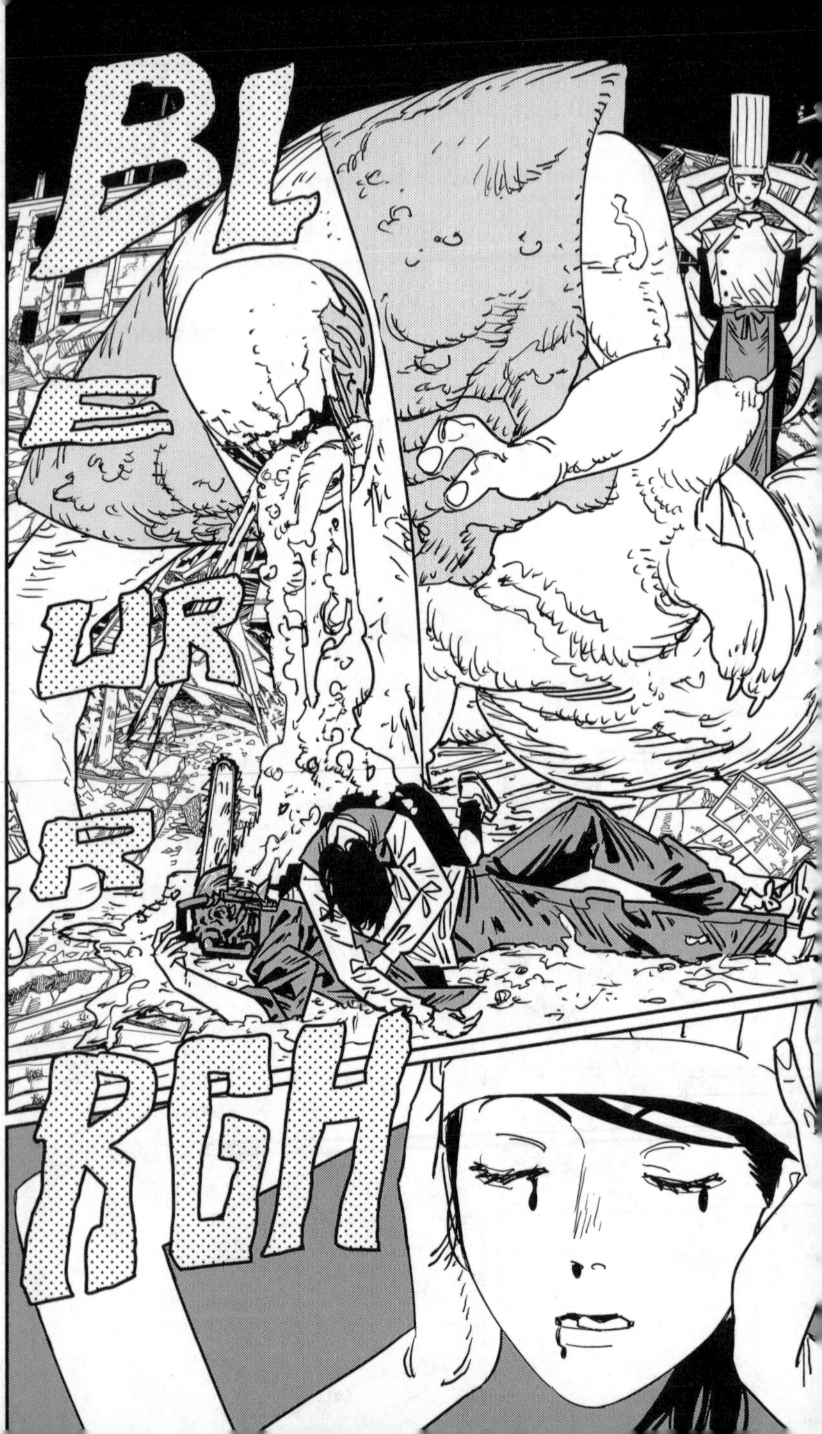
BLEURRRGH

I MADE
THAT
MEAL
WITH
LOVE...

I...
I MUH—

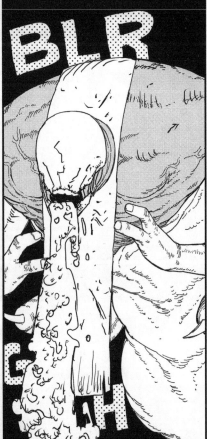

...
THROW
IT
UP?!

HOW
DARE
YOU...

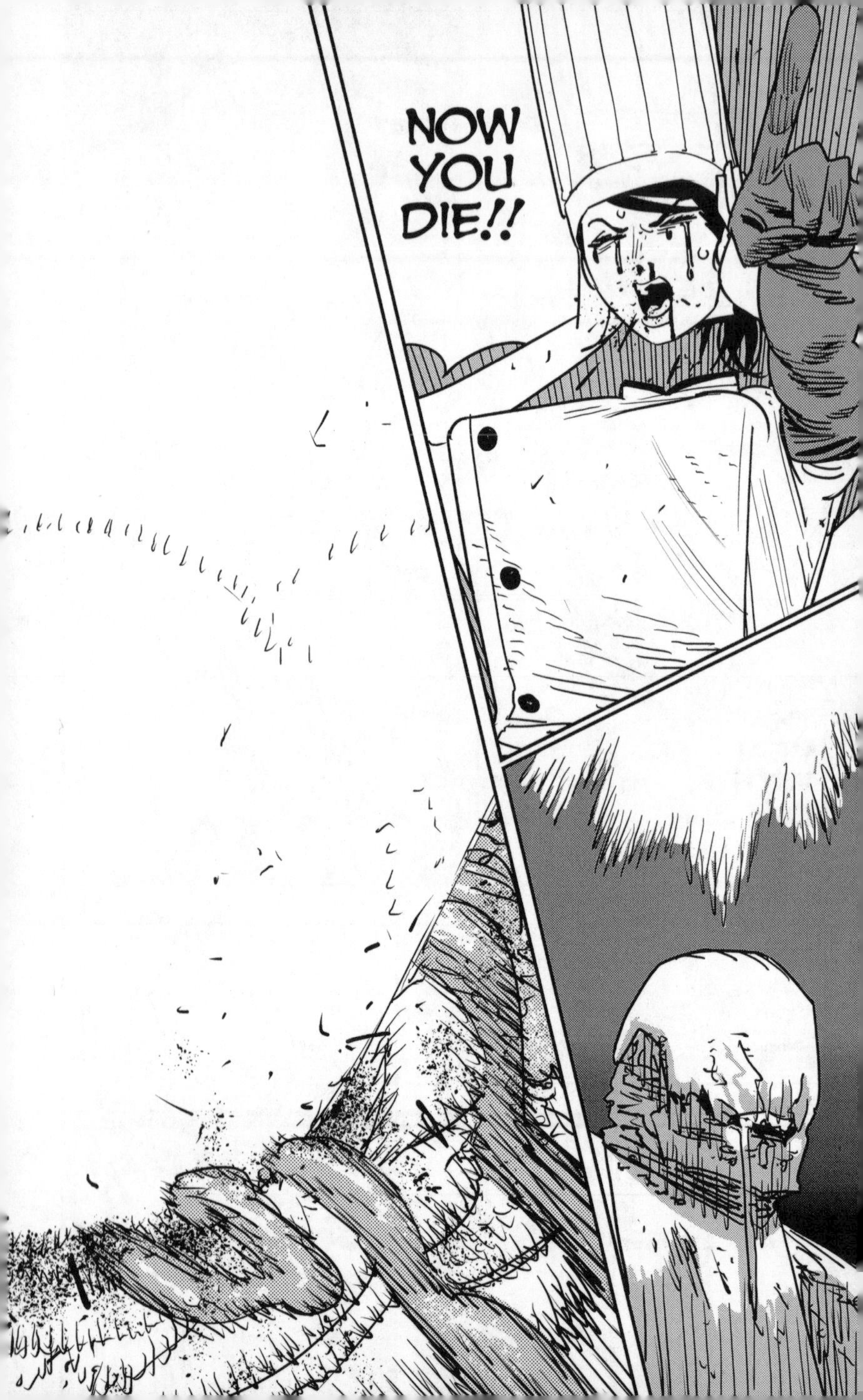
NOW YOU DIE!!

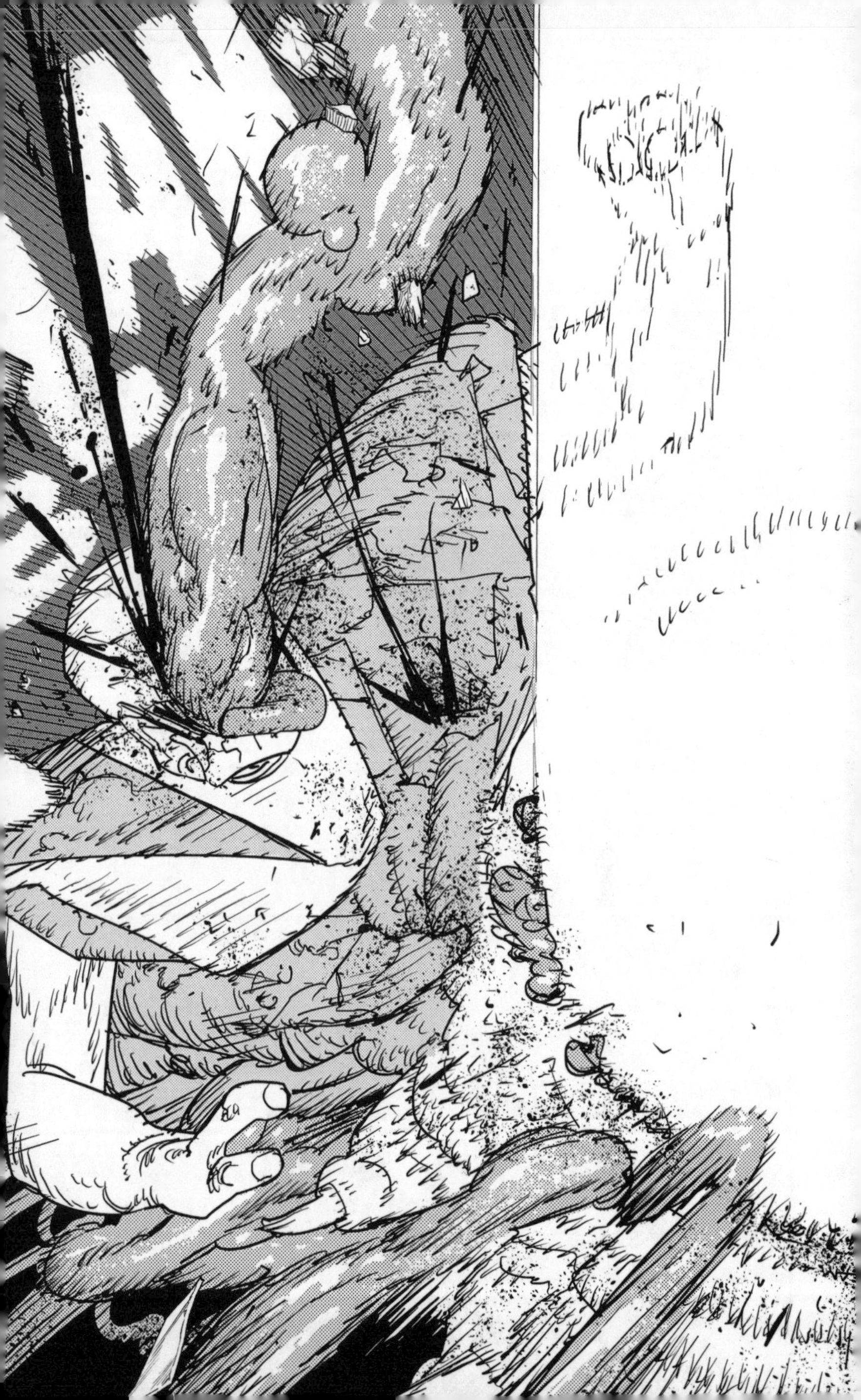

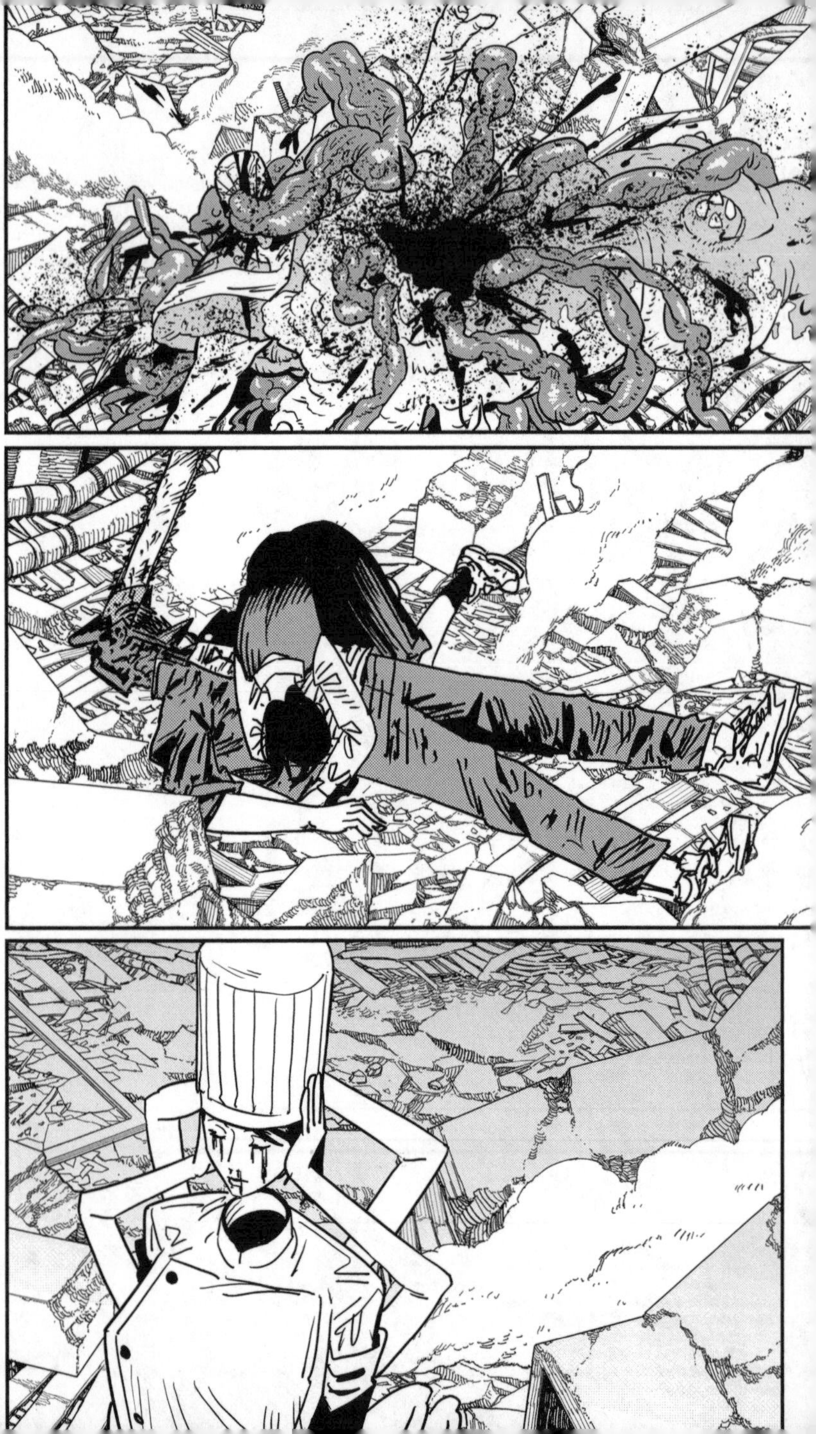

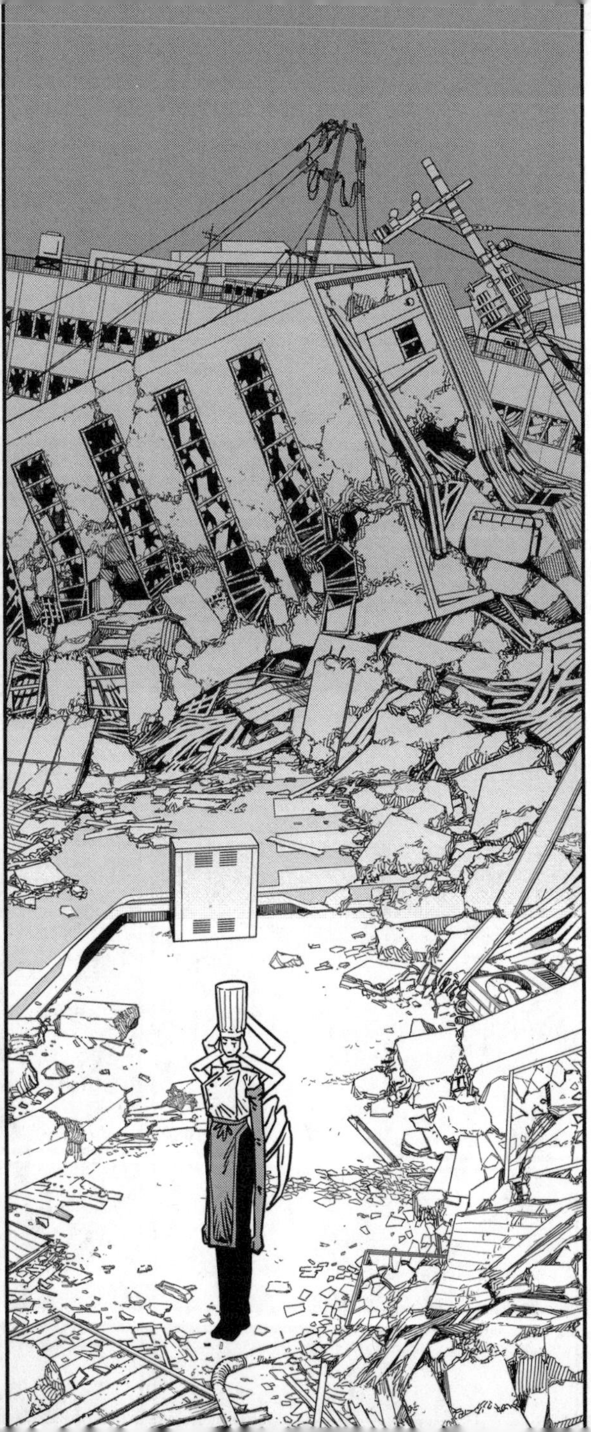

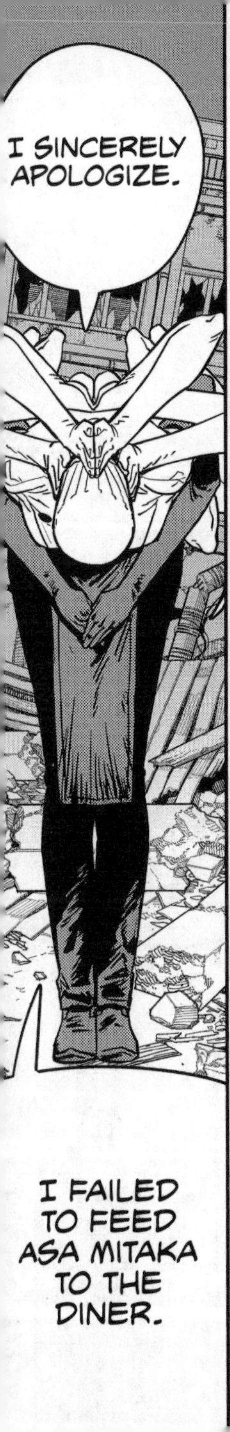
I SINCERELY APOLOGIZE.
I FAILED TO FEED ASA MITAKA TO THE DINER.

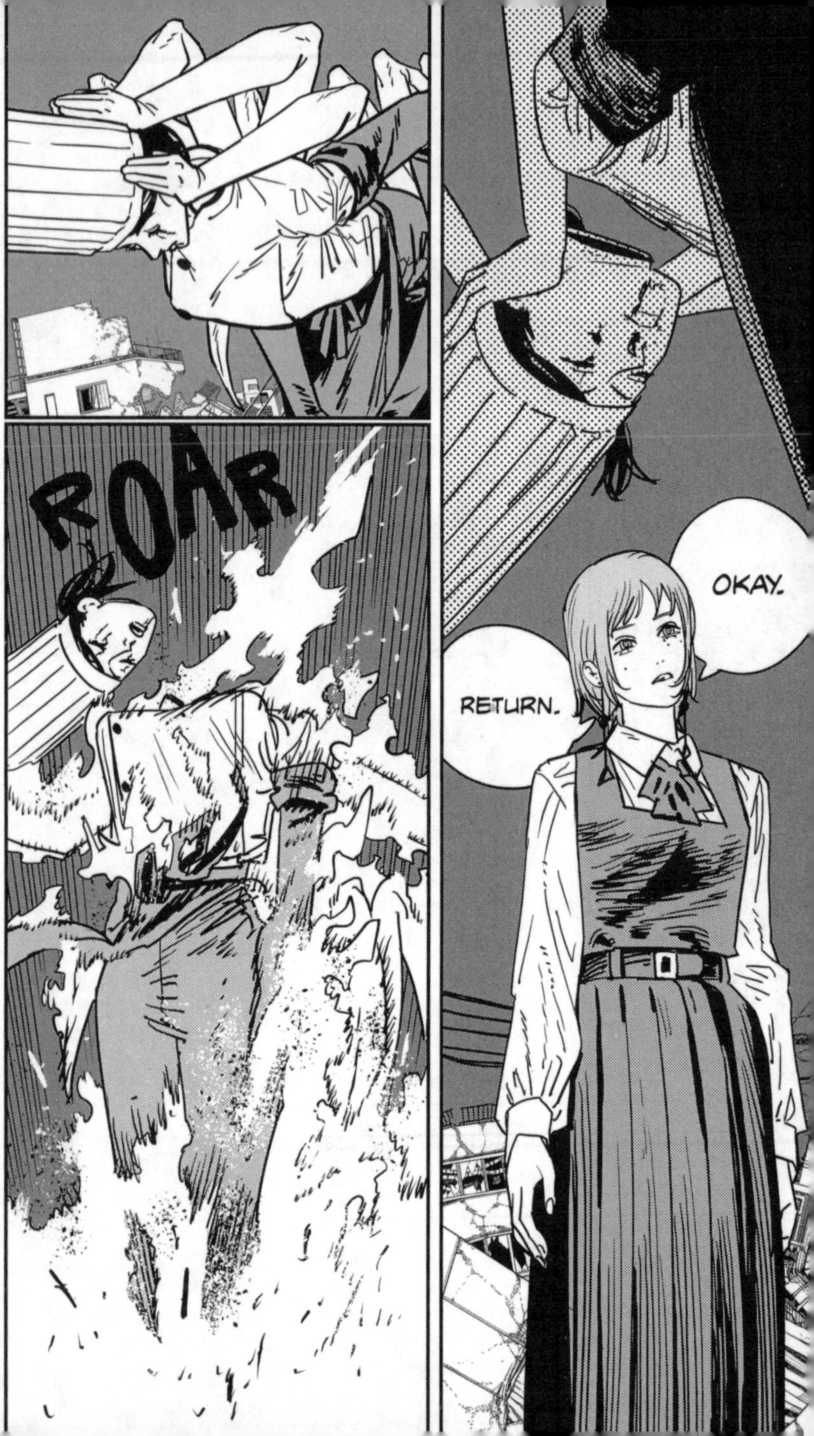
OKAY.
RETURN.
ROAR

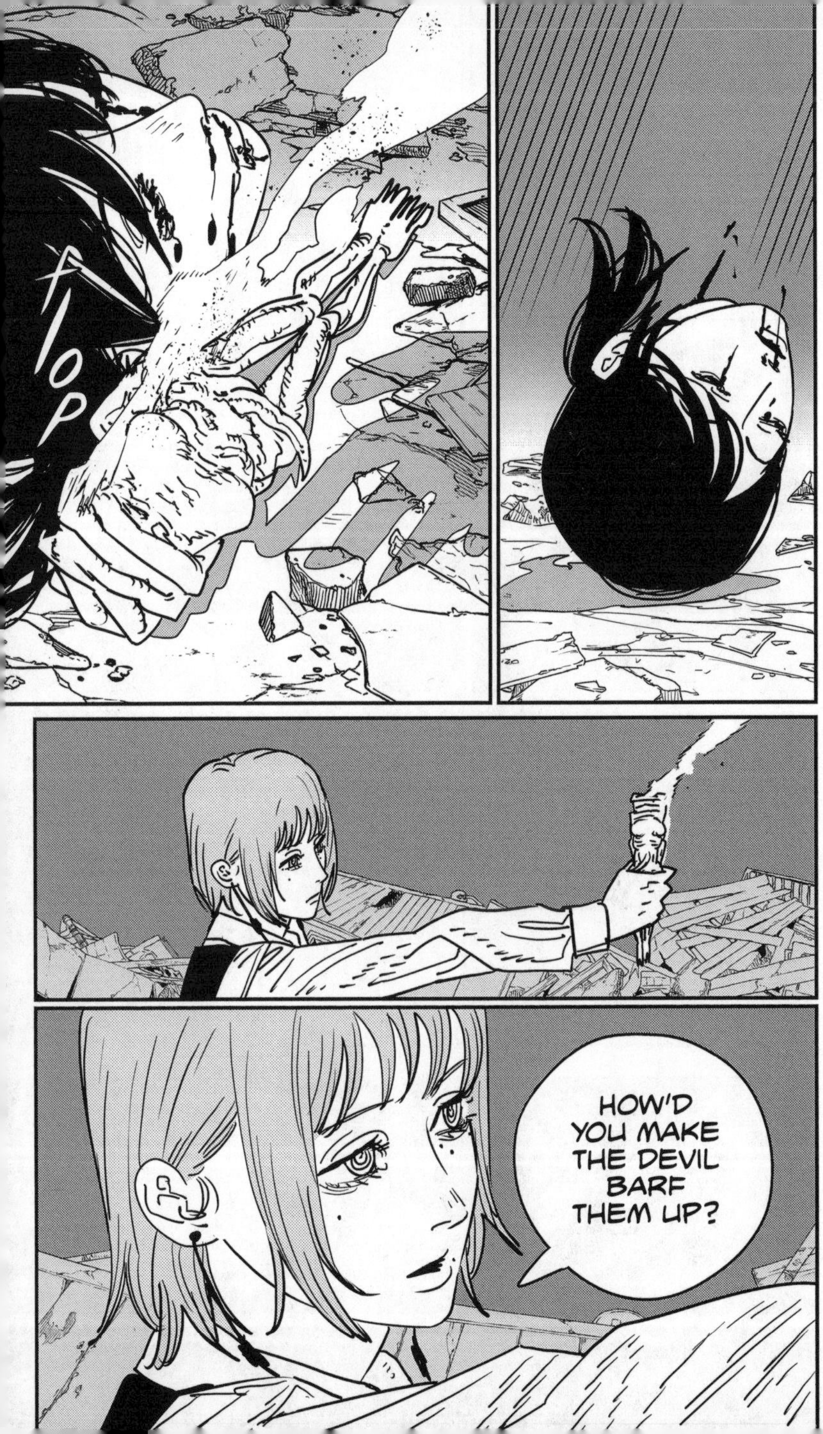
FLOP
HOW'D YOU MAKE THE DEVIL BARF THEM UP?

I CONTROLLED THAT DEVIL'S BRAIN A TEENSY BIT...

CONTROL.

...TO MAKE HUMANS TASTE LIKE LITERAL CRAP.

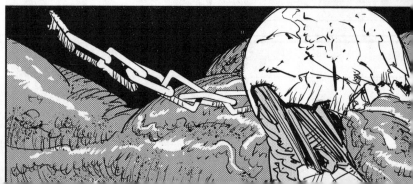

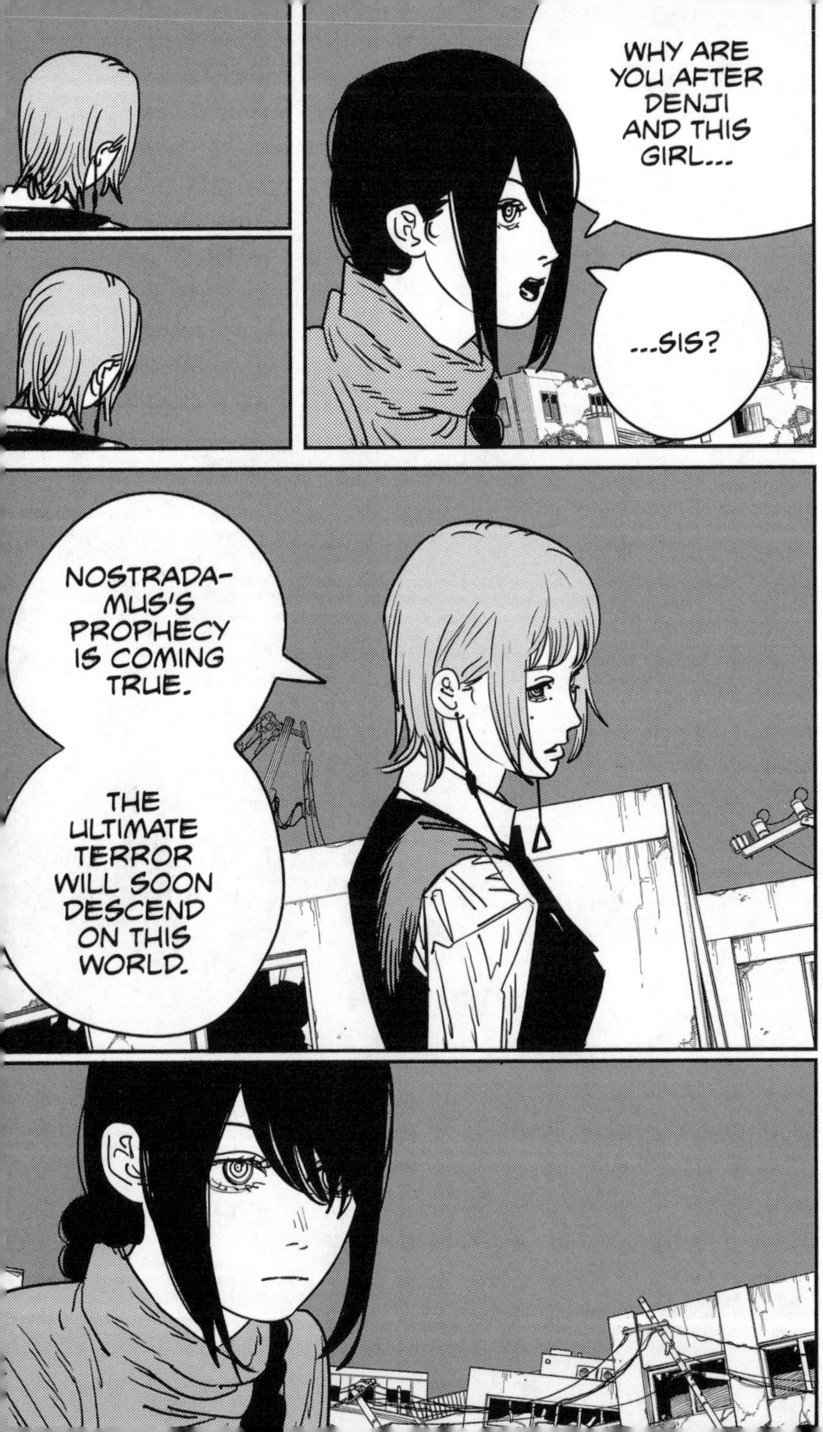
WHY ARE YOU AFTER DENJI AND THIS GIRL...
...SIS?
NOSTRADAMUS'S PROPHECY IS COMING TRUE.
THE ULTIMATE TERROR WILL SOON DESCEND ON THIS WORLD.

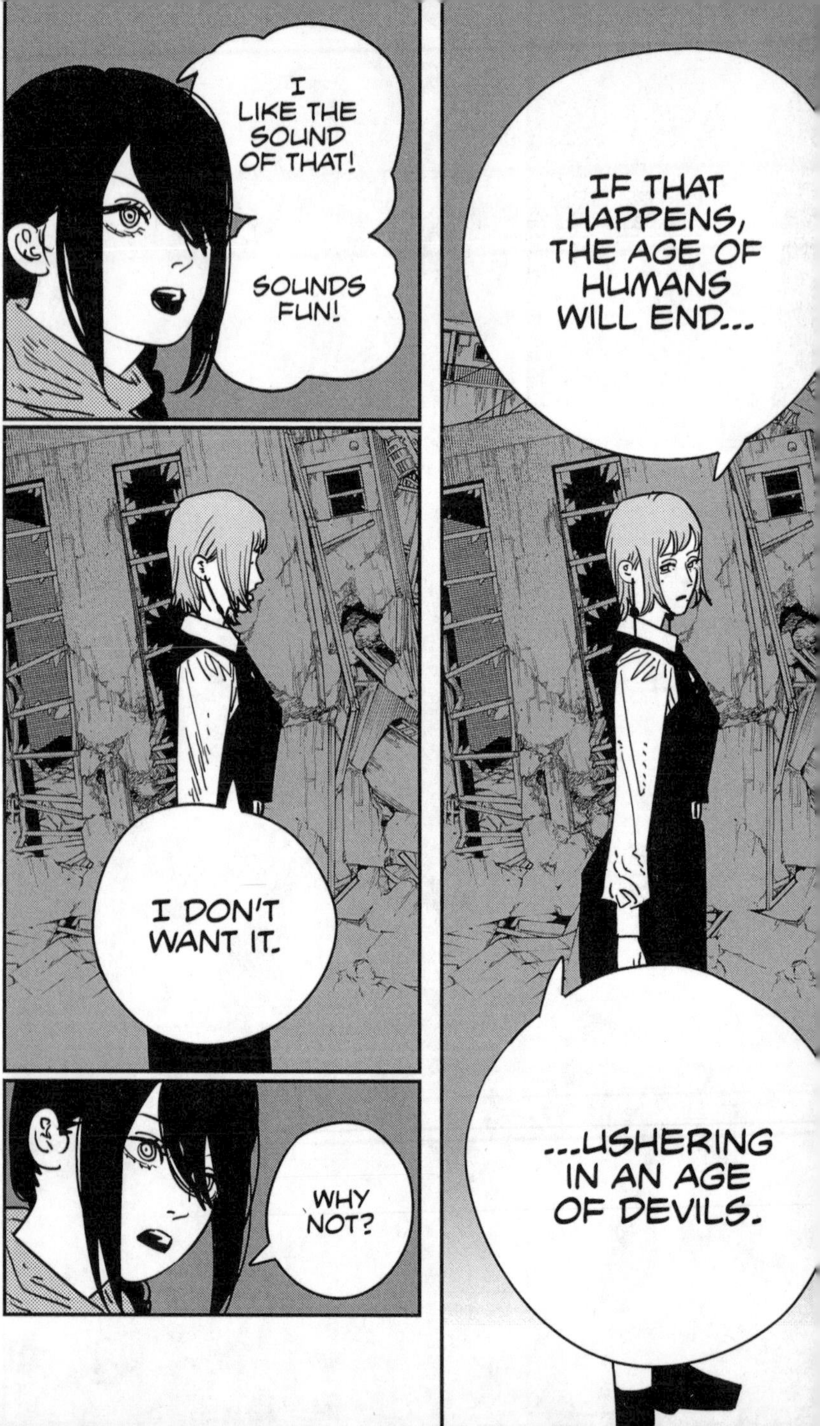
IF THAT HAPPENS, THE AGE OF HUMANS WILL END...
...USHERING IN AN AGE OF DEVILS.
I LIKE THE SOUND OF THAT!
SOUNDS FUN!
I DON'T WANT IT.
WHY NOT?

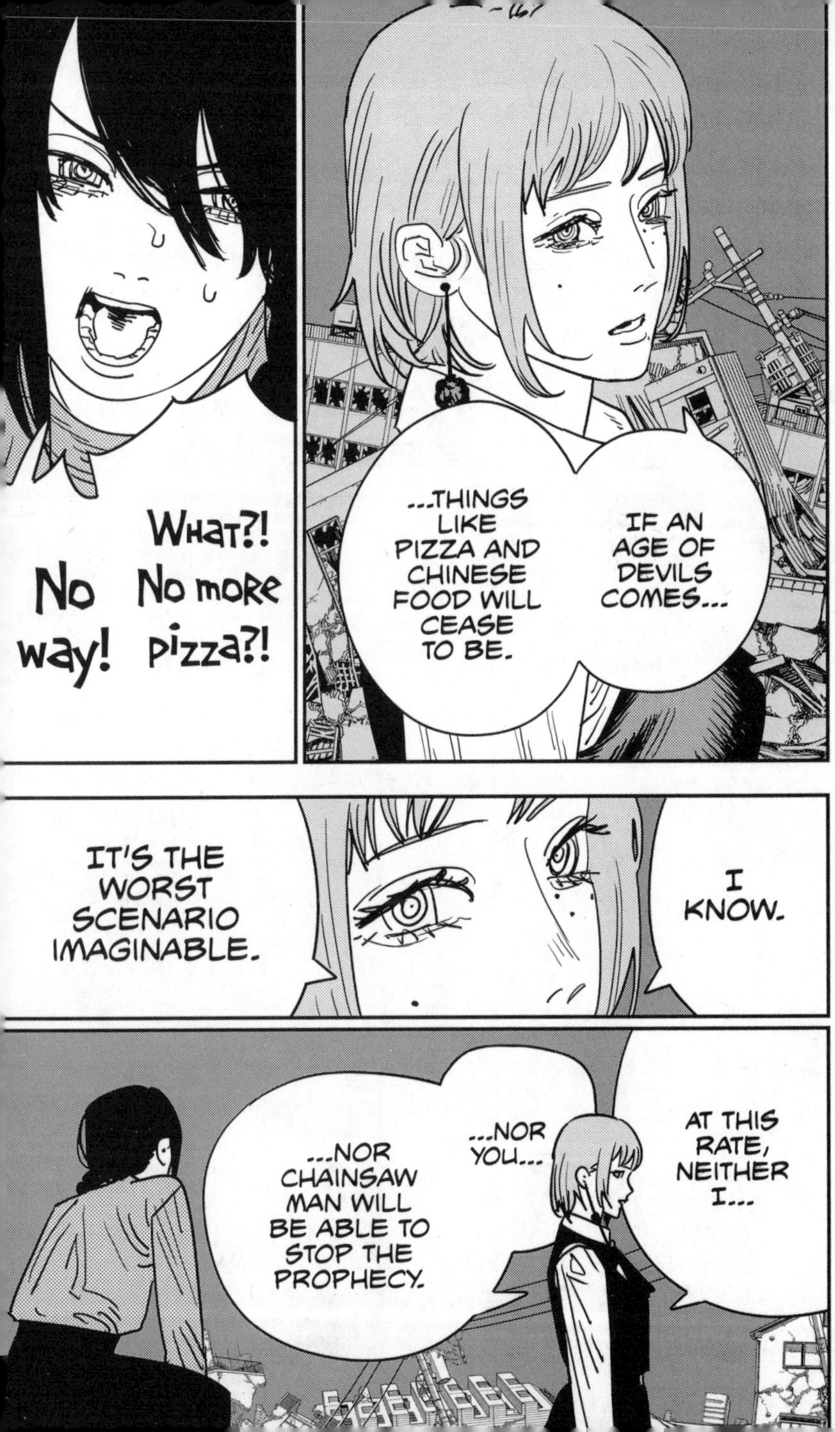
IF AN AGE OF DEVILS COMES...
...THINGS LIKE PIZZA AND CHINESE FOOD WILL CEASE TO BE.
What?! No more pizza?!
No way!
I KNOW.
IT'S THE WORST SCENARIO IMAGINABLE.
AT THIS RATE, NEITHER I...
...NOR YOU...
...NOR CHAINSAW MAN WILL BE ABLE TO STOP THE PROPHECY.

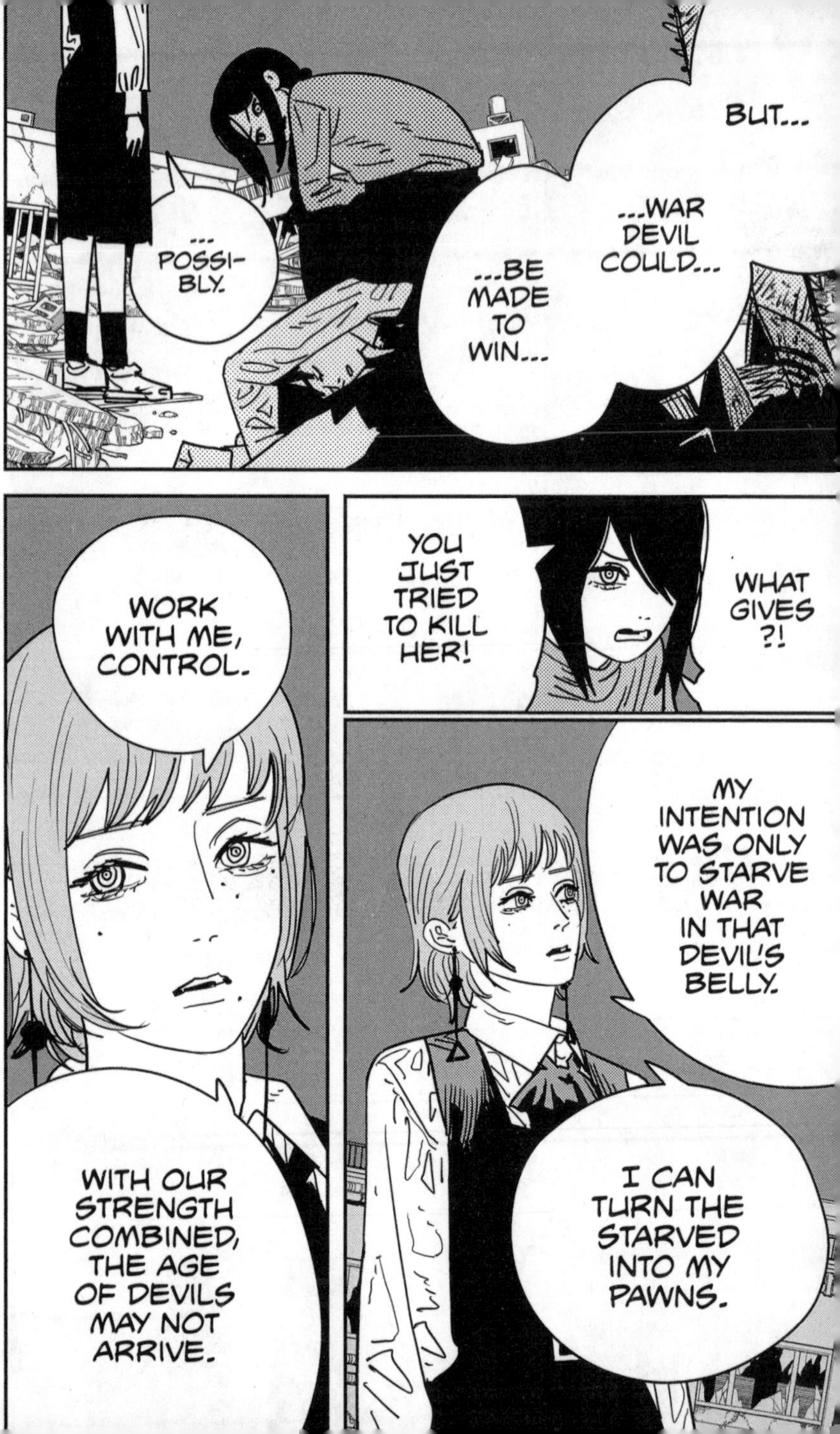
BUT...
...WAR DEVIL COULD...
...BE MADE TO WIN...
...POSSIBLY.
WHAT GIVES?!
YOU JUST TRIED TO KILL HER!
MY INTENTION WAS ONLY TO STARVE WAR IN THAT DEVIL'S BELLY.
I CAN TURN THE STARVED INTO MY PAWNS.
WORK WITH ME, CONTROL.
WITH OUR STRENGTH COMBINED, THE AGE OF DEVILS MAY NOT ARRIVE.

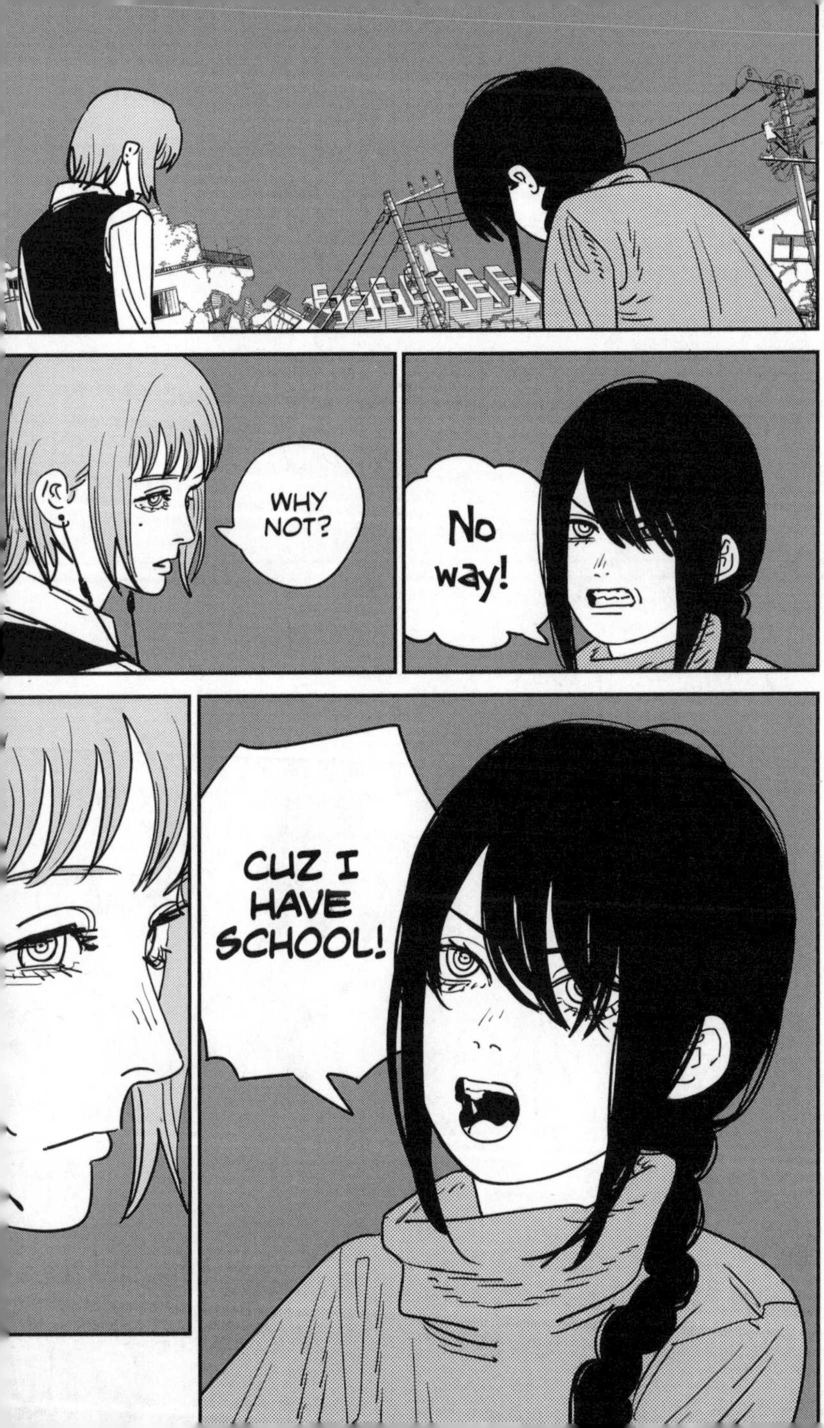
No way!
WHY NOT?
CUZ I HAVE SCHOOL!

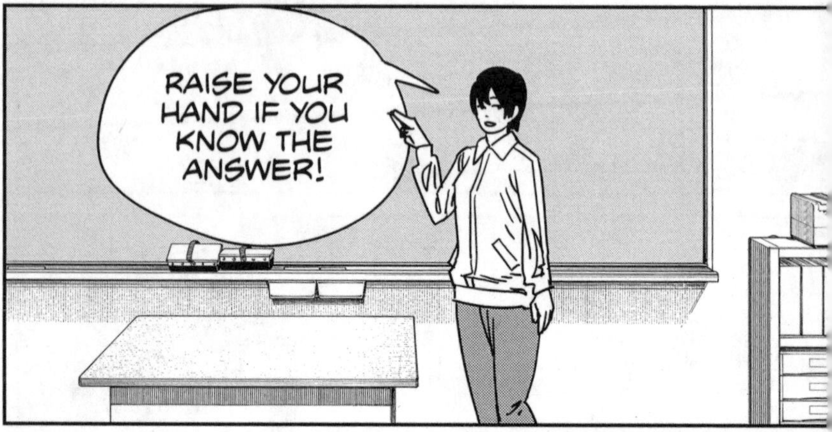
RAISE YOUR HAND IF YOU KNOW THE ANSWER!
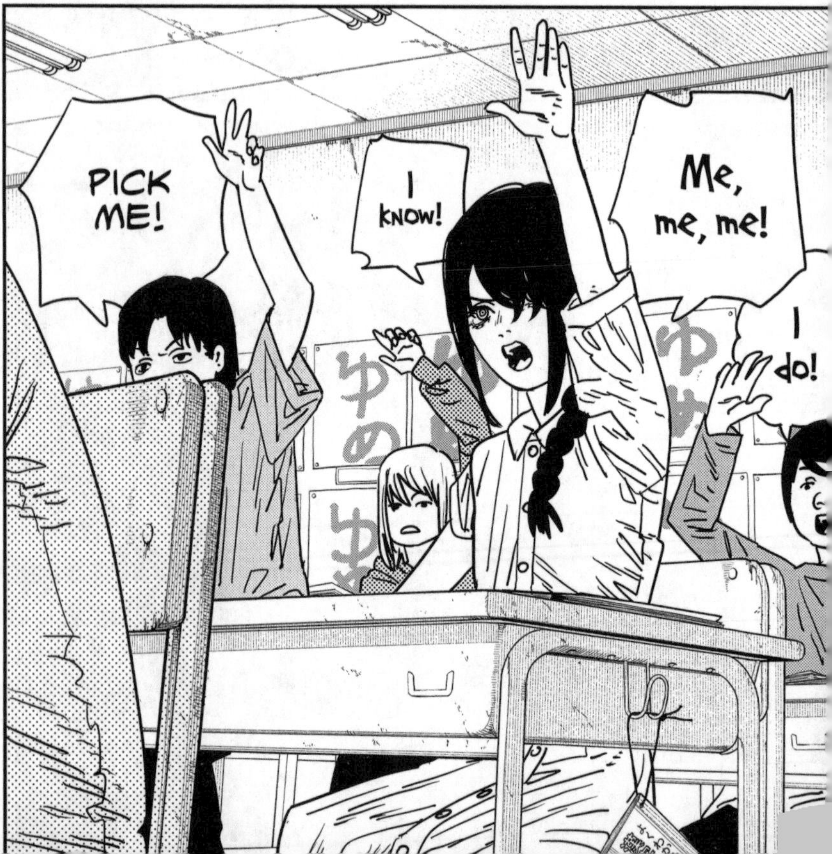
Me, me, me!
I do!
I KNOW!
PICK ME!

Chainsawman

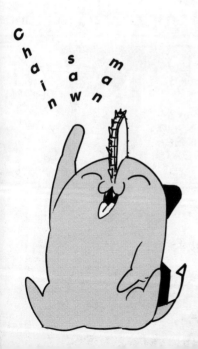

Chapter 132: Protection

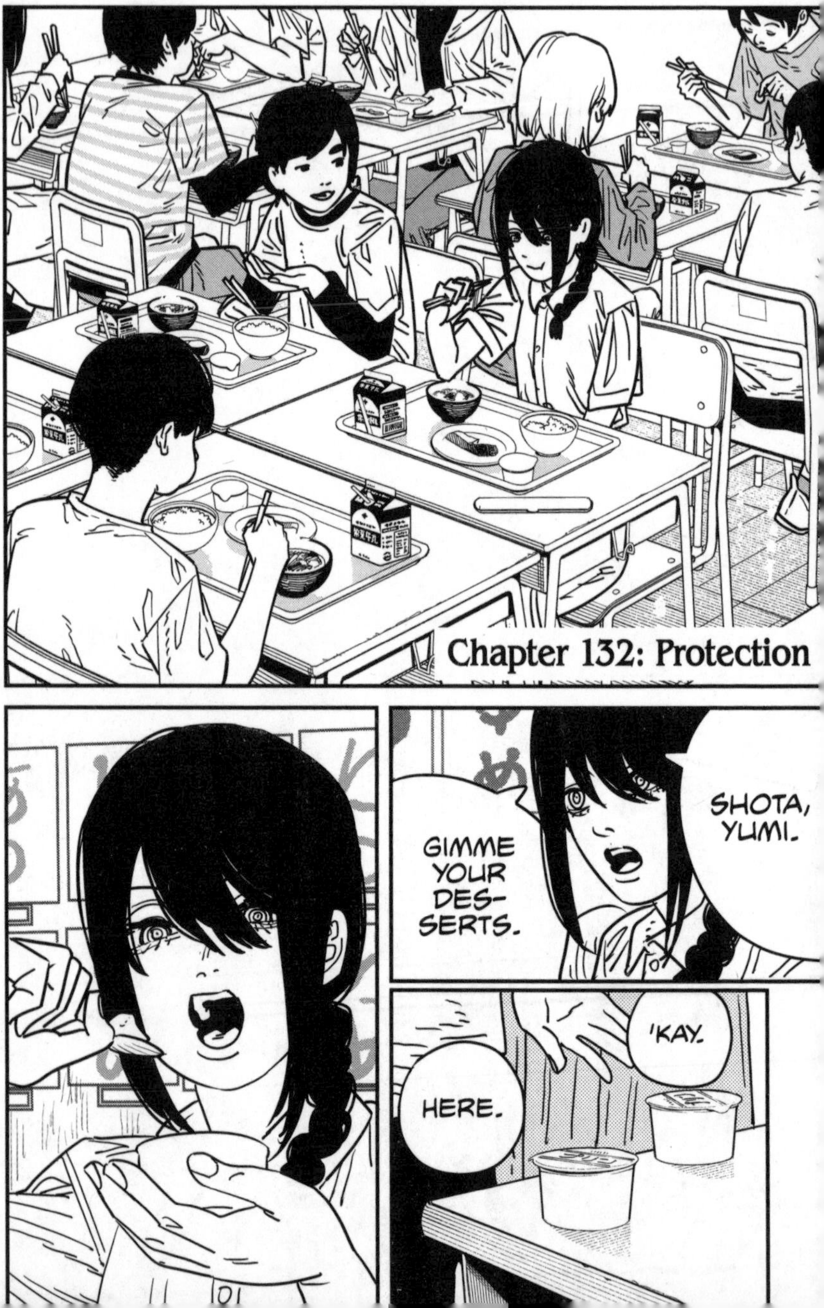
SHOTA, YUMI.
GIMME YOUR DES-SERTS.
'KAY.
HERE.

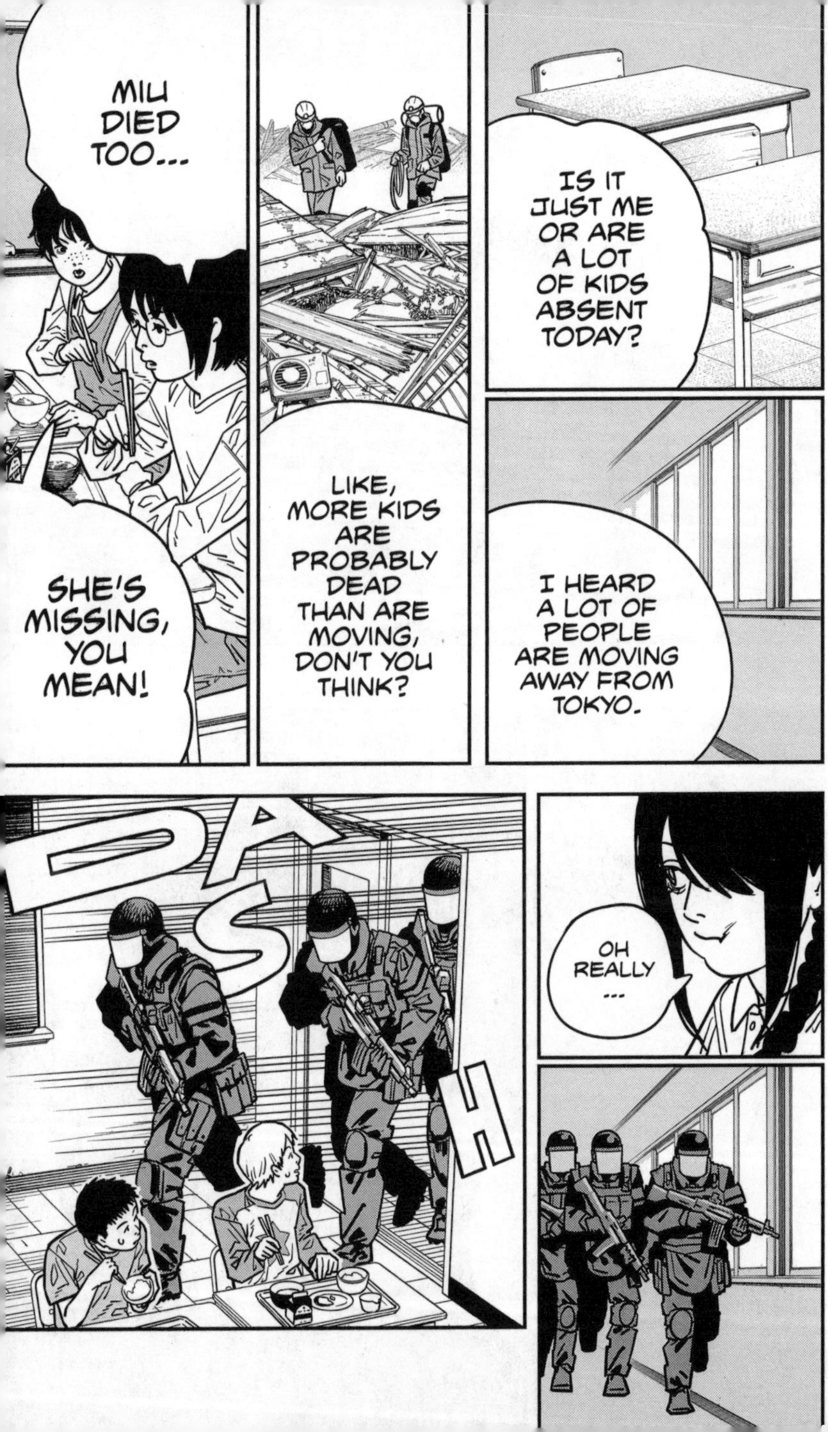
IS IT JUST ME OR ARE A LOT OF KIDS ABSENT TODAY?
I HEARD A LOT OF PEOPLE ARE MOVING AWAY FROM TOKYO.
LIKE, MORE KIDS ARE PROBABLY DEAD THAN ARE MOVING, DON'T YOU THINK?
MIU DIED TOO...
SHE'S MISSING, YOU MEAN!
OH REALLY ...
DASH

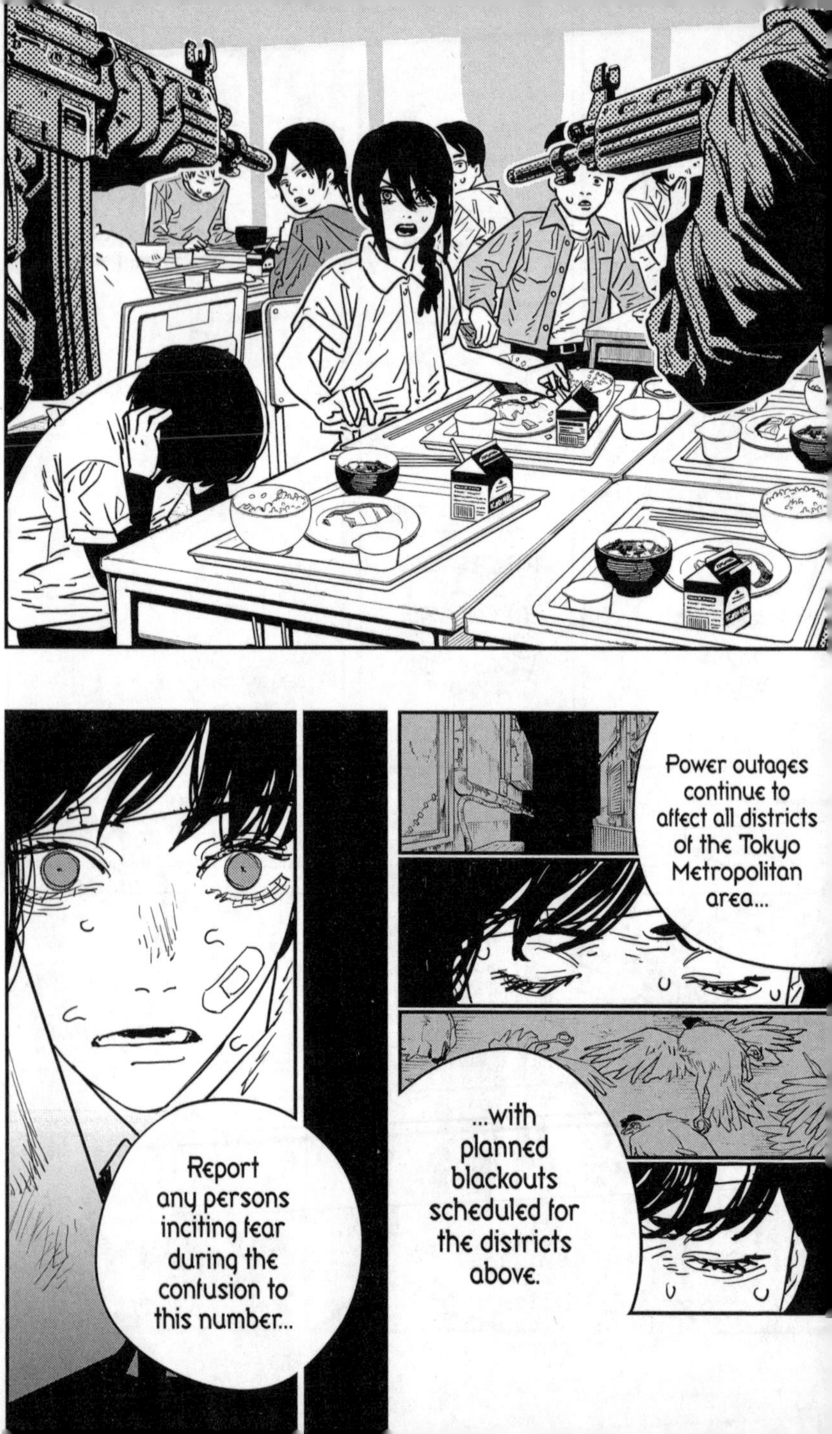
Power outages continue to affect all districts of the Tokyo Metropolitan area...
...with planned blackouts scheduled for the districts above.
Report any persons inciting fear during the confusion to this number...

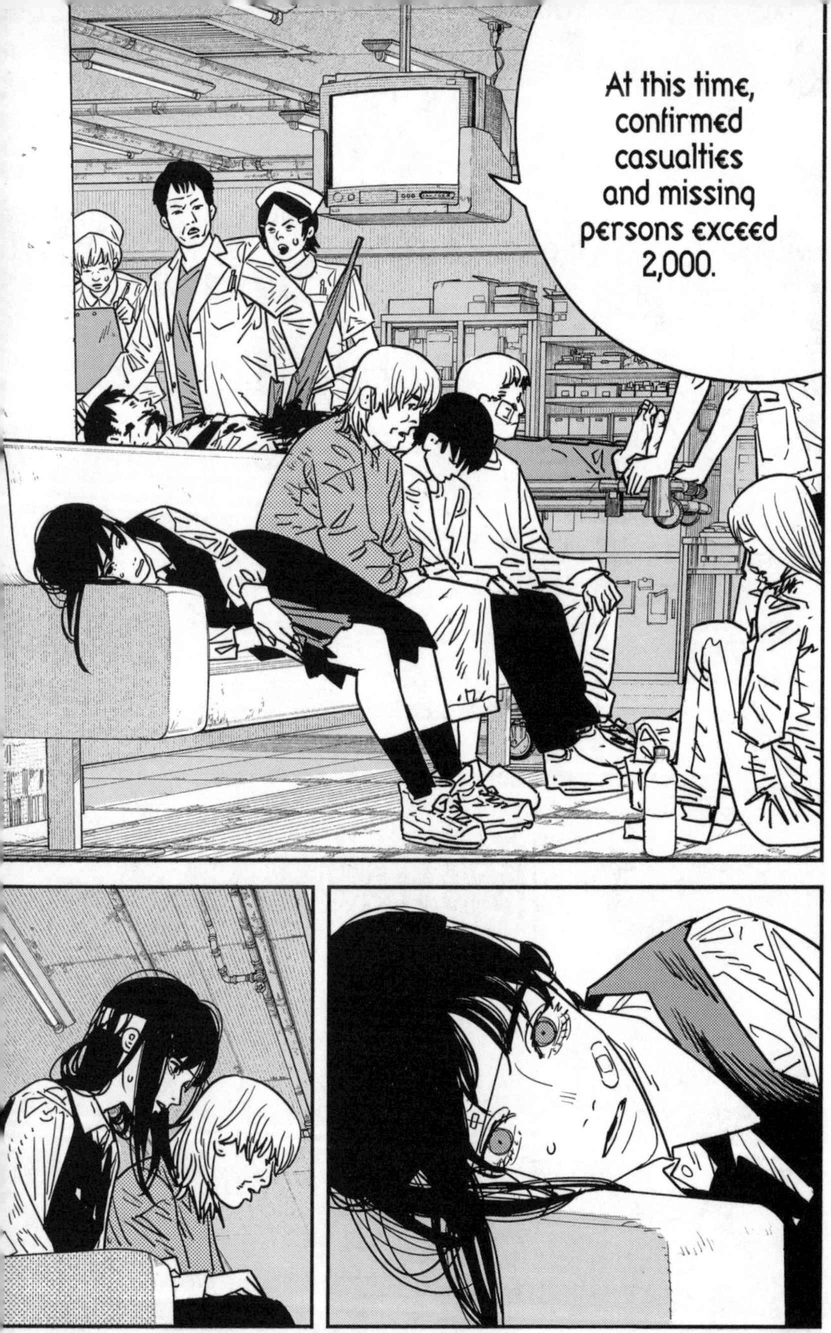
At this time, confirmed casualties and missing persons exceed 2,000.

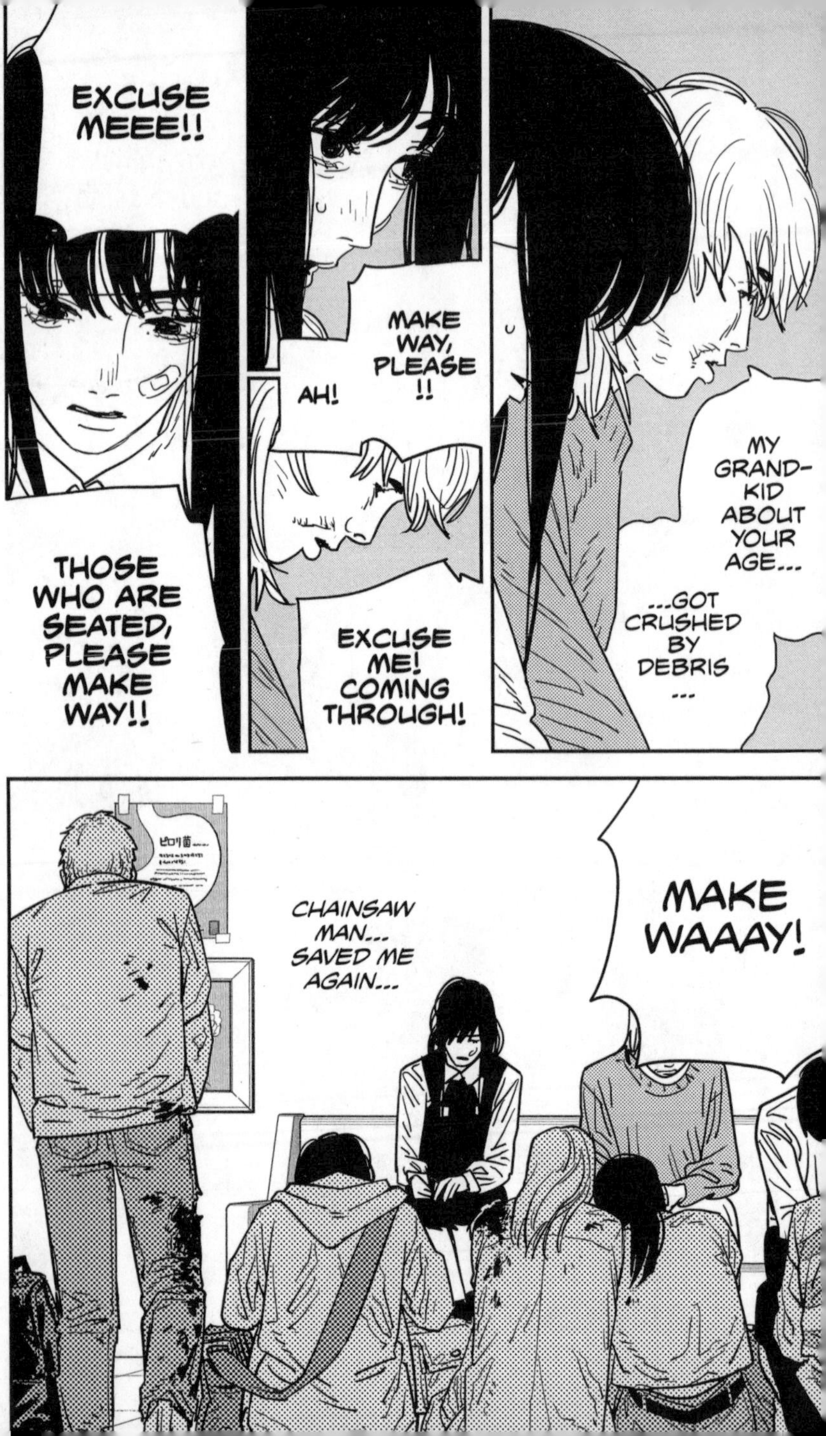
MY GRAND-KID ABOUT YOUR AGE...
...GOT CRUSHED BY DEBRIS ...
MAKE WAY, PLEASE !!
AH!
EXCUSE ME! COMING THROUGH!
EXCUSE MEEE!!
THOSE WHO ARE SEATED, PLEASE MAKE WAY!!
MAKE WAAAY!
CHAINSAW MAN... SAVED ME AGAIN...

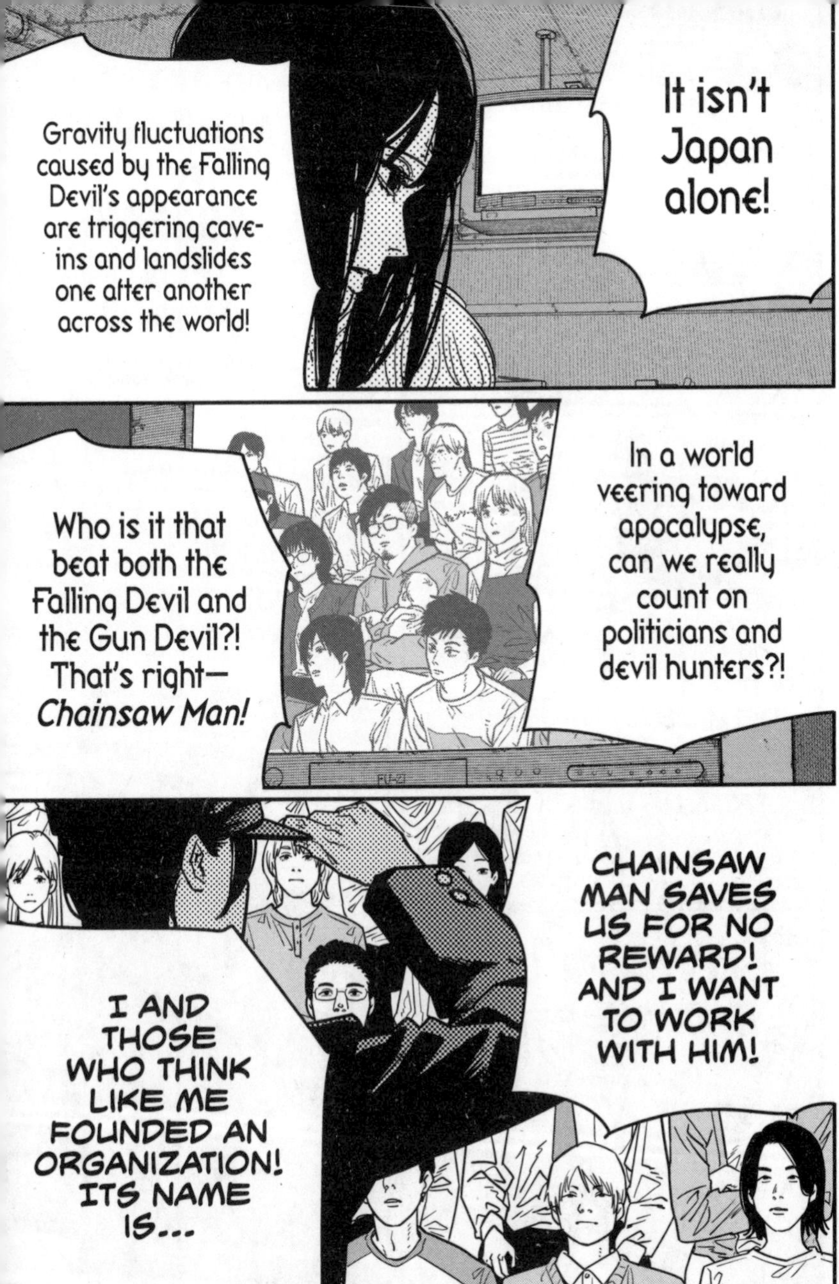
It isn't Japan alone!
Gravity fluctuations caused by the Falling Devil's appearance are triggering cave-ins and landslides one after another across the world!
In a world veering toward apocalypse, can we really count on politicians and devil hunters?!
Who is it that beat both the Falling Devil and the Gun Devil?! That's right—*Chainsaw Man!*
CHAINSAW MAN SAVES US FOR NO REWARD! AND I WANT TO WORK WITH HIM!
I AND THOSE WHO THINK LIKE ME FOUNDED AN ORGANIZATION! ITS NAME IS...

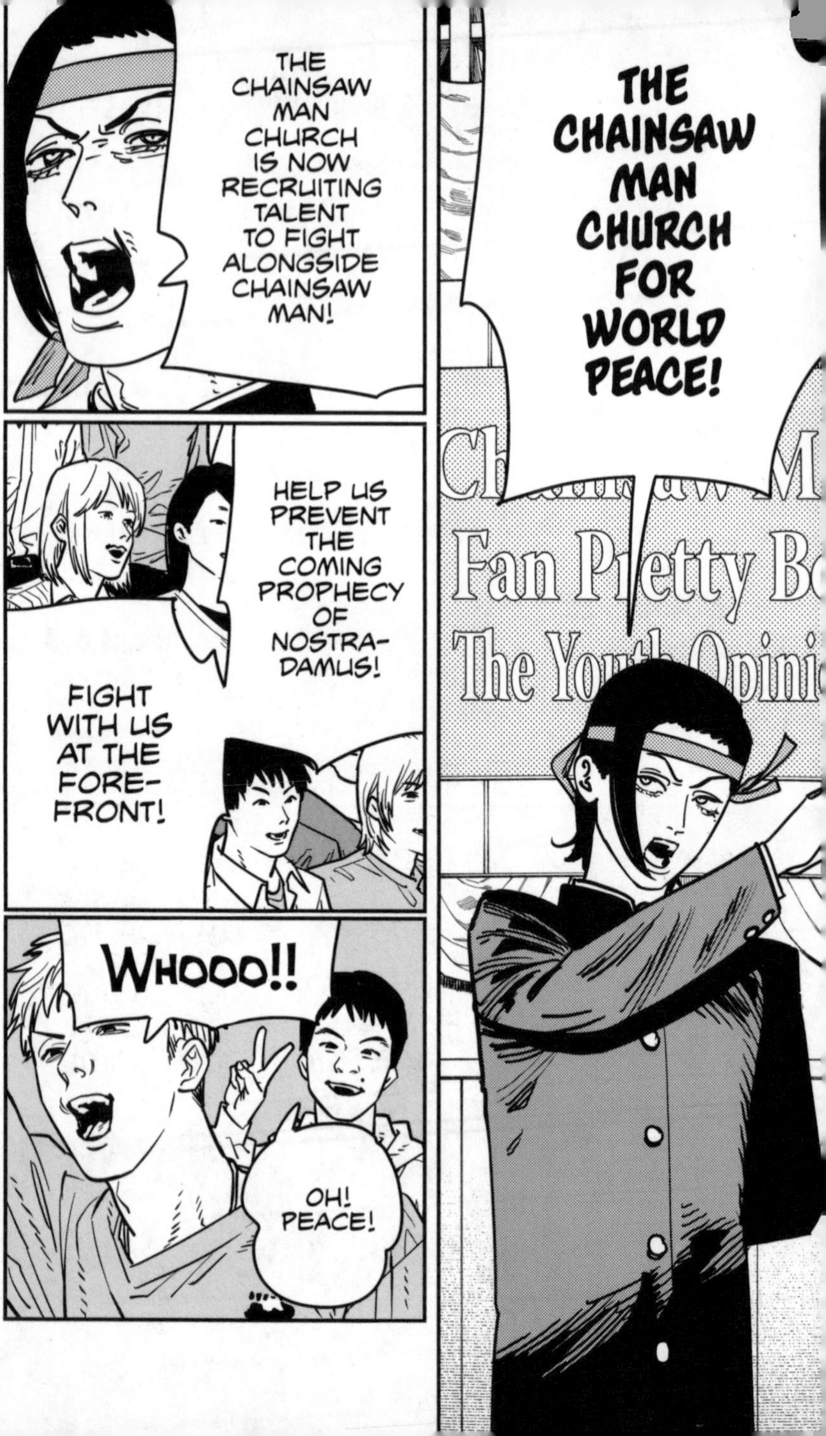
THE CHAINSAW MAN CHURCH FOR WORLD PEACE!
THE CHAINSAW MAN CHURCH IS NOW RECRUITING TALENT TO FIGHT ALONGSIDE CHAINSAW MAN!
HELP US PREVENT THE COMING PROPHECY OF NOSTRA-DAMUS!
FIGHT WITH US AT THE FORE-FRONT!
WHOOO!!
OH! PEACE!

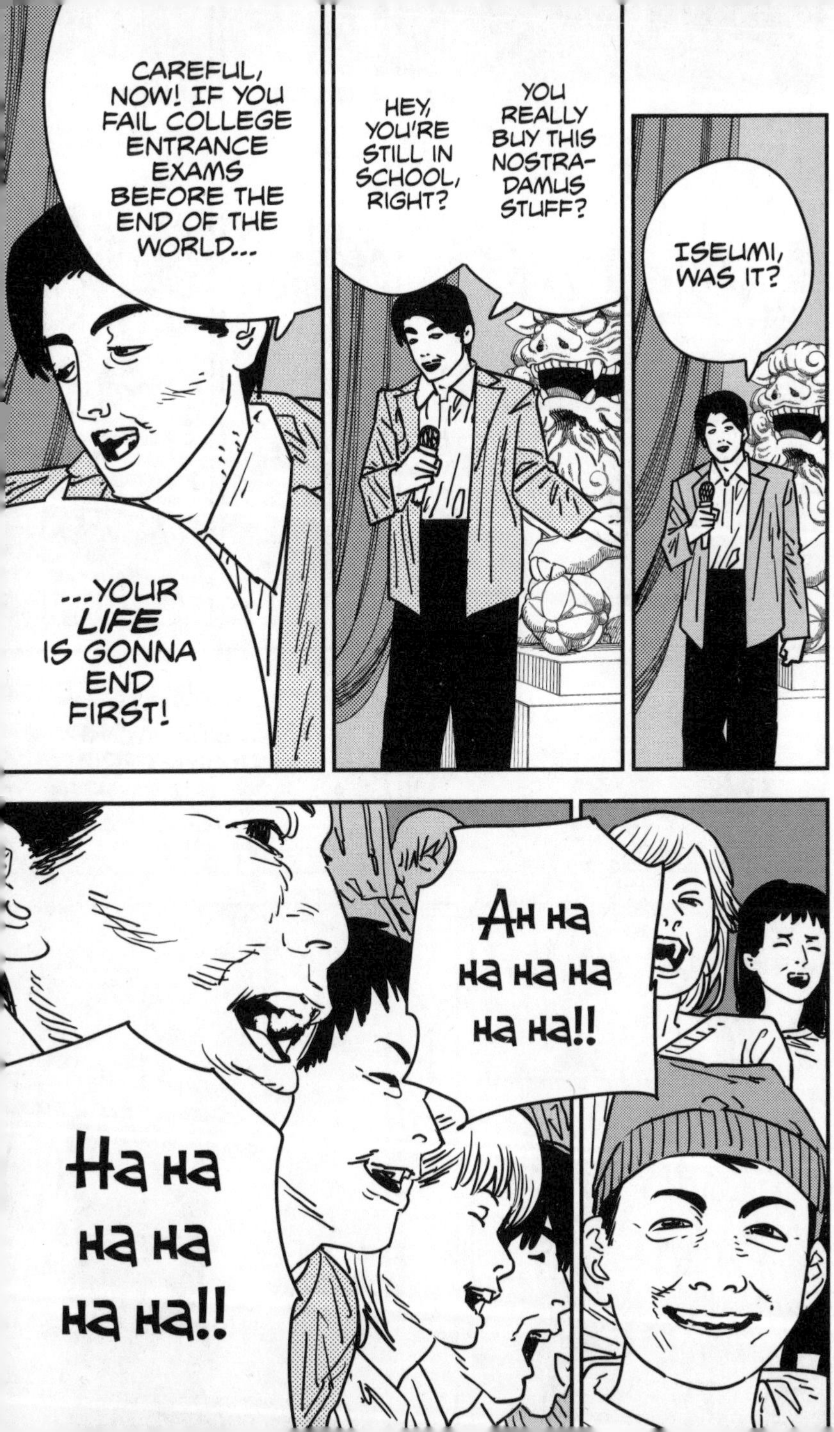
ISEUMI, WAS IT?
YOU REALLY BUY THIS NOSTRA-DAMUS STUFF?
HEY, YOU'RE STILL IN SCHOOL, RIGHT?
CAREFUL, NOW! IF YOU FAIL COLLEGE ENTRANCE EXAMS BEFORE THE END OF THE WORLD...
...YOUR *LIFE* IS GONNA END FIRST!
AH HA HA HA HA HA HA!!
HA HA HA HA HA HA!!

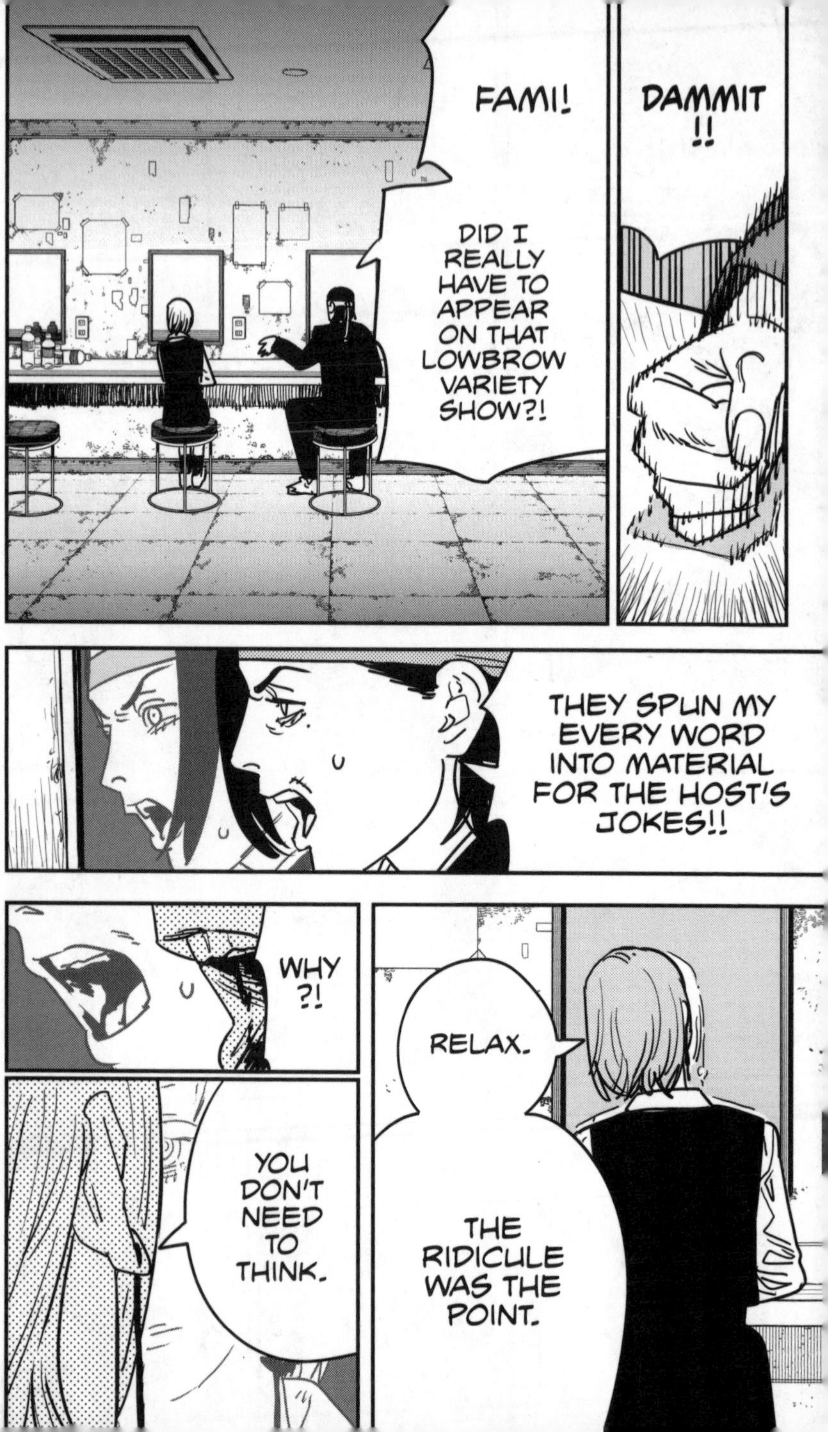
DAMMIT!!
FAMI!
DID I REALLY HAVE TO APPEAR ON THAT LOWBROW VARIETY SHOW?!
THEY SPUN MY EVERY WORD INTO MATERIAL FOR THE HOST'S JOKES!!
WHY?!
RELAX.
YOU DON'T NEED TO THINK.
THE RIDICULE WAS THE POINT.

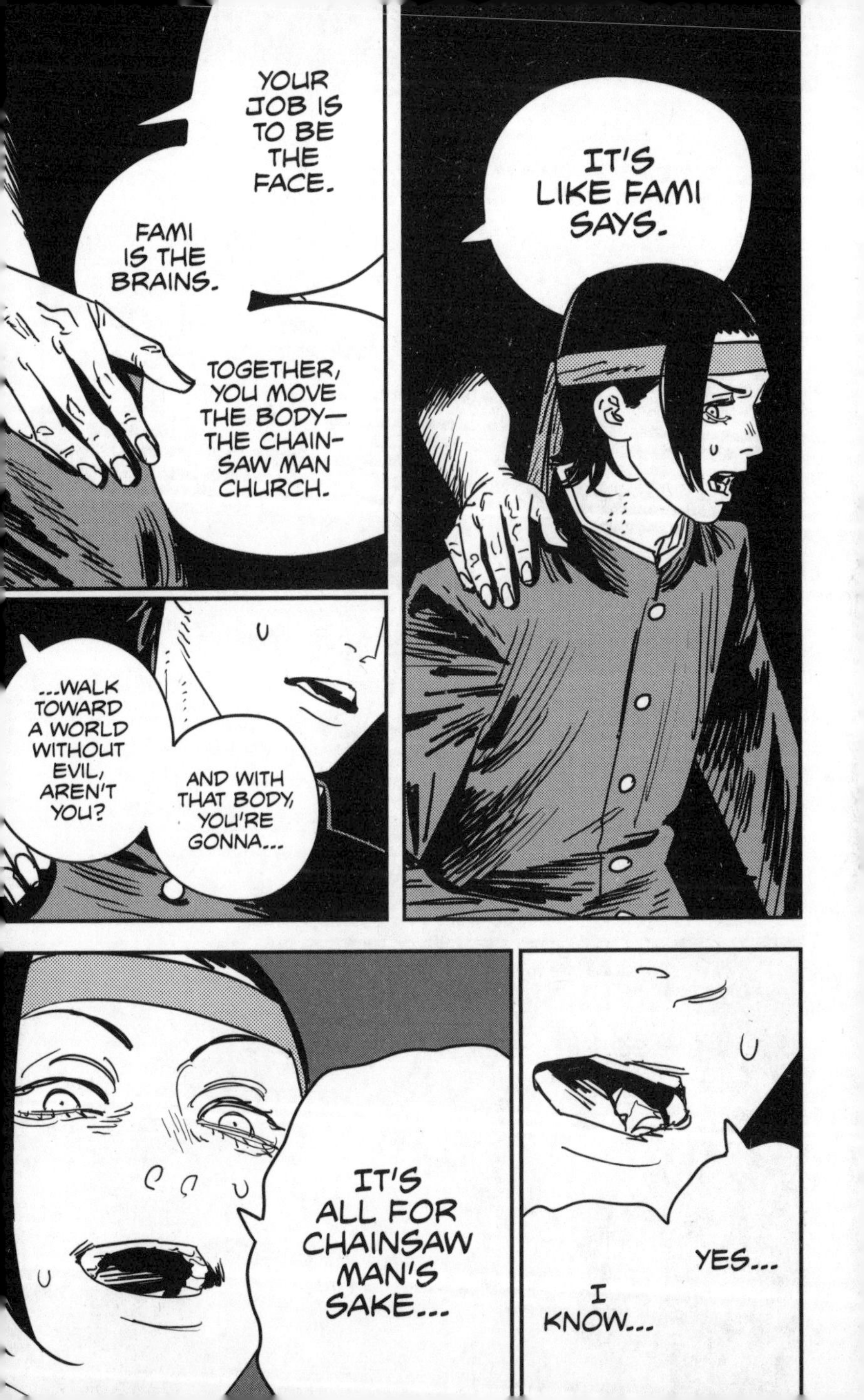
YOUR JOB IS TO BE THE FACE.
FAMI IS THE BRAINS.
TOGETHER, YOU MOVE THE BODY— THE CHAIN-SAW MAN CHURCH.
AND WITH THAT BODY, YOU'RE GONNA...
...WALK TOWARD A WORLD WITHOUT EVIL, AREN'T YOU?
IT'S LIKE FAMI SAYS.
IT'S ALL FOR CHAINSAW MAN'S SAKE...
YES... I KNOW...

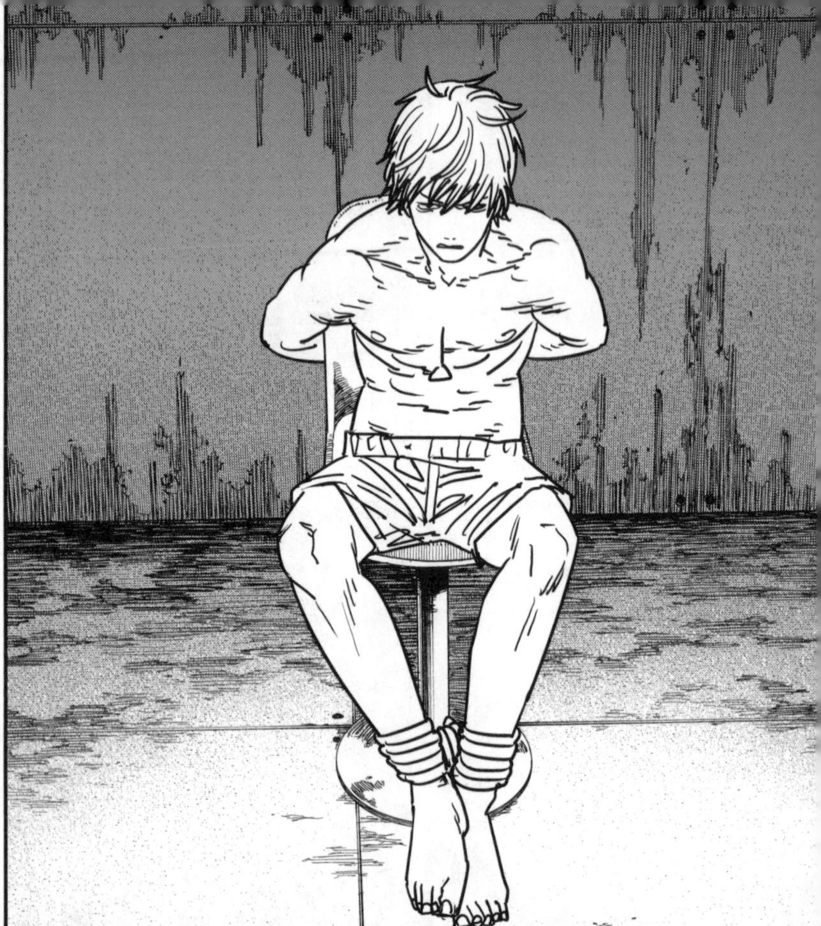

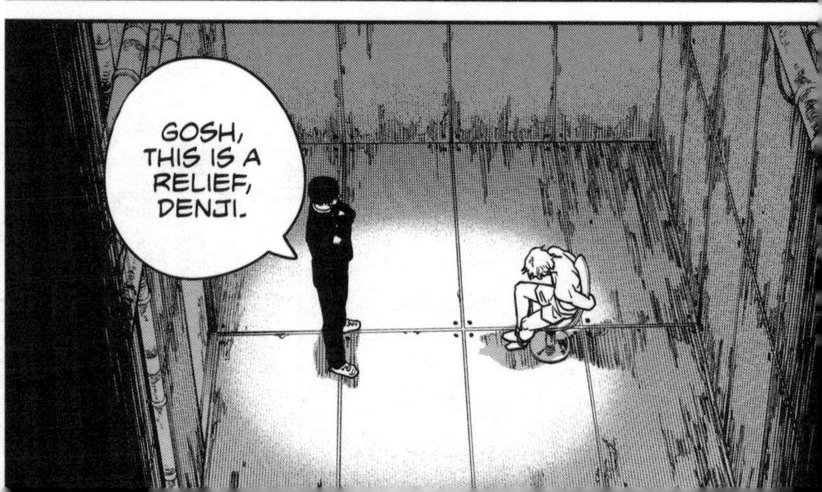
GOSH, THIS IS A RELIEF, DENJI.

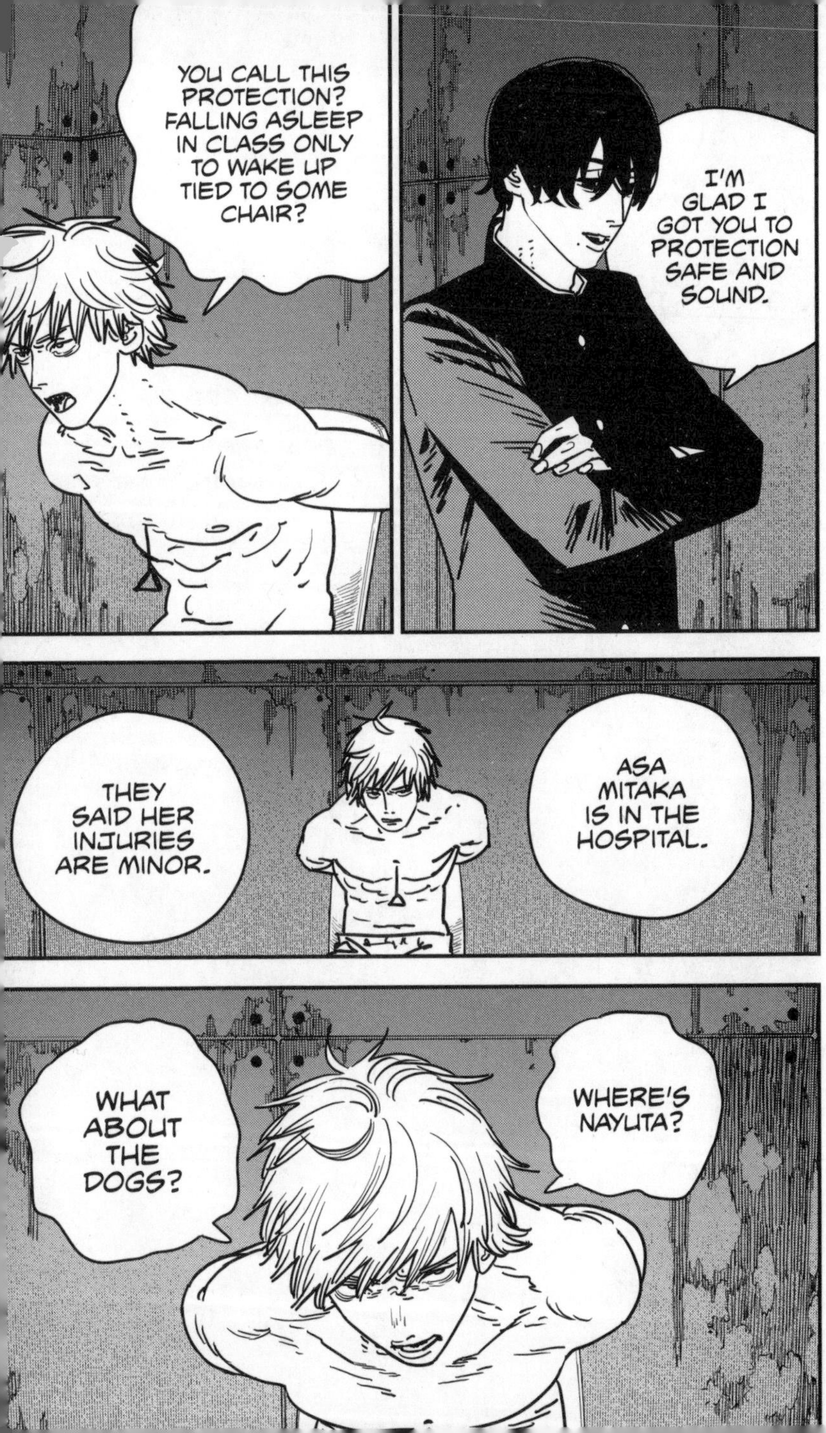
I'M GLAD I GOT YOU TO PROTECTION SAFE AND SOUND.
YOU CALL THIS PROTECTION? FALLING ASLEEP IN CLASS ONLY TO WAKE UP TIED TO SOME CHAIR?
ASA MITAKA IS IN THE HOSPITAL.
THEY SAID HER INJURIES ARE MINOR.
WHERE'S NAYUTA?
WHAT ABOUT THE DOGS?

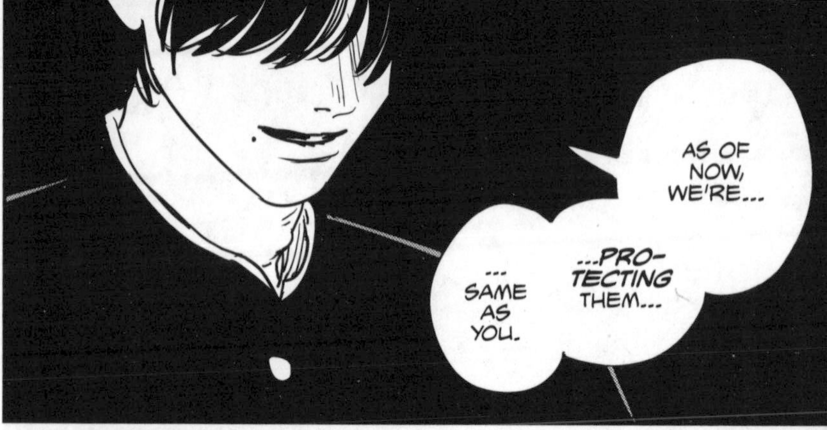
AS OF NOW, WE'RE...
...PROTECTING THEM...
... SAME AS YOU.
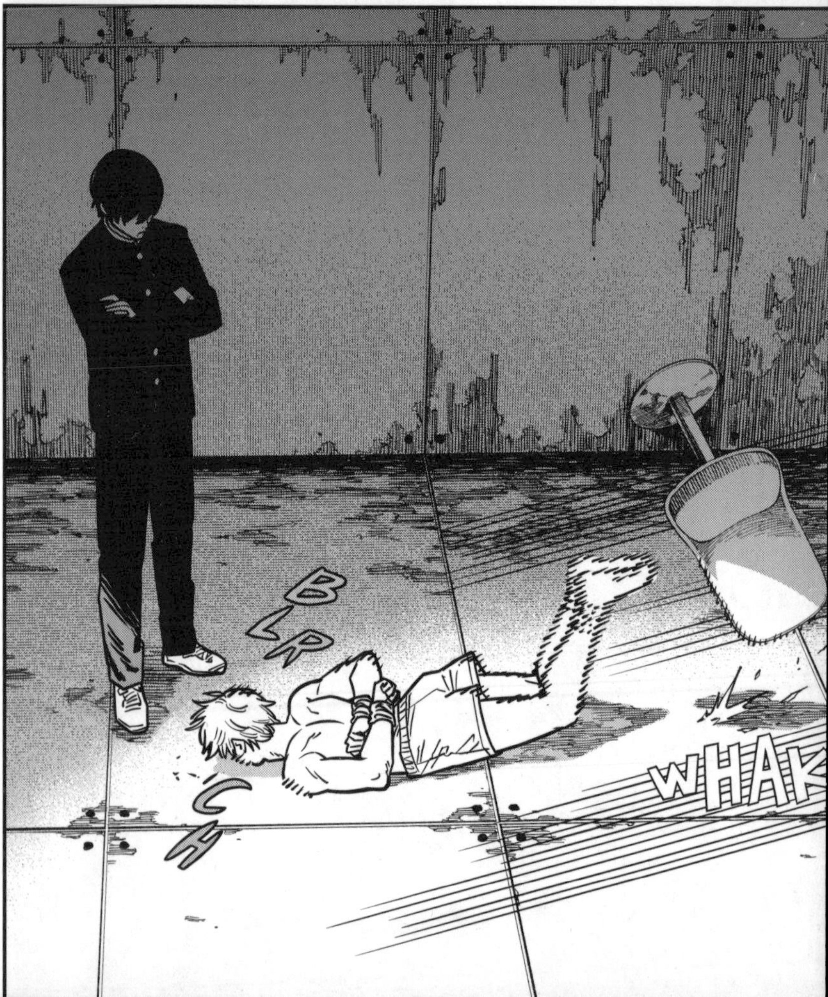
WHAK
BLRCH

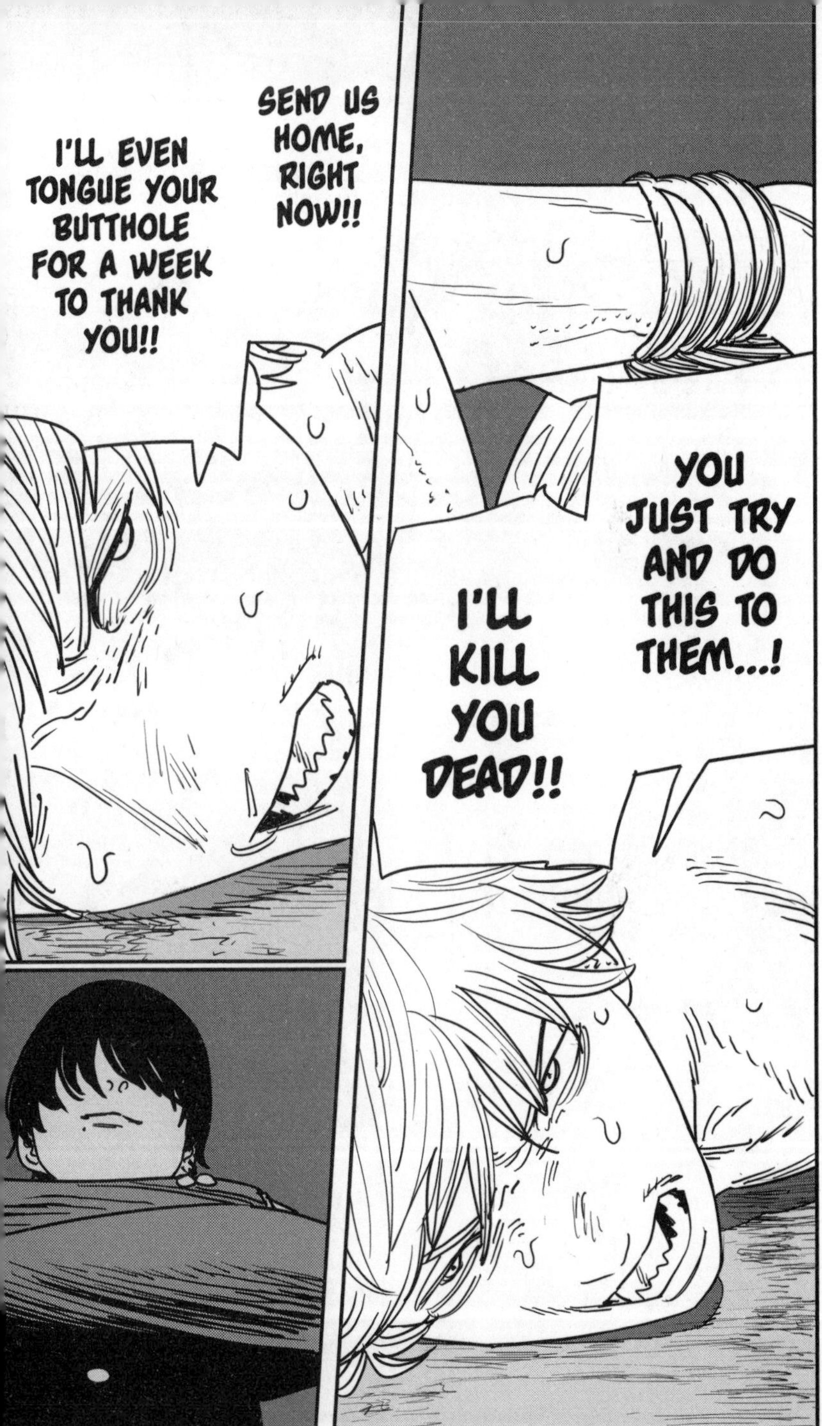
YOU JUST TRY AND DO THIS TO THEM...!
I'LL KILL YOU DEAD!!
SEND US HOME, RIGHT NOW!!
I'LL EVEN TONGUE YOUR BUTTHOLE FOR A WEEK TO THANK YOU!!

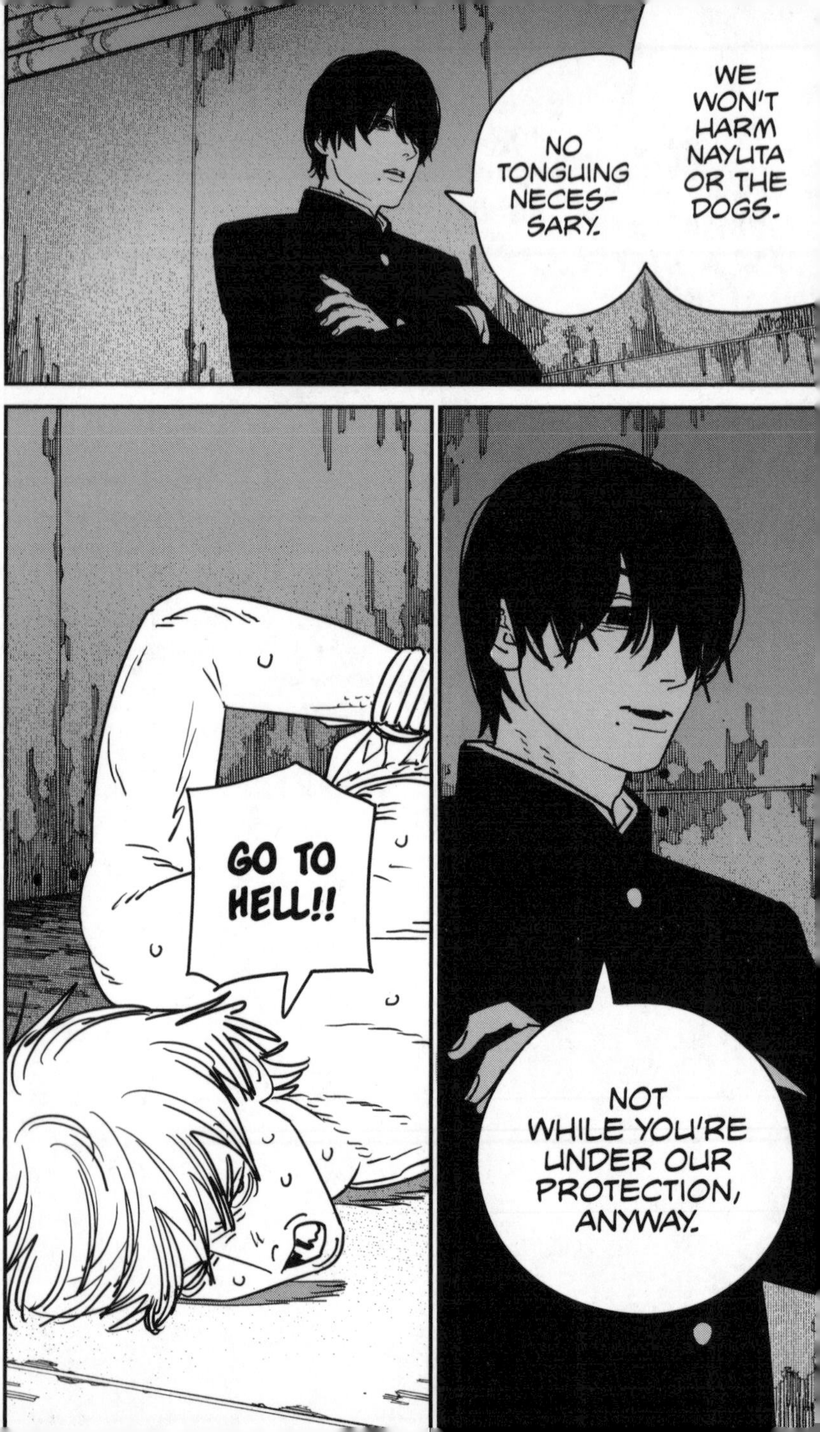
WE WON'T HARM NAYUTA OR THE DOGS.
NO TONGUING NECES-SARY.
NOT WHILE YOU'RE UNDER OUR PROTECTION, ANYWAY.
GO TO HELL!!

Chain saw man

Chapter 133: Chainsaw Man Protest

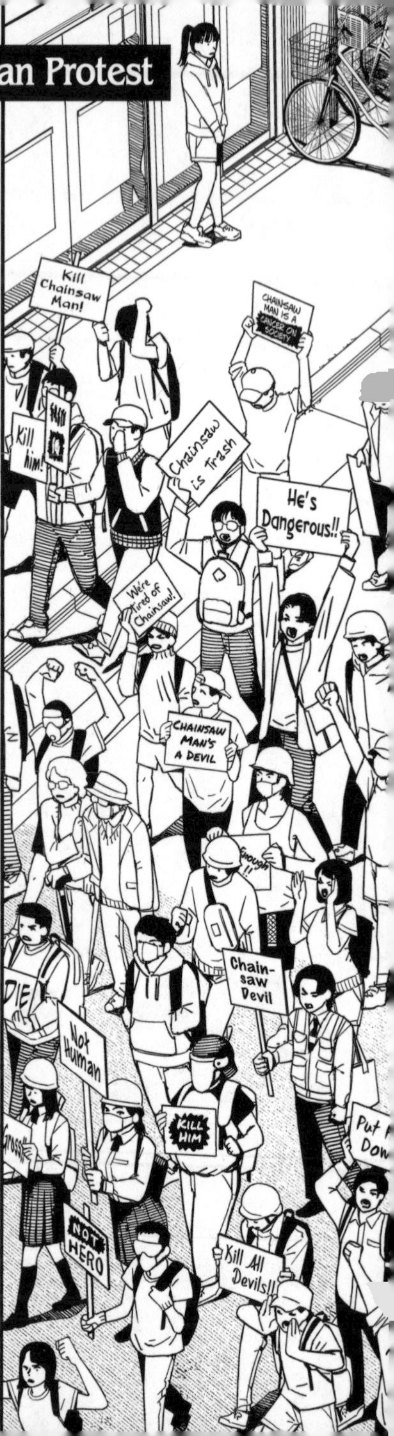
Kill Chainsaw Man!
CHAINSAW MAN IS A CANCER ON SOCIETY
Kill him!
Chainsaw is Trash
He's Dangerous!!
We're tired of Chainsaw!
CHAINSAW MAN'S A DEVIL
Enough!!
Chain-saw Devil
DIE
Not Human
KILL HIM
Gross!!
NOT HERO
Kill All Devils!!

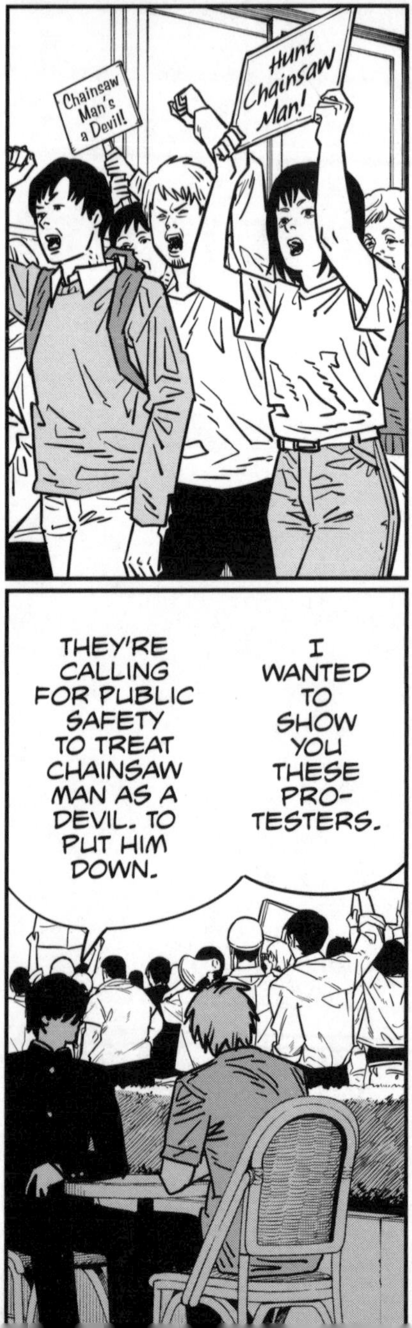
Hunt Chainsaw Man!
Chainsaw Man's a Devil!
I WANTED TO SHOW YOU THESE PRO-TESTERS. THEY'RE CALLING FOR PUBLIC SAFETY TO TREAT CHAINSAW MAN AS A DEVIL. TO PUT HIM DOWN.

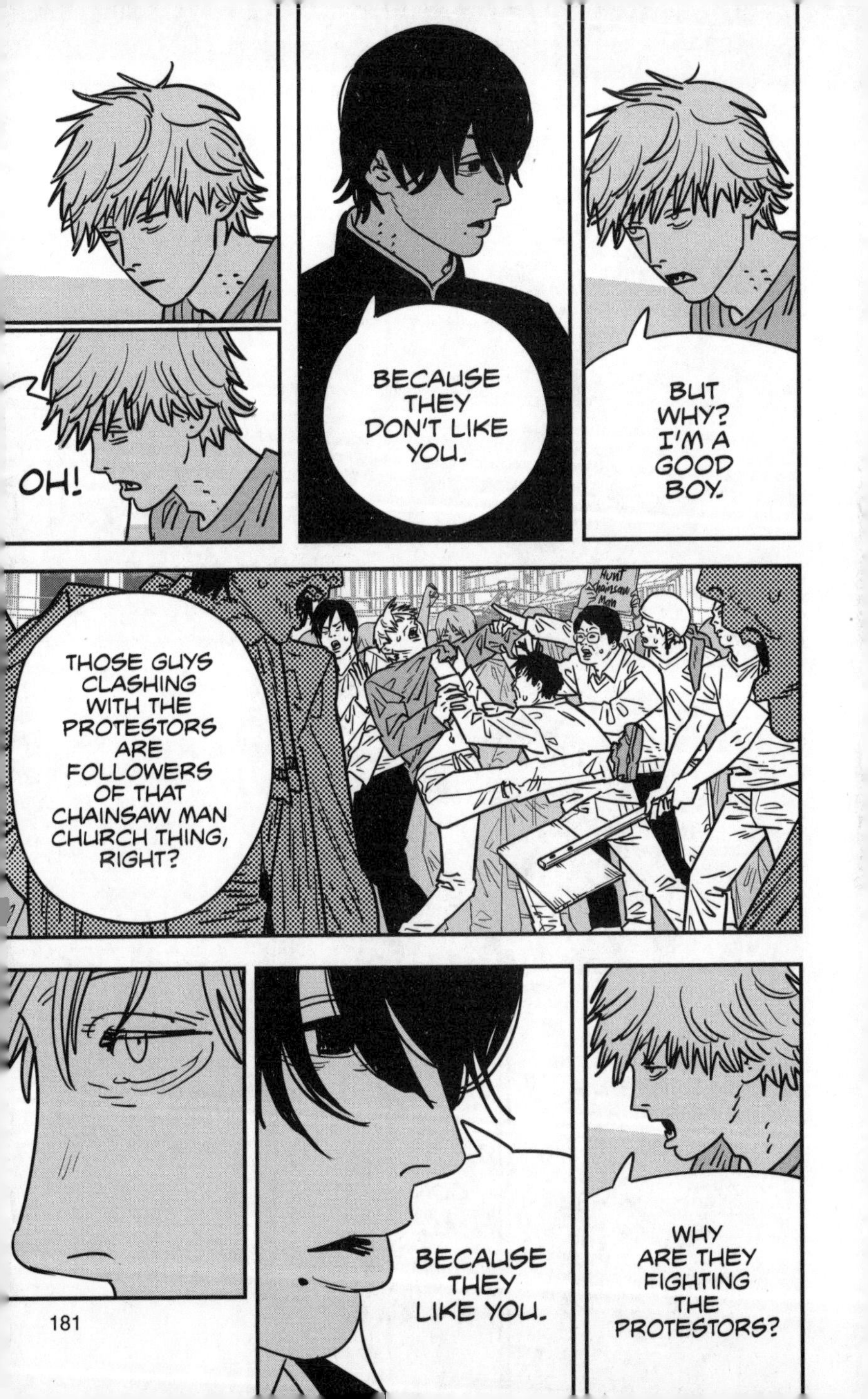
BUT WHY? I'M A GOOD BOY.
BECAUSE THEY DON'T LIKE YOU.
OH!
Hunt Chainsaw Man
THOSE GUYS CLASHING WITH THE PROTESTORS ARE FOLLOWERS OF THAT CHAINSAW MAN CHURCH THING, RIGHT?
WHY ARE THEY FIGHTING THE PROTESTORS?
BECAUSE THEY LIKE YOU.

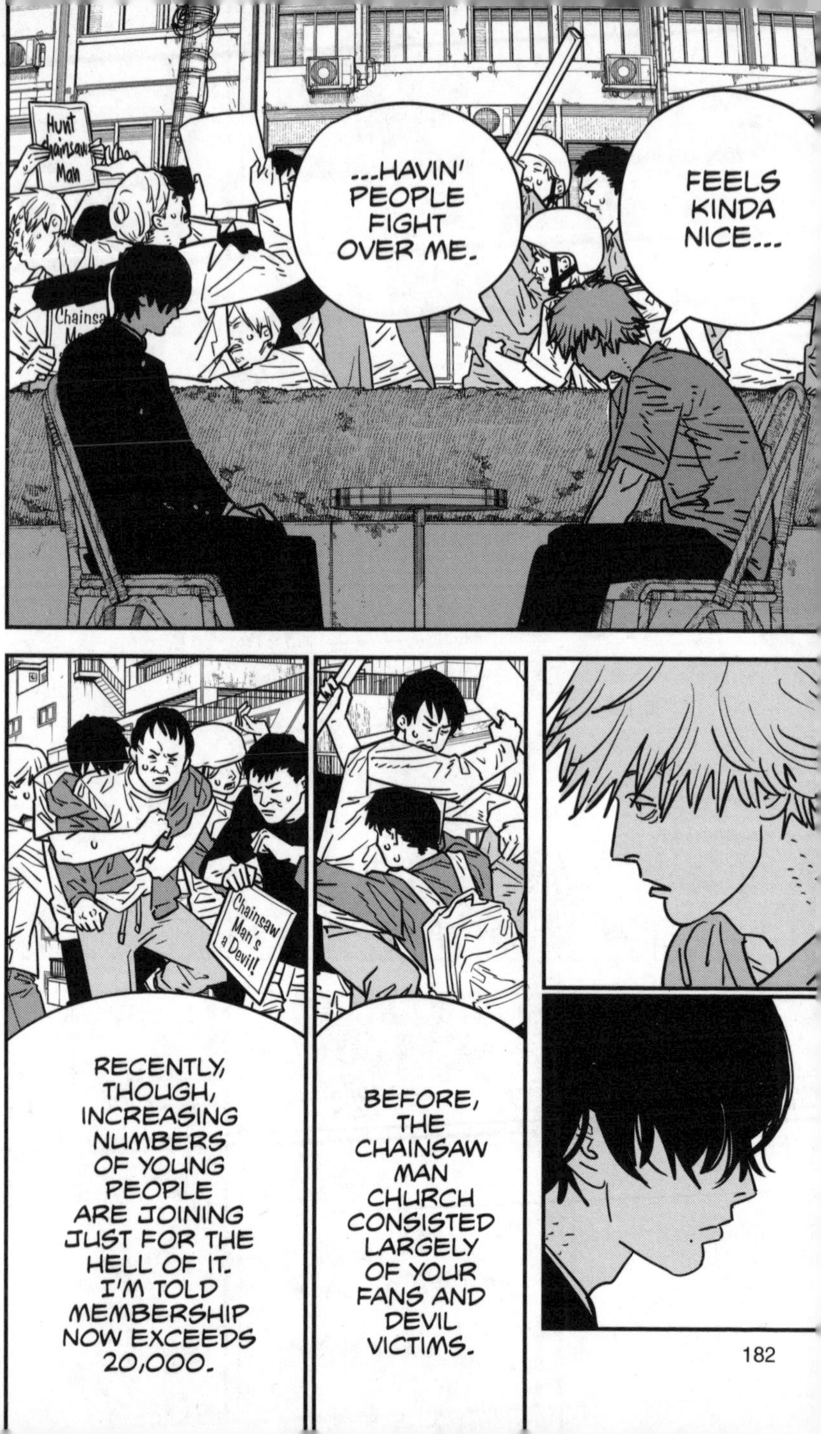
FEELS KINDA NICE...
...HAVIN' PEOPLE FIGHT OVER ME.
Hunt chainsaw Man
Chainsaw Man's a Devil!
BEFORE, THE CHAINSAW MAN CHURCH CONSISTED LARGELY OF YOUR FANS AND DEVIL VICTIMS.
RECENTLY, THOUGH, INCREASING NUMBERS OF YOUNG PEOPLE ARE JOINING JUST FOR THE HELL OF IT. I'M TOLD MEMBERSHIP NOW EXCEEDS 20,000.

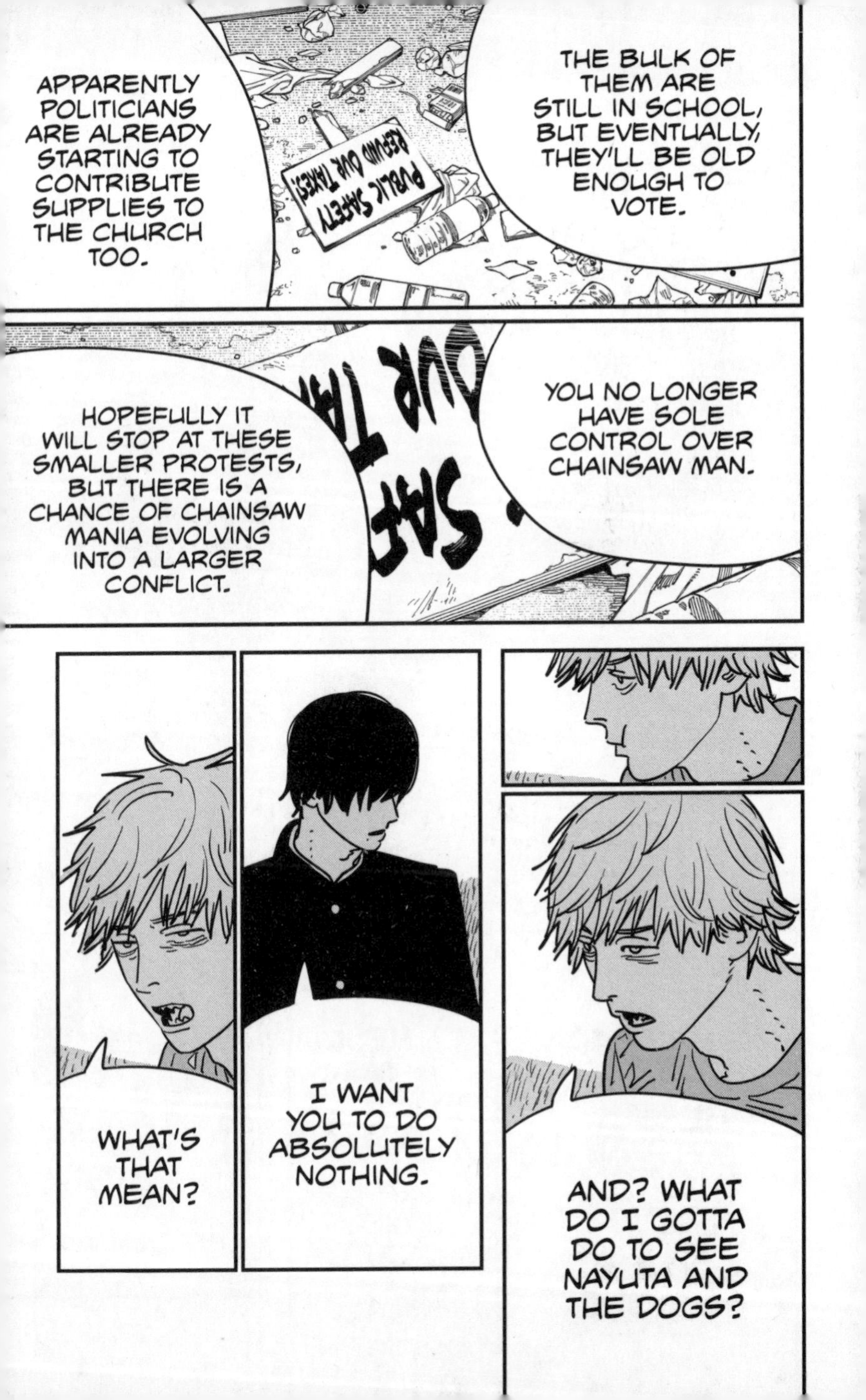
THE BULK OF THEM ARE STILL IN SCHOOL, BUT EVENTUALLY, THEY'LL BE OLD ENOUGH TO VOTE.
PUBLIC SAFETY
REFUND OUR TAXES!
APPARENTLY POLITICIANS ARE ALREADY STARTING TO CONTRIBUTE SUPPLIES TO THE CHURCH TOO.
YOU NO LONGER HAVE SOLE CONTROL OVER CHAINSAW MAN.
HOPEFULLY IT WILL STOP AT THESE SMALLER PROTESTS, BUT THERE IS A CHANCE OF CHAINSAW MANIA EVOLVING INTO A LARGER CONFLICT.
AND? WHAT DO I GOTTA DO TO SEE NAYUTA AND THE DOGS?
I WANT YOU TO DO ABSOLUTELY NOTHING.
WHAT'S THAT MEAN?

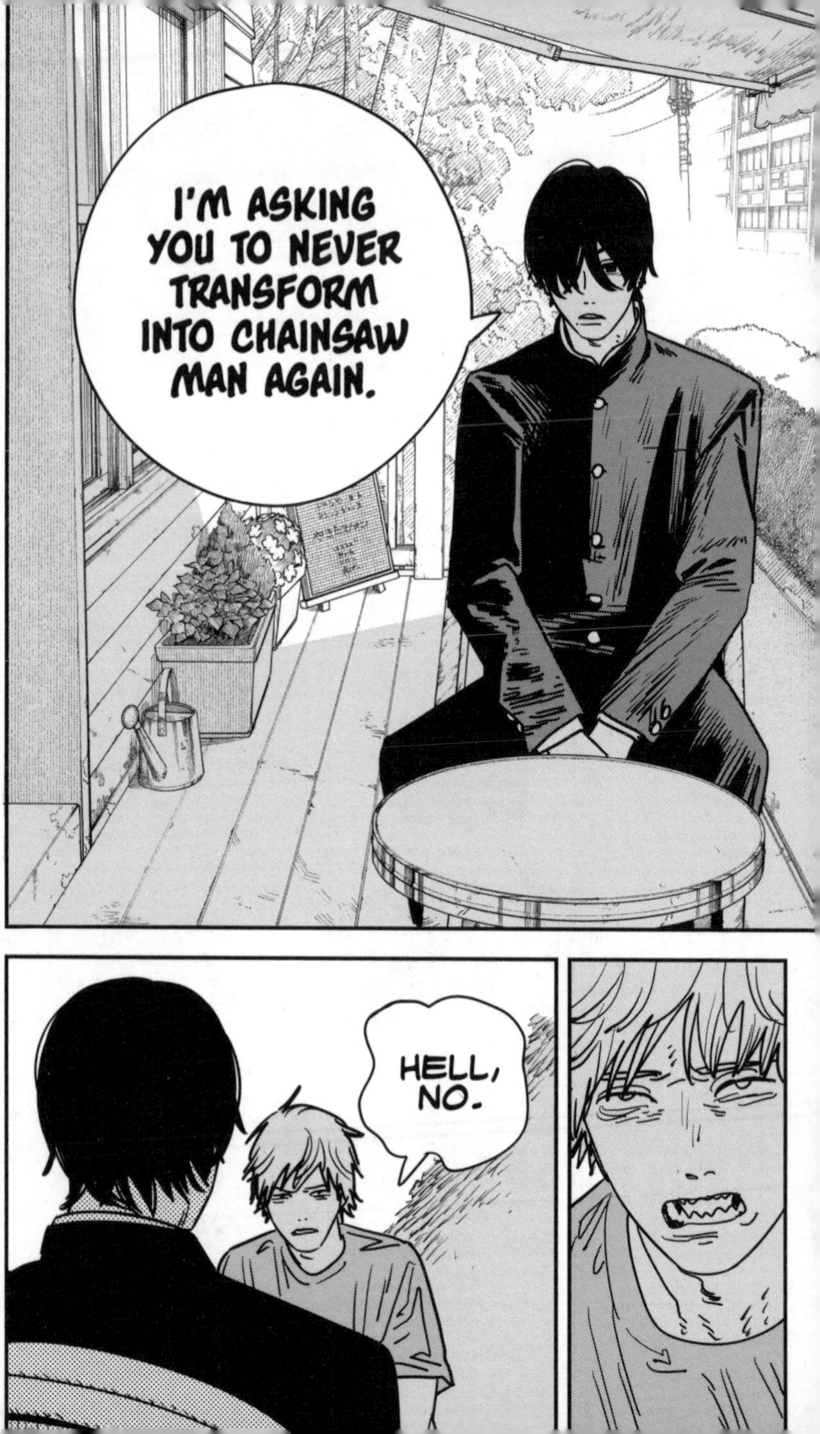
I'M ASKING YOU TO NEVER TRANSFORM INTO CHAINSAW MAN AGAIN.
HELL, NO.

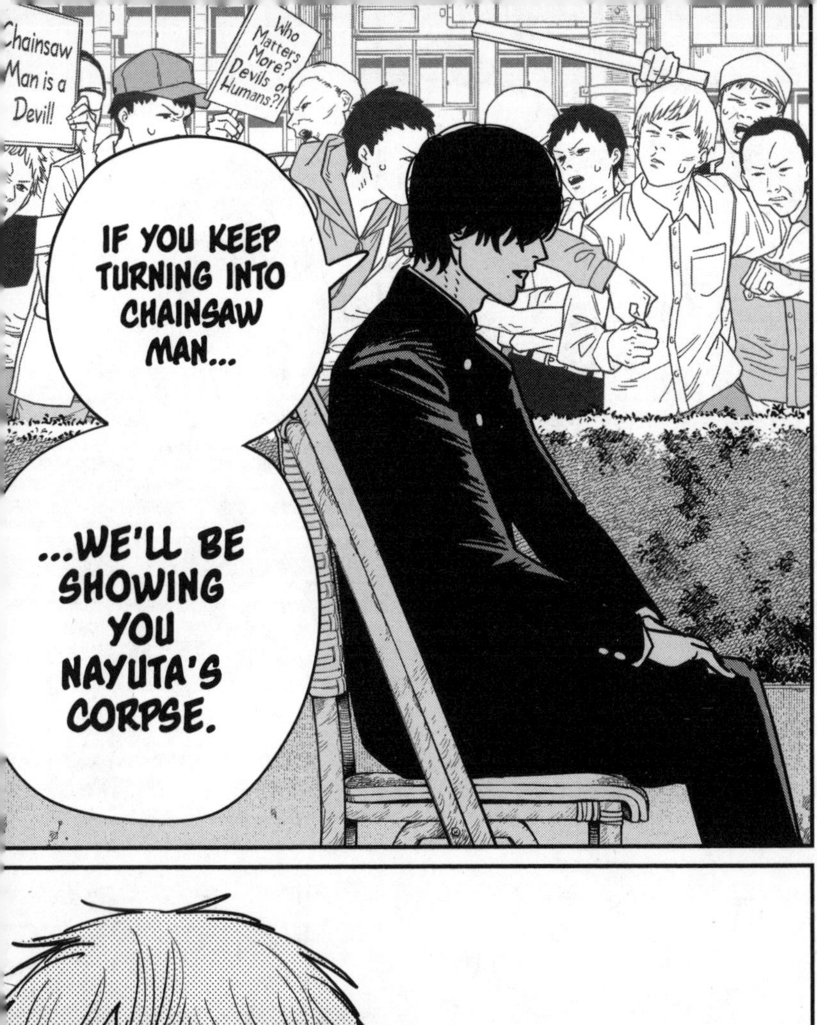
Who Matters More? Devils or Humans?!
Chainsaw Man is a Devil!
IF YOU KEEP TURNING INTO CHAINSAW MAN...
...WE'LL BE SHOWING YOU NAYUTA'S CORPSE.
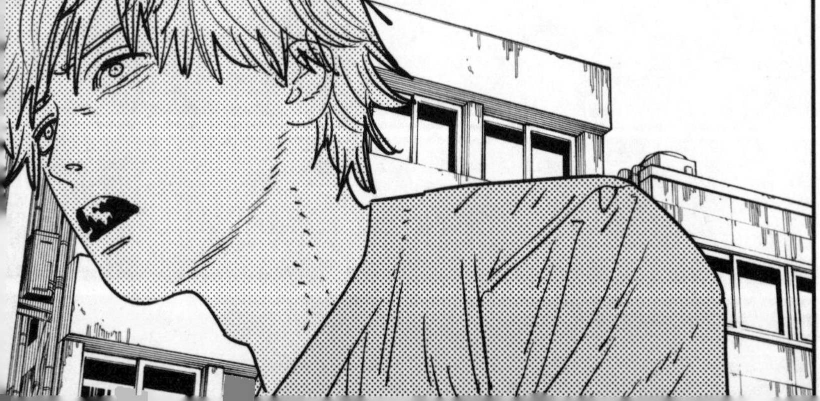

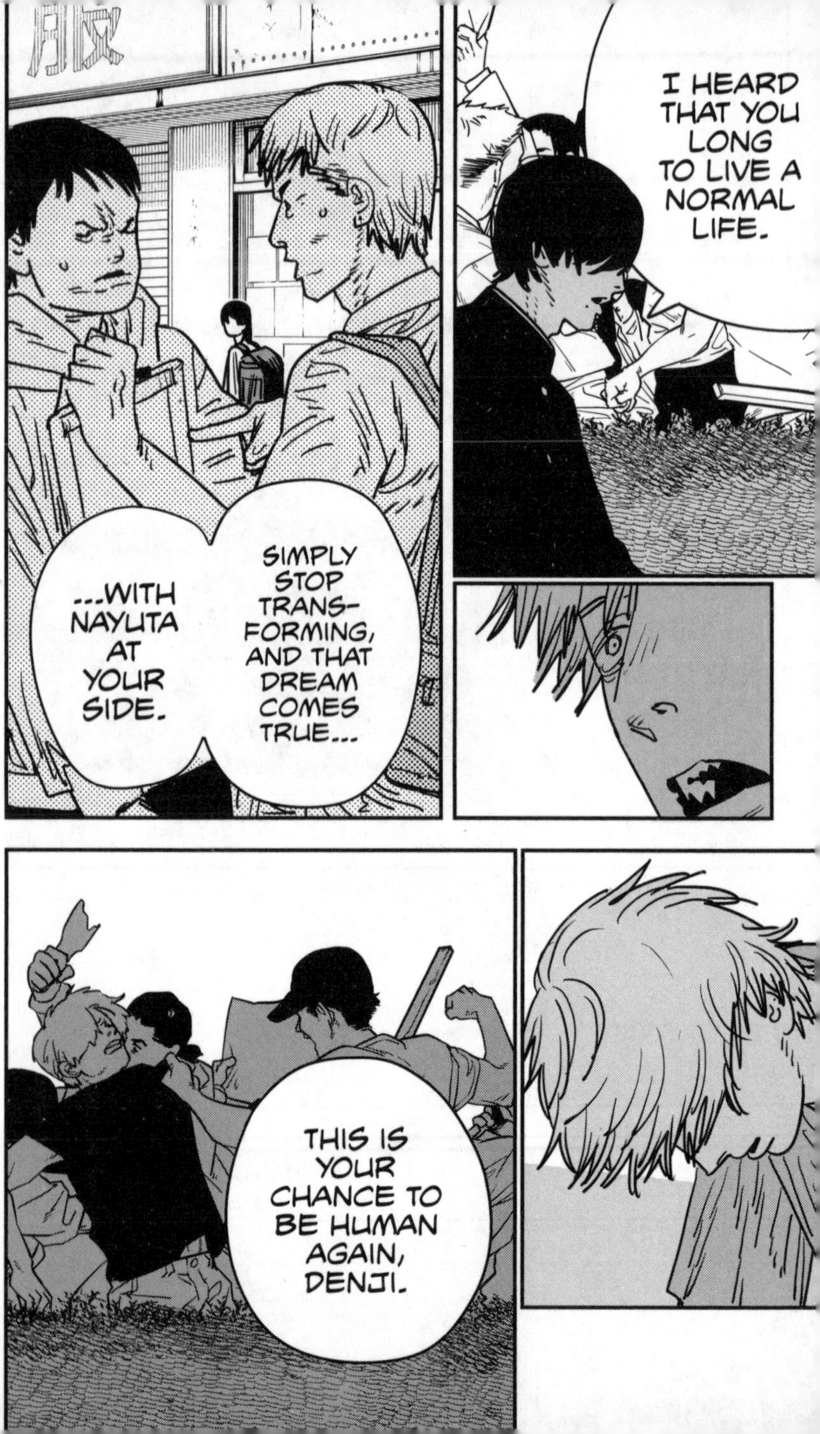
I HEARD THAT YOU LONG TO LIVE A NORMAL LIFE.
SIMPLY STOP TRANS-FORMING, AND THAT DREAM COMES TRUE...
...WITH NAYUTA AT YOUR SIDE.
THIS IS YOUR CHANCE TO BE HUMAN AGAIN, DENJI.

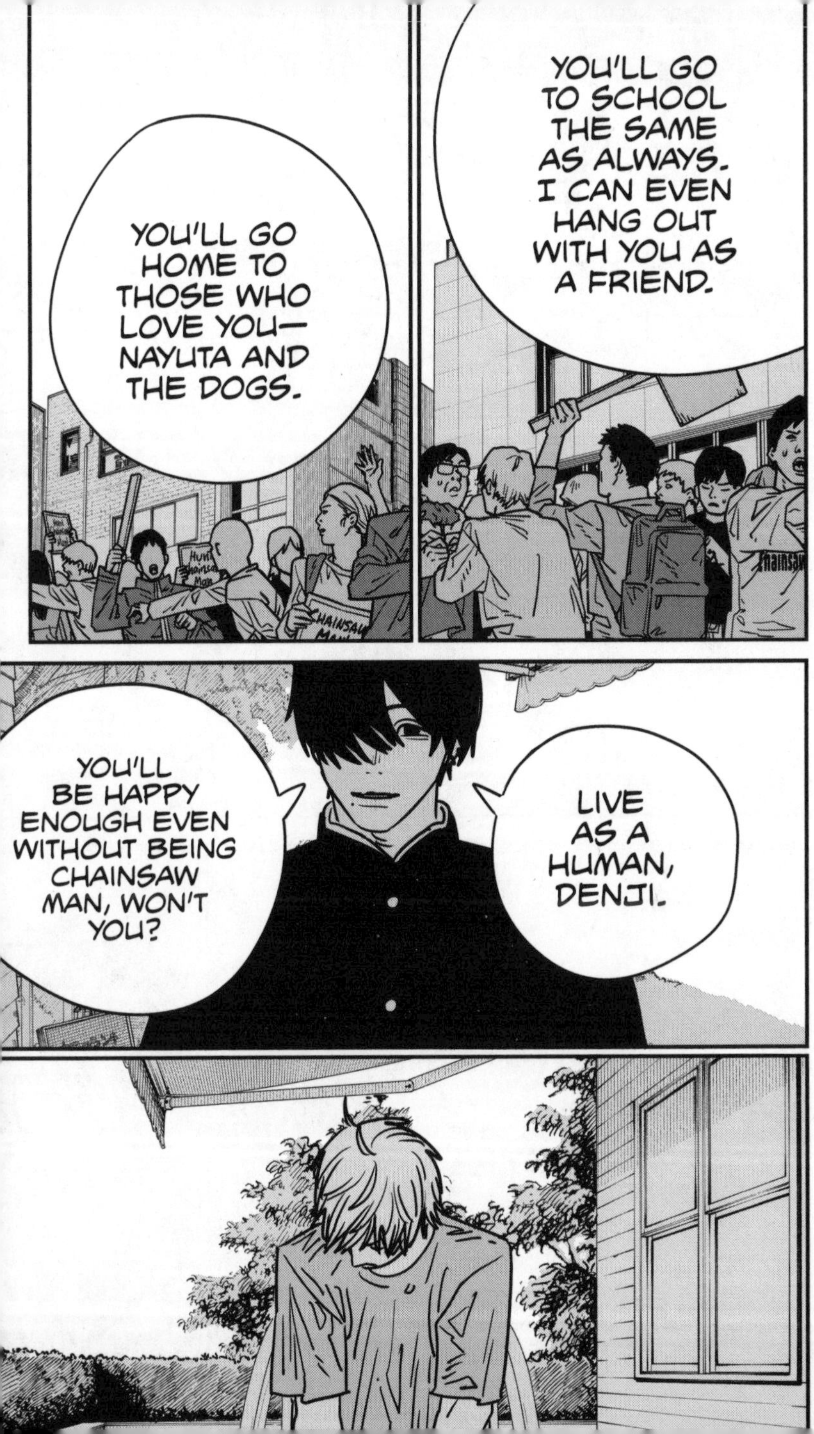
YOU'LL GO TO SCHOOL THE SAME AS ALWAYS. I CAN EVEN HANG OUT WITH YOU AS A FRIEND.
YOU'LL GO HOME TO THOSE WHO LOVE YOU—NAYUTA AND THE DOGS.
LIVE AS A HUMAN, DENJI.
YOU'LL BE HAPPY ENOUGH EVEN WITHOUT BEING CHAINSAW MAN, WON'T YOU?

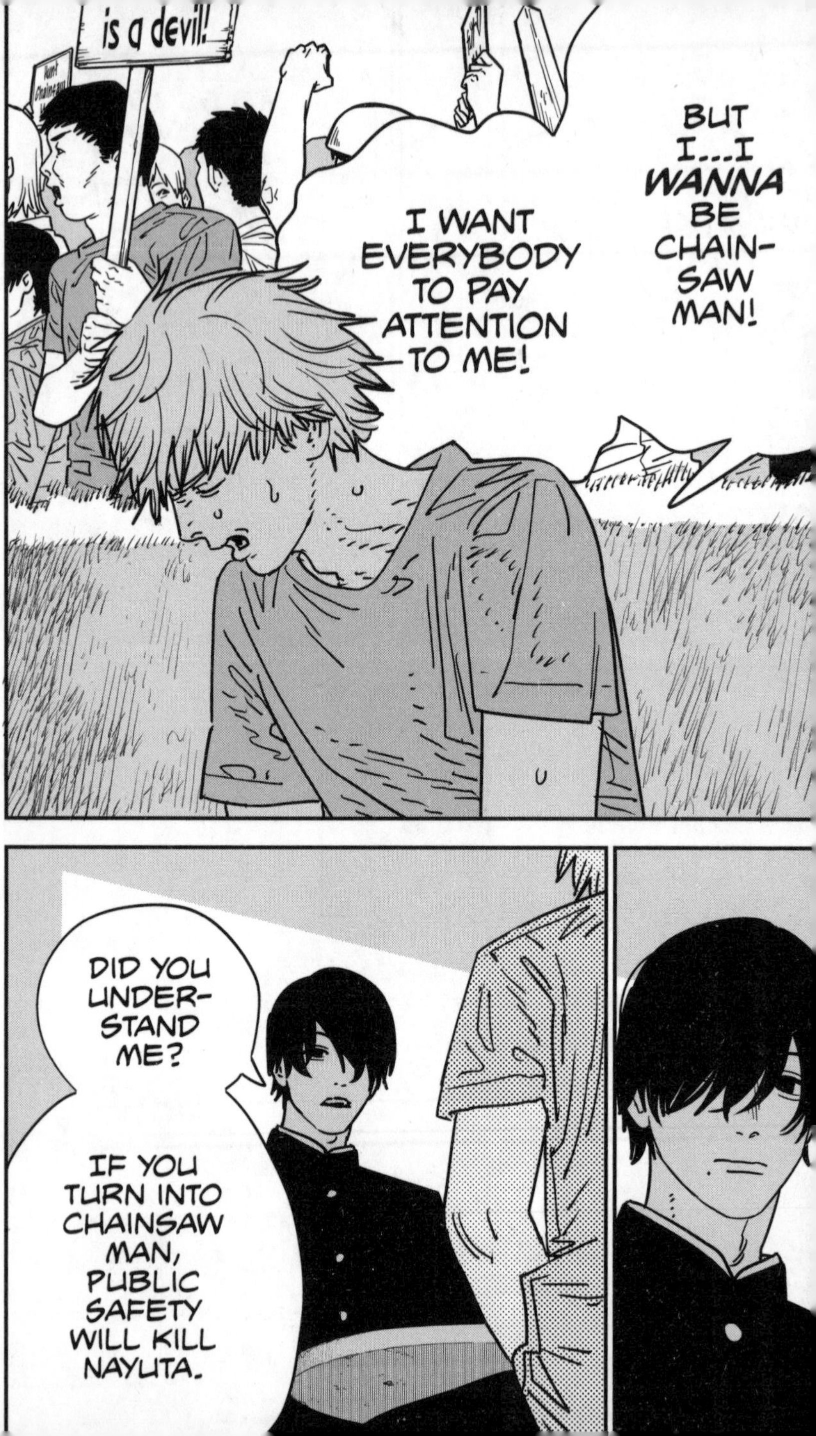
is a devil!
BUT I...I *WANNA* BE CHAINSAW MAN!
I WANT EVERYBODY TO PAY ATTENTION TO ME!
DID YOU UNDERSTAND ME?
IF YOU TURN INTO CHAINSAW MAN, PUBLIC SAFETY WILL KILL NAYUTA.

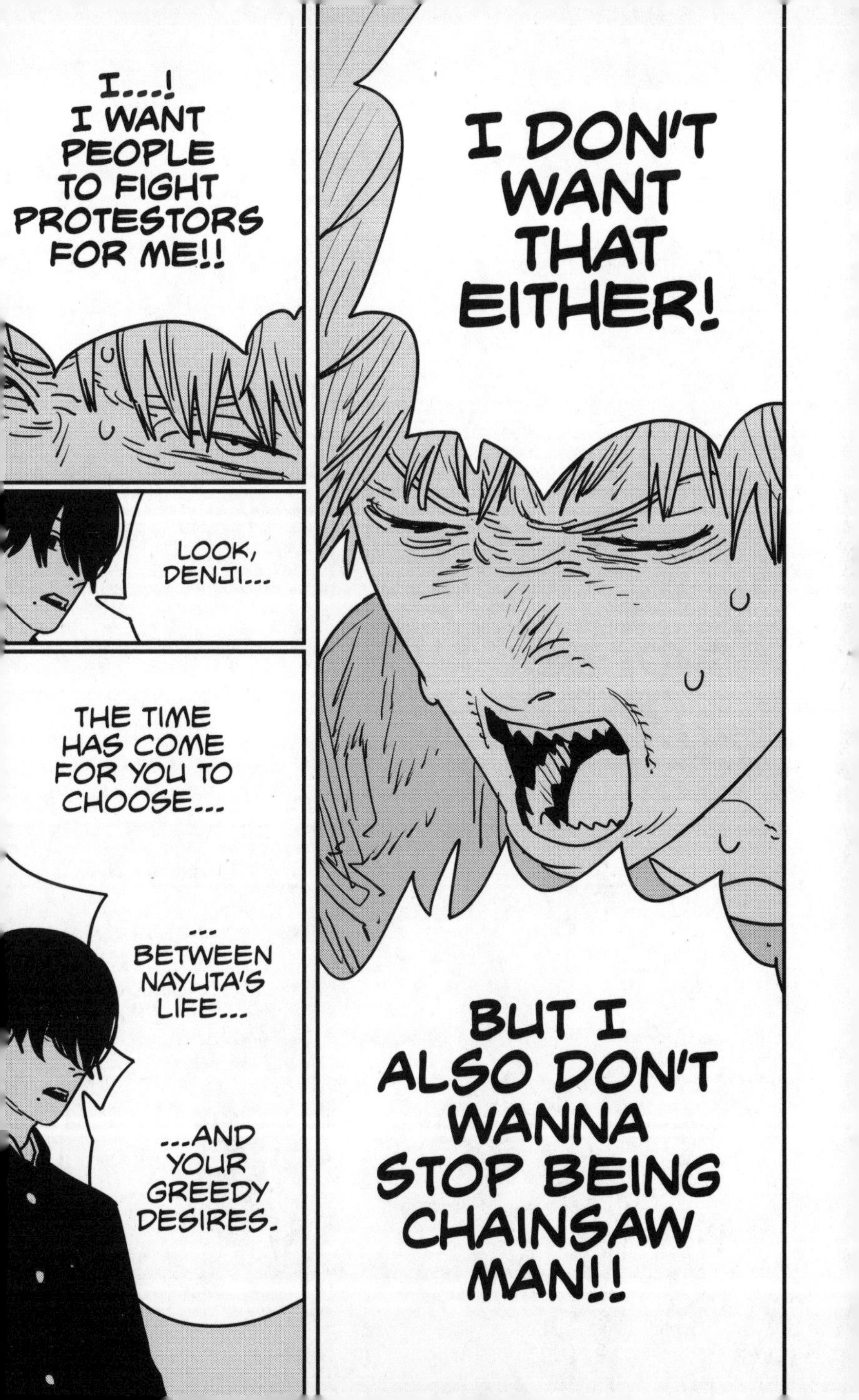
I...! I WANT PEOPLE TO FIGHT PROTESTORS FOR ME!!
LOOK, DENJI...
THE TIME HAS COME FOR YOU TO CHOOSE...
...BETWEEN NAYUTA'S LIFE...
...AND YOUR GREEDY DESIRES.
I DON'T WANT THAT EITHER!
BUT I ALSO DON'T WANNA STOP BEING CHAINSAW MAN!!

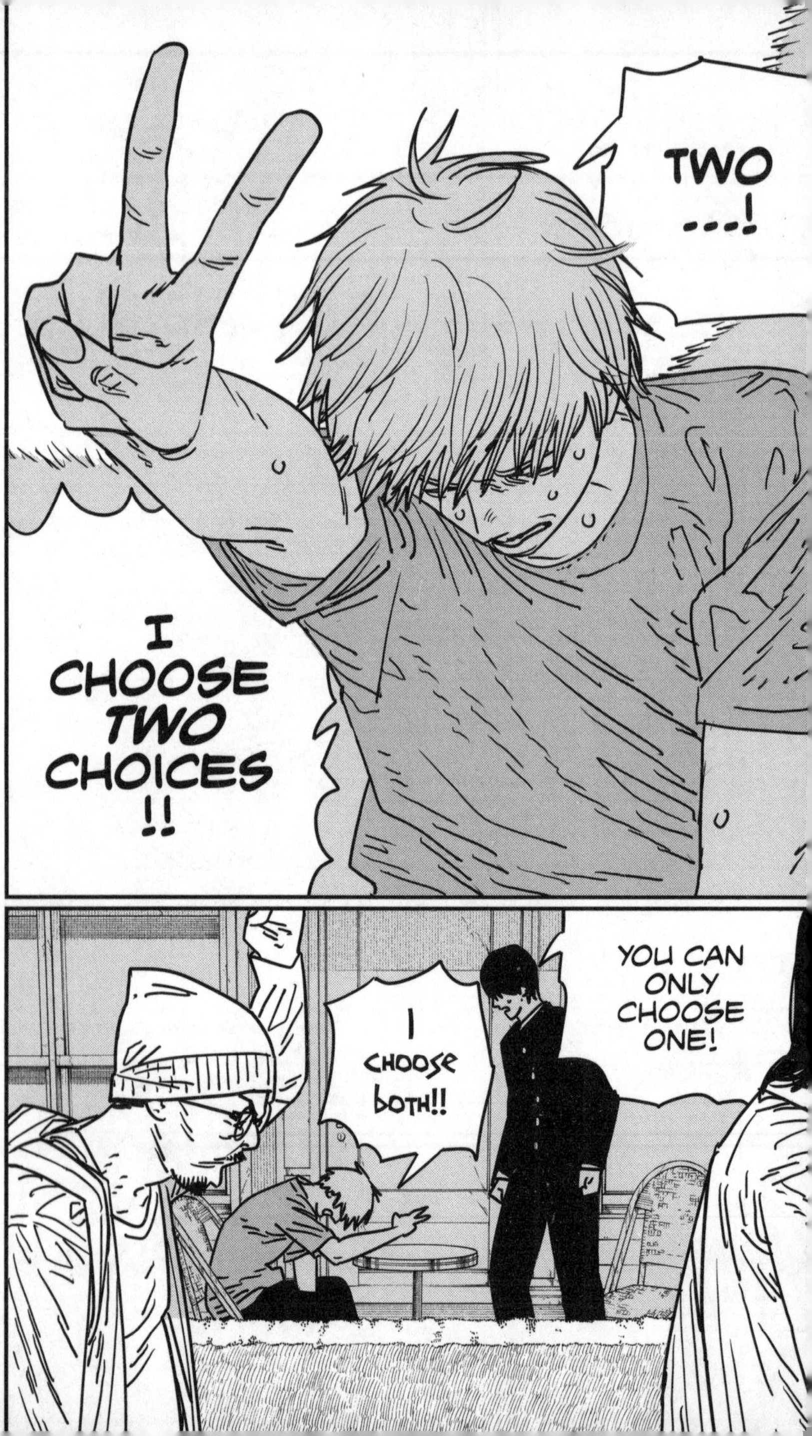
TWO...!
I CHOOSE *TWO* CHOICES!!
YOU CAN ONLY CHOOSE ONE!
I CHOOSE BOTH!!

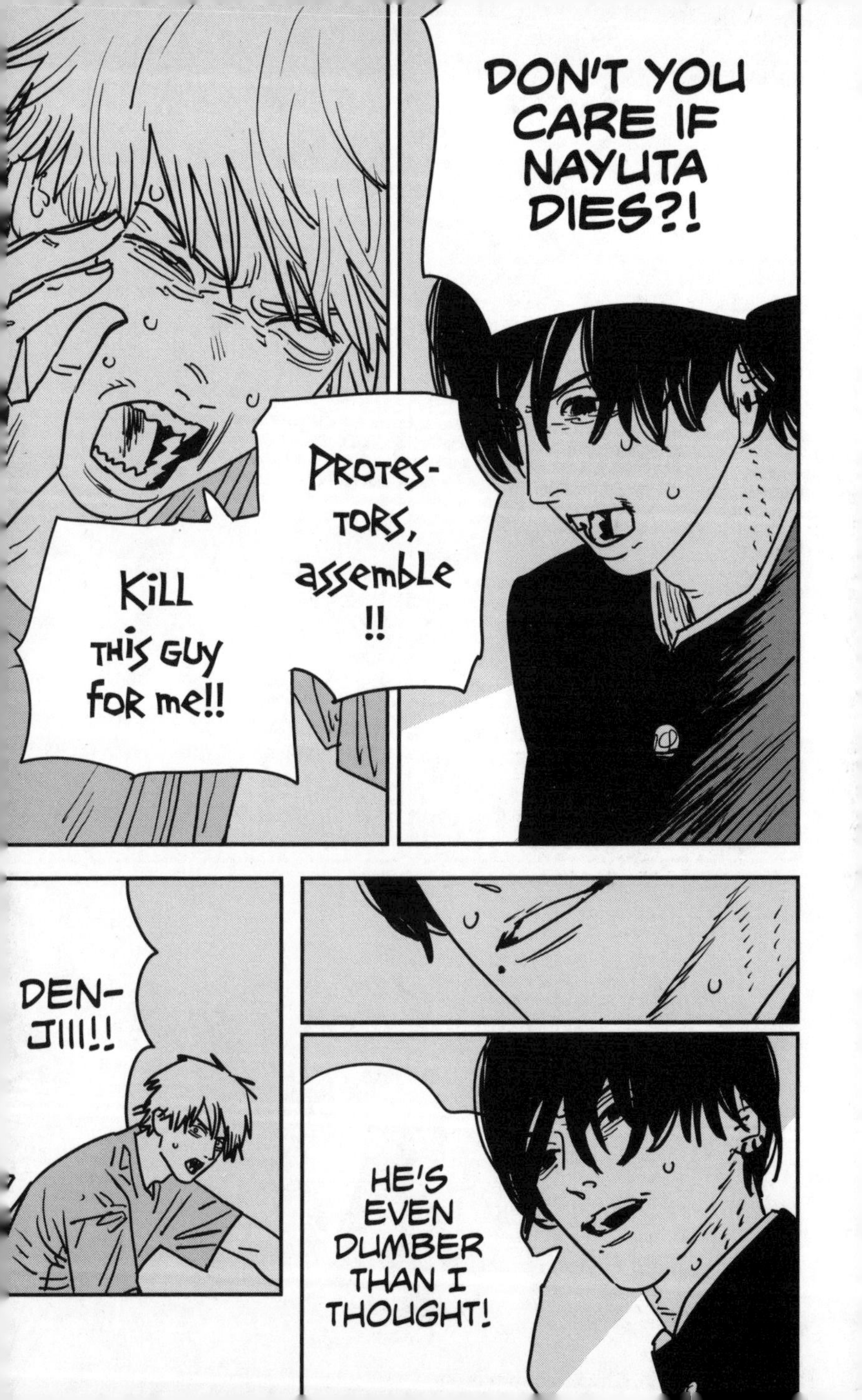
DON'T YOU CARE IF NAYUTA DIES?!
PROTES-TORS, assemble!!
Kill THIS GUY FOR me!!
HE'S EVEN DUMBER THAN I THOUGHT!
DEN-JIIII!!

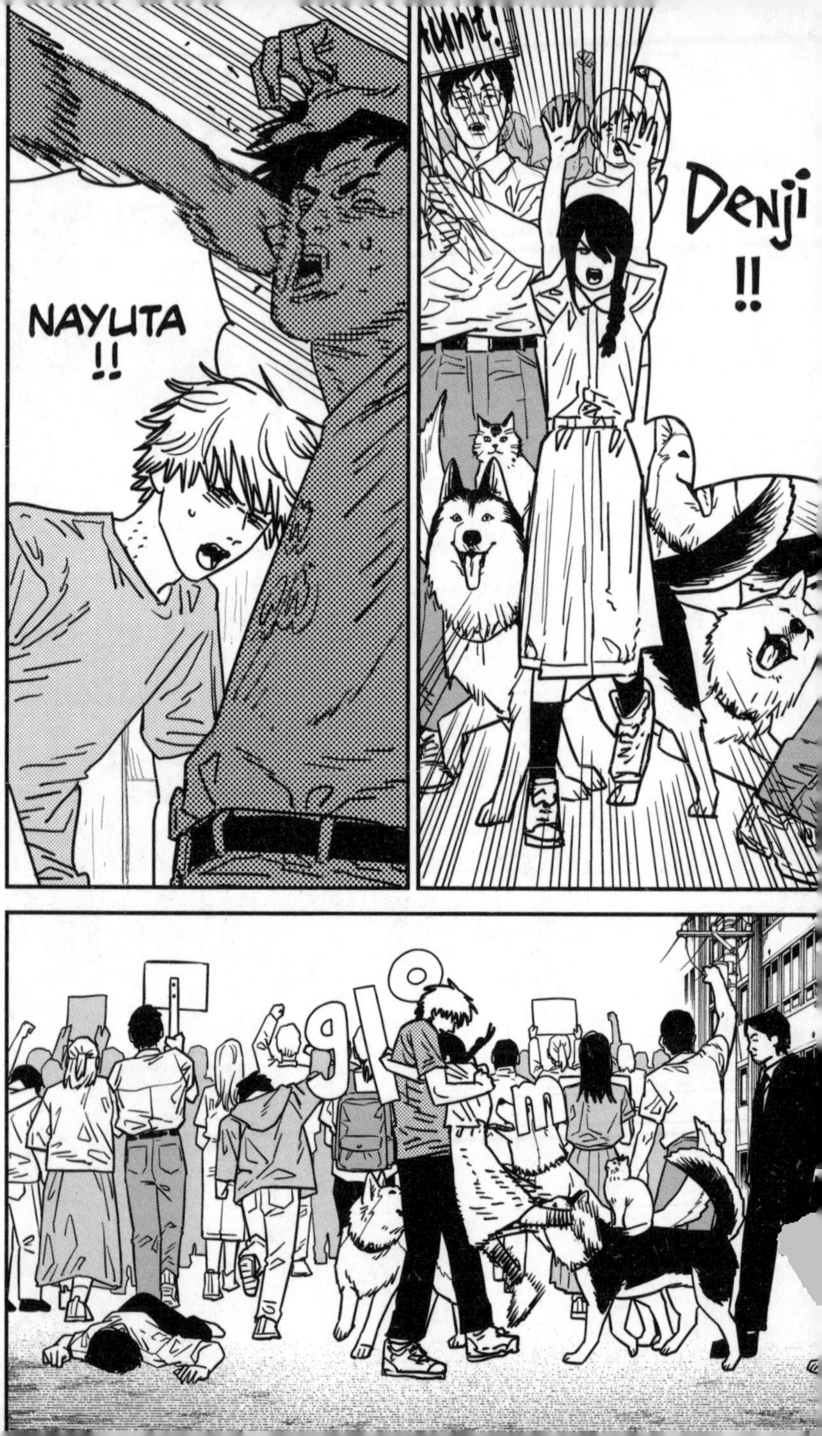
Denji !!
NAYUTA !!
glom

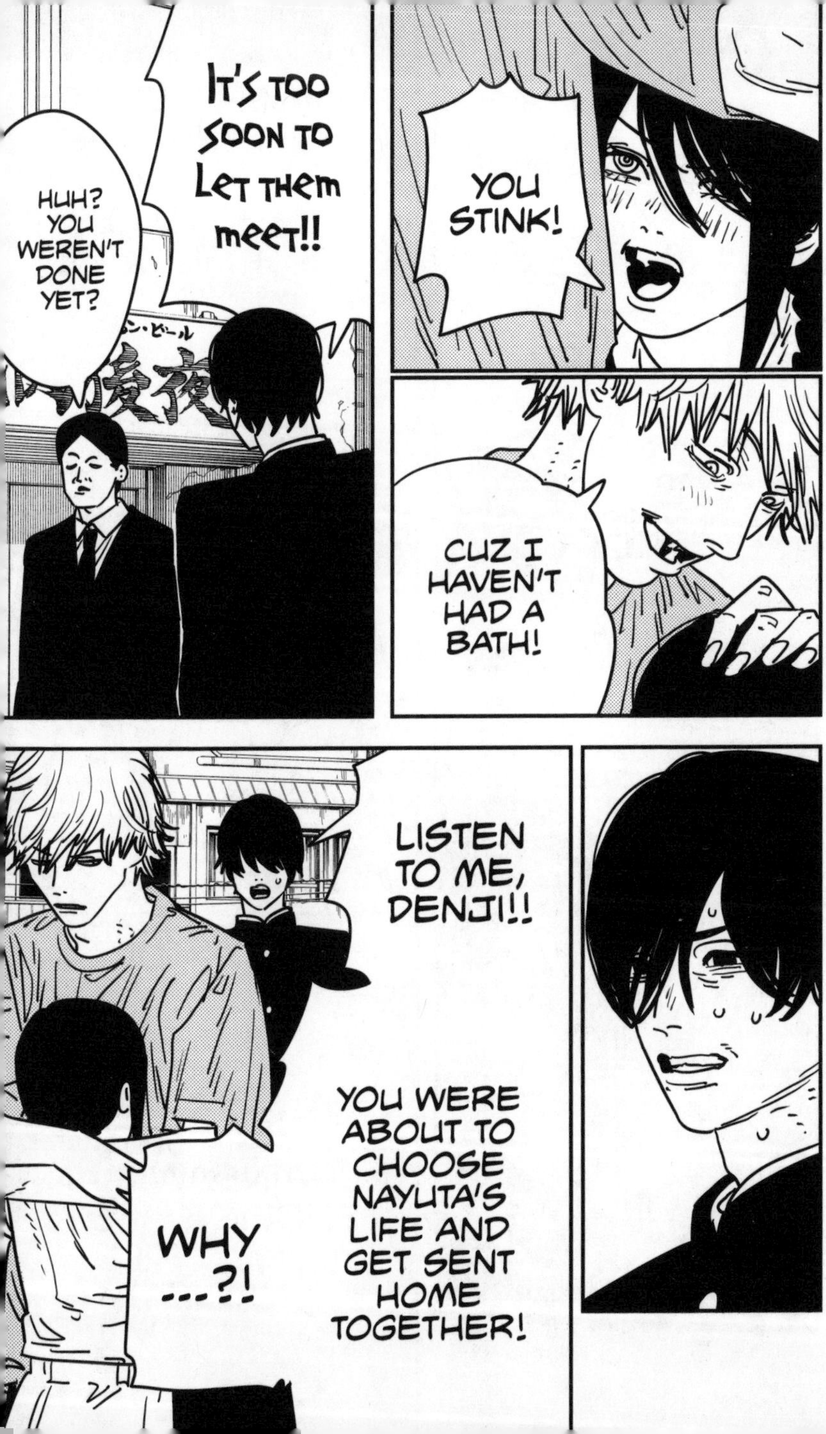
YOU STINK!
CUZ I HAVEN'T HAD A BATH!
IT'S TOO SOON TO LET THEM MEET!!
HUH? YOU WEREN'T DONE YET?
LISTEN TO ME, DENJI!!
YOU WERE ABOUT TO CHOOSE NAYUTA'S LIFE AND GET SENT HOME TOGETHER!
WHY ...?!

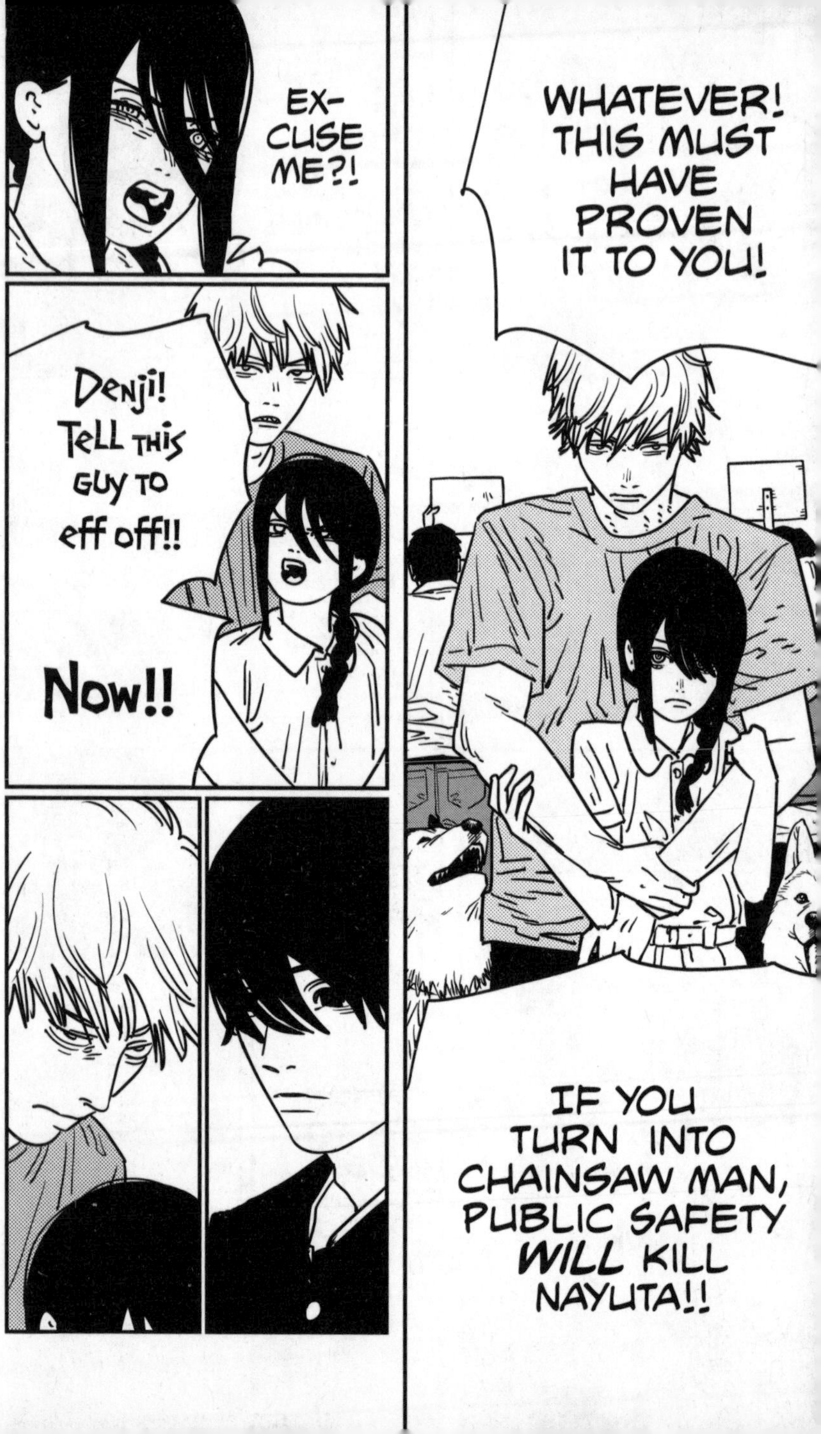
WHATEVER! THIS MUST HAVE PROVEN IT TO YOU!
IF YOU TURN INTO CHAINSAW MAN, PUBLIC SAFETY WILL KILL NAYUTA!!
EX-CUSE ME?!
Denji! Tell this guy to eff off!!
Now!!

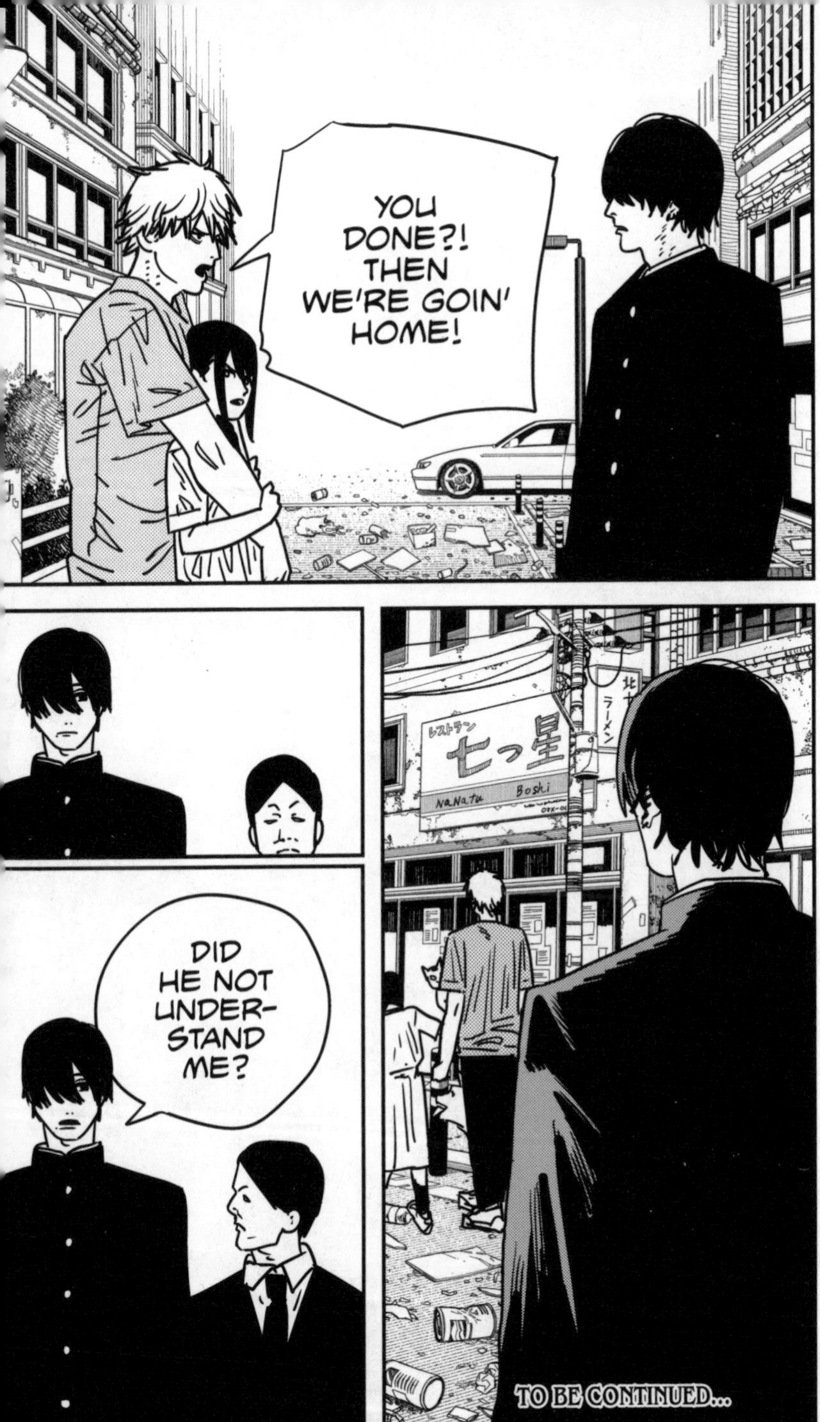
YOU DONE?! THEN WE'RE GOIN' HOME!
レストラン
七っ星
NaNatu Boshi
ラーメン
TO BE CONTINUED...
DID HE NOT UNDER-STAND ME?

Chain saw man

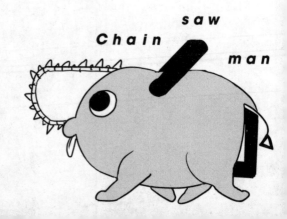

CHAINSAW

MAN

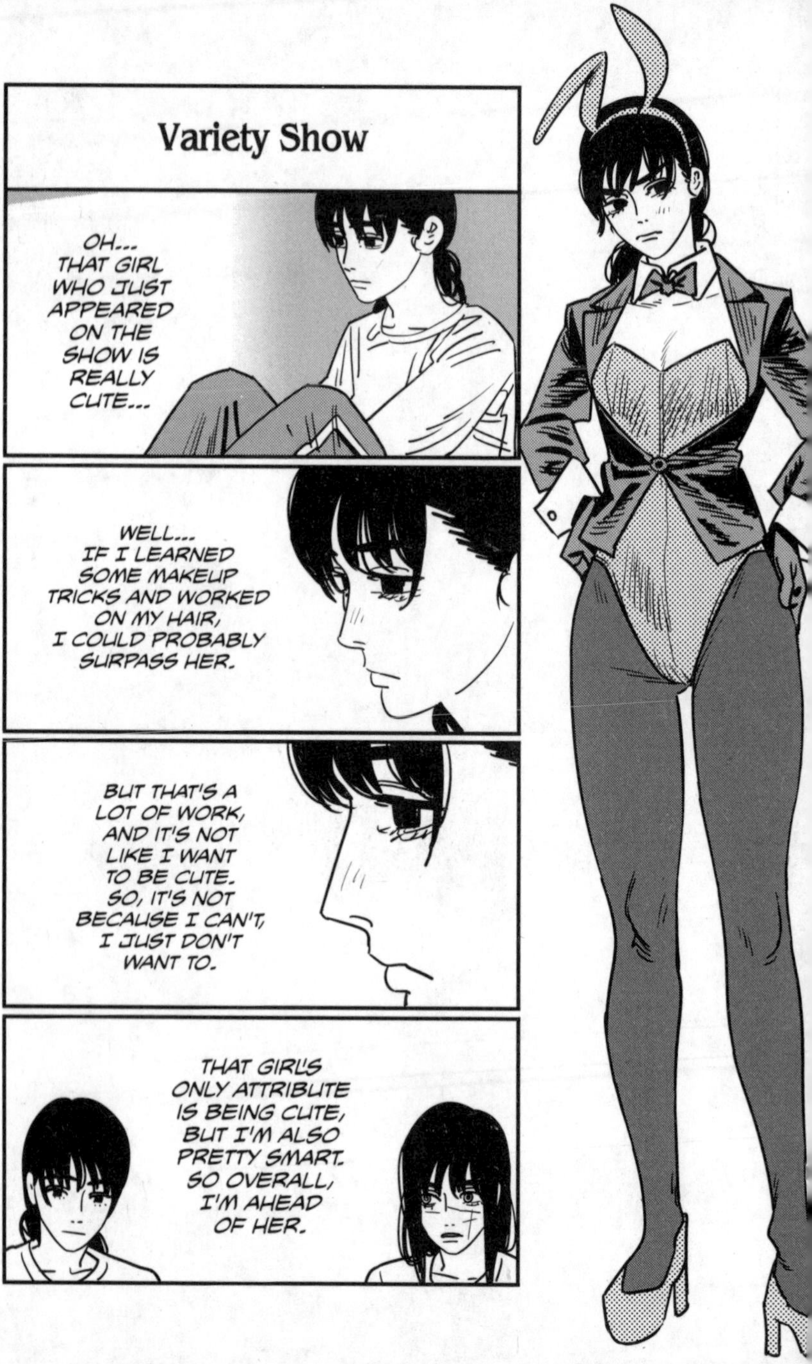
Variety Show
OH... THAT GIRL WHO JUST APPEARED ON THE SHOW IS REALLY CUTE...
WELL... IF I LEARNED SOME MAKEUP TRICKS AND WORKED ON MY HAIR, I COULD PROBABLY SURPASS HER.
BUT THAT'S A LOT OF WORK, AND IT'S NOT LIKE I WANT TO BE CUTE. SO, IT'S NOT BECAUSE I CAN'T, I JUST DON'T WANT TO.
THAT GIRL'S ONLY ATTRIBUTE IS BEING CUTE, BUT I'M ALSO PRETTY SMART. SO OVERALL, I'M AHEAD OF HER.

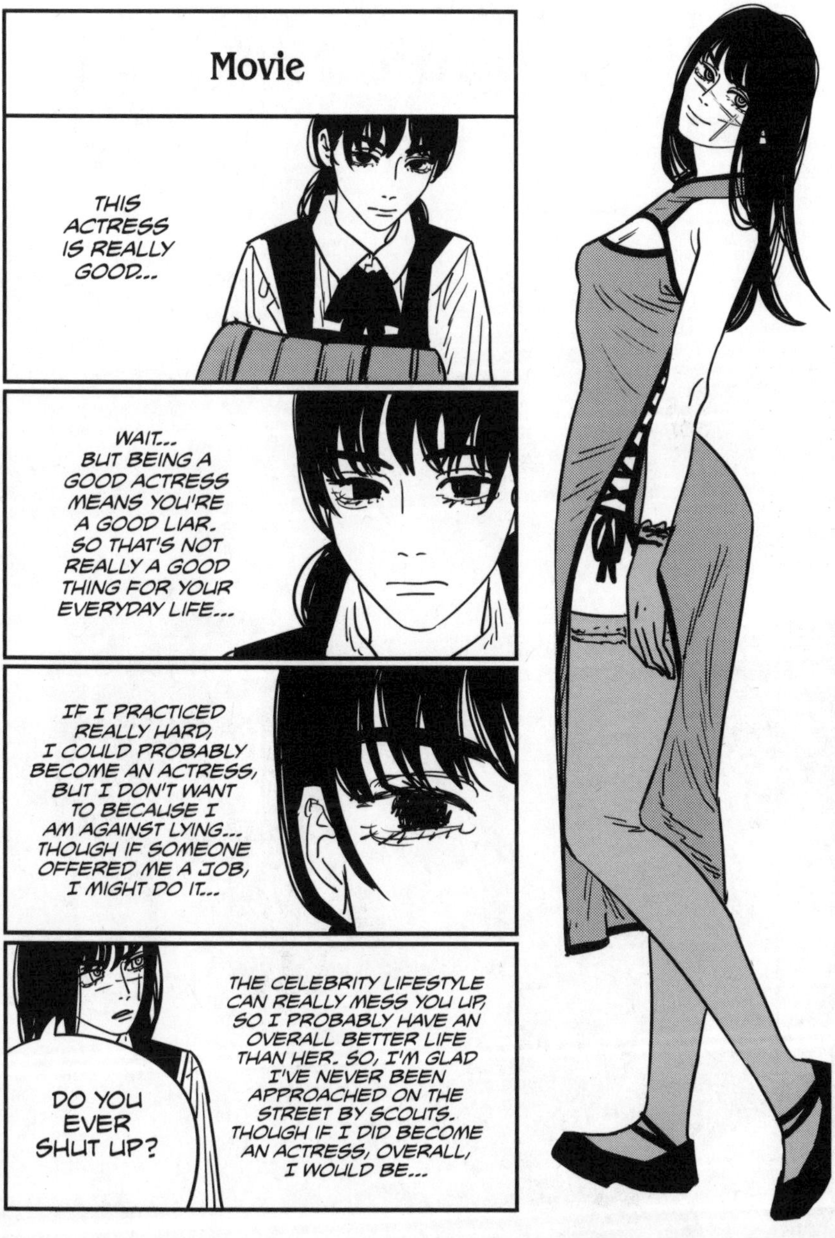
Movie
THIS ACTRESS IS REALLY GOOD...
WAIT... BUT BEING A GOOD ACTRESS MEANS YOU'RE A GOOD LIAR. SO THAT'S NOT REALLY A GOOD THING FOR YOUR EVERYDAY LIFE...
IF I PRACTICED REALLY HARD, I COULD PROBABLY BECOME AN ACTRESS, BUT I DON'T WANT TO BECAUSE I AM AGAINST LYING... THOUGH IF SOMEONE OFFERED ME A JOB, I MIGHT DO IT...
THE CELEBRITY LIFESTYLE CAN REALLY MESS YOU UP, SO I PROBABLY HAVE AN OVERALL BETTER LIFE THAN HER. SO, I'M GLAD I'VE NEVER BEEN APPROACHED ON THE STREET BY SCOUTS. THOUGH IF I DID BECOME AN ACTRESS, OVERALL, I WOULD BE...
DO YOU EVER SHUT UP?

YOU'RE READING THE WRONG WAY!

CHAINSAW MAN

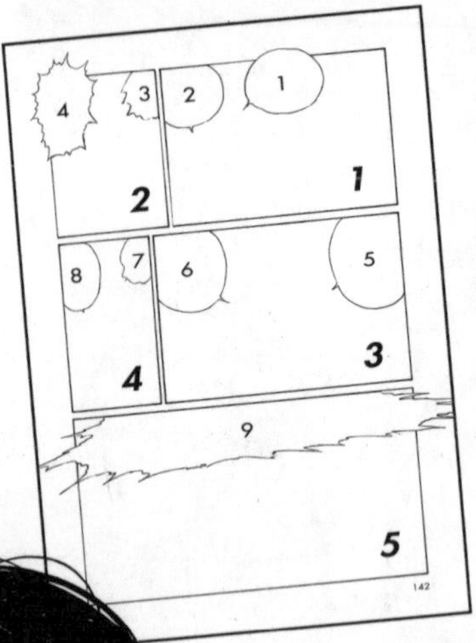

1
2
1
3
4
2
5
6
3
7
8
4
9
5
142

Chainsaw Man reads from right to left, starting in the upper-right corner. Japanese is read from right to left, meaning that action, sound effects, and word-balloon order are completely reversed from English order.

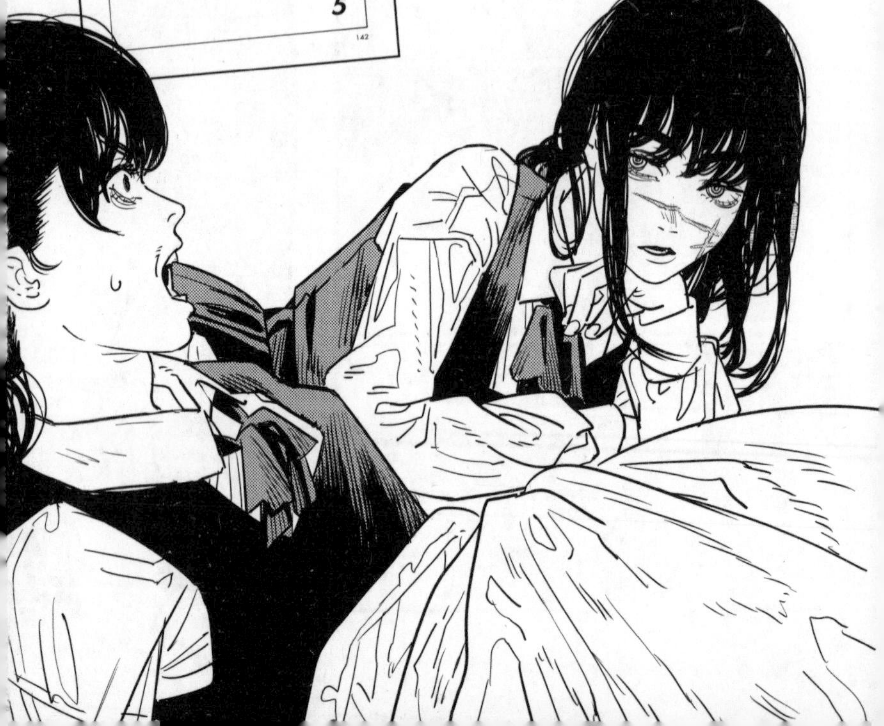